Across Cultures

A Reader for Writers

Across Cultures

A Reader for Writers

SEVENTH EDITION

Sheena Gillespie
Robert Becker

Queensborough Community College
City University of New York

PEARSON
Longman

New York   San Francisco   Boston
London   Toronto   Sydney   Tokyo   Singapore   Madrid
Mexico City   Munich   Paris   Cape Town   Hong Kong   Montreal

Publisher: Joseph Opiela

Senior Marketing Manager: Sandra McGuire

Production Manager: Ellen MacElree

Project Coordination, Text Design, Electronic Page Makeup:
    TexTech International

Cover Designer/Manager: Wendy Ann Fredericks

Cover Art: Jose Ortega/Images.com

Senior Manufacturing Buyer: Dennis J. Para

Printer and Binder: R. R. Donnelley and Sons Company/Harrisonburg

Cover Printer: Phoenix Color Corps.

For permission to use copyrighted material, grateful acknowledgment is made
to the copyright holders on pp. 523–527, which are hereby made part of this
copyright page.

Library of Congress Cataloging-in-Publication Data

Across cultures: a reader for writers / [compiled by] Sheena Gillespie,
Robert Becker—7th ed.

        p.   cm.

Includes Index

ISBN 13: 978-0-321-47529-9

ISBN 10:   0-321-47529-1

    1. College readers.   2.   English language—Rhetoric—Problems,
exercises, etc.   3.   Multiculturalism—Problems, exercises, etc.
4.   Report writing—Problems, exercises, etc.   5.   Culture—Problems,
exercises, etc.   6.   Reader—Multiculturalism.   7.   Readers—Culture.
I. Gillespie, Sheena,   II. Singleton, Robert.

PE1417.A27   2008

808'.0427—dc22   2007018468

Please visit us at http://www.ablongman.com

2 3 4 5 6 7 8 9 10—DOH—10 09 08 07

To Gabe, Amanda, and 彭迅 *(Anna)*

In memory of my parents,
Florence and Lou Becker

Contents

Asterisks after titles identify student writings.

Rhetorical Contents

COMPARISON AND CONTRAST

CAUSE AND EFFECT

PERSUASION

Preface for the Teacher

There is no such thing as a neutral educational process. Education either functions as an instrument which is used to facilitate the integration of the younger generation into the logic of the present system and bring conformity to it, or becomes "the practice of freedom," the means by which men and women deal critically and creatively with reality and discover how to participate in the transformation of their world.

—Richard Shaull

ACROSS CULTURES: A READER FOR WRITERS is a reader that invites students to look beyond their own society and culture. The title embodies our guiding image of a reaching out—moving beyond the immediate and the parochial to an acknowledgment and acceptance of pluralism and diversity within and among cultures. In our usage, such reaching out does not mean blending or blurring or assimilating (or hybridizing, in the biological sense). The outreach we mean may be found, first, in the selection of readings by authors from and about many countries: by North Americans writing about other cultures and about United States culture and subcultures; by members of ethnic subcultures in the United States, such as immigrants or their children, African-Americans, or Native Americans, writing about the United States; and by persons from other cultures writing about those cultures. Second, this reaching out is encouraged by the text's apparatus, in aids to the student. Perspectives (quotations); chapter introductions; text selection headnotes; the end-of-lesson trio Interpretations, Correspondences, Applications; The Knowing Eye (reading images); and Additional Writing Topics are found in every chapter.

We began the first edition of *Across Cultures* in 1989, and since then, the number of students coming from homes that are at least bilingual and bicultural has doubled, and although we hear daily about the many facets of globalization, there has been little progress in developing pedagogy that addresses the impact of these new linguistic realities. The seventh edition of *Across Cultures* reflects this concern and we have endeavored to address the complexities of this issue by adding texts, apparatus, and assignments that will assist us in learning more about the ramifications of tapping into the rich cultures, languages, experiences, and values of our students.

In the seventh edition of *Across Cultures* we have:

- Expanded the literacy narratives beyond the linguistic to better reflect the other kinds of literacies that students are engaged in, including the visual arts, performing arts, and technology. We have also included more questions that encourage students to utilize additional forms of literacy such as musical, drawing, and speaking skills.

- Recast the ninth chapter, "Popular Culture," to include contemporary topics such as computer gaming and text messaging. Three new essays address music and are presented as a unit within the chapter to facilitate discussion about popular music and increase interactivity among the texts.

- Updated and increased the number of images in most chapters. Our students live in a visual world, and multimedia has become the primary vehicle for the way our students learn. Prompts invite students to sharpen their observational skills, and by reading images, to make connections between the photographs and the chapter's written texts.

- Created additional "Web topics." These activities, placed in "Applications" or "Additional Writing Topics," are intended to help students use the Internet as a resource for additional thinking about essays they have read. Synthesizing additional—and sometimes contradictory—information will help students to further their own thinking.

- Included more student essays and replaced many others with new and fresh works.

The world of culture is a world of values. Although the good may be immaterial—truth, beauty, honor, glory—cultural good must be realized in temporal and material form. Culture consists as much in conserving values as in realizing them.

Each chapter begins with Perspectives, brief provocative quotations that stimulate thought and discussion on the chapter topic. Next come the texts—myths, folktales, essays, and short stories. Whereas many of the essays and stories reflect the seemingly endless—often tumultuous—changes in current events, our rationale for including myths and folktales is to show culture in its conserving role. Although *Across Cultures* probably pays more attention to shifts in population and to political and economic changes around the world, these changes occur against backgrounds of centuries of history and tradition, of treasured stories of origins and beginnings that give direction to the current shifting allegiances. Such stories may actually revive and sustain some cultures. As N. Scott Momaday says of the storyteller in Native American tradition: "[He] creates himself and his listeners through the power of his perception, his imagination, his expression, his devotion to important details. He is a holy man; his function is sacred."

The selections we offer in *Across Cultures* cover a much greater variety of cultural trends than the table of contents indicates. For example, work, the subject of Chapter 5, leads to such related subjects as affirmative action, immigration, cultural displacement, family narratives, and definitions of success. Traditions, the subject of Chapter 6, leads to questions of family life, the roles of men and women, class differences, and rituals and ceremonies of all kinds.

Each text is preceded by a biographical/cultural headnote and is followed by questions—Interpretations—that provoke thinking and discussion, probe comprehension, call attention to important rhetorical features, and help the reader relate the text to the chapter topic. Comparison or cross-examination is the purpose of the questions called Correspondences, which also follow each text. The Applications section provides writing and discussion topics and follows each group of Perspectives and each text. These activities call on the student to analyze cross-cultural similarities and differences and sometimes to place themselves at crossroads. The Knowing Eye section of each chapter features images for analysis and discussion. Additional Writing Topics at the end of the chapter provide added opportunities for students to engage the chapter's theme.

Cultural commentary in our text is direct and explicit. Each chapter includes one section on general American culture by an American writer, two or three texts by writers from diverse ethnic groups within the United States writing either on the experience of those groups or on individuals within them, and several texts by writers from cultures elsewhere in the world. A Geographical Index at the back of the book indicates the worldwide scope of these texts, the better to place American culture and its own diversity in a world context for comparison.

We are grateful to the following reviewers for their excellent critiques and suggestions for the seventh edition of the text: Syble Simon, Richard Dennison, Alexander Howe, Diana Gruendler, Lori Lipoma, Lori Stoltz, Chella Courington, Jane Womack, Stasia Callan, Amy Martin.

Special thanks are due to our colleagues at Queensborough and elsewhere for the essays they contributed: Todd Craig, Martin Kutnoswski, John Misak, and Tom Montgomery-Fate. We are proud to include student essays by Gillianne N. Duncan, James Geasor, Laura Kuehn, and Tom Lee.

Dora Sofia Caputo, Ridley Gunderson, Bianca Henriquez, Thomas Lee, Elissa R. Schlau, and Amanda Stellman provided the new images for this edition that highlight the cross cultural themes of the texts.

We acknowledge our gratitude to Robert Singleton for writing and updating the biographical headnotes, to Gladys deBuccio, James Geasor, and Anna Howard for their generous assistance in the preparation of the manuscript, and to Isabel Pipolo for her meticulous work on the instructor's manual.

Our colleagues Ann Agranoff, Roslyn Andela, Thea Callendar, Jean Darcy, Pat Hickey, Carol McHugh, Jean Murley, and John Talbird reviewed readings, gathered student essays, and shared their knowledge of *Across Cultures*.

Finally, we acknowledge the encouragement and support of Joe Opiela who has guided us through yet another edition of *Across Cultures*.

Sheena Gillespie
Robert Becker

Preface for the Student

We are in the middle of an extraordinary social experiment: the attempt to provide education for all members of a vast pluralistic democracy.
                                                                    —Mike Rose

Narrative is radical, creating us at the very moment it is being created.
                                                                    —Toni Morrison

AS TEACHERS, WE SHARE MIKE ROSE'S EXCITEMENT at being part of a unique intellectual and social experiment that seeks to provide education for a culturally diverse student population. In the seventh edition of *Across Cultures*, we invite you to celebrate and participate in this historically unprecedented multicultural experiment by reading the narratives of writers from other cultures, both within the United States and in many other parts of the world. Toni Morrison, in her 1993 Nobel Lecture, talked about the power of narrative to help us understand ourselves and others. Morrison is particularly concerned that the writer's words and stories be the windows through which both writer and reader gain knowledge not only of the self but also of the self in relation to other people and cultures.

Old cultures, and even some not so old, such as that of the United States, like to think that their cultures are superior. But once cultures cross—whether such meetings add to or subtract from the sum of their parts—they are never again the same: they can never again claim absoluteness, exclusivity, or monopoly. To promote and foster such meetings, or crossings, is the purpose of *Across Cultures: A Reader for Writers*. We hope that the readings in each chapter, several of which are written by students, will stimulate creative conversations about cultural differences as you share ideas about family, friends, gender issues, community, education, work, choices, traditions, and popular culture with your classmates.

At the center of each chapter are readings on a common subject or meeting ground, but you are introduced to the chapter through a group of brief quotations (Perspectives) to stimulate personal responses in journal entries and collaborative explorations in group projects. Each text is introduced with a biographical headnote that places the author in a particular historical-geographical context. After most texts are three sets of questions: Interpretations, to provoke thinking and discussion and to call attention to specific rhetorical features; Correspondences, to encourage comparisons of cultures; and Applications, exercises to develop critical thinking and writing skills. Accordingly, you will often be asked to compare texts within, between, and among chapters.

In each chapter there is also a paired reading. Correspondences and Applications follow the second reading.

The first chapter on "Writing, the 'Writing Process,' and You" will assist you in applying the readings to your study of writing. We ask you to think of yourselves as writers joining a community of writers who will help one another as you engage in the various stages of writing narratives. The Perspective section can be used to stimulate journal writing. Application questions provide specific opportunities for you to convey what you think on a particular issue to a wider audience than just your peers through more structured writing and discussion activities. The Additional Writing Topics at the end of each chapter require you to conduct interviews, engage in debate, take positions, or reach conclusions. We have also expanded the range of writing topics to include creative writing, topics that draw upon different kinds of intelligences, as well as topics that ask/assist/require you to use the Web.

As you are also a creatively visual generation, we have added images in each chapter to encourage more complex and varied writing topics. The new prompts invite you to sharpen your observational skills, play with different voices, and make connections between the images and the chapter's texts.

When you look around your classes and your campus, you probably see a student body diverse in its many countries, ethnicities, and ages. We hope that *Across Cultures* will stimulate and encourage you to tap into the rich cultures, languages, experiences, and values of your peers.

S. G.
R. B.

Across Cultures

A Reader for Writers

1

Writing, the "Writing Process," and You

W HO ARE YOU?
What is your name? How old are you? Where are you from? Who is in your family? What are you interested in? Why are you here? Where do you want to be in five years? Your answers to these questions will help you to define yourself, to place you in a context, to help you to realize your self-identity. You are a man or a woman. Maybe you are eighteen years old, or twenty-five, or forty, or seventy, or any number between or beyond. You're from the city, the suburbs, the country. You want to be an accountant, a physician, a musician, a teacher, a professional athlete, a movie star.

Whatever your thoughts and responses are to the above questions, one thing is for certain—you are a writer. While you may not have included this answer among those offered to the questions above, as a member of the class you are enrolled in you are a writer. Sure, in the outside world you are a son or daughter, a mother or sister, a brother or uncle. You are an artist, a someday All-Star, entrepreneur of the year, or attorney of the month. You want to become a fashion designer, a Grammy winner, a Nobel Prize winner, the president.

However, when you walk through the door into your English class, you are a writer participating in a community of writers. Here your thoughts and ideas will be committed to the written page, and the identity you establish for yourself as a writer will prove to be as important as any you might have invented prior to this time. The sooner you commit to this perception of yourself, the sooner you will trust yourself to get your words down on paper, and the easier the process of writing will become.

Yet this transformation into and acceptance of being a writer is demanding.

First of all, writing is not the same as speaking. Writing utilizes different physical actions as well as unique cognitive processes. Rather than merely translating speech into a written form, writing allows one to select more consciously the language that will be used to communicate. When you speak, you probably don't spend much time considering each word that you will use—words usually just seem to flow. Sometimes they seem to flow much too easily and quickly! Did you ever experience having words come out of your mouth and as you were saying them you thought to yourself, "Whoops! I probably shouldn't have said that!" Too late! Sometimes it seems as if words bypass our brains and emerge into the ears of our listeners all by themselves!

Writing, on the other hand, is a more deliberate and physical act. The words we want to use are still there, but now we can take our time and luxuriate in our choice of them as we put them down on the page. In fact, we can often change a word before it is committed to paper, and even when it's down we can still modify it to suit our needs. It is our ability to control more carefully the presentation of language that makes writing a unique verbal act; however, this uniqueness is—as you will see—a double-edged sword.

In this day of e-mail and instant messaging, we are closer than ever to emulating speech in our writing. It is quite possible to have the same "Whoops" response after replying to an IM all too quickly! The incorporation of technology into writing is a revelation that has sprouted a revolution.

Despite the changes that technology (specifically computer-based word processing programs, e-mail, and instant messaging) has brought to writing, there is still one fundamental truth concerning writers and writing—as a writer, you are unique. Although many writers may share similarities, it is most unlikely that two writers will do *exactly* the same thing. In fact, it is not unusual for any single writer to alter how she or he approaches writing depending upon the task at hand. This approach to writing—the *writing process*—is unique to each writer, and, it may be argued, unique to each project undertaken. Yet there are important lessons to be learned from an examination of the choices that all writers make when encountering a writing task.

The first choice a writer makes is how to begin. How do you actually start a writing project? Some people like to sit quietly before they write, giving themselves a chance to gather their thoughts before committing them to paper. Other people like to engage in some physical activity—taking a walk or shooting some baskets—to help them clear their minds before starting. Others like to jump in, get that first sentence down and keep on going from there. While one of these actions might describe the way that you get started, there are other techniques that writers use to get them past that blank piece of paper staring them in the face. Three of these are freewriting, brainstorming, and journal-writing. Since you are a unique person and a unique writer, not all of these techniques will work for you. However, by giving each a serious try (indeed, the old "college try"), you might discover a tool that will help make you a more comfortable and effective writer. When this occurs, take this technique with you and incorporate it into your own writing process.

For many writers getting started is the hardest part. A bare sheet of paper can be intimidating, and the sooner that you can put words on it, the better. *Freewriting* is a technique where you write down whatever comes into your mind without consideration of language, grammar, or content. But all you'll get is garbage, you say? The idea is not to evaluate your thoughts but merely to generate them. You will have much time to consider and reconsider the words and ideas that will become your final text, but the real trick for a writer is just to get going! Sit down in a quiet place. Set a timer for five minutes and begin to write. Don't let yourself be interrupted. Don't stop for anything. If you have an itch, don't scratch it—write about scratching it. If you are feeling hungry, don't stop to grab for that cookie—write about the intensity of your hunger pains. If you get stuck and have nothing to write about, write down the colors of the rainbow, the days of the week, or the months of the year until your mind picks up a thread and starts going along it. One thing about your mind: it moves pretty quickly, and keeping up with it might prove a challenge. Do the best you can to follow it. If it stops in midthought and moves to another, stay with it! When freewriting, try to train yourself to stop in midsentence to follow your brain as it moves through the back alleys of your consciousness.

At the end of five minutes, or whenever you have set your timer to go off, go back and read what you have written. (Note how your handwriting may have deteriorated as you have gone forward!) What is the most interesting (or important) idea that you have written? What topic seems to crop up more than any other? What intriguing idea would you like to pursue? The best piece of writing that you can create is the one about something that you are interested in. Practice freewriting regularly and use it to help you find those topics that are meaningful to you.

Another technique to help you to get started is *brainstorming*. Brainstorming is similar to freewriting in that you may use it to generate ideas, but it is different in that you simply create a list of those points you think you want to make about a topic. Often, brainstorming is done as a group activity. When used in this way, group members call out responses to a recorder who sets down on paper or a chalkboard the ideas that are generated. As with freewriting, the idea is not to make judgments about the contributions that are being brainstormed. That will come later, in preparation for creating a first draft of a writing task. Rather, the object of brainstorming is to get those juices flowing and place ideas out there!

Yet another means of generating ideas is *journal-writing*. Setting your ideas to paper three or more times a week is a way to create a record of your thoughts and feelings. Note, however, that keeping a journal is not like writing in a diary. Whereas a diary is primarily a posting of daily events, journals may be quite varied and contain many kinds of entries. Sure, you might write about what happened to you during the day, but you should also be experimenting with new forms and diverse topics. Write a letter to a friend or a famous person, create lyrics to a song or a poem, sketch a landscape or a portrait, cut out and paste in a quotation, picture, or recipe that you find interesting. Of course, as you include material in your journal, be sure to comment on it. What is it about those lyrics that you find most interesting? How do they apply to your life? That picture you cut out of the magazine—what do you find intriguing about it? Why would you want to visit that place? What do you think you would find there? And that recipe you included in your journal so as not to forget it—what was the response to it when you served it to your family and/or friends? What was the verdict? Was it worth making or did you have to order in a couple of pizzas as an emergency measure?

Whatever you decide to do with your journal, remember that it should be a representation of who you are and what you think. If you choose to write only daily diary-like entries, don't be surprised if the sameness of that form causes you to lose interest in the enterprise. By giving a journal a fair try—by making it as unique as *you* are—you will not only see more clearly who you are, but you will also discover many topics to write about, some of which you might never have thought about before.

Freewriting, brainstorming, and *journal-writing* are techniques that will help you to generate ideas and get your writing started. Now that you no longer have a blank page or screen in front of you, what will you do with all that stuff?

Once you have some raw material for an essay, there are certain questions that you—and all writers—need to answer to create an effective piece. Primarily, you must consider *what* you want to say, to *whom* you want to say it, and *why* you want to convey the information.

The first decision you have to make concerns the "what"—what is it that you want to communicate? Generating ideas about your topic might have opened up several aspects of your topic to you; now you need to think about what the main point is that you want to express. This main idea about your general topic, when stated as a clear and direct sentence, is your *thesis*. There's nothing fancy about a thesis statement. It's simply a one-sentence expression of the main idea that you want to convey to your readers.

Another matter that you need to address concerns the person or people who will read your writing. This readership is called an audience and you need to take them into account when you create your work. Who will your readers be? How old are they? How much formal education do they have? What are their interests? Why are they reading your work? Your answers to these questions will help you to target your audience. Depending upon your topic and whom you are writing for, you may need to adjust your vocabulary, treatment of ideas, the complexity of language, and even the form that your writing takes.

Yet another concern that writers take into account when considering audience is *tone*—how one presents himself or herself to an audience. How do you want yourself and your topic to appear to your readers? Do you want to take a forceful stance with them, letting them know who's boss and in control of the information being presented? Do you want to win their sympathies and come over to your way of seeing things? Do you want to appear impartial and sway your audience with a logical presentation of information? The relationship you form with your readers—the tone that you supply to your writing—will be created by your choice of language, how you appeal to their hearts and minds, and your approach to your topic.

One final consideration you need to address is *why* you are writing your piece. Yes, you are in a writing class and you want to get a good grade. However, this answer to the question addresses your *motives* for writing rather than your *purpose*. Basically, if you are seeking some kind of tangible, material compensation—primarily either grades or money— then you are talking about motives. Your purpose for writing concerns nonmaterial objectives: you may want to entertain your readers, inform them, vent your emotions to them, or even provide a memory for them to preserve in their own minds. Chances are, you won't be able to settle on a single purpose for writing; indeed, it seems the more complex the work, the more purposes a writer has in mind for writing it. However, by assessing your purpose, audience, and meaning before creating your first draft, you will be able to more closely approach what it is that you want to convey to your readers and how you want to say it.

So now we get to putting all of this preparatory work into action, into that work of writing that we have called a first draft. Just its name implies that there will be (at least!) one more, so what's unique about a first, as opposed to a second, third, or fourth, draft?

First drafts are where you get to work out on paper the real answers to those questions asked earlier. While you have generated ideas and thought about your meaning, purpose, and audience, a first draft is the place where you get to try out your ideas and intentions.

When you create this draft, try to stick to your main idea (thesis), and organize information in a way that best addresses your view of audience and that achieves your purpose for writing. However, don't be surprised if when you complete this draft and read it over, you have found a new main point or discovered additional answers to some of the questions you asked yourself earlier. Quite often a first draft is where a writer truly discovers what he or she has to say. It is not unusual for a writer to declare after completing a first draft, "*Now* I have found what I really want to talk about!" There's a simple truth to this statement. How do we know what we want to say until we have said it?

Going back to the earlier discussion of speech and writing, sometimes when we speak we discover the truth of a statement only when it is too late. However, making such a discovery when creating a first draft is like finding gold! Now that you have found what you want to say, you may create a second draft that capitalizes on this knowledge. Now an opportunity presents itself for you to refine and sharpen your topic in view of your discovery. You might also re-evaluate your assessment of your audience and how you might best approach your readers. In essence, a first draft is a critical step in creating an interesting and effective final essay.

But wait! With your first draft in hand, how will you go about transforming it into a completed essay? Most students try to touch up a first draft by making surface changes to it. They may alter the structure of a sentence or two, and are likely to change a few words and fix spelling errors and minor grammatical slips. While these changes will help to increase the clarity of the essay, they will not capitalize on the hard work you have already done creating the first draft and then reassessing your meaning, purpose, and audience. To improve a first draft significantly most often calls for a writer to revise it thoroughly. Those changes mentioned above really concern *editing* and will be discussed later. What experienced writers do to a first draft almost always involves the use of *revising strategies*. These strategies are available to all writers and are the only techniques available to transform a promising first draft into a truly effective piece of writing. Here are the revising techniques available to you:

Addition: Use this technique to offer additional information to your reader. You might add only a phrase to clarify an idea, but sometimes you might need to add a sentence or even a whole paragraph to make your point strongly and clearly.

Deletion: The exact opposite of addition, deletion is used when you have too much information in your essay. Perhaps you repeat yourself or stray from your thesis. In these instances, remove that information to create a tighter, more effective, essay.

Substitution: A combination of addition and deletion, substitution requires you to replace ineffective text with phrases, sentences, or paragraphs that convey your ideas more exactly and clearly.

Rearrangement: Whereas the previous techniques have to do with the amount and effectiveness of the information you provide, rearrangement concerns the *organization* of the information in your essay. There are three techniques involved in rearranging an essay:

Moving: Use this technique to take information from one place in the essay and position it elsewhere. Sometimes a sentence or group of sentences really belongs somewhere else—move them to where they will function more effectively.

Combining: On occasion you will notice that sentences referring to the same idea appear in varied places in your essay. If you determine that these ideas ought to be placed together, you would use combining to bring them to a new location, perhaps creating a new paragraph to accommodate them.

Redistributing: The opposite of *combining*, this technique would be used to de-emphasize information by taking ideas from one location and placing them in several related areas. Sometimes a body paragraph that supports your thesis tangentially can be broken up and the relevant sentences placed in other paragraphs. This will eliminate the digression you have made and strengthen the body paragraphs that are already in place.

These techniques—*adding, deleting, substituting, rearranging*—will help you to change the substance of your essay. By doing so, they will enable you to change your meaning and better adapt it to your purpose and audience. These revision strategies will encourage you to do much more than alter a word or punctuation mark, and they will help you make the kinds of changes that first drafts require to bring them to completion.

Let the power of your computer's word-processing program help you use these revising strategies. Your text is flexible and not set in stone. Highlight and cut and paste those sentences that are giving you a problem. How do they look in their new location? Not too good you say? Hit the undo icon and your text is as it was. To be doubly sure that no harm will come to your original, save the first draft (as Draft1), open the file, and immediately save the working copy as Draft2. Now if something goes terribly wrong and you can no longer undo the changes you have made, you can always revert back to your original document, Draft1. Play with your text—add, delete, substitute, and rearrange—but be sure to save your work often! Becoming familiar with the power of revision is a prerequisite to becoming a more effective writer.

By now your revised essay is pretty much where you want it. You have said what you had intended to say and have achieved your purpose in view of your intended audience. Before handing your work to your instructor or submitting it for publication, you need to take the final two steps to maximize its effectiveness—*editing* and *proofreading*.

Both of these stages have been discussed briefly earlier. *Editing* occurs when you read over your draft and examine and modify each sentence for clarity and effectiveness. Sharpen your choice of language to make certain that every word is accurate, that every word says what you want it to say. You might add, delete, or substitute a word or phrase here and there to increase the effectiveness of your text.

Proofreading is when you go over your piece for the last time, paying attention to the accuracy of every word and punctuation mark. Check the spelling of each and every word sentence by sentence—don't trust a spellchecker to find and correct errors since it will not recognize wrong word choices (*form* instead of *from*, for example). Check grammar and punctuation to make sure that minor slips are corrected.

One problem with proofreading is that you are probably the worst person to check your work at this time! Since you have read your essay so many times, your mind often will tell your eye what to see and slight errors will go unnoticed. It's helpful to exchange papers with a classmate and to alert each other to those minor errors that fall into the proofreading category. Should you be unable to share your work, you might read your essay backwards, beginning with the last sentence and ending with the first. Doing this will decontextualize your essay so that your mind does not know what to expect and your eyes will be put to work! After completing this final stage of the "writing process," your essay should be one that you are proud of and that represents your best efforts. Indeed, you have done the work that all writers need to do to write effectively.

Even so, this process of writing and revising might not be completed. Perhaps, after reading your essay, your peer group or instructor may suggest additional revisions or things to think about. In that case, assess the comments that were made and use your writing process to accommodate a new set of changes. This exchange of ideas and perceptions between a writer and his or her audience is invaluable. Learning how readers view your work and respond to your words is an important experience and an essential part of any writer's writing process. Indeed, it is by exposing yourself to these writing situations that you earn the title and identity of "writer."

What has been summarized above are those techniques that make up the writing process. Remember, however, that every writer formulates his or her own plan to successfully complete a writing task. *Your* writing process is the sequence of steps that you find to be most helpful in creating an essay. You do not need to apply each of these steps, and frequently, steps are not followed in order. It is the nature of writing that makes these processes recursive; that is, a writer usually goes back and forth among them as the written work is produced. Oftentimes, writers revise works in process—even in the most preliminary stages. Conversely, it is plausible to generate ideas even when a piece is nearing completion.

Most important, experiment with your writing process to find the most effective way to write for *you*! Make those techniques and strategies that work best part of your personal armory of writing techniques. For example, some writers, when composing an essay, begin with the essay's body and leave the introduction for last. Their rationale is that they need to know what they have written before creating the paragraph that introduces the work. Whatever your personal preferences, keep your mind open to new techniques. Allow yourself to enjoy the freedom and potential for self-discovery that every writer may experience when setting ideas to paper.

Literacy Narratives

In *Across Cultures*, the essays by Sherman Alexie (p. 71), Susan G. Madera (p. 76), Paule Marshall (p. 196), Vincent Cremona (p. 206), Gloria Naylor (p. 379), and Kenneth Woo (p. 383) are "literacy narratives." A *narrative* may be defined as a story that makes a point. What, however is *literacy*? According to *The American Heritage Dictionary of the English Language, Fourth Edition*, one definition of literacy is "The condition or quality of being literate, especially the ability to read and write." Certainly, the authors named above are concerned with reading and writing; this kind of literacy—linguistic literacy—is central to their personal stories. Yet, perhaps other kinds of literacy are also being addressed in these stories.

A second definition presented in *The American Heritage Dictionary* is of literacy as "the condition or quality of being knowledgeable in a particular subject or field." In this case, our representation of literacy must expand to encompass what we know and how we know it. In these instances, who we are as individuals and as individuals within society will help to form our knowledge of ourselves and our world. The things we do and the people we do them with will help to shape our definitions.

- What kind of literacy is required when hiking a trail or negotiating a subway system?

- What does one have to know to work in an office or a factory?

- How does one begin to master the technological literacy required by today's world?

- What kinds of literacy are required to play a song or create a painting?

- If you attend a house of worship, what kinds of literacy are invoked? What would someone who practices another religion need to know in order to become literate in your faith?

- How does one know how to dance, ice skate, or perform gymnastics?

- What kind of literacy is required to participate in a team sport, to be involved in a relationship, to be a member of a family?

- What does "literacy" mean to you? What kinds of literacy have you mastered? Which are you currently in the midst of learning?

Sometime this semester, your instructor might ask you to write your own literacy narrative. Perhaps, if you are asked to share your story with a classmate, a group of your peers, or with your whole class, you might observe types of literacy that you had not thought about. As your classmates share their stories, what do you notice about their literacy narratives? How is the general idea of literacy being described? What kinds of literacy are being addressed? How do these narratives compare with those published in this book?

And, as you read the literary narratives in *Across Cultures*, think about what common themes or kinds of literacy the authors are writing about. Consider how their stories resemble yours, how their depictions of literacy relate to your story and the stories of your classmates.

Composing Your Own Literacy Narratives

If you have been asked to write a literacy narrative, there are several approaches to the assignment that you may take. Below is a method to help you formulate your ideas about your involvement with language. By following the sequence of assignments from beginning to end, you will create the kind of essay that is represented by the authors who have published their literacy narratives in the chapters of this book.

PROMPTS

- Remember back to your first writing memory, either at home or at school.

- When was the first time you realized that a piece of your writing had an effect on someone?

- When have you seen or felt language doing "harm" or causing "hurt"?

- Describe the physical location where you do your writing in as much detail as you can.

- Characterize your writing process using the metaphor of a meal. For example: What kinds of food? Home cooked? Fast food? A holiday celebration? How many courses and of what kind? Who is present when you eat? What does the table look like where you eat? Silverware? Napkins? Drinks? Rests between parts of the meal? While watching TV? Is there dessert?

- What is your favorite book? When did you read it? Why is it your favorite?

- Describe a person who has been an influence on your writing/reading/language use.

- When did you first become aware of your private voice in a public context?

- What kind of stories did you enjoy hearing as a child? Can you remember creating a story of your own?

JOURNAL-WRITING

Select one of the prompts above and, without stopping, write for five minutes on anything that comes to mind related to the prompt. When the five minutes are up, select another prompt and write again for five minutes. Repeat the process again so that you have three freewritten chunks of text. Now go back and look for connections across the three chunks and rewrite them so that they form one comprehensive journal entry.

CONNECTIONS

Based upon what you have written, look through the texts in the chapter and find at least one that you can link to. Are there issues in the text that help you make sense of your journal entry? How can you use these to expand on your literacy narrative? Remember that points of conflict may be as helpful as those in common as you think about them in relation to your own writing.

REFLECTIONS

Read over the new material you have added to your narrative. How did the process of reading literacy narratives, reseeing other texts as literacy narratives, and writing your own narrative help you to think of these issues in different contexts? What insights did you gain about yourself coming into language? Do you better understand the differences between your public and private voices? How might you develop them? As you negotiate among your various roles and cultures, how will you use language to create understanding? In what contexts might you engage in the discourse of persuasion? Write a journal entry on any of these issues that seem pertinent to your literacy narrative.

2

Family and Community

A REVIEW OF THE PERSPECTIVES on family, friends, and community in this chapter reflect incredible variations in cross-cultural views of social relationships, but one theme remains constant: we are social beings. The variations that exist in family, friendship, and community have been built on the changeless desire and need to reach out to one another.

The thousand-year-old parable of the Good Samaritan establishes a clear definition of *neighbor*, a definition that transcends tribal and even family differences and calls on us to value service to others over our own comfort. Even those who accept this definition as an ideal, however, admit that it is very difficult to practice.

The American poet Walt Whitman described the self as a "miracle of miracles, beyond statement, most spiritual and vaguest of earth's dreams, yet hardest basic fact, and only entrance to all facts." The self, as Whitman indicates, is indeed paradoxical, and if it is to remain dynamic, it must constantly evolve. To ensure self-growth, we must evaluate all that happens to us, however seemingly insignificant.

What you will encounter as you read the texts on these issues is that regardless of their ethnic and cultural backgrounds, the writers have a common interest in knowing and understanding themselves and others. You will meet people like yourself with complex personalities composed of conflicting desires, attitudes, and expressions. Like them, you play many roles—parent, child, sibling, friend, lover, employee, student. Although each of us is unique, we are also influenced by those who share our daily and communal lives. When our own personality, individualism, and sense of identity become all-important, who helps us reconcile self and society, independence and interdependence? The cross-cultural examples in this chapter may suggest some answers, but they also raise difficult questions and make complex choices.

David Brooks, for example, in "People Like Us," presents credible evidence to support his thesis that "we don't really care about diversity all that much in America, even though we talk about it a great deal," challenging the whole notion to use Toni Morrison's words that "we are people in search of a national community." Tom Rosenberg makes a courageous decision to reclaim his Jewish heritage after three decades by changing not only his last name but also his first, and Lewis Johnson Sawaquat, despite the prejudice that he experienced as a Native American, shares his aspirations that his daughter will be more fortunate.

Family members and the places we grew up are often important catalysts for reconstructing and understanding ourselves. Dana Wehle and Mahwash Shoaib, for example, invite us to their family homes in New York and Pakistan respectively, to present their responses to the deaths of a parent and grandparent.

Immigrant family relationships add different voices to this conversation by sharing the gains and losses of diasporic experiences. Amy Tan confesses in "Mother Tongue" that at as a child she was ashamed of her mother's "limited English," which in turn diminished her perception of her mother. In "Two Lives," Maylasian immigrant Shirley Geok-Lin Lim reflects on her lack of communal identity as a "resident alien" seeing "herself through the eyes of citizens: guest, stranger, outsider, misfit, beggar."

The basic importance and influence of family members, even those about whom we are ambivalent, are apparent in this cross-cultural survey of relationships. All of the texts reinforce how much of our personal and cultural identities are rooted in our need for community.

Perspectives

Civilization progresses at the expense of individual happiness.
—*Sigmund Freud*

No people are ever as divided as those of the same blood.
—*Mavis Gallant*

All parents realize, or should realize, that children are not possessions, but are only lent to us, angel boarders, as it were.
—*John Gregory Dunne*

"Family" is not just a buzz word for reactionaries; for women, as for men, it is the symbol of the last area where one has any hope of control over one's destiny, of meeting one's most basic human needs, of nourishing that core of personhood, threatened now by vast impersonal institutions and uncontrollable corporate and government bureaucracies.
—*Betty Friedan*

Relationships and communion are the most significant clues surrounding the mystery of our human nature. They tell us the most about who we are.
—*Susan Cahill*

Friendship is by its very nature freer of deceit than any other relationship we can know because it is the bond least affected by striving for power, physical pleasure, or material profit, most liberated from any oath of duty or constancy.
—*Francine du Plessix Gray*

Some people are your relatives but others are your ancestors, and you choose the ones you want to have as ancestors. You create yourself out of those.
—*Ralph Ellison*

Talents are best nurtured in solitude; character is best formed in the stormy billows of the world.
—*Johann Wolfgang von Goethe*

Friendship marks a life even more deeply than love.
—*Elie Wiesel*

Virtue never stands alone. It is bound to have neighbors.
—*Confucius*

Your children need your presence more than your presents.

—Jesse Jackson

The price of hating other human beings is loving oneself less.

—Eldridge Cleaver

In search of my mother's garden I found my own.

—Alice Walker

Every man's neighbor is his looking glass.

—English proverb

Fate makes relatives, but choice makes friends.

—DeLile

I have three chairs in my house; one for solitude, two for friendship, three for society.

—Henry David Thoreau

Each friend represents a world in us, a world possibly not born until they arrive, and it is only by this meeting that a new world is born.

—Anaïs Nin

The family, not the individual, is the real molecule of society, the key link in the social chain of being.

—Robert Nisbet

Home is the place, when you have to go there, they have to take you in.

—Robert Frost

The moment we cease to hold each other, the minute we break faith with one another, the sea engulfs us and the light goes out.

—James Baldwin

We are people in search of a national community.

—Toni Morrison

Children have more need of models than of critics.

—Joseph Joubert

The family is the basic cell of government: it is where we are trained to believe that we are human beings or that we are chattel, it is where we are trained to see the sex and race divisions and become callous to injustice even if it is done to ourselves, to accept as biological a full system of authoritarian government.

—Gloria Steinem

The Good Samaritan

LUKE 10:29–37

The parable of the Good Samaritan is one of a number of stories told by Jesus to his followers. The original city of Samaria was the center of a sect whose worship at a separate temple (on Mt. Gerizim) and whose recognition of the authority of only the Pentateuch (the first five books of the Bible) led to continual tension with the Jews of Jerusalem and elsewhere. As you read the parable, brainstorm on your associations with the word "neighbor."

THEN ONE OF THE EXPERTS IN THE LAW stood up to test him and said,

"Master, what must I do to be sure of eternal life?"

"What does the Law say and what has your reading taught you?" said Jesus.

"The Law says, 'Thou shalt love the Lord thy God with all thy heart and with all thy soul and with all thy strength and with all thy mind—and thy neighbor as thyself,'" he replied.

"Quite right," said Jesus. "Do that and you will live."

But the man, wanting to justify himself, continued, "But who is my 'neighbor'?"

And Jesus gave him the following reply:

"A man was once on his way down from Jerusalem to Jericho. He fell into the hands of bandits who stripped off his clothes, beat him up, and left him half dead. It so happened that a priest was going down that road, and when he saw him he passed by on the other side. A Levite also came on the scene, and when he saw him he too passed by on the other side. But then a Samaritan traveler came along to the place where the man was lying, and at the sight of him he was touched with pity. He went across to him and bandaged his wounds, pouring on oil and wine. Then he put him on his own mule, brought him to an inn and did what he could for him. Next day he took out two silver coins and gave them to the innkeeper with the words: 'Look after him, will you? I will pay you back whatever more you spend, when I come through here on my return.' Which of these three seems to you to have been a neighbor to the bandits' victim?"

"The man who gave him practical sympathy," he replied.

"Then you go and give the same," returned Jesus.

INTERPRETATIONS

1. The lawyer wants to "test" Jesus and, after hearing Jesus's first answer, to "justify himself." How do you think he feels after hearing the parable and correctly answering Jesus' question? How do you explain the change?

2. Jesus connects salvation (inheriting "eternal life") with kind service to needy people. How important do *you* consider service to needy people? What's the best way to be of service? Can one do wrong in doing right? Do good works also require sensitivity and intelligence? Health and wealth? Why or why not?

3. "Love thy neighbor" turns out to be, in this parable, something quite practical. What is *your* idea of love?

4. Jesus answers the lawyer's second question—"And who is my neighbor?"—with a story instead of a definition. What definition does the story imply? Do you agree with the definition? Why or why not? How does Jesus tailor his story to his audience? Why does he choose a Samaritan as the hero of his story?

CORRESPONDENCES

1. "Every man's neighbor is his looking glass." What point is this English proverb making about behavior? How might that point apply to the parable of the Good Samaritan?

2. Review Goethe's perspective (page 17) and discuss its application to "The Good Samaritan."

APPLICATIONS

1. Discuss with your group the concept of community, a central theme in "The Good Samaritan." What emotional, sensory, and visual associations does the word evoke for you? When did you most feel part of a community? Is it possible to have a sense of community living in a city as opposed to a small town? What images do you associate with community? Can people from different cultures share a sense of community? Write a summary of your group's discussion, citing specifics.

2. Write a journal entry describing your concept of an ideal community and the roles you can imagine yourself fulfilling in such a place.

3. Brainstorm on your associations with the word "neighbor." What images does it evoke? How has the concept of neighbor changed with time? What factors have contributed? How well do you know your next-door neighbor? Write a concise summary of the points discussed in your group.

People Like Us

DAVID BROOKS

The gently satirical David Brooks (b. 1961 in Toronto) has become familiar to a large audience through his books, his column in the New York Times *(2003–), and his appearances on National Public Radio and the* News Hour with Jim Lehrer. *He grew up in New York City and a suburb of Philadelphia and graduated from the University of Chicago in 1983. Brooks has worked for the* Wall Street Journal *(1986–95) as book review editor, movie critic, foreign correspondent, and op-ed editor, and as senior editor of* The Weekly Standard *(1995–2003). He edited* Backward and Upward: The New Conservative Writing *(1995). Brooks's* Bobos in Paradise: The New Upper Class and How They Got There *(2000) describes that class as "bourgeois bohemians," i.e., yuppie-hippies who are both well-educated and self-indulgent, gently mocking their consumption habits and disdain for conformity. Brooks strongly implies that he himself is a Bobo. His next book,* On Paradise Drive: How We Live Now (and Always Have) in the Future Tense *(2004), continued to describe this group. Do you agree with Brooks that our attitude toward diversity is rather hypocritical?*

MAYBE IT'S TIME to admit the obvious. We don't really care about diversity all that much in America, even though we talk about it a great deal. Maybe somewhere in this country there is a truly diverse neighborhood in which a black Pentecostal minister lives next to a white antiglobalization activist, who lives next to an Asian short-order cook, who lives next to a professional golfer, who lives next to a postmodern-literature professor and a cardiovascular surgeon. But I have never been to or heard of that neighborhood. Instead, what I have seen all around the country is people making strenuous efforts to group themselves with people who are basically like themselves.

Human beings are capable of drawing amazingly subtle social distinctions and then shaping their lives around them. In the Washington, D.C., area Democratic lawyers tend to live in suburban Maryland, and Republican lawyers tend to live in suburban Virginia. If you asked a Democratic lawyer to move from her $750,000 house in Bethesda, Maryland, to a $750,000 house in Great Falls, Virginia, she'd look at you as if you had just asked her to buy a pickup truck with a gun rack and to shove chewing tobacco in her kid's mouth. In Manhattan the owner of a

$3 million SoHo loft would feel out of place moving into a $3 million. Fifth Avenue apartment. A West Hollywood interior decorator would feel dislocated if you asked him to move to Orange County. In Georgia a barista from Athens would probably not fit in serving coffee in Americus.

It is a common complaint that every place is starting to look the same. But in the information age, the late writer James Chapin once told me, every place becomes more like itself. People are less often tied down to factories and mills, and they can search for places to live on the basis of cultural affinity. Once they find a town in which people share their values, they flock there, and reinforce whatever was distinctive about the town in the first place. Once Boulder, Colorado, became known as congenial to politically progressive mountain bikers, half the politically progressive mountain bikers in the country (it seems) moved there; they made the place so culturally pure that it has become practically a parody of itself.

But people love it. Make no mistake—we are increasing our happiness by segmenting off so rigorously. We are finding places where we are comfortable and where we feel we can flourish. But the choices we make toward that end lead to the very opposite of diversity. The United States might be a diverse nation when considered as a whole, but block by block and institution by institution it is a relatively homogeneous nation.

When we use the word "diversity" today we usually mean racial integration. But even here our good intentions seem to have run into the brick wall of human nature. Over the past generation reformers have tried heroically, and in many cases successfully, to end housing discrimination. But recent patterns aren't encouraging: according to an analysis of the 2000 census data, the 1990s saw only a slight increase in the racial integration of neighborhoods in the United States. The number of middle-class and upper-middle-class African-American families is rising, but for whatever reasons—racism, psychological comfort—these families tend to congregate in predominantly black neighborhoods.

In fact, evidence suggests that some neighborhoods become more segregated over time. New suburbs in Arizona and Nevada, for example, start out reasonably well integrated. These neighborhoods don't yet have reputations, so people choose their houses for other, mostly economic reasons. But as neighborhoods age, they develop personalities (that's where the Asians live, and that's where the Hispanics live), and segmentation occurs. It could be that in a few years the new suburbs in the South-west will be nearly as segregated as the established ones in the Northeast and the Midwest.

Even though race and ethnicity run deep in American society, we should in theory be able to find areas that are at least culturally diverse.

But here, too, people show few signs of being truly interested in building diverse communities. If you run a retail company and you're thinking of opening new stores, you can choose among dozens of consulting firms that are quite effective at locating your potential customers. They can do this because people with similar tastes and preferences tend to congregate by ZIP code.

The most famous of these precision marketing firms is Claritas, which breaks down the U.S. population into sixty-two psycho-demographic clusters, based on such factors as how much money people make, what they like to read and watch, and what products they have bought in the past. For example, the "suburban sprawl" cluster is composed of young families making about $41,000 a year and living in fast-growing places such as Burnsville, Minnesota, and Bensalem, Pennsylvania. These people are almost twice as likely as other Americans to have three-way calling. They are two and a half times as likely to buy Light n' Lively Kid Yogurt. Members of the "towns & gowns" cluster are recent college graduates in places such as Berkeley, California, and Gainesville, Florida. They are big consumers of DoveBars and *Saturday Night Live*. They tend to drive small foreign cars and to read *Rolling Stone* and *Scientific American*.

Looking through the market research, one can sometimes be amazed by how efficiently people cluster—and by how predictable we all are. If you wanted to sell imported wine, obviously you would have to find places where rich people live. But did you know that the sixteen counties with the greatest proportion of imported-wine drinkers are all in the same three metropolitan areas (New York, San Francisco, and Washington, D.C.)? If you tried to open a motor-home dealership in Montgomery County, Pennsylvania, you'd probably go broke, because people in this ring of the Philadelphia suburbs think RVs are kind of uncool. But if you traveled just a short way north, to Monroe County, Pennsylvania, you would find yourself in the fifth motor-home-friendliest county in America.

Geography is not the only way we find ourselves divided from people unlike us. Some of us watch Fox News, while others listen to NPR. Some like David Letterman, and others—typically in less urban neighborhoods—like Jay Leno. Some go to charismatic churches: some go to mainstream churches. Americans tend more and more often to marry people with education levels similar to their own, and to befriend people with backgrounds similar to their own.

My favorite illustration of this latter pattern comes from the first, noncontroversial chapter of *The Bell Curve*. Think of your twelve closest friends, Richard J. Herrnstein and Charles Murray write. If you had chosen them randomly from the American population, the odds that half of your twelve closest friends would be college graduates would be six in a thousand. The odds that half of the twelve would have advanced degrees would be less than one in a million. Have any of your twelve closest friends graduated from Harvard, Stanford, Yale, Princeton, Caltech, MIT, Duke, Dartmouth, Cornell, Columbia, Chicago, or Brown? If you chose your friends randomly from the American population, the odds against your having four or more friends from those schools would be more than a billion to one.

Many of us live in absurdly unlikely groupings, because we have organized our lives that way.

It's striking that the institutions that talk the most about diversity often practice it the least. For example, no group of people sings the diversity anthem more frequently and fervently than administrators at just such elite universities. But elite universities are amazingly undiverse in their values, politics, and mores. Professors in particular are drawn from a rather narrow segment of the population. If faculties reflected the general population, 32 percent of professors would be registered Democrats and 31 percent would be registered Republicans. Forty percent would be evangelical Christians. But a recent study of several universities by the conservative Center for the Study of Popular Culture and the American Enterprise Institute found that roughly 90 percent of those professors in the arts and sciences who had registered with a political party had registered Democratic. Fifty-seven professors at Brown were found on the voter-registration rolls. Of those, fifty-four were Democrats. Of the forty-two professors in the English, history, sociology, and political-science departments, all were Democrats. The results at Harvard, Penn State, Maryland, and the University of California at Santa Barbara were similar to the results at Brown.

What we are looking at here is human nature. People want to be around others who are roughly like themselves. That's called community. It probably would be psychologically difficult for most Brown professors to share an office with someone who was pro-life, a member of the National Rifle Association, or an evangelical Christian. It's likely that hiring committees would subtly—even unconsciously—screen out any such people they encountered. Republicans and evangelical Christians have sensed that they are not welcome at places like Brown, so they don't even consider working there. In fact, any registered Republican who contemplates a career in academia these days is both a hero and a fool. So, in a semi–self-selective pattern, brainy people with generally liberal social mores flow to academia, and brainy people with generally conservative mores flow elsewhere.

The dream of diversity is like the dream of equality. Both are based on ideals we celebrate even as we undermine them daily. (How many times have you seen someone renounce a high-paying job or pull his child from an elite college on the grounds that these things are bad for equality?) On the one hand, the situation is appalling. It is appalling that Americans know so little about one another. It is appalling that many of us are so narrow-minded that we can't tolerate a few people with ideas significantly different from our own. It's appalling that evangelical Christians are practically absent from entire professions, such as academia, the media, and filmmaking. It's appalling that people should be content to cut themselves off from everyone unlike themselves.

The segmentation of society means that often we don't even have arguments across the political divide. Within their little validating communities, liberals and conservatives circulate half-truths about the supposed awfulness of the other side. These distortions are believed because it feels good to believe them.

On the other hand, there are limits to how diverse any community can or should be. I've come to think that it is not useful to try to hammer diversity into every neighborhood and institution in the United States. Sure, Augusta National should probably admit women, and university sociology departments should probably hire a conservative or two. It would be nice if all neighborhoods had a good mixture of ethnicities. But human nature being what it is, most places and institutions are going to remain culturally homogeneous.

It's probably better to think about diverse lives, not diverse institutions. Human beings, if they are to live well, will have to move through a series of institutions and environments, which may be individually homogeneous but, taken together, will offer diverse experiences. It might also be a good idea to make national service a rite of passage for young people in this country: it would take them out of their narrow neighborhood segment and thrust them in with people unlike themselves. Finally, it's probably important for adults to get out of their own familiar circles. If you live in a coastal, socially liberal neighborhood, maybe you should take out a subscription to *The Door*, the evangelical humor magazine; or maybe you should visit Branson, Missouri. Maybe you should stop in at a megachurch. Sure, it would be superficial familiarity, but it beats the iron curtains that now separate the nation's various cultural zones.

Look around at your daily life. Are you really in touch with the broad diversity of American life? Do you care?

INTERPRETATIONS

1. Brooks maintains that people like to group themselves with others who are similar to themselves. What factors are mentioned that might provide a center of association for individuals?

2. According to Brooks, what accounts for the segregation of neighborhoods? Describe the social mechanism that he sees at work.

3. In paragraphs 13 and 14, Brooks argues that "the institutions that talk most about diversity often practice it the least." What evidence does he use to support this statement?

4. After you finish reading the essay, what conclusion do you come to about how Brooks feels about the segmentation that exists in America? What are some concrete effects of seeking out "people like us"?

CORRESPONDENCES

1. To what extent might Brooks's essay be used to explain what happens to John Wideman in "The Night I Was Nobody"?

2. Compare Brooks's essay to Linda Stanley's "Passion and the Dream" in Chapter 7. How well are Brooks's theories about community supported by Stanley's experiences?

APPLICATIONS

1. In paragraph 14, Brooks defines community as people wanting "to be around others who are roughly like themselves." Do you agree or disagree with this definition? Write a journal entry explaining your responses.

2. Draw a limited genealogical chart that shows your family (grandparents, your immediate family, and first cousins). Using some of the criteria mentioned by Brooks, try to assess how similar or different these people are. In a few paragraphs, explain your conclusions stating directly the criteria you are applying.

   Now, add to this chart those relatives who have married into the family. How do they compare to the original grouping? How do your findings compare to those of Brooks? Present your conclusions in a few paragraphs.

3. "Do you care?" What are the implications of people surrounding themselves with similar individuals? Write an essay that argues for or against the need to pursue diversity in America.

4. "Who are 'us'?"

   At a computer that has access to the Internet, point your browser to www.google.com. Type your ZIP code into the search bar and click on "Search." One of the first results you get should be something like "XXXXX Zip Code Detailed Profile—residents and real estate info" (where XXXXX is the ZIP code you initially entered) and have a Web address that starts with www.city-data.com/zips/. Click on this link. Now you should have a Web page listing some demographics for the ZIP code you initially entered. Next, for additional information, click on the highlighted text next to "City" toward the top center of the page.

What information have you learned about people in this ZIP code? How does this data relate to what Brooks has mentioned in his essay?

Changing My Name after Sixty Years

TOM ROSENBERG

Tom Rosenberg was born in Berlin, Germany, but in 1938 his family fled Nazi persecution, settling in New York City when Rosenberg was six years old. In an attempt to downplay their Jewish heritage, the Rosenbergs changed their surname to Ross upon arriving in the United States. As Tom Ross, Rosenberg grew up in New York, graduated from the University of Pittsburgh, then joined the Marines and served in the Korean War. He moved to the West Coast upon returning to the United States and served as a political consultant for nearly thirty years, spearheading environmental and outdoor recreation initiatives. He published his first novel, Phantom on His Wheels *in 2000, which draws upon his interests in journalism, environmentalism, and politics. The following essay, which appeared in the July 17, 2000, issue of* Newsweek, *shows how Rosenberg spent most of his life denying his heritage and explains why he has chosen to embrace it now.*

MY PARENTS LEFT NAZI GERMANY in 1938, when I was six and my mother was pregnant with my sister. They arrived in America with a lot of baggage—guilt over deserting loved ones, anger over losing their home and business, and a lifelong fear of anti-Semitism.

Shortly thereafter, whether out of fear, a desire to assimilate, or a combination of both, they changed our family name from Rosenberg to Ross. My parents were different from the immigrants who landed on Ellis Island and had their names changed by an immigration bureaucrat. My mother and father voluntarily gave up their identity and a measure of pride for an Anglicized name.

Growing up a German-Jewish kid in the Bronx in the 1940s, a time when Americans were dying in a war fought in part to save Jews from the hated Nazis, was difficult. Even my new name failed to protect me from bigotry; the neighborhood bullies knew a "sheenie" when they saw one.

The bullying only intensified the shame I felt about my family's religious and ethnic background. I spent much of my youth denying my roots and vying for my peers' acceptance as "Tom Ross." Today I look back and wonder what kind of life I might have led if my parents had kept our family name.

In the '50s, I doubt Tom Rosenberg would have been accepted as a pledge by Theta Chi, a predominantly Christian fraternity at my college. He probably would have pledged a Jewish fraternity or had the self-confidence and conviction to ignore the Greek system altogether. Tom Rosenberg might have married a Jewish woman, stayed in the East, and maintained closer ties to his Jewish family.

As it was, I moved west to San Francisco. Only after I married and became a father did I begin to acknowledge my Jewish heritage.

My first wife, a liberal Methodist, insisted that I stop running from Judaism. For years we attended both a Unitarian church and a Jewish temple. Her open-minded attitude set the tone in our household and was passed on to our three kids. As a family, we celebrated Christmas and went to temple on the High Holidays. But even though my wife and I were careful to teach our kids tolerance, their exposure to either religion was minimal. Most weekends, we took the kids on ski trips, rationalizing that the majesty of the Sierra was enough of a spiritual experience.

So last year, when I decided to tell my children that I was legally changing my name back to Rosenberg, I wondered how they would react. We were in a restaurant celebrating the publication of my first novel. After they toasted my tenacity for staying with fiction for some thirty years, I made my announcement: "I want to be remembered by the name I was born with."

I explained that the kind of discrimination and stereotyping still evident today had made me rethink the years I'd spent denying my family's history, years that I'd been ashamed to talk about with them. The present political climate—the initiatives attacking social services for immigrants, bilingual education, Affirmative Action—made me want to shout "I'm an immigrant!" My children were silent for a moment before they smiled, leaned over, and hugged me.

The memories of my years of denial continued to dog me as I told friends and family that I planned to change my name. The rabbi at the Reform temple that I belong to with my second wife suggested I go a step further. "Have you thought of taking a Hebrew first name?" he asked.

He must have seen the shocked look on my face. I wondered, is he suggesting I become more religious, more Jewish? "What's involved?" I asked hesitatingly.

The rabbi explained that the ceremony would be simple and private, just for family and friends. I would make a few remarks about why I had selected my name, and then he would say a blessing.

It took me a moment to grasp the significance of what the rabbi was proposing. He saw my name change as a chance to do more than reclaim a piece of my family's history: it was an opportunity to renew my commitment to Jewish ideals. I realized it was also a way to give my kids the sense of pride in their heritage that they had missed out on as children.

A few months later I stood at the pulpit in front of an open, lighted ark, flanked by my wife and the rabbi. Before me stood my children, holding their children. I had scribbled a few notes for my talk, but felt too emotional to use them. I held on to the lectern for support and winged it.

"Every time I step into a temple. I'm reminded that Judaism has survived for 4,000 years. It's survived because it's a positive religion. My parents, your grandparents, changed their name out of fear. I'm changing it back out of pride. I chose the name Tikvah because it means hope."

INTERPRETATIONS

1. In the last paragraph, Rosenberg says to his children, "My parents, your grandparents, changed their name out of fear. I'm changing it back out of pride." What, specifically, were Rosenberg's parents afraid of? What is the source of Rosenberg's pride?

2. In what ways does Rosenberg's decision reflect his awareness of family and community?

3. According to Rosenberg, how might his life had been different had his parents not changed their name?

CORRESPONDENCES

1. Compare Rosenberg's essay to the one by Lewis Sawaquat (page 61). What similarities do you notice in the writers' lives? What similarities do you notice in their narratives?

2. In the first paragraph of his narrative, Rosenberg describes the situation surrounding his coming to America. Why did his parents leave Germany? What was the reality confronting them in 1938? Read "Janushinka" by Hana Wehle in Chapter 8. How does this narrative help you to understand Rosenberg's early life?

APPLICATIONS

1. If you had the opportunity to give yourself a name, what would you choose? You might consider a name that describes you, or one in

another language that is meaningful to you. Now, imagine yourself at a naming ceremony similar to the one Rosenberg describes. Write out a speech that explains the significance of your new name that you will deliver to your close friends and family.

2. In paragraph 7, Rosenberg briefly mentions religion and spirituality. What relationship do you think exists between these terms? How might you explain your definition of these terms and how they relate to each other?

3. What religious beliefs or customs are followed by your parents or grandparents? Do you actively participate in these beliefs and/or practices? Why or why not? What general idea governs what you choose to believe and follow?

We Kissed the Tomato and Then the Sky

DANA WEHLE

Dana Wehle (b. 1954), born in Queens, New York, now lives in Brooklyn. She is a classically trained painter with a masters of fine arts. The daughter of two Holocaust survivors, her work has been recognized for its effectiveness in communicating the impact of the Holocaust on the second generation. She has a master's degree in social work and is a certified psychoanalyst with a private psychotherapy practice in New York. Her chapter on the suppression of creativity in oppressive environments is included in a forthcoming book entitled Psychoanalytic Approaches to Cult Recovery. *As you read her essay, list in your journal her conflicting emotions about her mother. To what extent does she resolve them?*

MY PARENTS' BIG BED was not the kind to take refuge in when I was little. The two twin beds, connected by an elegant walnut headboard, were each clearly assigned. One was his, one was hers. After my father died, my mother made the monumental decision to make his side hers after forty-three years of it being the other way. She defensively explained that her motive was not to help resolve her loss, but simply to be closer to the door. In fact, the increasing number of times she got up during the night became a matter of concern to us all.

When I visited her once she was alone, I knew she would have preferred my sleeping next to her but, always needing my space, I awkwardly told her I preferred to sleep upstairs in my old room. Our love was deep and passionate, but our differences were equally as strong. For years, I had perched on a ledge waiting patiently, and sometimes not so patiently, for an opening for her to let me love her and for her to return that love for an extended period of time without tense interruption. It might have happened that the clock ran out before that opening presented itself. But, like a seagull watching for signs of food, I didn't miss my chance.

Just a year and a half after my father died, as cancer slowed her down and her need to lead was increasingly balanced by her willingness to be led, I cherished sleeping next to her. Two grown women, mother and daughter in corny, flowery nightgowns, filled this once forbidding bed in precious unity. Night after night, our arms stretched across the crack between the beds as our hands warmly joined. With just one reading light easing the darkness, I now viewed the room from her vantage point. In this space that enveloped us both, my mother would share her disbelief at her illness, her increasing symptoms and pains and even her unanswerable questions. I would say, "Pfeh!"; and she would say, "That's right. Pfeh!" Each lying on our own side, we were fully on the same side in sharing the sadness and the anger. We talked about Karl, her first husband, and my father and how blessed she felt for having loved two such loving men. She asked me if I was happy with my husband, and I said "very." We bonded as two women who shared the thankfulness of knowing this type of love.

Once, I crawled on her side and kissed her soft cheek. She gave me her special "Safta"* kiss. I kissed her hand and retreated to my side of the enormous bed. In the middle of the night, I was awakened by her moans of pain, which she did not recall in the morning. Keeping to her routine, I made the bed in just the right way: the bedspread did not touch the floor, the quilts were not bumpy, and the throw pillows were not carelessly placed. In spite of this, she became cold when the temperature was warm; full when she ate only a spoonful; and tired when her day had barely begun.

The big bed, now perfectly made in its flowery pastel-colored spread with matching pillows, holds all these memories plus the last— her lying there no longer able to warmly hold my hand.

• • •

Who would have believed that in my lifetime I would have gotten to share meditation space with my mother? But in her last weeks, when the pain of cancer slowed her down, this fast-moving, always self-sufficient woman was too tired to run. She did not stop running all at once, however. It was gradual, more like the increasing presence of the left hand in a piano composition, where the effect of the grave bass notes emerges in time.

For my mother, shopping was once the beginning of a long day that included swimming forty laps, cooking up a storm, writing letters, doing "administrative work," and trying to sit down to write the last essay in a series on her Holocaust experiences. At this time, shopping alone wore her out. As she would say, "she couldn't anymore." How trapped she must have felt. Her survivor instincts told her she had to

---

*"Safta" means grandmother in Hebrew. This kiss had no name when my siblings and I were young but my mother called it "the safta kiss" with the grandchildren. It can't be described, it has to be experienced.

find new doors. Though she could no longer will her body to do more, she still had command over her mind and soul. At seventy-nine, this Czech Jewish woman who was set in her ways opened herself up to a "New Age" experience.

We meditated in two green-and-white lawn chairs, inhaling and exhaling as we felt the earth's energy travel through our bodies. We visualized ourselves as eagles flying above Floral Park and landing at Jones Beach. We watched the ocean come forward and recede as we observed our breathing doing the same. We felt the rhythm of nature and the universe and experienced ourselves being part of the whole. Guided by ancient wisdom, we tried to find balance within the extremes and centeredness in the moment. After we embraced memories of the past at Jones Beach and absorbed the ocean's lessons, we slowly traveled back to Queens. We landed and gently opened our eyes. My mother and I were sitting in the driveway in the sun, hearing the birds sing, the neighbors rattle their garbage cans, and the dogs bark as we listened to the silence.

One week later, two weeks before her death, we sat in a sculpture park with two dear friends. My mother enthusiastically suggested that she lead us through a meditation. I got to share this sacred space with her; this space she could create only because even at this desperate time, she was open to expansion. I still hear her saying "I feel the wind caressing my face."

• • •

She sat there with a weak smile on her face as her fading eyes suddenly filled with the recognition of a world once known. Around the large dining room table, my mother, my sisters, and I were assembled. My brother went between this room and another, changing CDs as we all tried to decide which music to play at her funeral. The surrealism of the moment was not lost.

I sat directly across from her and caught the flash of light in her sunken eyes as the Beethoven piece we played at my father's funeral filled the air. I think the others missed this flash as they continued to discuss the options. I requested that we be silent and share the experience.

If music can be worn out, this Beethoven concerto would have been destroyed by how often my mother listened to it after my father's death. After a year or so, however, this same CD became lethal for her as she could no longer bear the pain that it evoked. On this day before her own death and one and a half years after my father's, with fresh ears, she received this music as an offering from heaven.

My mother described our relationship as love/hate. But at that time, when only I seemed to know what filled her heart, I knew what she meant by her last direct words to me: "It always amazed me how you would sometimes know what I was feeling without my saying the words."

Dear Ma, I had a dream a few days after you died and all I remember is you sitting at the end of the table smiling at me as you knew I knew the profound joy you were feeling at the moment Daddy's music filled your soul.

• • •

Oddly, my mother's death has given me a sense of completion in a way similar to my finishing a painting. Drawn studies, painted studies, notes, and art materials fill my studio as the residue of final works. Audio tapes and journals crammed with ponderings about my parents' future deaths fill my drawers, which, with my memories, are the stuff of my latest final work. I prepared for the day when I could no longer hear their voices by taping their sweetest answering machine messages. One year after my father's death Ma left these:

Are you home? Daninko? OK. I just came from the city. I wanted to report to you, OK? Thank you, Bye-bye. (October 1996)

Hi Dana. Are you there? Are you home? Oh. What a pity. Channel 13. Danny Kaye. So, I thought you would laugh. Anyhow, Bye-bye. (December 1996)

My mother's urgency defined her life-affirming existence, yet it was also a constant reminder to me of her emotional scars. She beat death so many times, from the gas chambers to critical illnesses. She was just beginning to beat her paralyzing grief after my father's death. Now, her obsessive race, which she so ably finessed over her lifetime, was over.

This seventy-nine-year-old woman was a juggler extraordinaire, but a juggler's art is both exhilarating and unsettling to watch. Warding off the sound of shattering plates, my mother looked straight ahead till the very end. One quiet night, however, she did confess that she was not sure whether she or the cancer was in control. When the terror of death found its way through her thick defenses, my mother found solace in knowing she would be with my father when she died.

The last of her messages was left thirty-four days before her end, and it went like this:

Hi Dana. I am just reporting. I am chewing my breakfast very slowly. I came from swimming . . . and I will rest . . . and then

I will go to get the drug. And I had a very good, peaceful night. And also Dr. Li called me, how I am feeling after that tea. So, that was very nice. I hope you are fine. I am just reporting. Bye-bye. (May 1997)

I suppose it's because she had no regrets, and because I now have many answers to questions that occupied me since I was young, that I feel some sense of completion. Both finishing a painting and saying goodbye to someone you love require time to reflect upon moments that are just right as well as unanswered questions.

Hello? Dani? Are you home? That's Ma. Are you there? Dana? OK, so I just wanted to know what is going on. I didn't hear from you, so I wanted to make sure that you are OK. So call me if you feel up to it. OK? Bye-bye. (March 1997)

Ma. I'm here. Where are you?

• • •

The house is still intact; the pillows on the couch are still scrunched from someone's weight; the flowers in the vases are still more alive than dead; the mail is still coming to a woman who was alive less than a month ago and to a man long gone. My home. My house where I grew up. My parents' house. My mother's house.

Soon my mother's beloved tomato plants, still green, will bear the red harvest that she knew she would not live to see. The piano, which once eloquently spoke for my father through his strong fingers and passionate heart, will be among the things removed. The smell of cardboard boxes mingling with the sight of frenzied dust particles will signal that the pain of saying goodbye is near.

I comfort myself by knowing that my mother's refined artistic sensibility will filter into my home when some of her artwork and belongings will become my own. I look forward to honoring my promise to my father to organize "the stuff downstairs" into an archive. This stuff (rare, browning photographs and documents from before the war; my parents' published writings as witnesses to the Holocaust; materials from my father's years as administrative head of the Jewish Community in Prague, hospital administrator, and Czech Jewish historian; as well as newer family memorabilia) has always been, and will always be, a defiant symbol of their survival. I feel calmed by the honor of this task.

Though the breakdown has not yet started, I have already felt compelled to rescue a remnant of my mother's favorite shirt from being used simply as a rag. The familiar battle between a need to hold on and a voice that says let go has begun. I guess that saying good-bye to her, to him again, and to the house will mean separating from the rags. I guess that the struggle itself will bestow honor upon them and the home they created.

• • •

Today is September 4, 1997, and always counting the time since my father died, I just realized that today is exactly one year and ten months since his death. Ma died on June 11 and I now count both their days, though hers is still counted only in months. The house has been totally dismantled, and its stark emptiness is especially pronounced when strangers come to check out whether they want to make it their home. Like the sound of a wailing Greek chorus, the lamenting of old neighbors, family, and dear friends counters the silent indifference of those who pass through with no feeling. A sweet, subtle reminder of the way Ma sounded when she answered the phone by one of those who loved her the most brings it all back.

Last week, my husband and I picked a juicy red tomato off the stem. Holding each other tightly, we kissed this symbol of life, each other, and then the sky. Our hands could not part. This was our good-bye. Later on, my sister and I held each other. We cried. We prayed. We laughed in our childhood bedroom, as we got one last touch of the textured linoleum tiles that used to bruise our hands while we endlessly practiced to be in the "Jacks Olympics." Filled with the joy of sharing, we said our goodbye.

• • •

Today is September 4, 2000 and I still have not stopped saying goodbye. Tonight, about five years since my father died and about three years since my mother died, the beautiful bright moon suddenly appeared outside my window. Memories of my parents, like the moon, often emerge unexpectedly as sources of light surrounded by darkness. Some nights, when sleep is eluding me, I am struck by the power of memory. Once, while thinking about someone's wedding plans, my eyes got overwhelmed with tears because all I could think about was how gleaming my father's eyes were when he shared in the joy of my wedding just two weeks before he died. Another time, while watching a poignant late night "Roseanne" rerun, I suddenly cried reckless tears because all I could think about was how loving my mother was when she brought me homemade soup while I was recovering from surgery one year before she died.

Each time my tears of loss turn into tears of gratitude, I say good-bye again. Each time my tears of loss turn into tears of gratitude, I feel the wind caressing my face.

INTERPRETATIONS

1. The author refers several times to her mother's urgency. Does this word also describe the author? What examples can you cite? What is the underlying reason for her urgency?
2. Time is an important theme in this essay. What direct and indirect techniques does the author use to suggest the passing of time?
3. Characterize the author's relationship with her mother. What different aspects of this relationship does she portray in the essay?
4. Analyze her father's role in the essay. What symbols does the author associate with him? How do these add unity to the memoir?

CORRESPONDENCES

1. Walker's perspective reflects upon the links between her mother and herself. To what extent is this also true of Wehle's text?
2. Cahill's perspective addresses relationships and communion. Find examples of each in Wehle's text and analyze their effect.

APPLICATIONS

1. Wehle uses many literary techniques to enhance theme. With your group members, cite examples of foreshadowing, similes, and metaphors. To what senses do they appeal? Are there examples that indicate Wehle's interest in the visual arts? Why does she end her essay with a line that occurs earlier? How has its meaning changed?
2. Wehle discusses part of her mother's history and the values she communicated. Write an essay analyzing the impact that your family's history and values has had on you. Be specific.
3. Review the answering machine tapes in Wehle's essay. What do they reveal about her mother? What do they add to knowledge of the author? Is this an effective method for writing memoirs? Why or why not?

Focusing on Friends

STEVE TESICH

Steve Tesich (1943–1996) was born in Yugoslavia and immigrated to the United States when he was fourteen. He is best known for the original screenplay Breaking Away *(1979), for which he won an Academy Award. He also wrote the screenplays* Eyewitness *(1981) and* Four Friends *(1981); many plays for the theater, including* Passing Game *(1977),* The Road *(1978), and* Division Street *(1980); and a novel,* Summer Crossing *(1982). A recurring theme in Tesich's work is the plight of the outsider. Before reading Tesich's essay, brainstorm on the word "friend."*

WHEN I THINK OF PEOPLE who were my good friends, I see them all, as I do everything else from my life, in cinematic terms. The camera work is entirely different for men and women.

I remember all the women in almost extreme close-ups. The settings are different—apartments, restaurants—but they're all interiors, as if I had never spent a single minute with a single woman outside. They're looking right at me, these women in these extreme close-ups; the lighting is exquisite, worthy of a Fellini or Fosse film, and their lips are moving. They're telling me something important or reacting to something even more important that I've told them. It's the kind of movie where you tell people to keep quiet when they chew their popcorn too loudly.

The boys and men who were my friends are in an entirely different movie. No close-ups here. No exquisite lighting. The camera work is rather shaky but the background is moving. We're going somewhere, on foot, on bicycles, in cars. The ritual of motion, of action, makes up for the inconsequential nature of the dialogue. It's a much sloppier film, this film that is not really a film but a memory of real friends: Slobo, Louie, Sam. Male friends. I've loved all three of them. I assumed they knew this, but I never told them.

Quite the contrary is true in my female films. In close-up after close-up, I am telling every woman who I ever loved that I love her, and then lingering on yet another close-up of her face for a reaction. There is a perfectly appropriate musical score playing while I wait. And if I wait long enough, I get an answer. I am loved. I am not loved. Language clears up the suspense. The emotion is nailed down.

Therein lies the difference, I think, between my friendships with men and with women. I can tell women I love them. Not only can I tell them, I am compulsive about it. I can hardly wait to tell them. But I can't tell the men. I just can't. And they can't tell me. Emotions are never nailed down. They run wild, and I and my male friends chase after them, on foot, on bicycles, in cars, keeping the quarry in sight but never catching up.

My first friend was Slobo. I was still living in Yugoslavia at the time, and not far from my house there was an old German truck left abandoned after the war. It had no wheels. No windshield. No doors. But the steering wheel was intact. Slobo and I flew to America in that truck. It was our airplane. Even now, I remember the background moving as we took off down the street, across Europe, across the Atlantic. We were inseparable. The best of friends. Naturally, not one word concerning the nature of our feelings for one another was ever exchanged. It was all done in actions.

The inevitable would happen at least once a day. As we were flying over the Atlantic, there came, out of nowhere, that wonderful moment: engine failure! "We'll have to bail out," I shouted. "A-a-a-a-a!" Slobo made the sound of the failing engine. Then he would turn and look me in the eye: "I can't swim," he'd say. "Fear not." I put my hand on his shoulder. "I'll drag you to shore." And, with that, both of us would tumble out of the truck onto the dusty street. I swam through the dust. Slobo drowned in the dust, coughing, gagging. "Sharks!" he cried. But I always saved him. The next day the ritual would be repeated, only then it would be my turn to say "I can't swim," and Slobo would save me. We saved each other from certain death over a hundred times, until finally a day came when I really left for America with my mother and sister. Slobo and I stood at the train station. We were there to say goodbye, but, since we weren't that good at saying things and since he couldn't save me, he just cried until the train started to move.

The best friend I had in high school was Louie. It now seems to me that I was totally monogamous when it came to male friends. I would have several girl friends but only one real male friend. Louie was it at that time. We were both athletes, and one day we decided to "run till we drop." We just wanted to know what it was like. Skinny Louie set the pace as we ran around our high-school track. Lap after lap. Four laps to a mile. Mile after mile we ran. I had the reputation as being a big-time jock. Louie didn't. But this was Louie's day. There was a bounce in his step and, when he turned back to look at me, his eyes were gleaming with the thrill of it all. I finally dropped. Louie still looked fresh; he seemed capable, on that day, of running forever. But we were the best of friends, and so he stopped. "That's it," he lied,

"I couldn't go another step farther." It was an act of love. Naturally, I said nothing.

Louie got killed in Vietnam. Several weeks after his funeral, I went to his mother's house, and, because she was a woman, I tried to tell her how much I had loved her son. It was not a good scene. Although I was telling the truth, my words sounded like lies. It was all very painful and embarrassing. I kept thinking how sorry I was that I had never told Louie himself.

Sam is my best friend now, and has been for many years. A few years ago, we were swimming at a beach in East Hampton. The Atlantic! The very Atlantic I had flown over in my German truck with Slobo. We had swum out pretty far from the shore when both of us simultaneously thought we spotted a shark. Water is not only a good conductor of electricity but of panic as well. We began splashing like madmen toward shore. Suddenly, at the height of my panic, I realized how much I loved my friend, what an irreplaceable friend he was, and, although I was the faster swimmer, I fell back to protect him. Naturally, the shark in the end proved to be imaginary. But not my feelings for my friend. For several days after that I wanted to share my discovery with him, to tell him how much I love him. Fortunately, I didn't.

I say fortunately because on reflection, there seems to be sufficient evidence to indicate that, if anybody was cheated and shortchanged by me, it was the women, the girls, the very recipients of my uncensored emotions. Yes, I could hardly wait to tell them I loved them. I did love them. But once I told them, something stopped. The emotion was nailed down, but, with it, the enthusiasm and the energy to prove it was nailed down, too. I can remember my voice saying to almost all of them, at one time or another: "I told you I love you. What else do you want?" I can now recoil at the impatient hostility of that voice but I can't deny it was mine.

The tyranny of self-censorship forced me, in my relations with male friends, to seek alternatives to language. And just because I could never be sure they understood exactly how I felt about them, I was forced to look for ways to prove it. That is, I now think how it should be. It is time to make adjustments. It is time to pull back the camera, free the women I know, and myself, from those merciless close-ups and have the background move.

INTERPRETATIONS

1. Contrast Tesich's treatment of male and female friends in his cinematic imagination and in his real life.

2. To what extent do you agree with Tesich that telling a person you love him or her "nails down" the emotion?

3. By moving from the general to the specific, Tesich is able to present Slobo, Louie, and Sam in some detail. How do his portrayals of them clarify his purpose? How do they affect you as his audience?

CORRESPONDENCES

1. Review the Nin perspective on friendship. How does it apply to Tesich's relationships with his male friends?

2. Apply the du Plessix Gray perspective on friendship to Tesich's portrayal of his friendships with women. To what extent do you treat male and female friends differently?

APPLICATIONS

1. In addition to contrasting friendships between men and women and women and men, Tesich also defines friendship in general. Discuss his ideas about friendship with your group. To what extent do you agree with his gender distinctions? Do your friendships fit into the categories he discusses? Write a summary of your conclusions.

2. From the title to the last sentence, much of the language is from the world of filmmaking. How does this language help Tesich clarify his meaning and purpose? Support your point of view with specific examples.

3. How do you differentiate between an acquaintance and a friend? Do you consider someone you "hang out" with frequently your friend? Write a journal entry on these questions.

Mother Tongue

AMY TAN

Amy Tan (b. 1952 in Oakland, CA) has a variety of hobbies, such as billiards and piano-playing with a rock band, and before writing The Joy Luck Club *(1989), for which she won the LA Book Award and the National Book Award, she had a wide variety of jobs, such as bartending and caring for developmentally disabled children. Mother–daughter relationships are frequently important in her work. She was raised by her mother, a vocational nurse; her father, a Baptist minister and electrical engineer, died when Tan was a teenager. Other books of Tan's include* The Kitchen God's Wife *(1991),* The Moon Lady *(2000), and* The Bonesetter's Daughter *(2001).* The Opposite of Fate, *a work of nonfiction, was published in 2003. With* Saving Fish from Drowning *(2005) she returned to novel writing. Are you, like Tan, aware of using "different Englishes"?*

I AM NOT A SCHOLAR OF ENGLISH or literature. I cannot give you much more than personal opinions on the English language and its variations in this country or others.

I am a writer. And by that definition, I am someone who has always loved language. I am fascinated by language in daily life. I spend a great deal of my time thinking about the power of language—the way it can evoke an emotion, a visual image, a complex idea, or a simple truth. Language is the tool of my trade. And I use them all—all the Englishes I grew up with.

Recently, I was made keenly aware of the different Englishes I do use. I was giving a talk to a large group of people, the same talk I had already given to half a dozen other groups. The nature of the talk was about my writing, my life, and my book, *The Joy Luck Club.* The talk was going along well enough, until I remembered one major difference that made the whole talk sound wrong. My mother was in the room. And it was perhaps the first time she had heard me give a lengthy speech, using the kind of English I have never used with her. I was saying things like, "The intersection of memory upon imagination" and "There is an aspect of my fiction that relates to thus-and-thus"—a speech filled with carefully wrought grammatical phrases, burdened, it suddenly seemed to me, with nominalized forms, past perfect tenses, conditional phrases, all the forms of standard English that I had learned in school and through books, the forms of English I did not use at home with my mother.

Just last week, I was walking down the street with my mother, and I again found myself conscious of the English I was using, the English I do use with her. We were talking about the price of new and used furniture and I heard myself saying this: "Not waste money that way." My husband was with us as well, and he didn't notice any switch in my English. And then I realized why. It's because over the twenty years we've been together I've often used that same kind of English with him, and sometimes he even uses it with me. It has become our language of intimacy, a different sort of English that relates to family talk, the language I grew up with.

So you'll have some idea of what this family talk I heard sounds like, I'll quote what my mother said during a recent conversation which I videotaped and then transcribed. During this conversation, my mother was talking about a political gangster in Shanghai who had the same last name as her family's, Du, and how the gangster in his early years wanted to be adopted by her family, which was rich by comparison. Later, the gangster became more powerful, far richer than my mother's family, and one day showed up at my mother's wedding to pay his respects. Here's what she said in part:

"Du Yusong having business like fruit stand. Like off the street kind. He is Du like Du Zong—but not Tsung-ming Island people. The local people call putong, the river east side, he belong to that side local people. That man want to ask Du Zong father take him in like become own family. Du Zong father wasn't look down on him, but didn't take seriously, until that man big like become a mafia. Now important person, very hard to inviting him. Chinese way, came only to show respect, don't stay for dinner. Respect for making big celebration, he shows up. Mean gives lots of respect. Chinese custom. Chinese social life that way. If too important won't have to stay too long. He come to my wedding. I didn't see, I heard it. I gone to boy's side, they have YMCA dinner. Chinese age I was nineteen."

You should know that my mother's expressive command of English belies how much she actually understands. She reads the *Forbes* report, listens to *Wall Street Week*, converses daily with her stockbroker, reads all of Shirley MacLaine's books with ease—all kinds of things I can't begin to understand. Yet some of my friends tell me they understand 50 percent of what my mother says. Some say they understand 80 to 90 percent. Some say they understand none of it, as if she were speaking pure Chinese. But to me, my mother's English is perfectly clear, perfectly natural. It's my mother tongue. Her language, as I hear it, is vivid, direct, full of observation and imagery. That was the language that helped shape the way I saw things, expressed things, made sense of the world.

Lately, I've been giving more thought to the kind of English my mother speaks. Like others, I have described it to people as "broken" or "fractured" English. But I wince when I say that. It has always bothered me that I can think of no way to describe it other than "broken," as if it were damaged and needed to be fixed, as if it lacked a certain wholeness and soundness. I've heard other terms used, "limited English," for example. But they seem just as bad, as if everything is limited, including people's perceptions of the limited English speaker.

I know this for a fact, because when I was growing up, my mother's "limited" English limited *my* perception of her. I was ashamed of her English. I believed that her English reflected the quality of what she had to say. That is, because she expressed them imperfectly her thoughts were imperfect. And I had plenty of empirical evidence to support me: the fact that people in department stores, at banks, and at restaurants did not take her seriously, did not give her good service, pretended not to understand her, or even acted as if they did not hear her.

My mother has long realized the limitations of her English as well. When I was fifteen, she used to have me call people on the phone to pretend I was she. In this guise, I was forced to ask for information or even to complain and yell at people who had been rude to her. One time it was a call to her stockbroker in New York. She had cashed out her small portfolio and it just so happened we were going to go to New York the next week, our very first trip outside California. I had to get on the phone and say in an adolescent voice that was not very convincing, "This is Mrs. Tan."

And my mother was standing in the back whispering loudly, "Why he don't send me check, already two weeks late. So mad he lie to me, losing me money."

And then I said in perfect English, "Yes, I'm getting rather concerned. You had agreed to send the check two weeks ago, but it hasn't arrived."

Then she began to talk more loudly. "What he want, I come to New York tell him front of his boss, you cheating me?" And I was trying to calm her down, make her be quiet, while telling the stockbroker, "I can't tolerate any more excuses. If I don't receive the check immediately, I am going to have to speak to your manager when I'm in New York next week." And sure enough, the following week there we were in front of this astonished stockbroker, and I was sitting there red-faced and quiet, and my mother, the real Mrs. Tan, was shouting at his boss in her impeccable broken English.

We used a similar routine just five days ago, for a situation that was far less humorous. My mother had gone to the hospital for an appointment, to find out about a benign brain tumor a CAT scan had revealed a month ago. She said she had spoken very good English, her best English, no mistakes. Still, she said, the hospital did not apologize when they said they had lost the CAT scan and she had come for nothing. She said they did not seem to have any sympathy when she told them she was anxious to know the exact diagnosis, since her husband and son had both died of brain tumors. She said they would not give her any more information until the next time and she would have to make another appointment for that. So she said she would not leave until the doctor called her daughter. She wouldn't budge. And when the doctor finally called her daughter, me, who spoke in perfect English—lo and behold—we had assurances the CAT scan would be found, promises that a conference call on Monday would be held, and apologies for any suffering my mother had gone through for a most regrettable mistake.

I think my mother's English almost had an effect on limiting my possibilities in life as well. Sociologists and linguists probably will tell you that a person's developing language skills are more influenced by peers. But I do think that the language spoken in the family, especially in immigrant families which are more insular, plays a large role in shaping the language of the child. And I believe that it affected my results on achievement tests, IQ tests, and the SAT. While my English skills were never judged as poor, compared to math, English could not be considered my strong suit. In grade school I did moderately well, getting perhaps B's, sometimes B-pluses, in English and scoring perhaps in the sixtieth or seventieth percentile on achievement tests. But those scores were not good enough to override the opinion that my true abilities lay in math and science, because in those areas I achieved A's and scored in the ninetieth percentile or higher.

This was understandable. Math is precise; there is only one correct answer. Whereas, for me at least, the answers on English tests were always a judgment call, a matter of opinion and personal experience. Those tests were constructed around items like fill-in-the-blank sentence completion, such as, "Even though Tom was_____, Mary thought he was_____." And the correct answer always seemed to be the most bland combinations of thoughts, for example, "Even though Tom was shy, Mary thought he was charming," with the grammatical structure "even though" limiting the correct answer to some sort of semantic opposites, so you wouldn't get answers like, "Even though Tom was foolish, Mary thought he was ridiculous." Well, according to my mother, there were very few limitations as to what Tom could have been and what Mary might have thought of him. So I never did well on tests like that.

The same was true with word analogies, pairs of words in which you were supposed to find some sort of logical, semantic relationship—for example, "*Sunset* is to *nightfall* as_____ is to_____." And here you would be presented with a list of four possible pairs, one of which showed the same kind of relationship: *red* is to *stoplight, bus* is to *arrival, chills* is to *fever, yawn* is to *boring.* Well, I could never think that way. I knew what the tests were asking, but I could not block out of my mind the images already created by the first pair, "*sunset* is to *nightfall*"—and I would see a burst of color against a darkening sky, the moon rising, the lowering of a curtain of stars. And all the other pairs of words—red, bus, stoplight, boring—just threw up a mass of confusing images, making it impossible for me to sort out something as logical as saying: "A sunset precedes nightfall" is the same as "a chill precedes a fever." The only way I would have gotten that answer right would have been to imagine an associative situation, for example, by being disobedient and staying out past sunset, catching a chill at night which turns into feverish pneumonia as punishment, which indeed did happen to me.

I have been thinking about all this lately, about my mother's English, about achievement tests. Because lately I've been asked, as a writer, why there are not more Asian Americans represented in American literature. Why are there few Asian Americans enrolled in creative writing programs? Why do so many Chinese students go into engineering? Well, these are broad sociological questions I can't begin to answer. But I have noticed in surveys—in fact, just last week—that Asian students, as a whole, always do significantly better on math achievement tests than in English. And this makes me think that there are other Asian-American students whose English spoken in the home might also be described as "broken" or "limited." And perhaps they also have teachers who are steering them away from writing and into math and science, which is what happened to me.

Fortunately, I happen to be rebellious in nature and enjoy the challenge of disproving assumptions made about me. I became an English major my first year in college, after being enrolled as pre-med. I started writing nonfiction as a freelancer the week after I was told by my former boss that writing was my worst skill and I should hone my talents toward account management.

But it wasn't until 1985 that I finally began to write fiction. And at first I wrote using what I thought to be wittily crafted sentences, sentences that would finally prove I had mastery over the English language. Here's an example from the first draft of a story that later made its way into *The Joy Luck Club,* but without this line: "That was my mental quandary in its nascent state." A terrible line, which I can hardly pronounce.

Fortunately, for reasons I won't get into today, I later decided I should envision a reader for the stories I would write. And the reader I decided upon was my mother, because these were stories about mothers. So with this reader in mind—and in fact she did read my early drafts—I began to write stories using all the Englishes I grew up with: the English I spoke to my mother, which for lack of a better term might be described as "simple"; the English she used with me, which for lack of a better term might be described as "broken"; my translation of her Chinese, which could certainly be described as "watered down"; and what I imagine to be her translation of her Chinese if she could speak in perfect English, her internal language, and for that I sought to preserve the essence, but neither an English nor a Chinese structure. I wanted to capture what language ability tests can never reveal: her intent, her passion, her imagery, the rhythms of her speech and the nature of her thoughts.

Apart from what any critic had to say about my writing, I knew I had succeeded where it counted when my mother finished reading my book and gave me her verdict: "So easy to read."

INTERPRETATIONS

1. Tan states in her second paragraph that she is "fascinated by language in daily life." Cite examples from her essay that support that statement.

2. What several "Englishes" do you speak and why? What determines the English you use in a particular situation? Cite examples.

3. Tan cites several examples of "family talk" in her essay. Which did you enjoy most?

4. How does she also use "family talk" to create portraits of her mother? Be specific.

5. How effectively does Tan's essay illustrate that being bilingual can make a writer better in both languages?

CORRESPONDENCES

1. Review Ellison's perspective and discuss its relevance to Tan's essay. To what extent can Tan's mother be considered "her ancestor?" Explain.

2. Review Gallant's perspective on families. To what extent do you agree or disagree? How does it apply to Tan's essay?

APPLICATIONS

1. Good writing, according to Tan, is easy reading. How good according to this criterion is Tan's essay? Write a journal entry citing specific examples from "Mother Tongue."

2. Point of view concerns the narrative of a written text and answers the question "who is telling the story?" Review Tan's text and imagine how different it might be if told from her mother's point of view. Rewrite a section of Tan's essay, paying close attention to what that character is thinking, feeling, and experiencing. Also, be sure to include specific details that capitalize on the character's knowledge of the event you are writing about.

3. Sometimes we can best illustrate the importance of a relationship by focusing on a particular event. Choose an event, action, or conversation to best explain a relationship that is important to you.

4. Write a journal entry on the significance of Tan's title "Mother Tongue."

Treasures

MAHWASH SHOAIB

Mahwash Shoaib (b. 1973), a native of Pakistan, is a graduate of the University of Punjab and currently a graduate student at the Graduate School and University Center of CUNY in New York City. She is a poet, a writer, and a translator of poetry from her native Urdu language into English. Keenly interested in philosophy as a way of life, she devotes her time between the study of language and literature, writing, and bibliophilia. Her aim is to realize her creative potential in both fiction and poetry. Before reading Shoaib's essay, freewrite on one of your "treasures."

Pakistan, formerly a part of India, became a dominion in 1947. In 1956, an Islamic Republic was proclaimed. For the next thirty-five years, government consisted of a series of elected prime ministers alternating with military coup d'etats. In 1988, Benazir Bhutto became the first female leader of a Muslim nation when she was elected prime minister. In the nine years that followed, three governments were successively dissolved on the allegation of corruption and mismanagement. Although Nawaz Sharif was appointed the prime minister in 1996 through a landslide vote, the country itself faces an uncertain future on the fiftieth anniversary of its conception.

THEY ARE ALL WAITING FOR ME. *I slowly lift the dress out of the wrappings of tissue. It is indeed beautiful. The velvet is a majestic russet color; the embroidery is of real silver thread and fills the neck of the* kameez[1] *in the shape of a bow. The slightly dull sequins still blink on the velvet. There are solid creases where the cloth was folded; here the velvet shines with a fiercer intensity than below the folds which reveal lighter mysteries. When I pass my hand over it, the velvet smooths down. As I wear the dress for the first time, I am amazed at how snugly it fits me, as if it were made just for me. The dress is not mine; it was a part of my grandmother's trousseau. In fact, this is what my grandfather brought for her to wear on their* nikkah.[2] *She wore it only once and then put it away; then my youngest* khala,[3] *her last daughter to be married, wore it; and now, the dress is being worn for the third time by me. I feel it on my body and try to imagine how my grandmother must have felt on the nuptial day, adorned*

[1]A long shirt worn with pants called shalwar.
[2]Traditional Muslim marriage ceremony.
[3]Aunt, mother's sister.

51

in this dress. My young cousins ask me impatiently from outside the door if I need any help. I open the door and come out feeling a little shy. Everyone stops talking and tells me how nice I look in her dress, the women admiring how immaculately preserved it is and how much it would cost today to have something like that made.

Everyone, young and old, his children and grandchildren, called him Abbaji, with love. Last year, January 1 was a very joyous occasion for us because we celebrated Abbaji's ninety-fifth birthday. Eleven of his fifteen children managed to gather in the same house that day. I promised him that five years from now we would celebrate his century-marking birthday and everyone would be there.

Today there is an unusual number of people in my grandfather's house because it is Eid, *the day at the end of* Ramazan, *when we celebrate the end of fasting and offer prayers of gratitude to Allah. Not only are two of my* khalas *here with their families, but just a few moments ago my grandmother's brother, my mother's* mamoon,[4] *came in with his wife and daughters. Their bright, jocund voices shimmering through the walls, now everyone is sitting together in the living room talking and drinking tea while the children are playing all over the house. Spicy aromas emanating from the family kitchen are mingling with delicate perfumes on crisply-ironed clothes to form one warm embrace.*

Although every time the phone rang at night we would be filled with dread, no one was prepared for the news. This year on the midnight of January 1, we were awakened by a phone call telling us that Abbaji had died. Later on I found out that Abbaji had died calling out for every one of his children, few of whom were with him at that time. That is why I cannot reconcile the fact that I wasn't there at the time when he wanted to gather all his seeds. The distance does nothing to dissipate the agony and anger; only it makes the grief more unbearable. How can you triumph distance and time to tell someone that you love him, something you thought you would always have time for?

After a few minutes I excuse myself and go to my grandfather's room to show him the dress. My eldest mamoon *is sitting beside my grandfather and when he sees me entering with my cousins behind me, he leaves the room grumbling that these children do not leave any corner of the house in peace. The girls, somewhat bored now, run off to play. As I sit down on his bed, my* khala *also comes in the room after having served the latest guests. Abbaji is*

---

[4]Uncle, mother's brother.

lying in his bed, supported by pillows, and smiles at me kindly. Through the open door I see the tree casting a long shadow in the coral evening.

My earliest memories are associated with Abbaji because I spent my early childhood under the eyes of my grandparents in their *haveli*, the huge fort-like house that Abbaji had before he moved to the smaller house, after my grandmother's death. His voracious appetite for reading instilled in me a respect for books. Once when I was ten or eleven years old, we went to spend our winter vacations with him. I brought along my arsenal of books to while away time and one of the books was Robert Louis Stevenson's *Treasure Island*. One afternoon when I was tired of playing with my cousins, I went to look for the novel. After a long search I came out on the veranda and found Abbaji basking in the hazy sunlight and reading the book. I remember feeling a concoction of mild surprise and delectation even then that my own grandfather was reading and enjoying the same book that had made me so happy. Then at times he would tell me a tale within a tale. One evening very long ago when he was young, Abbaji was sitting on a rock by a frothy river reading a book. In the book an incident was described in great detail in which a snake slithers off a rock and falls into the river; at that very moment, a snake, out of nowhere, sprang on the rock right in front of him and landed into the gushing waters. At the end of the tale, Abbaji would chuckle with merry perplexity; I would try to picture a young boy with a book in his hands at the edge of a river, his shadow extending before him, frightened by the sudden appearance of a lithe snake, and my blood would race with adventure. This is what a child's trove of bright and diffused memories is made up of—shared words and shared silences.

I ask him, Abbaji, how does the dress look? He puts on his glasses and looks at me from head to toe, tells me that it is very beautiful and asks when did I have it made. I do not realize but my khala *guesses immediately and laughingly asks him if he does not recognize it. My grandfather, with a short embarrassed laugh, says no. I then tell him that it is the dress that my grandmother wore for her wedding. He asks incredulously if it is true, and we talk about how many people came to visit us today and how much I'll miss this day when I go back. After some time I come out of his room a little hurt and disappointed.*

When I look at the pictures I took of Abbaji last year, I still wonder at the kind smile touching the tired liquid eyes of a man who had seen life and still found it amusing. His presence was a spiritual focus to which his scattered progeny drifted back time and again. Family legend has it that when he was sixteen or seventeen, Abbaji ran away from his home in Afghanistan because of an escalating bloody dispute about his father's estate, to which he was the sole heir. And I ask myself, what do I truly know of my grandfather? I do remember so many times when he came to visit us at our house in Lahore, the weddings, births and birthdays we celebrated. But I also remember the times when he used to pick up the loosened skin from his hands remorsefully. So, in sad nostalgia, what matters most . . . the freedom from pain of a loved one or the lost inert moments of happiness induced by him?

There are still a lot of guests in the living room and I mingle with them. One of my cousins and I pose for a special picture of me in the dress. Just when the camera flashes, I remember that I forgot to take off the thick woolen socks peeking from under it.

I have lost my bearings. It seems that right when I was beginning to convince myself that the tunnel was not so dimly lit, life slapped me full in the face of my meager certitude. A catharsis is unwelcome and the fear for the mortality of my loved ones is fresh. I have found that treasures that bind you by the spirit are hard to keep. The dress, the pictures are still tangible; the person whose presence was hope is no more. I keep returning to times and events and places and images in a tiding circuit until I am unsure of where I started from. Suddenly I am frightened of the new year.

INTERPRETATIONS

1. Why do you think Shoaib begins her essay with a detailed description of her grandmother's wedding dress?

2. Shoaib's memoir juxtaposes past and present in alternating paragraphs. Analyze the effects of this technique on her purpose and meaning. How does she use this technique to reflect on her relationship with Abbaji?

3. Characterize Abbaji. Which of his traits have most influenced the author? How would you describe their relationship? Do you have a similar relationship with any member of your family?

CORRESPONDENCES

1. Review Friedan's perspective on families and discuss its relevance to the texts by Shoaib and Lim (page 56).

2. Shoaib and Wehle write about the death of a close family member. Compare and contrast their responses to loss.

APPLICATIONS

1. Shoaib's essay focuses on her portrayal of her grandfather, but in the italicized passages she also reveals herself. Write a portrait of the author using these paragraphs.

2. Freewrite about an older family member who intrigues you and about whom you would like to know more. Interview family members or friends for information about him or her, and write a description based on your interviews.

3. Shoaib and Wehle recall an experience that represents a turning point in their lives. If you have had such an experience (it need not be about death), write an essay comparing its effects when it first occurred and now as you view it in retrospect.

4. Note how Shoaib uses visual cues in the text to signal different voices and tones. If you examine the italicized and the non-italicized sections of the essay, what kinds of music are evoked by each of these font types? How would you describe these kinds of music to a reader?

5. It is possible to look at Shoaib's first paragraph as a journal entry. Try to write a journal entry about something that is happening in this essay from the perspective of one of the other participants.

Two Lives

SHIRLEY GEOK-LIN LIM

Shirley Geok-Lin Lim (b. 1944 in a small town in Malaysia where the languages she heard were Malay, Hokkien, and English) received her B.A. at the University of Malaysia, Kuala Lumpur, and her M.A. and Ph.D. in English and American Literature from Brandeis University. She was a Fulbright Scholar in the years 1969–1972. Her first book of poems, Crossing the Peninsula *(1980), won the Commonwealth Poetry Prize. Lin has published four additional books of poetry and three collections of short stories. Her work is represented in many anthologies. Her memoir,* Among the White Moon Faces: An Asian-American Memoir of Homelands *(1997), received the American Book Award Lim's first novel* Joss and Gold *was published in 2001. Her career has been "across cultures": she is currently the Chair Professor of English and head of the English Department at the University of Hong Kong, as well as Professor of English and Women's Studies at the University of California, Santa Barbara. She has also taught in her native Malaysia, and in Australia. Ask yourself, before you read the selection, what the phrase "resident alien" means to you.*

NO ONE WHO HAS NOT LEFT EVERYTHING behind her—every acquaintance, tree, corner lamp post, brother, lover—understands the peculiar remorse of the resident alien. Unlike the happy immigrant who sees the United States as a vast real-estate advertisement selling a neighborly future, the person who enters the country as a resident alien is neither here nor there. Without family, house, or society, she views herself through the eyes of citizens: guest, stranger, outsider, misfit, beggar. Transient like the drunks asleep by the steps down to the subway, her bodily presence is a wraith, less than smoke among the 250 million in the nation. Were she to fall in front of the screeching wheels of the Number Four Lexington line, her death would be noted by no one, mourned by none, except if the news should arrive weeks later, twelve thousand miles away.

A resident alien has walked out of a community's living memory, out of social structures in which her identity is folded, like a bud in a tree, to take on the raw stinks of public bathrooms and the shapes of shadows in parks. She holds her breath as she walks through the American city counting the afternoon hours. Memory for her is a great mourning, a death of the living. The alien resident mourns even as she chooses to abandon. Her memory, like her guilt and early love, is involuntary but her choice of the United States is willful.

For what? She asks the question over and over again. At first, she asks it every day. Then as she begins to feel comfortable in the body of a stranger, she asks it occasionally, when the weekend stretches over the Sunday papers and the television news does not seem enough, or when the racks of dresses in the department stores fail to amuse. Finally, she forgets what it feels like not to be a stranger. She has found work that keeps her busy, or better still, tired. She has found a lover, a child, a telephone friend, the American equivalents for the opacity of her childhood. The dense solidity of Asian society becomes a thin story. At some point, she no longer considers exchanging the remote relationships that pass as American social life for those crowded rooms in Asia, the unhappy family circles. And were those rooms really that crowded, the family so intensely unhappy? . . .

It was the waste of time I minded most, a sludgy feeling that took over October and November. In September, almost a year after my arrival at Brandeis, Father had written to say he had been diagnosed with throat cancer. He was seeking medical care in Malacca. "Don't come home," his letter ended, "I don't want you to interrupt your studies."

I told no one. Food stuck in my throat whenever I thought of Father. The thought was like a fishbone, sharp and nagging. I couldn't speak of him.

Another short letter arrived from China without a return address. I read it over and over in the safety of my room. "I am doing well," it said. "My white blood cells have gone up, and I am feeling stronger." The small black-and-white photograph that fell out of the envelope showed that he was lying. The shirt draped over his body like a sheet over a child, although his face was old and sad.

For a few months, the letters came from China without a forwarding address: he was staying near the clinic in Canton, noted for its cancer cures. He wrote irregularly. Like a careful student, perhaps because he was lonely, he sent the laboratory reports on his white blood count. His letters were optimistic to begin with. The white blood-cell numbers had improved; he was enjoying this Chinese city he had never seen before, visiting parks, zoos, and museums, with a new friend also undergoing treatment at the clinic. Then a letter arrived complaining of homesickness. He wanted to be home with the family; he missed Malaysian food.

When Thanksgiving came, the Castle emptied out. Julie and Carol returned to Brooklyn and Missouri. On Friday I picked up a letter from my mailbox. The rice-paper-fine aerogramme rustled as I spread it out to read the ball-point print that smeared across the crumpled blue surface. It was a letter from Second Brother, and I was immediately afraid, for Second Brother had never written to me before. "We buried Father two weeks ago," he wrote.

I stared at the words and calculated the time. Two weeks ago, and a week for the aerogramme to cross the world to reach me in Massachusetts. It was unimaginable that Father, the source of whatever drove me, that total enveloping wretchedness of involuntary love, my eternal bond, my body's and heart's DNA, had been dead for almost a month. The world had a hole in it, it was rent, and I would never heal.

Maggie came knocking at my door just as I finished reading Second Brother's letter. An orphan left with a trust fund, she was slowly completing her graduate studies, while spending most of her time volunteering to help with the animals in the zoo. She wanted to know if I had had any pumpkin pie yet for Thanksgiving. Would I go with her to the cafeteria for a piece of pie? I was still holding Second Brother's blue aerogramme in my hand.

"My father's dead," I said to her. Why was I telling her this? Would I have said the same thing if the janitor had knocked on the door to fix the radiator? "He died three weeks ago."

"Oh," she said. "I'm sorry." I could see that she was. Tall and big-boned, Maggie was deep water, quiet-spoken, all reserve.

I paid for my pie and coffee at the cafeteria and watched her eat. She left the crust and scraped the brown gooey filling carefully with her fork till it was all gone. My throat hurt. Then I returned alone to my room. I knew Maggie would never visit me again. I had been too painful for her.

At first I didn't cry. It wasn't Father's death that drove hardest at me, it was that he had been dead for more than two weeks already, and I hadn't known all that time that he had gone. "We didn't think you should come home," Second Brother wrote. The grief and the guilt lay beyond tears. Months later, in Brooklyn where I was sharing a studio apartment with Charles, the Brandeis graduate student whom I would later marry, I woke up in the middle of the night my face drenched with tears. I had wept in my sleep for Father.

A month after the news of Father's death, Second Brother sent me a package of papers from Father's belongings. Father had kept all my old school record books, annual school certificates of achievement, examination diplomas, yellowed letters of recommendation from high school teachers, and Malaysian citizenship documents. On an unmailed aerogramme sheet, Father had scrawled in a shaky hand, "I want you to come home now."

My brother also sent me a diary Father had kept in the last weeks of his life. Only a few pages were filled, and all the entries were addressed to me. In the early entries, he wrote he was hopeful he would recover, and he did not want me to return home because it was so important for me to continue my studies. In the second to last entry, he asked that I hurry home; he didn't believe he had much time left and he wanted to see me. In the very last entry, addressing me as his dear daughter, he wrote that although he knew I would do so, still he asked that I promise to take care of my brothers and sister, Peng's children. The entry was very short and the handwriting erratic. My father had willed his children to me.

The day I received the package, I emptied my bank account and sent the few hundred dollars in it to Peng. With it, my letter promised that I would send her as much as I could each month. For a long time, every U.S. dollar rang as precious Malaysian currency for me to remit. A ten-dollar shirt? I paid for it and guiltily counted the groceries the money could have bought for Father's family. I disapproved of my growing consumerism. The pastries that gleamed, sugar-encrusted, at Dunkin' Donuts, which I eyed longingly, would buy copy books for my half-brothers. For the next few years, I carried my father's ghostly presence through department stores and restaurants. His sad smile was a mirage of poverty. I saw my half-siblings ragged and hungry whenever I glanced at a sales tag, and every month, I made out a bank draft to Peng and mailed it out as an exorcism.

An exorcism I could not explain to Charles, my American husband. How could one eat well if one's family was starving? For Chinese, eating is both material and cultural. We feed our hungry ghosts before we may feed ourselves. Ancestors are ravenous, and can die of neglect. Our fathers' children are also ourselves. The self is paltry, phantasmagoric; it leaks and slips away. It is the family, parents, siblings, cousins, that signify the meaning of the self, and beyond the family, the extended community.

In writing the bank drafts I remained my father's daughter, returning to Father the bargain we had made. This is the meaning of blood—to give, because you cannot eat unless the family is also eating. For years, I woke up nights, heart beating wildly. Oh Asia, that nets its children in ties of blood so binding that they cut the spirit.

INTERPRETATIONS

1. How does Lim characterize the "resident alien" in paragraphs 1 and 2? What is the connection between the "resident alien" and the "alien resident"?

2. What is the effect of Lim's recording the process of her father's illness and death?

3. Why does she include the entries from her father's diaries? How would you describe the relationship she and her father shared?

4. How do you interpret the last line of her essay? What examples of her spirit's being "cut" can you cite?

CORRESPONDENCES

1. Wehle and Lim record their responses to the death of a parent. Compare and contrast their reactions to that experience.

2. How do Shoaib and Lim use mood and tone to enhance theme?

APPLICATIONS

1. Write a journal entry on the title of Lim's essay.

2. Lim writes that she disapproves of her "growing consumerism." What examples does she cite? Do you and your group members think of yourselves as consumers? Is it easy to resist being a consumer in today's society? Summarize your group's discussion.

3. Lim writes about her sorrow and guilt as she distances herself from her native culture. If you have had a similar experience, write a short essay describing how you resolved the paradox of being a "resident alien" and "an alien resident."

4. Who is Lim describing in paragraphs 1 and 2 of this essay? What do you imagine this person to look like? Draw a sketch of this individual. Then, using your sketch to guide you, write a detailed description of this person.

For My Indian Daughter

LEWIS (JOHNSON) SAWAQUAT

Lewis (Johnson) Sawaquat (b. 1935) was raised in Harbor Springs, Michigan, where his great-grandfather was the last official chief of the Potawatomi Ottawas. A retired surveyor, Sawaquat is currently the cultural adviser of The Grand Travers Band of Ottawa and Chippewa Indians. In "For My Indian Daughter," the author portrays his personal odyssey toward greater ethnic pride and cultural awareness. He adopted his Indian name after this essay was published.

According to tradition, the Ottawas, the Ojibway, and the Potawatomi were originally one tribe living north of the Great Lakes. After the Ottawas separated, they were active in the Indian Wars as allies of the French. After joining the Huron at Mackinaw in Michigan (adjacent to the area of Johnson's home town of Harbor Springs and nearby Burt Lake), the Ottawa dispersed over a wide area. When first encountered by whites (in the seventeenth century), the Potawatomi lived mainly near the mouth of the Green Bay in Wisconsin. By the end of the century, they had settled along both sides of the southern end of Lake Michigan. The majority of the tribe still lives in Michigan.

MY LITTLE GIRL IS SINGING HERSELF to sleep upstairs, her voice mingling with the sounds of the birds outside in the old maple trees. She is two and I am nearly 50, and I am very taken with her. She came along late in my life, unexpected and unbidden, a startling gift.

Today at the beach my chubby-legged, brown-skinned daughter ran laughing into the water as fast as she could. My wife and I laughed watching her, until we heard behind us a low guttural curse and then an unpleasant voice raised in an imitation war whoop.

I turned to see a fat man in a bathing suit, white and soft as a grub, as he covered his mouth and prepared to make the Indian war cry again. He was middle-aged, younger than I, and had three little children lined up next to him, grinning foolishly. My wife suggested we leave the beach, and I agreed.

I knew the man was not unusual in his feelings against Indians. His beach behavior might have been socially unacceptable to more civilized whites, but his basic view of Indians is expressed daily in our small town, frequently on the editorial pages of the county newspaper, as white people speak out against Indian fishing rights and land rights, saying in essence, "Those Indians are taking our fish, our land." It doesn't matter to them that we were here first, that the U.S. Supreme Court has ruled in our favor. It matters to them that we have something they want, and they hate us for it. Backlash is the common explanation of the attacks on Indians, the bumper stickers that say, "Spear an Indian, Save a Fish," but I know better. The hatred of Indians goes back to the beginning when white people came to this country. For me it goes back to my childhood in Harbor Springs, Michigan.

Harbor Springs is now a summer resort for the very affluent, but a hundred years ago it was the Indian village of my Ottawa ancestors. My grandmother, Anna Showanessy, and other Indians like her, had their land there taken by treaty, by fraud, by violence, by theft. They remembered how whites had burned down the village at Burt Lake in 1900 and pushed the Indians out. These were the stories in my family.

When I was a boy my mother told me to walk down the alleys in Harbor Springs and not to wear my orange football sweater out of the house. This way I would not stand out, not be noticed, and not be a target.

I wore my orange sweater anyway and deliberately avoided the alleys. I was the biggest person I knew and wasn't really afraid. But I met my comeuppance when I enlisted in the U.S. Army. One night all the men in my barracks gathered together and, gang-fashion, pulled me into the shower and scrubbed me down with rough brushes used for floors, saying, "We won't have any dirty Indians in our outfit." It is a point of irony that I was cleaner than any of them. Later in Korea I learned how to kill, how to bully, how to hate Koreans. I came out of the war tougher than ever and, strangely, white.

I went to college, got married, lived in La Porte, Indiana, worked as a surveyor and raised three boys. I headed Boy Scout groups, never thinking it odd when the Scouts did imitation Indian dances, imitation Indian lore.

One day when I was 35 or thereabouts I heard about an Indian powwow. My father used to attend them and so with great curiosity and a strange joy at discovering a part of my heritage, I decided the thing to do to get ready for this big event was to have my friend make me a spear in his forge. The steel was fine and blue and iridescent. The feathers on the shaft were bright and proud.

In a dusty state fairground in southern Indiana, I found white people dressed as Indians. I learned they were "hobbyists," that is, it was their hobby and leisure pastime to masquerade as Indians on weekends. I felt ridiculous with my spear, and I left.

It was years before I could tell anyone of the embarrassment of this weekend and see any humor in it. But in a way it was that weekend, for all its silliness, that was my awakening. I realized I didn't know who I was. I didn't have an Indian name. I didn't speak the Indian language. I didn't know the Indian customs. Dimly I remembered the Ottawa word for dog, but it was a baby word, *kahgee*, not the full word, *muhkahgee*, which I was later to learn. Even more hazily I remembered a naming ceremony (my own). I remembered legs dancing around me, dust. Where had that been? Who had I been? "Suwaukquat," my mother told me when I asked, "where the tree begins to grow."

That was 1968, and I was not the only Indian in the country who was feeling the need to remember who he or she was. There were others. They had powwows, real ones, and eventually I found them. Together we researched our past, a search that for me culminated in the Longest Walk, a march on Washington in 1978. Maybe because I now know what it means to be Indian, it surprises me that others don't. Of course there aren't very many of us left. The chances of an average person knowing an average Indian in an average lifetime are pretty slim.

Still, I was amused one day when my small, four-year-old neighbor looked at me as I was hoeing in my garden and said, "You aren't a real Indian, are you?" Scotty is little, talkative, likable. Finally I said, "I'm a real Indian." He looked at me for a moment and then said, squinting into the sun, "Then where's your horse and feathers?" The child was simply a smaller, whiter version of my own ignorant self years before. We'd both seen too much TV, that's all. He was not to be blamed. And so, in a way, the moronic man on the beach today is blameless. We come full circle to realize other people are like ourselves, as discomfiting as that may be sometimes.

As I sit in my old chair on my porch, in a light that is fading so the leaves are barely distinguishable against the sky, I can picture my girl asleep upstairs. I would like to prepare her for what's to come, take her each step of the way saying, there's a place to avoid, here's what I know about this, but much of what's before her she must go through alone. She must pass through pain and joy and solitude and community to discover her own inner self that is unlike any other and come through that passage to the place where she sees all people are one, and in so seeing may live her life in a brighter future.

INTERPRETATIONS

1. What audience besides his daughter is Sawaquat writing for? Cite evidence. Why do you suppose he waited until he was nearly fifty and had a daughter—he has three other children, boys—to express these thoughts?

2. "I didn't know who I was." What do we have to know about ourselves before we know who we are? How important is ancestry to a sense of identity? What should be our attitude toward our ancestry—or ancestries?

3. Until he asked his mother, Sawaquat did not know his Indian name. Why do you suppose she withheld it? How do you think you would feel to discover that you had another name? Why?

4. What was involved in Sawaquat "finding himself"? Why must such a search be conducted with others? How did white society delay the search and make it difficult?

CORRESPONDENCES

1. Feelings of alienation and displacement are expressed by both Lim and Sawaquat. Explain their causes and effects. How are they reconciled in each text?

2. Review Morrison's perspective and discuss its relevance to Sawaquat's essay. Does pursuing ethnic identity preclude searching for a national community? Explain.

APPLICATIONS

1. "We come full circle to realize other people are like ourselves, as discomfiting as that may be sometimes." To what extent do you agree with Sawaquat? Write a summary of your group's discussions.

2. Write an essay on a part of your cultural heritage you might someday want to share with your children.

3. In paragraph 14 Sawaquat says of his daughter: "She must pass through pain and joy and solitude and community to discover her own inner self that is unlike any other . . ." To what extent do you agree? Write a journal entry of an experience that corresponds to Sawaquat's comment.

4. In this essay Lewis Sawaquat writes: "The chances of an average person knowing an average Indian in an average lifetime are pretty slim." Hopefully, the following Web sites will help a reader begin to bridge this knowledge gap.

   http://www.indiancountry.com

   http://www.turtletrack.org

   http://www.navajohopiobserver.com

The Night I Was Nobody

JOHN EDGAR WIDEMAN

John Edgar Wideman (b. 1941 in Washington DC) has written nine other novels since A Glance Away *was published in 1967, only a year after he graduated from Oxford University on a Rhodes scholarship. Having grown up in a Pittsburgh ghetto, he was recruited by the University of Pennsylvania on a basketball scholarship. Although he also writes in other forms, such as short story and autobiography (e.g.,* Brothers and Keepers *[1984]), his usual subject is black urban experience, juxtaposing his own personal life with national issues. He was professor of English at the University of Massachusetts–Amherst after 1986 and was named Distinguished Professor in 2001. He is now professor of African Studies at Brown University. In 2005 he published* God's Gym *(2005), a collection of stories, and reissued in paperback his 1990 novel* Philadelphia Fire *This novel, based on 1985 events when Philadelphia police bombed the headquarters of an armed group named Move, killing six adults and five children, and destroying fifty-three homes, shows Wideman's characteristic blending of his personal life with broader issues. Watch for this juxtaposition in the following selection.*

ON JULY 4TH, THE FIREWORKS DAY, the day for picnics and patriotic speeches, I was in Clovis, New Mexico, to watch my daughter, Jamila, and her team, the Central Massachusetts Cougars, compete in the Junior Olympics Basketball national tourney. During our ten-day visit to Clovis the weather had been bizarre. Hailstones as large as golf balls. Torrents of rain flooding streets hubcap deep. Running through the pelting rain from their van to a gym, Jamila and several teammates cramming through a doorway had looked back just in time to see a funnel cloud touch down a few blocks away. Continuous sheet lightning had shattered the horizon, crackling for hours night and day. Spectacular, off-the-charts weather flexing its muscles, reminding people what little control they had over their lives.

Hail rat-tat-tatting against our windshield our first day in town wasn't exactly a warm welcome, but things got better fast. Clovis people were glad to see us and the mini-spike we triggered in the local economy. Hospitable, generous, our hosts lavished upon us the same hands-on affection and attention to detail that had transformed an unpromising place in the middle of nowhere into a very livable community.

On top of all that, the Cougars were kicking butt, so the night of July 3rd I wanted to celebrate with a frozen margarita. I couldn't pry anybody else away from "Bubba's," the movable feast of beer, chips, and chatter the adults traveling with the Cougars improvised nightly in the King's Inn Motel parking lot, so I drove off alone to find one perfect margarita.

Inside the door of Kelley's Bar and Lounge I was flagged by a guy collecting a cover charge and told I couldn't enter wearing my Malcolm X hat. I asked why; the guy hesitated, conferred for a moment with his partner, then declared that Malcolm X hats were against the dress code. For a split second I thought it might be that *no* caps were allowed in Kelley's. But the door crew and two or three others hanging around the entrance-way all wore the billed caps ubiquitous in New Mexico, duplicates of mine, except theirs sported the logos of feed stores and truck stops instead of a silver *X*.

What careened through my mind in the next couple of minutes is essentially unsayable but included scenes from my own half-century of life as a black man, clips from five hundred years of black/white meetings on slave ships, auction blocks, plantations, basketball courts, in the Supreme Court's marble halls, in beds, back alleys and back rooms, kisses and lynch ropes and contracts for millions of dollars so a black face will grace a cereal box. To tease away my anger I tried joking with folks in other places. Hey, Spike Lee. That hat you gave me on the set of the Malcolm movie in Cairo ain't legal in Clovis.

But nothing about these white guys barring my way was really funny. Part of me wanted to get down and dirty. Curse the suckers. Were they prepared to do battle to keep me and my cap out? Another voice said, Be cool. Don't sully your hands. Walk away and call the cops or a lawyer. Forget these chumps. Sue the owner. Or should I win hearts and minds? Look, fellas, I understand why the *X* on my cap might offend or scare you. You probably don't know much about Malcolm. The incredible metamorphoses of his thinking, his soul. By the time he was assassinated he wasn't a racist, didn't advocate violence. He was trying to make sense of America's impossible history, free himself, free us from the crippling legacy of race hate and oppression.

While all the above occupied my mind, my body, on its own, had assumed a gunfighter's vigilance, hands ready at sides, head cocked, weight poised, eyes tight and hard on the doorkeeper yet alert to anything stirring on the periphery. Many other eyes, all in white faces, were checking out the entranceway, recognizing the ingredients of a racial incident. Hadn't they witnessed Los Angeles going berserk on their TV screens just a couple months ago? That truck driver beaten nearly to death in the street, those packs of black hoodlums burning and looting? Invisible lines were being drawn in the air, in the sand, invisible chips bristled on shoulders.

The weather again. Our American racial weather, turbulent, unchanging in its changeability, its power to rock us and stun us and smack us from our routines and tear us apart as if none of our cities, our pieties, our promises, our dreams, ever stood a chance of holding on. The racial weather. Outside us, then suddenly, unforgettably, unforgivingly inside, reminding us of what we've only pretended to have forgotten. Our limits, our flaws. The lies and compromises we practice to avoid dealing honestly with the contradictions of race. How dependent we are on luck to survive—*when* we survive—the racial weather.

One minute you're a person, the next moment somebody starts treating you as if you're not. Often it happens just that way, just that suddenly. Particularly if you are a black man in America. Race and racism are a force larger than individuals, more powerful than law or education or government or the church, a force able to wipe these institutions away in the charged moments, minuscule of mountainous, when black and white come face to face. In Watts in 1965,[1] or a few less-than-glorious minutes in Clovis, New Mexico, on the eve of the day that commemorates our country's freedom, our inalienable right as a nation, as citizens, to life, liberty, equality, the pursuit of happiness, those precepts and principles that still look good on paper but are often as worthless as a sheet of newspaper to protect you in a storm if you're a black man at the wrong time in the wrong place.

None of this is news, is it? Not July 3rd in Clovis, when a tiny misfire occurred, or yesterday in your town or tomorrow in mine? But haven't we made progress? Aren't things much better than they used to be? Hasn't enough been done?

We ask the wrong questions when we look around and see a handful of fabulously wealthy black people, a few others entering the middle classes. Far more striking than the positive changes are the abiding patterns and assumptions that have not changed. Not all black people are mired in social pathology, but the bottom rung of the ladder of opportunity (and the space *beneath* the bottom rung) is still defined by the color of the people trapped there—and many *are* still trapped there, no doubt about it, because their status was inherited, determined generation after generation by blood, by color. Once, all black people

---

[1]*Watts in 1965:* In August of 1965, a police traffic stop provoked six days of rioting in which thirty four people died in the Watts neighborhood of Los Angeles—Eds.

were legally excluded from full participation in the mainstream. Then fewer. Now only some. But the mechanisms of disenfranchisement that originally separated African Americans from other Americans persist, if not legally, then in the apartheid mind-set, convictions and practices of the majority. The seeds sleep but don't die. Ten who suffer from exclusion today can become ten thousand tomorrow. Racial weather can change that quickly.

How would the bouncer have responded if I'd calmly declared, "This is a free country, I can wear any hat I choose"? Would he thank me for standing up for our shared birthright? Or would he have to admit, it pushed, that American rights belong only to *some* Americans, white Americans?

We didn't get that far in our conversation. We usually don't. The girls' faces pulled me from the edge—girls of all colors, sizes, shapes, gritty kids bonding through hard clean competition. Weren't these guys who didn't like my X cap kids too? Who did they think I was? What did they think they were protecting? I backed out, backed down, climbed in my car and drove away from Kelley's. After all, I didn't want Kelley's. I wanted a frozen margarita and a mellow celebration. So I bought plenty of ice and the ingredients for a margarita and rejoined the festivities at Bubba's. Everybody volunteered to go back with me to Kelley's, but I didn't want to spoil the victory party, taint our daughters' accomplishments, erase the high marks Clovis had earned hosting us.

But I haven't forgotten what happened in Kelley's. I write about it now because this is my country, the country where my sons and daughter are growing up, and your daughters and sons, and the crisis, the affliction, the same ole, same ole waste of life continues across the land, the nightmarish weather of racism, starbursts of misery in the dark.

The statistics of inequality don't demonstrate a "black crisis"—that perspective confuses cause and victim, solutions and responsibility. When the rain falls, it falls on us all. The bad news about black men—that they die sooner and more violently than white men, are more ravaged by unemployment and lack of opportunity, are more exposed to drugs, disease, broken families, and police brutality, more likely to go to jail than college, more cheated by the inertia and callousness of a government that represents and protects the most needy the least—this is not a "black problem," but a *national* shame affecting us all. Wrenching ourselves free from the long nightmare of racism will require collective determination, countless individual acts of will, gutsy, informed, unselfish. To imagine the terrible cost of not healing ourselves, we must first imagine how good it would feel to be healed.

INTERPRETATIONS

1. Comment on the first sentence of Wideman's essay. Why does he choose to mention these particular events? What do they have in common?

2. Wideman uses the metaphor of weather throughout the essay beginning in the first paragraph with a literal description of the weather they encountered. To what extent does the last sentence foreshadow his encounter at Kelley's bar in paragraph 4?

3. What mood does he create in the second paragraph? What is the main reason that the people of Clovis are happy to entertain the fans attending the Junior Olympics?

4. Wideman is denied admission to Kelley's bar because of his Malcolm X hat. What associations do you have with Malcolm X? Why does Wideman mention that the hat was a present from Spike Lee?

5. Trace the course of the weather metaphor in paragraphs 8, 10, 11, and 15. What are the symbolic implications of the connections he makes between weather and racism?

6. Review Wideman's penultimate paragraph in which he states his reasons for writing about this incident. To what extent do you agree or disagree with his concluding sentence?

CORRESPONDENCES

1. Review Baldwin's perspective and discuss its relevance to Wideman's essay. What does each imply about the importance of community?

2. Wideman and Sawaquat record their experiences with racism initially because of their children but also because of their hope that it will be eradicated. To what extent do you share their hopes? What actions, if any, do you imagine taking to help eradicate racism?

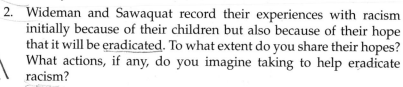

APPLICATIONS

1. Write a journal entry responding to the title of Wideman's essay. Under what circumstances can you imagine feeling like a nobody?

2. Check the Internet for more information on Malcolm X and/or Spike Lee and write an essay on your impressions of one or both of them.

3. Discuss with your group Wideman's response to the situation at Kelley's bar. Should he have confronted the bouncer and taken a stand or withdrawn because of the young girls, including his daughter, who were participating in the Junior Olympics? What can you imagine doing in his situation? Record your group's responses.

The Joy of Reading and Writing: Superman and Me

SHERMAN ALEXIE

Sherman Alexie (b. 1966) grew up on the Spokane Indian Reservation in Wellpinit, Washington. He attended the reservation school until the eighth grade, when he chose to travel thirty-two miles to the Reardan High School, where he was the only Indian until his twin sisters joined him a year later. From there he went to Gonzaga University, a Jesuit school in Spokane and received his B.A. from Washington State University. In 1992 Alexie published his first poetry collection, The Business of Fancydancing, *followed by eight more books of poetry. He published* The Lone Ranger and Tonto Fistfight in Heaven, *a collection of short stories, in 1993, which provided much of the material for the screenplay and film* Smoke Signals *(1998). The film was written, directed, and produced by Indians, and won two awards at the Sundance Film Festival* Reservation Blues, *Alexie's first novel, was published in 1995. His second novel,* Indian Killer *(1996) was a* New York Times *Notable Book. To date, Alexie has published fourteen books, including his most recent collection of short stories,* Ten Little Indians *(2003). Alexie continues to live on the Spokane reservation, where he is sometimes accused of "airing dirty laundry." He is a popular speaker and reader of his works at tribal events. What presuppositions do you have about Indian reading habits?*

Approximately 1,100 Spokane Tribal members live on the reservation where Alexie grew up. Alexie's father is a Coeur d'Alene Indian, and his mother is a Spokane Indian. The Spokane Indians are of the Interior Salish group, which has inhabited northeastern Washington, northern Idaho, and western Montana for centuries. "Spokane" is generally accepted as meaning "Sun People" or "Children of the Sun." The living cycle of the Spokane was integral to their economic and social life. In the spring, the winter camps dispersed to gather food, hunt, and fish. By early summer, salmon fishing, hunting, and rootdigging were the main activities. Summer was the time of year when intertribal activities were at the highest, since neighboring tribes joined the Spokanes for root and berry gathering. This tradition of socializing is carried on today with the Indian powwows, which begin in June and end in September. Visiting, games, and ceremonial dancing are important parts in the social life of today's Indians.

I LEARNED TO READ WITH A *SUPERMAN* COMIC BOOK. Simple enough, I suppose. I cannot recall which particular Superman comic book I read, nor can I remember which villain he fought in that issue. I cannot remember the plot, nor the means by which I obtained the comic book. What I can remember is this: I was three years old, a Spokane Indian boy living with his family on the Spokane Indian Reservation in eastern Washington state. We were poor by most standards, but one of my parents usually managed to find some minimum-wage job or another, which made us middle-class by reservation standards. I had a brother and three sisters. We lived on a combination of irregular paychecks, hope, fear, and government surplus food.

My father, who is one of the few Indians who went to Catholic school on purpose, was an avid reader of westerns, spy thrillers, murder mysteries, gangster epics, basketball player biographies, and anything else he could find. He bought his books by the pound at Dutch's Pawn Shop, Goodwill, Salvation Army, and Value Village. When he had extra money, he bought new novels at supermarkets, convenience stores and hospital gift shops. Our house was filled with books. They were stacked in crazy piles in the bathroom, bedrooms, and living room. In a fit of unemployment-inspired creative energy, my father built a set of bookshelves and soon filled them with a random assortment of books about the Kennedy assassination, Watergate, the Vietnam War, and the entire twenty-three book series of the Apache westerns. My father loved books, and since I loved my father with an aching devotion, I decided to love books as well.

I can remember picking up my father's books before I could read. The words themselves were mostly foreign, but I still remember the exact moment when I first understood, with a sudden clarity, the purpose of a paragraph. I didn't have the vocabulary to say "paragraph," but I realized that a paragraph was a fence that held words. The words inside a paragraph worked together for a common purpose. They had some specific reason for being inside the same fence. This knowledge delighted me. I began to think of everything in terms of paragraphs. Our reservation was a small paragraph within the United States. My family's house was a paragraph, distinct from the other paragraphs of the LeBrets to the north, the Fords to our south, and the Tribal School to the west. Inside our house, each family member existed as a separate paragraph but still had genetics and common experiences to link us. Now, using this logic, I can see my changed family as an essay of seven paragraphs: mother, father, older brother, the deceased sister, my younger twin sisters, and our adopted little brother.

At the same time I was seeing the world in paragraphs, I also picked up the *Superman* comic book. Each panel, complete with picture, dialogue, and narrative, was a three-dimensional paragraph. In one panel, Superman breaks through a door. His suit is red, blue, and yellow. The brown door shatters into many pieces. I look at the narrative above the picture. I cannot read the words, but I assume it tells me that "Superman is breaking down the door." Aloud, I pretend to read the words and say, "Superman is breaking down the door." Words, dialogue, also float out of Superman's mouth. Because he is breaking down the door, I assume he says, "I am breaking down the door." Once again, I pretend to read the words and say aloud, "I am breaking down the door." In this way, I learned to read.

This might be an interesting story all by itself. A little Indian boy teaches himself to read at an early age and advances quickly. He reads *Grapes of Wrath* in kindergarten when other children are struggling through Dick and Jane. If he'd been anything but an Indian boy living on the reservation, he might have been called a prodigy. But he is an Indian boy living on the reservation and is simply an oddity. He grows into a man who often speaks of his childhood in the third-person, as if it will somehow dull the pain and make him sound more modest about his talents.

A smart Indian is a dangerous person, widely feared and ridiculed by Indians and non-Indians alike. I fought with my classmates on a daily basis. They wanted me to stay quiet when the non-Indian teacher asked for answers, for volunteers, for help. We were Indian children who were expected to be stupid. Most lived up to those expectations inside the classroom but subverted them on the outside. They struggled with basic reading in school but could remember how to sing a few dozen powwow songs. They were monosyllabic in front of their non-Indian teachers but could tell complicated stories and jokes at the dinner table. They submissively ducked their heads when confronted by a non-Indian adult but would slug it out with the Indian bully who was ten years older. As Indian children, we were expected to fail in the non-Indian world. Those who failed were ceremonially accepted by other Indians and appropriately pitied by non-Indians.

I refused to fail. I was smart. I was arrogant. I was lucky. I read books late into the night, until I could barely keep my eyes open. I read books at recess, then during lunch, and in the few minutes left after I had finished my classroom assignments. I read books in the car when my family traveled to powwows or basketball games. In shopping malls, I ran to the bookstores and read bits and pieces of as many books as I could. I read the books my father brought home from the pawnshops and secondhand. I read the books I borrowed from the library. I read the backs of cereal boxes. I read the newspaper. I read the bulletins posted on the walls of the school, the clinic, the tribal offices, the post office. I read junk mail. I read auto-repair manuals. I read magazines. I read anything that had words and paragraphs. I read with equal parts joy and desperation. I loved those books, but I also knew that love had only one purpose. I was trying to save my life.

Despite all the books I read, I am still surprised I became a writer. I was going to be a pediatrician. These days, I write novels, short stories, and poems. I visit schools and teach creative writing to Indian kids. In all my years in the reservation school system, I was never taught how to write poetry, short stories, or novels. I was certainly never taught that Indians wrote poetry, short stories, and novels. Writing was something beyond Indians. I cannot recall a single time that a guest teacher visited the reservation. There must have been visiting teachers. Who were they? Where are they now? Do they exist? I visit the schools as often as possible. The Indian kids crowd the classroom. Many are writing their own poems, short stories, and novels. They have read my books. They have read many other books. They look at me with bright eyes and arrogant wonder. They are trying to save their lives. Then there are the sullen and already defeated Indian kids who sit in the back rows and ignore me with theatrical precision. The pages of their notebooks are empty. They carry neither pencil nor pen. They stare out the window. They refuse and resist. "Books," I say to them. "Books," I say. I throw my weight against their locked doors. The door holds. I am smart. I am arrogant. I am lucky. I am trying to save our lives.

INTERPRETATIONS

1. The purpose of an introduction is to engage the reader. How well does Alexie's first paragraph accomplish this? Cite effective examples.

2. What role does his father play in his literacy acquisition? Is there someone who played a similar role in your learning to read?

3. How effectively does Alexie use the metaphor of a fence as a framing device for his essay? Trace its development in each paragraph.

4. In paragraph 4, Alexie returns to the theme of literacy as empowerment. Why does he reintroduce Superman? To what effect?

5. Alexie devotes subsequent paragraphs to personal history and cultural stereotypes. Explain the effects of the latter with respect to teachers, non-Indian, and Indian students.

6. Review Alexie's conclusion. Why does he devote so much time to visiting Indian schools? What is the effect of his ending his essay with the symbol of the door?

APPLICATIONS

1. "I read anything that had words and paragraphs. I read with equal parts of joy and desperation. I loved those books, but I also knew that love had only one purpose. I was trying to save my life." Write a journal response to each of Alexie's statements. What is the effect of juxtaposing joy and desperation? How do you react to his linking reading with saving his life?

2. Alexie writes ". . . I realized that a paragraph was a fence that held words." To what extent is this metaphor dependent upon an understanding of another kind of literacy? What literacy is being invoked?

3. In his second paragraph, Alexie writes: "My father, who is one of the few Indians who went to Catholic school on purpose . . ." What do the last two words of this quoted phrase tell you about the literacies present on the reservation?

One Voice

SUSAN G. MADERA

Susan G. Madera was born and raised in Little Italy, in Manhattan. She lives with her husband and two children in Queens, New York. She received her Associate in Arts degree from Queensborough Community College in 2003, and graduated from Queens College (CUNY) with a B.A. in English and Secondary Education. Record in your journal your responses to Madera's first paragraph.

GROWING UP, I KNEW TWO LANGUAGES: English, and neighborhood. The former was taught at school, and the latter was learned at home, from family and friends. I could read and write in English, but I spoke neighborhood. "What is neighborhood?" you may ask. That is the language spoken in the neighborhood of my youth, Little Italy. It is a language full of slang words, and colloquialisms. Where I grew up, almost everyone spoke neighborhood.

As a child, I attended Transfiguration, a small Catholic grammar school in Chinatown. This school was several blocks away from our cramped, fifth floor apartment in a walk-up building on Broome Street. It was a financial hardship for all five children in our family to attend this school. My father worked two strenuous jobs so that we could enjoy the benefits of a good education. I wore my plaid jumper, crisp white blouse, and red uniform tie with pride each day. I was getting the best education that money could buy. My father said that if I studied hard, I was going to be "someone" when I grew up.

In grammar school, the most difficult subject I studied was English. There were so many complicated rules to memorize! To me, it was a foreign language—mysterious, and intriguing, but not a language that I spoke fluently. I was not alone in my feelings of dismay. Many of the students in my class were having difficulty learning this new language.

I remember Dominick Mazzocchi asking, "How can you say *ain't* ain't a word?"

The teacher responded, "Not only is it not a word, but that was a double negative!"

Dominick responded, "Double what? I wish you would talk English! None of us is understanding you."

"You mean, none of us *are* understanding you," remarked the teacher.

Dominick screamed, "We don't talk like you do!" He was sent to the principal's office.

The truth is, we did not speak alike. Although we were getting a great education in school, it was the language we learned outside of school that determined our speech. Amy Tan writes that the way your friends speak to you, while you are growing up, will have a great impact on you (page 45). The effect on my language skills was a tremendous one, albeit negative. I could not speak English properly.

Once outside the neighborhood, this language hindered me. I was not always understood clearly, or was mocked. "What do you mean, you want to 'take' a haircut?," asked the hairdresser. "Where do you want to take it?" He began to laugh at me. I was so embarrassed. How could he not understand me? The language I picked up on the streets was a part of me, but as I grew up I wanted to get as far away from it as possible. It embarrassed me. In this case, being bilingual was not a blessing, it was a curse.

In high school, I began to use the rules taught to me in my English classes in grammar school. More than anything, I wanted to speak like everyone else. I tried my best, but was unsuccessful. The only way I could stop speaking neighborhood was to take a knife and cut the tongue from my mouth! In my junior year, I was approached by my English teacher who asked if I would like to write for the school paper. "I can't do that!," I exclaimed, "I don't talk right!" She then told me that although I did not speak correctly, I wrote correctly. My written work showed no trace of my flawed speech. She had so much confidence in me that she wanted me to edit the paper as well. I was flabbergasted, and quickly accepted the position. When my first story was published, I was amazed at the response I received from my peers. No one believed that I had written it! I could, indeed, write in proper English. This gave me hope. Perhaps, one day, I might also be able to speak correctly. I felt very much like M. Bella Mirabella, who described how she felt when she accomplished her goals. She wrote, "I was no longer the proverbial small child looking in the shop window."[1] I too was no longer on the outside looking in.

Success at last!

After high school, I attended Brooklyn College. Walking on campus for the first time was like browsing through a travel brochure. I was transformed into a tourist. There were trees everywhere. Although I was only in Brooklyn, I felt far from the city streets of Manhattan. I was in

---

[1]M. Bella Mirabella. "The Education of an Italian-American Girl Child." *Liberating Memory*. Ed. Janet Zandy (Rutgers University Press, 1995), pp. 162–172.

a different world. This was not like the small Catholic schools I had attended. I was alone, and afraid, but determined.

On the first day of classes, I was overwhelmed with feelings of anxiety. I was so excited, I could hardly breathe. That feeling of excitement was soon transformed into a feeling of terror. One of my professors had decided to make my life miserable. He taught Speech 101. On the first day of class, he had each student read aloud from our text book to determine the quality of their speech. He then proceeded to demean me, my heritage and my education. That day was only the first of many. He proceeded to make a fool of me each and every day our class met. That first, and last, semester at Brooklyn College was a dream that turned into a nightmare. José Torres (page 161) writes that you should not let someone else's opinion of you affect your self-worth. Unfortunately, this professor's opinion of me was so low, and his personal attacks were so painful, that I had lost all confidence in myself. It took years for me to gain that confidence back. I decided that college was not for me, and I went into the working world.

I was lucky enough to get a position as a typist in a very prestigious company, Morgan Guaranty. I began my career in the typing pool, typing on an IBM typewriter. Within a year, word processors came into the office, and I was thrilled to be picked as one of the people trained to use one. During this time, I met a wonderful man who would change my life forever—Michael. We dated for two years, and were married at Most Precious Blood Church, in Little Italy.

My personal life was wonderful, so too was my professional life. Over the next few years, I got small promotions within my department. Each promotion brought much more responsibility, with a little more money. One day, at review time, I was called into a meeting. When I walked into the dimly lit conference room, I was surprised to see several assistant vice presidents and a vice president with my supervisor. I immediately broke into a cold sweat. What had I done wrong? My years of "dedication, hard work, and knowledge of the English language" had brought me to their attention. Knowledge of the English language! They were joking, they had to be. They proceeded to make me an offer I could not refuse—my own department. I was dumbfounded when offered this position, but accepted quickly, before they changed their minds. I headed a department of word processors in the investment research department. This success was much larger than the one achieved in high school. I was now being accepted in the business world.

I eventually left Morgan on maternity leave with my first child. Upon my return, I was to be trained on the new IBM computers, and become supervisor of an even larger group of people. Once our son was born and I looked into his sparkling eyes, I knew I could not leave him to the care of a baby-sitter. When I returned three months later, it was to resign my position.

I am still a supervisor, but of our home. Michael is now twelve years old, and Matthew is six. Unfortunately, our children have a bit of neighborhood in them. I take the blame for this. As Dr. Benjamin Spock says about childhood development, "Between 3 and 5 years they were, generally, cozy, affectionate family children who proudly patterned their activities, table manners, and speech after their parents."[2] Our children's speech patterns were picked up from the main caregiver in our home, me. When I hear one of our boys say something incorrectly, I explain why it is wrong, and tell him the correct way to say it. My husband often tells me that I should be an English teacher because I am always correcting their grammar. I want our children to have the benefit of a strong background in English. I know the downfalls of not speaking properly, and I do not want them to experience them, as I have.

To say that I have conquered all my fears of the English language would be untrue. Twenty-one years after walking away from Brooklyn College, I am back in school at Queensborough Community College. What was the first class I decided to take? Why English, of course. I am as determined as ever to speak English as well as possible. I am doing well in my class, and I am proud of myself. I am also quite glad that QCC has decided to give me the three credits I earned in Speech at Brooklyn College, although I barely passed, with a grade of D. I could not have taken that class again.

Over the years, I have gained confidence in myself as a writer. The way I speak does not exemplify who I am; however, my writing is a true expression of the person I am inside. When I write, words come from deep inside of me, and spill out onto the page. I never stop to correct myself, as I would if I were speaking. I may speak two languages, but I write with one voice.

INTERPRETATIONS

1. What distinctions does Madera make between the language of school and the language of the neighborhood?

2. Why does she regard being bilingual as a "curse" rather than a "blessing"?

3. What roles do her teachers play in her acquisition of written language?

---

[2]Dr. Benjamin Spock and Michael B. Rothenberg, M.D., *Dr. Spock's Baby and Child Care* (New York: Pocket Books, 1985).

4. What point does she make about her "two languages" in her conclusion?

APPLICATIONS

1. Do you, like Madera, have a "writing self" and a "speaking self"? How do they differ? What does each express about your identity?

2. The opening sentence to Susan G. Madera's essay is: "Growing up, I knew two languages: English, and neighborhood." What literacies are implied in this statement? What is involved in the literacy of "neighborhood"? What knowledge do you bring to your understanding of your neighborhood?

3. What literacy is presented in Madera's anecdote about Dominick Mazzocchi? What assumptions about literacy are made?

4. How does Madera ultimately resolve the conflict between the literacies of English and neighborhood? To what extent have you negotiated these same literacies and the demands they make upon you?

The Knowing Eye

Bianca Henriquez

Alan S. Maltz

Zack Rutkin

READING IMAGES

1. Which of these photographs depict "family"? Which show "community"? Explain your answers.

2. Crucial to many definitions of family or community is the idea of sharing or giving. As you examine these photographs, what do you think is being shared or given?

MAKING CONNECTIONS

1. Which essay (or essays) in this chapter seem(s) to match these photographs? What similarities do you notice?

2. Select one "Perspective" (see pages 17–18) to summarize each photograph. After making your choices, are the quotations and photographs interchangeable? What have you learned about the interplay of words and images?

WORDS AND IMAGES

1. Which image do you like more? Why? Present your findings in an argumentation and persuasion essay.

2. As you examine the photograph of the people on the sofa, what do you think they might have said to each other immediately after the

picture was taken? First, write a dialogue of ten lines that illustrates the conversation they might have *as a family*. Now, write another dialogue of ten lines with the assumption that they are *not related*. What do you observe about the dialogues that you have created? How does the presence or absence of family relations influence the dialogues that you have written?

Additional Writing Topics

1. Motherhood is an important theme in the texts by Wehle and Tan. Analyze their respective viewpoints in an essay on motherhood that also includes your evaluation of the topic.

2. Although your lifestyle may differ greatly from that of your parents and/or grandparents, are there issues pertaining to family on which you agree? Discuss this subject with your group, including in your considerations the role of the family in communicating and preserving human values. Write a summary of your discussion.

3. Assume the persona of a parent (if you are not one), and write an essay explaining why you would prefer your child to take risks despite the fact that doing so may make life more difficult for him or her.

4. Several writers in this unit focus on the complex roles that memory plays in constructing the self. Write an essay in which you recount at least two memories and explain their significance in shaping your identity.

5. Several selections focus on family members and their influence. Why are families so important? Write an essay answering this question. Use examples from this chapter and your own experience.

6. Review Nin's perspective on friendship (page 18). What does it suggest about possibilities in relationships? Are old friends necessarily one's best friends? Write an essay comparing two friendships of varying durations. How has each contributed to your knowledge of yourself? How do the relationships differ?

7. You have been introduced to several families in this chapter. Imagine being invited to spend a weekend with one of them. Which family would you choose and why? What would you expect from such a visit? Cite evidence from the text to support your expectations.

8. Create a brainstorming list on your association with your name. How has your name affected and enhanced your identity? How might you have been different without your name? Write an essay based on your responses.

9. "The dream of diversity is like the dream of equality. Both are based on the ideals we celebrate even as we undermine them daily." To what extent do you agree with Brooks that there is a dichotomy between our beliefs and our actions regarding these issues? (Consider, for example, Wideman's experience at Kelley's Bar and Grill.) Do we in fact want to live in communities with people like ourselves? Write an essay refuting or supporting Brooks's views on these issues.

CHAPTER

3

Gender Issues

FEW ASPECTS OF CONTEMPORARY LIFE in North America and other parts of the world have changed more radically in the last two decades than those focusing on women in the workplace, gender roles in marriage, women's sexuality, divorce, communication between men and women, child custody, and sexual preference.

The texts on gender issues present a number of points of view on the relationship between men and women and their perceptions of each other. The writers explore, among other things, why various cultures have constructed different images of men and women at different points in their history.

They invite you to examine these changing cross-cultural concepts of masculinity and femininity and to evaluate the degree to which they have affected both men and women in their individual quests for identity, as well as the radical changes in the structure of the family. Some of the writers ask you to decide whether gender conflicts should be confronted or avoided, while others pose possibilities for freeing both sexes from the confines of traditional roles.

The most recurrent and controversial aspects of gender relations found in these texts is the debate between patriarchs and feminists. In some, the traditional idea of male supremacy has left its mark, and in others it is vigorously rejected, shattering intrapersonal and intracultural harmony.

Sexual orientation and sexual preference are current controversies particularly in the realm of "Queer Theory," in which scholars propose that human sexuality is a social construct based on culture rather than nature. They argue that in many cultures outside of the United States bisexuality and homosexuality are accepted, releasing both males and females from the confines of traditional sexual roles. Obviously, such reconsiderations are complex, involving not only individual and social values but moral and religious beliefs.

The texts in this chapter reflect the complexity of gender issues. Jerry Rockwood presents the difficulties of preparing a sensitive son to function in a culture in which masculinity and aggressiveness are considered synonymous. Paul Theroux critiques traditional concepts of masculinity, while Gary Soto asserts that being man should be measured in how well one can support himself. David Brooks in "The Power of Marriage" critiques contemporary attitudes toward fidelity and also makes a case for accepting gay marriages. Jason Barone and Leslie Norris write about an experience many children share: realizing that parents are fallible and cannot always protect them. Gelareh Asayesh in "Shrouded in Contradiction," reveals her ambivalence toward *hijab*— Islamic covering—"Sometimes I hate it. Sometimes I value it," and the controversial topic of sexual preference is the focus of the texts by Dennis Altman and Anna Quindlen.

As you join the debate concerning feminists, patriarchs, homosexuals, and lesbians in these texts from various cultures and traditions, you are invited to speculate on questions such as the following: Are men rightly in charge of the family and tribe? Should women be accorded the same personal, political, and economic rights as men? Can the family survive the challenge to traditionalism created by changing personal and economic gender roles? Are women who return to the workplace surrendering their matriarchal role of nurturing the family and tribe? How have cultural attitudes toward homosexuals and lesbians resulted in political and sexual exclusion? What new definitions are needed for the concept of love?

Perspectives

Masculinity and Femininity may stand on either side of a mile-high wall, yet women and men share beds and homes, histories and children. So while racial and ethnographic stereotypes are fueled by segregation and prohibit familiarity . . . sexual stereotypes are formed in intimacy. This is what makes them unique, and uniquely troubling.

—*Judith Levine*

Marriage is a lottery in which men stake their liberty and women their happiness.

—*Virginia des Rieux*

We need to draw on images of collaborative caring by both men and women as a model of responsibility.

—*Mary Catherine Bateson*

Marriage must be a relation either of sympathy or of conquest.

—*George Eliot*

In sum, "homophobia" is a form of acute conventionality. We should do our best to help humankind over this illness, since heterosexuals who are free of it tend to have much better lives than heterosexuals who are not.

—*George Weinberg*

Indeed, it is my experience that both men and women are fundamentally human, and that there is very little mystery about either sex, except for the exasperating mysteriousness of human beings in general.

—*Dorothy Sayers*

Marriage comes with more myths attached to it than a six-volume set of ancient Greek history.

—*Steven Tesich*

A good marriage is that in which each appoints the other the guardian of his solitude.

—*Rainer Maria Rilke*

Love will redeem a man and change his entire character and existence; lack of love will literally drive a woman crazy.

—*Jean Anouilh*

Not people die but worlds die in them.

—*Yevgeny Yevtushenko*

A child becomes an adult when he realizes that he has a right not only to be right but also to be wrong.

—*Thomas Szasz*

The word love has by no means the same sense for both sexes, and this is one of the serious misunderstandings that divide them.

—*Simone de Beauvoir*

Growing up homosexual was to grow up normally but displaced; to experience romantic love, but with the wrong person; to entertain grand ambitions, but of the unacceptable sort; to seek a gradual self-awakening, but in secret, not in public.

—*Andrew Sullivan*

Women have served all these centuries as looking-glasses possessing the magic and delicious power of reflecting the figure of man at twice its natural size.

—*Virginia Woolf*

The legal subordination of one sex to another is wrong in itself and now one of the chief hindrances to human improvement.

—*John Stuart Mill*

Males become so accustomed to masking their true emotions that it seems like second nature.

—*Mark Zmarzly*

APPLICATIONS

1. Review the various perspectives on marriage. What do they suggest about this intimate relationship? Select the one with which you are most in agreement and compare your choice with those of your group. What consensus, if any, did you reach?

2. Working with members of your group, devise a questionnaire that asks respondents about positive traits associated with masculinity and femininity. Distribute the questionnaire to ten or twelve classmates or co-workers. Write an analysis of their responses.

3. Discuss Zmarzly's perspective with your group. To what extent do you agree with him? What cultural and social factors account for males suppressing their emotions? What solutions are there?

Women

CHINESE FOLK TALE

Milton Rugoff in his A Harvest of World Folk Tales *introduced this old Chinese story this way:*

> *Popular conceptions of China's isolation notwithstanding, Chinese folktales have been no more free of international influence than those of Europe or America. Coming mostly from India through the medium of Buddhism, but also from the Near East, many familiar themes, including those of "Cinderella," the Master Thief, and the trapping of a jinni (genie) in a bottle, appear in Chinese folklore. But the national temperament asserts itself in many ways. Ripened by centuries of a religious philosophy that makes for serenity, the Chinese have lent their stories many distinctive qualities: a gentle whimsicality, fantasy, pathos, the uncanny, a quiet resignation to fate.*

AFTER HE WAS MARRIED, Chang the Third no longer wanted to go to work. He sat at home the whole day and played with his wife. He gazed endlessly at her beautiful face, and the longer he looked the less he wanted to go out. Finally, he gave up his job and remained night and day with his wife. He went on in this way for six months, and then for a year; but even the largest fortune is soon exhausted if one does nothing, and Chang had merely lived on his earnings. In two years, all his wife's jewels, the chairs, the tables, the linen, the clothes, in fact everything they had, was pawned or sold, and they were left without a penny.

His wife was really unusually beautiful, but she thought to herself, "Since his marriage, my husband has never left the house. Day and night he sits around doing nothing but eat. In a short while we shall no longer have the wherewithal to live." So she upbraided him, saying, "You really can't stay at home all day. All men must go to work." But Chang saw her beauty and he thought anxiously, "If I went out another man could come and make love to her." And instead of listening to her words, he remained at home, preferring to eat the most miserable food.

But eventually their poverty became unbearable. They could no longer live if he did not work. Finally, one morning, he said good-by to his wife and decided to go to a village. On his way he met a fine-looking man of about fifty years, who said to him, "Which is the way to such and such a village?" Chang answered, "I am going there myself, so we can go together." During their walk Chang told the stranger his story. "I am so unhappy at leaving my wife," he said. "But I must look for work to enable us to live."

The stranger replied, "The simplest thing is to bottle up your wife. I will give you the bottle, and every day, when you leave, you will only need to look at your wife and blow into the bottle, and she will vanish inside at once. As you can always take it with you, you will never lose your wife. I must now take another road, so farewell." Then he handed Chang a large three-inch bottle from his bag and disappeared. Chang dropped the bottle into his bag, noting what the man had said, and set off gaily for the village. The next day he tried the gift. As his wife was combing her hair before the mirror, he secretly blew into the bottle. The woman saw in the mirror the reflection of her husband blowing into a bottle, but then she lost consciousness and woke up to find herself inside the bottle. Chang put the bottle in his pocket and went off to his work in the village. He was quite contented, for now no other man could flirt with his wife. In the evening he tipped the bottle, and his beautiful wife stood before him as before.

One day, however, he was forced to leave his wife at home to do the washing. He begged her not to leave the house when the washing was finished, and then set off to the village, forgetting to take the bottle with him.

After her husband's departure, the wife went down to the river to wash the clothes. While she was rinsing a shirt she suddenly felt a long, hard thing between her fingers. She took it out and looked at it carefully. "It's a bottle," she said to herself. "Every morning my husband blows into it and I vanish inside. Why has he forgotten it today?" While she was pondering over the matter, a handsome young man passed by on the other bank. She looked up at him, and without thinking what she was doing blew into the bottle, whereupon the young man disappeared. When she had finished the washing, she replaced the bottle in her husband's clothes.

When the man arrived home, he immediately asked for the bottle he had left behind, and his wife handed it to him without a word. The next day when he went out he blew into the bottle as usual, and his wife disappeared, and again he flattered himself that she was safe from the caresses of other men.

That evening on his return he tipped the bottle, but this time two people appeared, his wife and a handsome young man. He was very much surprised and said to himself, "How strange! I thought my wife was quite safe shut up in the bottle, but now she has got a man with her! How odd it is! And how impossible it is to keep a beautiful wife to oneself."

INTERPRETATIONS

1. Describe the relationship between Chang and his wife. How does it change in the course of the story?
2. What type of marriage does the bottle symbolize? What does the mirror symbolize?
3. What seems to be the point (moral) of this tale?
4. Do you think the title works? Why or why not? Would an equally good title be "Men"?

Apollo and Daphne

GREEK LEGEND

*Greece reached the height of its achievements and power in the fifth century
B.C. Its accomplishments in art, architecture, science, mathematics, philosophy, drama, literature, and democracy became legacies for future generations
in countries all over the world. In later centuries, Greece fell under the rule of
Rome, Turkey, and other nations. In 1829, it won independence from Turkey
and became a kingdom. A republic was formed in 1924. During World War II,
occupation by Germans, Italians, and Bulgarians was met by guerrilla warfare against the occupying armies. Subsequent struggles led to the reestablish-
ment of the monarchy, juntas, and finally socialist government.*

DAPHNE [GREEK FOR "LAUREL"] was a wood nymph, the daughter of the
river god Peneus. She was one of those free-spirited women in mythology who was more interested in hunting and fishing than in men. Her
father despaired that she would ever marry; he was more interested in
grandchildren than in having still more game to eat.

The god Apollo saw Daphne one day and fell instantly in love
with her. He was unable to think of anything but her and he pursued
her to no avail. Daphne was absolutely indifferent to his attentions;
it mattered not whether he was god or mortal. She also knew that relationships with gods were often complicated and even dangerous.
She was, after all, half divine, yet mortal. Finally Apollo chased her
through the forests until she was stricken with fear. There was no way
that she could outrun him, so she cried for her father to save her with a
miracle.

Suddenly, she felt her feet become rooted in the earth. She could not
move. Leaves began to sprout from her arms—she had become a living
laurel tree. The gods have a way of sorting things out of the most desperate situations, so they made the laurel tree the sacred tree of Apollo.

To this day, whether at poetry contests or athletic events, both
within the purview of Apollo, the winner is crowned with laurels.

INTERPRETATIONS

1. Characterize Daphne. Might she be regarded as an early feminist?
   Explain.

CORRESPONDENCES

1. Review the Rilke perspective. To what extent do you agree with his point about solitude in relationships? What might Chang the Third (of "Women") have learned from Rilke?

2. To what extent are Apollo and Chang the Third responsible for their fates?

APPLICATIONS

1. Personal space and its effect on gender relationships differs among cultures. Using "Women" as a point of departure, compare your ideas on personal space and romance with group members from other cultures.

2. Discuss with your group the degree to which Daphne's being a free spirit conflicts with parental expectations. To what extent is this still the case? Write a summary of your group's conclusion.

3. Discuss the issue of possessiveness in intimate relationships. Focus on dating perspectives from male and female members of your group and discuss the degree to which they affect attitudes toward freedom in close gender relationships.

Shrouded in Contradiction

GELAREH ASAYESH

Born April 7, 1962, in Tehran, Iran, Gelareh Asayesh earned a B.A. in jour-
nalism at the University of North Carolina in 1983. She worked as a reporter
and staff writer for the Miami Herald, *Miami, FL, 1983–1988 and for the*
Baltimore Sun, *1989–1992, and as a freelance writer since 1992. In 1999 she*
published the memoir Saffron Sky: A Life between Iran and America,
which she says was "roughly fifteen years in the writing." "Shrouded in Con-
tradiction" was published in the New York Times Magazine *in November,*
2001. Asayesh believes that as an immigrant she has a "special agenda" to
retain her "essential core" while becoming "something new." Do you see a
connection between your essential core and your clothes? How do you feel
about using clothes as a "message"?

The Islamic Republic of Iran (formerly Persia), with a population of about
67 million people, lies between the Middle East and Southeast Asia, bordered
on the west by Turkey and Iraq and on the east by Pakistan. Since the Islamic
Revolution of 1979 (led by Shiite Ayatollah Ruholla Khomeini) established a
theocracy, the country has been ruled by a religious head, an ayatollah,
although a secular president and representatives are also elected. When mili-
tants seized sixty-two Americans at the U.S. Embassy in that same year, the
United States severed diplomatic relations. A more moderate president,
Mohammad Khatami, elected in 1997, gave promise of improved U.S.-Iranian
relations, but the current president, Mahmoud Ahmadinejad, and a crisis over
nuclear power, have set back relations between the two countries.

I GREW UP WEARING THE MINISKIRT to school, the veil to the mosque. In the
Tehran of my childhood, women in bright sundresses shared the sidewalk with women swathed in black. The tension between the two ways
of life was palpable. As a schoolgirl, I often cringed when my bare legs
got leering or contemptuous glances. Yet, at times, I long for the days
when I could walk the streets of my country with the wind in my hair.
When clothes were clothes. In today's Iran, whatever I wear sends a message. If it's a chador, it embarrasses my Westernized relatives. If it's a
skimpy scarf, I risk being accused of stepping on the blood of the martyrs
who died in the war with Iraq. Each time I return to Tehran, I wait until
the last possible moment, when my plane lands on the tarmac, to don the
scarf and long jacket that many Iranian women wear in lieu of a veil.

To wear *hijab*—Islamic covering—is to invite contradiction. Sometimes I hate it. Sometimes I value it.

Most of the time, I don't even notice it. It's annoying, but so is wearing pantyhose to work. It ruins my hair, but so does the humidity in Florida, where I live. For many women, the veil is neither a symbol nor a statement. It's simply what they wear, as their mothers did before them. Something to dry your face with after your ablutions before prayer. A place for a toddler to hide when he's feeling shy. Even for a woman like me, who wears it with a hint of rebellion, *hijab* is just not that big a deal.

Except when it is.

"Sister, what kind of get-up is this?" a woman in black, one of a pair, asks me one summer day on the Caspian shore. I am standing in line to ride a gondola up a mountain, where I'll savor some ice cream along with vistas of sea and forest. Women in chadors stand wilting in the heat, faces gleaming with sweat. Women in makeup and clunky heels wear knee-length jackets with pants, their hair daringly exposed beneath sheer scarves.

None have been more daring than I. I've wound my scarf into a turban, leaving my neck bare to the breeze. The woman in black is a government employee paid to police public morals. "Fix your scarf at once!" she snaps.

"But I'm hot," I say.

"You're hot?" she exclaims. "Don't you think we all are?"

I start unwinding my makeshift turban. "The men aren't hot," I mutter.

Her companion looks at me in shocked reproach. "Sister, this isn't about men and women," she says, shaking her head. "This is about Islam."

I want to argue. I feel like a child. Defiant, but powerless. Burning with injustice, but also with a hint of shame. I do as I am told, feeling acutely conscious of the bare skin I am covering. In policing my sexuality, these women have made me more aware of it.

The veil masks erotic freedom, but its advocates believe *hijab* transcends the erotic—or expands it. In the West, we think of passion as a fever of the body, not the soul. In the East, Sufi poets used earthly passion as a metaphor; the beloved they celebrated was God. Where I come from, people are more likely to find delicious passion in the mosque than in the bedroom.

There are times when I feel a hint of this passion. A few years after my encounter on the Caspian, I go to the wake of a family friend. Sitting in a mosque in Mashhad, I grip a slippery black veil with one hand and a prayer book with the other. In the center of the hall, there's a stack of Koranic texts decorated with green-and-black calligraphy, a vase of white gladioluses and a large photograph of the dearly departed. Along the walls, women wait quietly.

From the men's side of the mosque, the mullah's voice rises in lament. His voice is deep and plaintive, oddly compelling. I bow my head, sequestered in my veil while at my side a community of women pray and weep with increasing abandon. I remember from girlhood this sense of being exquisitely alone in the company of others. Sometimes I have cried as well, free to weep without having to offer an explanation. Perhaps they are right, those mystics who believe that physical love is an obstacle to spiritual love; those architects of mosques who abstained from images of earthly life, decorating their work with geometric shapes that they believed freed the soul to slip from its worldly moorings. I do not aspire to such lofty sentiments. All I know is that such moments of passionate abandon, within the circle of invisibility created by the veil, offer an emotional catharsis every bit as potent as any sexual release.

Outside, the rain pours from a sullen sky. I make my farewells and walk toward the car, where my driver waits. My veil is wicking muddy water from the sidewalk. I gather up the wet and grimy folds with distaste, longing to be home, where I can cast off this curtain of cloth that gives with one hand, takes away with the other.

INTERPRETATIONS

1. In the first paragraph, Asayesh longs for the days "when clothes were clothes." What do you think she means by this statement?
2. "For many women, the veil is neither a symbol nor a statement. It's simply what they wear, as their mothers did before them." Do you think that this statement applies to Asayesh? What specific examples can you find to support your answer?
3. In the incident that occurs on the Caspian shore, a woman who is employed to "police public morals" says to Asayesh, "Sister, this isn't about men and women. This is about Islam." Asayesh then writes, "I want to argue. I feel like a child. Defiant, but powerless." What arguments do you think Asayesh would present to the woman? What do you think is the primary issue—gender or religious belief?

CORRESPONDENCES

1. Asayesh and Gary Soto ("To Be a Man") both struggle against society. To what extent are their struggles dependent upon their gender?

2. In their essays, Asayesh and Paul Threoux ("The Male Myth")
    address the expectations that society has of them based upon their
    gender. What does society expect of Asayesh? What does it expect
    of Theroux? How are these demands similar or different?

APPLICATIONS

1. Was there a time in your life when your choice of clothing was in
    conflict with the expectations of others? Write a narrative about
    this event where you explain the incident and your feelings about
    it as it occurred. Also, include your thoughts and reflections about
    society and personal choice.

2. How does the clothing that men and women wear reflect society's
    views and expectations of them? Look through a couple of fashion
    magazines or watch a few music videos. In your journal, jot down
    what you notice about the clothing that the men and women are
    wearing. Now, in a formal essay, discuss similarities and differ-
    ences in the ways that men and women are portrayed. What mes-
    sages are presented about the roles of men and women in these
    visual media? What conclusions might you come to about the rela-
    tionship between gender, clothing, and society? Try to include spe-
    cific examples to support your views.

3. Enter a place of worship. What do you observe about the clothing
    that people are wearing? Is the clothing appropriate to the setting?
    Does the setting dictate behaviors to be followed?

    After returning from this place, try to recall specific details in
    your journal. Then, in class, discuss your findings with your
    group. What general conclusions has the group come to?

The Power of Marriage

DAVID BROOKS

A biographical sketch of David Brooks appears on p. 22. In "The Power of Marriage," Brooks clearly identifies himself as a conservative. What does that label mean to you? Can a conservative expect to influence the beliefs and behavior of a liberal?

ANYBODY WHO HAS SEVERAL SEXUAL PARTNERS in a year is committing spiritual suicide. He or she is ripping the veil from all that is private and delicate in oneself, and pulverizing it in an assembly line of selfish sensations.

But marriage is the opposite. Marriage joins two people in a sacred bond. It demands that they make an exclusive commitment to each other and thereby takes two discrete individuals and turns them into kin.

Few of us work as hard at the vocation of marriage as we should. But marriage makes us better than we deserve to be. Even in the chores of daily life, married couples find themselves, over the years, coming closer together, fusing into one flesh. Married people who remain committed to each other find that they reorganize and deepen each other's lives. They may eventually come to the point when they can say to each other: "Love you? I am you."

Today marriage is in crisis. Nearly half of all marriages end in divorce. Worse, in some circles, marriage is not even expected. Men and women shack up for a while, produce children and then float off to shack up with someone else.

Marriage is in crisis because marriage, which relies on a culture of fidelity, is now asked to survive in a culture of contingency. Today, individual choice is held up as the highest value: choice of lifestyles, choice of identities, choice of cellphone rate plans. Freedom is a wonderful thing, but the culture of contingency means that the marriage bond, which is supposed to be a sacred vow till death do us part, is now more likely to be seen as an easily canceled contract.

Men are more likely to want to trade up, when a younger trophy wife comes along. Men and women are quicker to opt out of marriages, even marriages that are not fatally flawed, when their "needs" don't seem to be met at that moment.

Still, even in this time of crisis, every human being in the United States has the chance to move from the path of contingency to the path of marital fidelity—except homosexuals. Gays and lesbians are banned from marriage and forbidden to enter into this powerful and ennobling institution. A gay or lesbian couple may love each other as deeply as any two people, but when you meet a member of such a couple at a party, he or she then introduces you to a "partner," a word that reeks of contingency.

You would think that faced with this marriage crisis, **we conservatives** would do everything in our power to move as many people as possible from the path of contingency to the path of fidelity. But instead, many argue that gays must be banished from matrimony because gay marriage would weaken all marriage. A marriage is between a man and a woman, they say. It is women who domesticate men and make marriage work.

Well, if women really domesticated men, heterosexual marriage wouldn't be in crisis. In truth, it's moral commitment, renewed every day through faithfulness, that "domesticates" all people.

Some conservatives may have latched onto biological determinism (men are savages who need women to tame them) as a convenient way to oppose gay marriage. But in fact we are not animals whose lives are bounded by our flesh and by our gender. We're moral creatures with souls, endowed with the ability to make covenants, such as the one Ruth made with Naomi: "Where you go I will go, and where you stay I will stay. Your people will be my people and your God my God. Where you die I will die, and there I will be buried."

The conservative course is not to banish gay people from making such commitments. It is to expect that they make such commitments. We shouldn't just allow gay marriage. We should insist on gay marriage. We should regard it as scandalous that two people could claim to love each other and not want to sanctify their love with marriage and fidelity.

When liberals argue for gay marriage, they make it sound like a really good employee benefits plan. Or they frame it as a civil rights issue, like extending the right to vote.

Marriage is not voting. It's going to be up to conservatives to make the important, moral case for marriage, including gay marriage. Not making it means drifting further into the culture of contingency, which, when it comes to intimate and sacred relations, is an abomination.

INTERPRETATIONS

1. To what extent do you agree with Brooks that "marriage is a sacred bond"? What connotations do you associate with "sacred"?

2. "Today marriage is in crisis." What evidence does Brooks cite in paragraphs 4–6 to support his thesis?

3. In paragraph 10, Brooks distinguishes between viewing human beings as "savages" or as "moral" creatures. Which point of view reflects yours? To what extent does it affect your support or non-support of gay marriage? Explain.

4. Should "conservatives" have a vested interest in supporting gay marriage? What, according to Brooks, motivates "liberals" to support this issue?

CORRESPONDENCES

1. Review des Rieux's perspective on marriage. To what extent does it apply to Brooks's essay?

2. Brooks and Theroux (page 101) hope to persuade their readers. Characterize the tone of both essays. Whose do you find more convincing? Cite evidence to support your answer.

APPLICATIONS

1. Discuss with your group the questions raised in the headnote on conservatives and liberals. How would you characterize yourself? What consensus, if any, did you reach?

2. Write a journal entry on your concepts of the power of marriage.

3. Discuss with your group the first paragraph of Brook's essay and record your responses. What consensus, if any, did you reach?

4. Write an essay responding to one of Brooks's Op-Ed columns in a current issue of *The New York Times*. Be sure to include specific evidence to support your point of view.

The Male Myth

PAUL THEROUX

Paul Theroux (b. 1941), who has had a successful career writing both fiction and nonfiction, was born in Medford, Massachusetts, and educated at the University of Maine, the University of Massachusetts, and Syracuse University. As a Peace Corps volunteer in the Congo, he became too friendly with local politicians who were not in good standing with the country's dictator and was deported. His numerous novels include The Mosquito Coast *(1982),* My Secret History *(1989),* Milroy the Magician *(1994),* Kowloon Tong *(1997), and* Blinding Light *(2005). Three of Theroux's novels have been adapted for film or TV. He has also published many collections of short stories. Theroux has been commercially, if not always critically, successful. He does not shy away from an argument. He has little patience with academic creative-writing programs and patronage provided by grants and fellowships. "The writer," he says, "doesn't want a patron half so badly as he wants a paying public." Theroux's travel books include* The Great Railway Bazaar *(1975),* Riding the Iron Rooster *(1988),* To the Ends of the Earth *(1990), and* Fresh Air Fiend *(2000). In* Dark Star Safari *(2003) Theroux revisits some of the places he served in the Peace Corps and gets into arguments with Christian missionaries. Theroux currently divides his time between Cape Cod and Hawaii, where he is a professional beekeeper. Are you personally affected by the argument in the following selection and if so, how?*

THERE IS A PATHETIC SENTENCE in the chapter "Fetishism" in Dr. Norman Cameron's book *Personality Development and Psychopathology*. It goes: "Fetishists are nearly always men; and their commonest fetish is a woman's shoe." I cannot read that sentence without thinking that it is just one more awful thing about being a man—and perhaps it is the most important thing to know about us.

I have always disliked being a man. The whole idea of manhood in America is pitiful, a little like having to wear an ill-fitting coat for one's entire life. (By contrast, I imagine femininity to be an oppressive sense of nakedness.) Even the expression "Be a man!" strikes me as insulting and abusive. It means: Be stupid, be unfeeling, obedient and soldierly, and stop thinking. Man means "manly"—how can one think "about men" without considering the terrible ambition of manliness? And yet it is part of every man's life. It is a hideous and crippling lie; it not only insists on difference and connives at superiority, it is also by its very nature destructive—emotionally damaging and socially harmful.

The youth who is subverted, as most are, into believing in the masculine ideal is effectively separated from women—it is the most savage tribal logic—and he spends the rest of his life finding women a riddle and a nuisance. Of course, there is a female version of this male affliction. It begins with mothers encouraging little girls to say (to other adults), "Do you like my new dress?" In a sense, girls are traditionally urged to please adults with a kind of coquettishness, while boys are enjoined to behave like monkeys toward each other. The nine-year-old coquette proceeds to become womanish in a subtle power game in which she learns to be sexually indispensable, socially decorative and always alert to a man's sense of inadequacy.

Femininity—being ladylike—implies needing a man as witness and seducer; but masculinity celebrates the exclusive company of men. That is why it is so grotesque; and that is also why there is no manliness without inadequacy—because it denies men the natural friendship of women.

It is very hard to imagine any concept of manliness that does not belittle women, and it begins very early. At an age when I wanted to meet girls—let's say the treacherous years of thirteen to sixteen—I was told to take up a sport, get more fresh air, join the Boy Scouts, and I was urged not to read so much. It was the 1950s and, if you asked too many questions about sex, you were sent to camp—boys' camp, of course; the nightmare. Nothing is more unnatural or prisonlike than a boys' camp, but if it were not for them, we would have no Elks' Lodges, no poolrooms, no boxing matches, no marines.

And perhaps no sports as we know them. Everyone is aware of how few in number are the athletes who behave like gentlemen. Just as high-school basketball teaches you how to be a poor loser, the manly attitude toward sports seems to be little more than a recipe for creating bad marriages, social misfits, moral degenerates, sadists, latent rapists and just plain louts. I regard high-school sports as a drug far worse than marijuana, and it is the reason that the average tennis champion, say, is a pathetic oaf.

Any objective study would find the quest for manliness essentially right wing, puritanical, cowardly, neurotic and fueled largely by a fear of women. It is also certainly philistine. There is no book hater like a Little League coach. But, indeed, all the creative arts are obnoxious to the manly ideal, because at their best the arts are pursued by uncompetitive and essentially solitary people. It makes it very hard for a creative youngster, for any boy who expresses the desire to be alone seems to be saying that there is something wrong with him.

It ought to be clear by now that I have an objection to the way we turn boys into men. It does not surprise me that when the President of the United States has his customary weekend off, he dresses like a cowboy—it is both a measure of his insecurity and his willingness to please. In many ways, American culture does little more for a man than prepare him for modeling clothes in the L. L. Bean catalogue. I take this as a personal insult because for many years I found it impossible to admit to myself that I wanted to be a writer. It was my guilty secret, because being a writer was incompatible with being a man.

There are people who might deny this, but that is because the American writer, typically, has been so at pains to prove his manliness. But first there was a fear that writing was not a manly profession—indeed, not a profession at all. (The paradox in American letters is that it has always been easier for a woman to write and for a man to be published.) Growing up, I had thought of sports as wasteful and humiliating, and the idea of manliness as a bore. My wanting to become a writer was not a flight from that oppressive role playing, but I quickly saw that it was at odds with it. Everything in stereotyped manliness goes against the life of the mind. The Hemingway personality is too tedious to go into here, but certainly it was not until this aberrant behavior was examined by feminists in the 1960's that any male writer dared question the pugnacity in Hemingway's fiction. All that bullfighting and arm-wrestling and elephant shooting diminished Hemingway as a writer: One cannot be a male writer without first proving that one is a man.

It is normal in America for a man to be dismissive or even somewhat apologetic about being a writer. Various factors make it easier. There is a heartiness about journalism that makes it acceptable—journalism is the manliest form of American writing and, therefore, the profession the most independent-minded women seek (yes, it is an illusion, but that is my point). Fiction writing is equated with a kind of dispirited failure and is only manly when it produces wealth. Money is masculinity. So is drinking. Being a drunkard is another assertion, if misplaced, of manliness. The American male writer is traditionally proud of his heavy drinking. But we are also very literal-minded people. A man proves his manhood in America in old-fashioned ways. He kills lions, like Hemingway; or he hunts ducks, like Nathanael West; or he makes pronouncements, like "A man should carry enough knife to defend himself with," as James Jones is said to have once told an interviewer. And we are familiar with the lengths to which Norman Mailer is prepared, in his endearing way, to prove that he is just as much a monster as the next man.

When the novelist John Irving was revealed as a wrestler, people took him to be a very serious writer. But what interests me is that it is inconceivable that any woman writer would be shown in such a posture. How surprised we would be if Joyce Carol Oates were revealed as a sumo wrestler or Joan Didion enjoyed pumping iron. "Lives in New York City with her three children" is the typical woman-writer's biographical note, for just as the male writer must prove he has achieved a sort of muscular manhood, the woman writer—or rather her publicists—must prove her motherhood.

There would be no point in saying any of this if it were not generally accepted that to be a man is somehow—even now in feminist-influenced America—a privilege. It is on the contrary an unmerciful and punishing burden. Being a man is bad enough; being manly is appalling. It is the sinister silliness of men's fashions that inspires the so-called dress code of the Ritz-Carlton Hotel in Boston. It is the institutionalized cheating in college sports. It is a pathetic and primitive insecurity.

And this is also why men often object to feminism, but are afraid to explain why: Of course women have a justified grievance, but most men believe—and with reason—that their lives are much worse.

INTERPRETATIONS

1. What is Theroux's definition of *manly*? To what extent do you agree with it?

2. How does Theroux define *femininity*? What observations does he make about society's attempts to stereotype women?

3. Theroux makes several comments about "the sinister silliness of men's fashions." What is the context for his analysis? To what extent do you agree with him?

CORRESPONDENCES

1. Create a dialogue between Soto (page 106) and Theroux on the topic of manhood.

2. To what extent do you agree with Soto and Theroux that societal values influence our concepts of masculininity and feminity. Is it possible or even desirable to deviate from stereotypical definitions? Explain your answer.

APPLICATIONS

1. "I have always disliked being a man." With this sentence, Paul Theroux begins the second paragraph of his essay "The Male

Myth." As you read through the essay, extract sentences that support this viewpoint. Now, imagine how someone who disagrees with Theroux would respond to these statements. (Perhaps, select someone famous who typifies the kind of "manliness" that Theroux seems to be questioning.) Try to create a conversation (dialogue) between these two individuals.

2. Discuss with your group the degree to which society and culture influence our concepts of masculinity and femininity. To what extent is it possible or desirable to go beyond stereotypical definitions?

3. Bring to class four advertisements from current magazines featuring dress styles for men and women. Analyze with your group the images they intend to communicate. To what extent are they based on gender stereotypes? What do they "promise" the consumer?

To Be a Man

GARY SOTO

*Gary Soto (b. 1952) was born in Fresno, California, to American-born
parents whose Mexican heritage was important in his upbringing. Soto was
raised by his mother after his father was killed in an industrial accident when
Soto was about five. He graduated magna cum laude in 1974 from California
State–Fresno, and in 1976 he received his master's degree in creative writing
from the University of California at Irvine. He is the author of numerous
poetry collections, among them his first volume of poetry,* The Elements of
San Joaquin *(1977), a grim picture of Mexican-American life, and* Black
Hair *(1985), which focuses on his friends and family.* New and Selected
Poems *(1995) was a finalist for the Los Angeles Book Award and the
National Book Award.* Shadow of the Plums: Poems *was published in
2002. One of Soto's memoirs,* Living Up The Street; Narrative Recollections, *received a Before Columbus Foundation American Book Award in
1985. He has written many books for young readers. In addition to writing,
Soto has produced a film and a libretto for the Los Angeles Opera. Soto also
serves as Young People's Ambassador for the California Rural Legal Assistance and the United Farm Workers of America. Before reading Soto's essay,
write a journal entry on the summer job you most hated. What did you learn
from the experience?*

HOW STRANGE IT IS to consider the dishevelled man sprawled out
against a store front with the rustling noise of newspaper in his lap.
Although we see him from our cars and say "poor guy," we keep
speeding toward jobs, careers, and people who will open our wallets,
however wide, to stuff them with money.

I wanted to be that man when I was a kid of ten or so, and told
Mother how I wanted my life. She stood at the stove staring down at
me, eyes narrowed, and said I didn't know what I was talking about.
She buttered a tortilla, rolled it fat as a telescope, and told me to eat it
outside. While I tore into my before-dinner-snack, I shook my head at
my mother because I knew what it was all about. Earlier in the week
(and the week before), I had pulled a lawn mower, block after block, in
search of work. I earned a few quarters, but more often screen doors
slapped shut with an "I'm sorry," or milky stares scared me to the next
house.

I pulled my lawn mower into the housing projects that were a block from where we lived. A heavy woman with veined legs and jowls like a fat purse, said, "Boy, you in the wrong place. We poor here."

It struck me like a ball. They were poor, but I didn't even recognize them. I left the projects and tried houses with little luck, and began to wonder if they too housed the poor. If they did, I thought, then where were the rich? I walked for blocks, asking at messy houses until I was so far from home I was lost.

That day I decided to become a hobo. If it was that difficult pulling quarters from a closed hand, it would be even more difficult plucking dollars from greedy pockets. I wanted to give up, to be a nobody in thrown-away clothes, because it was too much work to be a man. I looked at my stepfather who was beaten from work, from the seventeen years that he hunched over a conveyor belt, stuffing boxes with paperback books that ran down the belt quick as rats. Home from work, he sat in his oily chair with his eyes unmoved by television, by the kids, by his wife in the kitchen beating a round steak with a mallet. He sat dazed by hard labor and bitterness yellowed his face. If his hands could have spoken to him, they would have asked to die. They were tired, bleeding like hearts from the inside.

I couldn't do the same: work like a man. I knew I had the strength to wake from an alley, walk, and eat little. I knew I could give away the life that the television asked me to believe in, and live on fruit trees and the watery soup of the Mission.

But my ambition—that little screen in the mind with good movies—projected me as a priest, then a baseball coach, then a priest again, until here I am now raking a cracker across a cheesy dip at a faculty cocktail party. I'm looking the part and living well—the car, the house, and the suits in the closet. Some days this is where I want to be. On other days I want out, such as the day I was in a committee meeting among PhDs. In an odd moment I saw them as pieces of talking meat and, like meat we pick up to examine closely at supermarkets, they were soulless, dead, and fixed with marked prices. I watched their mouths move up and down with busy words that did not connect. As they finished mouthing one sentence to start on another, they just made up words removed from their feelings.

It's been twenty years since I went door to door. Now I am living this other life that seems a dream. How did I get here? What line on my palm arched into a small fortune? I sit before students, before grade books, before other professors talking about books they've yet to write, so surprised that I'm far from that man on the sidewalk, but not so far that he couldn't wake up one day, walk a few pissy steps saying, "It's time," and embrace me for life.

INTERPRETATIONS

1. Why do you think Soto's mother responds the way she does when he announced to her that he wanted to be like the man depicted in paragraph 1?
2. Why did Soto, as a child, decide to be a hobo? What do you think of his reasoning?
3. How do you think Soto feels about how he has chosen to live his life? How do his decisions represent his vision of what it means to be a man?

CORRESPONDENCES

1. Compare the societal pressures that Soto feels as a man with those felt by Asayesh as a woman (see "Shrouded in Contradiction," page 94).
2. Fathers and sons figure prominently in this chapter. How does Soto's portrayal of his stepfather relate to some of the other representations that appear? After reading a couple of the following essays, what do you learn about male gender roles? What qualities do grown men have or are they supposed to have? Possible readings: Rockwood, page 110; Quindlen, page 117; Barone, page 125; Norris, page 129.

APPLICATIONS

1. What does it mean to be a "man" or a "woman"? Write a definition essay that explores just one of these terms. Be sure to provide clear examples and to use details. (Note how Soto uses descriptive language to help you to see the people he presents in his essay.)
2. What is "the life that the television asked me to believe in" (paragraph 6)?

    Watch a commercial television station for one hour. As you watch, keep a list of those assumptions and expectations (regarding social status, consumerism, ethnicity, gender roles) that are being presented to you. Remember to log commercials as well as show content.

    After you have finished viewing the show or shows, consult your list. How has life been represented on the TV screen? More specifically, what "needs" or "wants" have been presented to you?

    Give careful consideration to your observations and your thoughts about them. Then, from your list, write an essay that explains your definition of both "needs" and "wants." Use examples from your TV viewing log to support your ideas.

3. Write a dialogue of ten lines that is derived from the exchange between the ten-year-old Soto and his mother that is described in paragraph 2. Now add a third person—Soto as the grown man described in paragraphs 7 and 8—who comments upon the ongoing exchange. What impact does Soto's life experiences have upon what he says to his mother and his younger self?

4. Three primary men are presented in Soto's essay: the man described in paragraph 1, the father described in paragraph 5, and the man (Soto) described in paragraph 7. From Soto's descriptions, draw a picture of each man, showing how each one illustrates what it is "to be a man." (Alternatively, you might cut out photos from a magazine or take the photographs yourself.) Share your drawings with your classmates, letting them explain the definitions that they interpret from your works.

Life Intrudes

JERRY ROCKWOOD

Jerry Rockwood (b. 1927) is an actor, director, and author who has taught at the Stella Adler Studio and the American Academy of Dramatic Art. Rockwood is the author of The Craftsmen of Dionysus: An Approach to Acting, *which was published in 1966. In 1988 Rockwood wrote the songs for a "musical play"* The Mandrake, *a loose adaptation of Machiavelli's* La Mandragola. *In that same year, "Life Intrudes" was originally published in* The New York Times Magazine *as part of the "About Men" series. Before you read Rockwood's essay, ask yourself what purpose could be served by criticizing your own or others' personalities?*

I NEVER SPOKE BACK. I was quiet and obedient. And so I grew up without aggression, at least the kind of aggression that can be seen on the surface.

It has cost me dearly. I think one reason I became an actor was to be able to vent my squelched aggression and hostility through the characters I played on the stage. But one needs loads of personal aggression to make it in the theater, and, as a result, I never had the success I wanted. Eventually, I turned to teaching acting in college.

Now I have been watching my son, Matthew, a year out of college, display a similar lack of aggression. He reminds me of myself—the way I used to find myself shrinking back or turning away from unpleasantness. Matthew uses "I choose not to" as an excuse for avoiding things he ought to face. It troubles me. It makes me wonder about the values we impose in raising our children.

Education, to a Cherokee father, meant teaching his son to hunt with a bow and arrow, to tread noiselessly through the woods. To an Eskimo father, it meant showing his boy how to tap ice for strength and thickness, how to gauge the depth of the water. Education for these boys meant learning to deal with the environment.

Was it so with Matthew when he was a boy? I think not. His was a good school. Private. Expensive. With all the right and beautiful philosophies intended to help kids grow up to be interested and sincere and sensitive and cooperative and creative and aware—to shun violence and war and vice and double-dealings. Disputes in Matthew's school were mediated by sympathetic and understanding teachers. Feelings were aired, points of view pointed out, alternatives proposed. The right stuff.

But I cannot forget an episode that occurred when Matthew was nine years old. A boy named Kevin, the leader of a small gang of bullies, had it in for him. I remember saying something like, "Look, Math, if Kevin calls you filthy names and teases you, then he's not a very nice kid, and the best thing to do is to ignore him. Laugh it off and walk away."

"But he follows me. And then he starts shoving me. And today he knocked over a bike on me. I don't know what to do!"

Well, what do you do? Tell me, educators and psychologists, what should I have told my son to do? He had discovered that the world inside his fabulously equipped, psychologist-staffed and superior-teacher-laden school was not like the real world outside.

What I did do is this: when I learned that Matthew was determined to fight with Kevin, I first tried to talk him out of it. I asked him if he could beat Kevin. He said yes. I saw that he was determined, and so I agreed and even accompanied him. "My father is coming," Matthew had explained to the other boys, "just to make sure that two of you guys don't jump me at once."

We all walked along the beach looking for a secluded place. "Whatever happens, Dad," Matthew said on the way, "don't break it up." I said I wouldn't break it up.

I stood against a telephone pole, gripping with one hand the lowest of the metal spikes used for climbing it. A dozen or more kids stood nearby. Matthew was sturdier than the wiry Kevin: they were the same height. Each waited for the other to move first. Kevin sprang and, in an instant, had Matthew down and in a headlock. His fist smashed again and again into Matthew's face. There was no contest. Kevin was an accomplished street fighter; Matthew simply didn't know how to fight. At last, "Do you give up?" "Yes."

Matthew rose to his feet, his nose bleeding, his lips bloody and swollen. He tried to hold back the tears, but the anger and humiliation were too much. He made a lunge, and Kevin reached all the way back with his right fist and threw all his weight into a solid punch in the neck. There was an audible intake of breath from the spectators at the sound of the punch. Matthew was stunned and gave a strangulated cry. "Do you give up?" A nod of the head. I put my arm around my son's shoulder and took him home to bathe his wounds.

Later, I tucked him in bed and kissed him goodnight. I knew that his bruises would heal, but I wasn't sure about the humiliation. Even now, all I'm sure of is that Matthew remembers the incident as vividly as I.

I am puzzled. I reluctantly allowed my son to have his confrontation, and he did not shrink from it. But was that enough? Should I have taught Matthew to be a street fighter, as well? Should he have been trained to co-exist in this other world? The idea is monstrous to me. But so is the idea of his being beaten up by any punk who comes along. Are we wrong in presenting only half the picture? Do you train a sailor by showing him the ropes and neglect to tell him about wind direction and tides?

"Life intrudes," was one of the pet expressions of Stella Adler, a wonderful acting teacher with whom I worked for years. Life intrudes. No matter how solidly we build our dream cabin, we can't ever completely seal up all the cracks. Life will sneak in, force itself upon us. It is there no matter how often we mutter our yeses and noes and ifs and buts and maybes. It is there, and it may be unwise to pretend it is not.

I don't have an answer, just the uncertainty of how to wish the best for Matthew and all of us. If we can't train the street fighters to be gentlemen, must we train the gentlemen to be street fighters? Should we all be Boy Scouts? Be Prepared? Or is that akin to the craziness of putting a hair trigger on the gun?

INTERPRETATIONS

1. What evidence does Rockwood present to support his point that being unaggressive has cost him? How has his lack of aggression affected his son?

2. What does the incident with the bully reveal about Matthew? About his father? To what extent do you agree that Matthew probably "remembers the incident" as vividly as does his father?

3. Review paragraphs 14–16. What is Rockwood puzzled about? Should he have taught Matthew to be a street fighter? Has he failed as a father? Why or why not?

CORRESPONDENCES

1. Create a conversation between Soto and Rockwood on the subject of masculinity. What issues or questions would you add to their discussion?

2. To what extent have rigid gender roles imposed emotional limitations on men? Compare Theroux's and Rockwood's points of view on these issues.

APPLICATIONS

1. Review paragraph 15 and discuss with your group the thematic significance of Rockwood's title. Can parents protect their children

from "dangers"? How do fathers help their sons (and daughters) to deal with violence and aggression? Summarize your discussion.

2. Write a journal entry on your first encounter with a bully. When and where did it occur? What emotions do you associate with the experience? Were the effects long-lasting? Did it involve your parents?

3. Assume Matthew's persona and write a portrait of his father referring to specific incidents and/or statements in Rockwood's essay.

Why Are Gay Men So Feared?

DENNIS ALTMAN

Born in 1943 in Sydney, Australia, Dennis Altman is a Reader in Politics at La Trobe University in Melbourne, Australia. Among his works are AIDS in the Mind *(1986) and* Paper Ambassadors *(1991). The excerpt from the article below appeared in the* New Internationalist *in November 1989.*

GAY MEN ARE THE VICTIMS of insults, prejudice, abuse, violence, sometimes murder. Why are gay men hated by so many other men? Some maintain that homosexuality is unnatural or a threat to the family. But celibacy is also unnatural, yet nuns and priests are not regularly attacked. And there is also a good case to be made that homosexuality actually *strengthens* the family by liberating some adults from child-bearing duties and so increasing the pool of adults available to look after children.

But the real objection to homosexuality (and lesbianism) is undoubtedly more deep-seated: It is threatening because it seems to challenge the conventional roles governing a person's sex, and the female and male roles in society. The assertion of homosexual identity clearly challenges the apparent naturalness of gender roles.

Men are particularly prone to use anger and violence against those they think are undermining their masculinity. And it is here that we can find at least some of the roots of homophobia and gay-bashing.

As Freud understood, most societies are built upon a set of relationships between men: Most powerful institutions like parliaments and business corporations are male-dominated. And this "male bonding" demands a certain degree of sexual sublimation.

In many societies, the links between men are much stronger than the relations that link them to women. But these bonds are social rather than individual, and for this reason need to be strictly governed. Armies, for example, depend upon a very strong sense of male solidarity, though this does not allow for too close an emotional tie between any *specific* pair of men.

Thus the most extreme homophobia is often found among tightly knit groups of men, who need to deny any sexual component to their bonding as well as boost their group solidarity by turning violently on "fags" or "queers," who are defined as completely alien. This is a phenomenon found among teenage gangs, policemen, and soldiers.

A particularly prominent example of this was Germany's Nazi Party, which shortly after coming to power purged those of its members who were tempted to turn the hypermasculinity of Nazism into an excuse for overt homosexual behavior.

Many observers of sexual violence have argued that the most virulent queer-basher is attacking the homosexual potential in himself—a potential that he has learned to suppress. Because homosexuality is "un-masculine," those who struggle with feelings of homosexuality (often unacknowledged) will be particularly tempted to resolve them through "masculine" expressions of violence. In court cases involving violence against gay men, the idea of preserving one's male honor is often pleaded as a defense.

Homophobia has effects that go far beyond those individuals against whom it is directed. Like racism and sexism, it is an expression of hatred that harms the perpetrator as well as the victim; the insecurities, fears, and sexual hang-ups that lead young men to go out looking for "fags" to beat up are dangerous to the entire society.

Those societies that are best able to accept homosexuals are also societies that are able to accept assertive women and gentle men, and they tend to be less prone to the violence produced by hypermasculinity.

INTERPRETATIONS

1. To what extent do you agree with Altman that homosexuality and lesbianism are feared because they challenge "the apparent naturalness of gender roles"?

2. What, according to Altman, is the connection between homosexuality and violence?

CORRESPONDENCES

1. Review Sullivan's perspective and discuss its application to Altman's essay.

2. Review Weinberg's perspective on homophobia and discuss its application to Altman's essay. How does it support or contradict Altman's point of view?

APPLICATIONS

1. Discuss with your group the question posed in Altman's title. To what extent do you agree that both homosexuals and lesbians are feared?

2. Review paragraph 8 of Altman's essay and write a persuasive essay agreeing or disagreeing with his point of view. You may include your emotional as well as your intellectual responses to his thesis.

3. Theroux and Rockwood share the difficulties of growing up male in a culture in which stereotypes of masculinity are pervasive. What conversation can you imagine their having with Altman? What would you add to the discussion?

Gay

ANNA QUINDLEN

Anna Quindlen (b. 1953 in Philadelphia) is well known as a columnist and a novelist, having won a Pulitzer Prize for Commentary in 1992. She has held a variety of positions at The New York Times *since 1977. From 1981 to 1983 she was deputy metropolitan editor. She was author of a biweekly column "About New York," 1983–1985, of a weekly column, "Life in the 30s," 1986–1988, and again of the biweekly column "Public & Private," 1990–1995. In 1991 she wrote her first novel,* Object Lessons, *followed by* One True Thing (1994) *(adapted as a film starting Renee Zellweger and Meryl Streep), and* Black and Blue (1998). Rise and Shine, *her most recent novel, was published in 2006. Quindlen is also the author of the nonfiction* Living Out Loud (1988), *(from which the following essay comes),* How Reading Changed My Life (1998), A Short Guide to a Happy Life (2000), *and* Being Perfect (2005). *She became a biweekly columnist for* Newsweek's *"Last Word" in 1999. Quindlen told an interviewer that she is most "at home in the rocky emotional terrain of marriage, parenthood, secret desires and self-doubts." A* Newsweek *chairman and editor-in-chief has praised Quindlen's "no-nonsense thinking and her unerring sense of justice and injustice." What evidence of these interests and qualities do you find in the following essay?*

WHEN HE WENT HOME LAST YEAR, he realized for the first time that he would be buried there, in the small, gritty industrial town he had loathed for as long as he could remember. He looked out the window of his bedroom and saw the siding on the house next door and knew that he was trapped, as surely as if he had never left for the city. Late one night, before he was to go back to his own apartment, his father tried to have a conversation with him, halting and slow, about drug use and the damage it could do to your body. At that moment he understood that it would be more soothing to his parents to think that he was a heroin addict than that he was a homosexual.

This is part of the story of a friend of a friend of mine. She went to his funeral not too long ago. The funeral home forced the family to pay extra to embalm him. Luckily, the local paper did not need to print the cause of death. His parents' friends did not ask what killed him, and his parents didn't talk about it. He had AIDS. His parents had figured out at the same time that he was dying and that he slept with men.

He tried to talk to them about his illness; he didn't want to discuss his homosexuality. That would have been too hard for them all.

Never have the lines between sex and death been so close, the chasm between parent and child so wide. His parents hoped almost until the end that some nice girl would "cure" him. They even hinted broadly that my friend might be that nice girl. After the funeral, as she helped with the dishes in their small kitchen with the window onto the backyard, she lost her temper at the subterfuge and said to his mother: "He was gay. Why is that more terrible than that he is dead?" The mother did not speak, but raised her hands from the soapy water and held them up as though to ward off the words.

I suppose this is true of many parents. For some it is simply that they think homosexuality is against God, against nature, condemns their sons to hell. For others it is something else, more difficult to put into words. It makes their children too different from them. We do not want our children to be too different—so different that they face social disapprobation and ostracism, so different that they die before we do. His parents did not know any homosexuals, or at least they did not believe they did. His parents did not know what homosexuals were like.

They are like us. They are us. Isn't that true? And yet, there is a difference. Perhaps mothers sometimes have an easier time accepting this. After all, they must accept early on that there are profound sexual differences between them and their sons. Fathers think their boys will be basically like them. Sometimes they are. And sometimes, in a way that comes to mean so much, they are not.

I have thought of this a fair amount because I am the mother of sons. I have managed to convince myself that I love my children so much that nothing they could do would turn me against them, or away from them, that nothing would make me take their pictures off the bureau and hide them in a drawer. A friend says I am fooling myself, that I would at least be disappointed and perhaps distressed if, like his, my sons' sexual orientation was not hetero. Maybe he's right. There are some obvious reasons to feel that way. If the incidence of AIDS remains higher among homosexuals than among heterosexuals, it would be one less thing they could die of. If societal prejudices remain constant, it would be one less thing they could be ostracized for.

But this I think I know: I think I could live with having a son who was homosexual. But it would break my heart if he was homosexual and felt that he could not tell me so, felt that I was not the kind of mother who could hear that particular truth. That is a kind of death, too, and it kills both your life with your child and all you have left after the funeral: the relationship that can live on inside you, if you have nurtured it.

In the days following his death, the mother of my friend's friend mourned the fact that she had known little of his life, had not wanted to know. "I spent too much time worrying about what he was," she said. Not who. What. And it turned out that there was not enough time, not with almost daily obituaries of people barely three decades old, dead of a disease she had never heard of when she first wondered about the kind of friends her boy had and why he didn't date more.

It reminded me that often we take our sweet time dealing with the things that we do not like about our children: the marriage we could not accept, the profession we disapproved of, the sexual orientation we may hate and fear. Sometimes we vow that we will never, never accept those things. The stories my friend told me about the illness, the death, the funeral and, especially, about the parents reminded me that sometimes we do not have all the time we think to make our peace with who our children are. It reminded me that "never" can last a long, long time, perhaps much longer than we intended, deep in our hearts, when we first invoked its terrible endless power.

INTERPRETATIONS

1. Why do you think the gay man's parents would prefer "to think that he was a heroin addict rather than that he was a homosexual"?

2. To what extent do you agree with Quindlen that parents are reluctant to accept children who are too different from them?

3. What is Quindlen's supposition about being the mother of a homosexual? Do you agree with her? Why or why not?

CORRESPONDENCES

1. Compare and contrast societal attitudes toward sexual preference in the texts by Quindlen and Altman.

2. Is Quindlen seeking only to inform her audience or does she wish also to persuade? Compare her purpose and tone with that of Altman.

APPLICATIONS

1. Imagine yourself as the young gay man and write a letter to your parents explaining your sexual preference.

2. Discuss with your group the implications of AIDS for your generation and its effects on gender relationships and on individual and family lives.

3. The film *Longtime Companion* portrays the responses of a group of friends confronting the reality of AIDS. Rent the videotape and write a review of the film, including the characters' reactions to their situation.

Why Do We Hate Our Bodies?

GILLIANNE N. DUNCAN

Gillianne Duncan enrolled in Queensborough Community College in 2000 but because of family and financial issues had to drop out. She grew up in a single mother household and her mother re-married when she was ten years old. She has four sisters and four nieces of varying ages and is disgusted by the images her nieces are surrounded by. Her co-workers and oldest niece were the inspirations for her essay as she listened to the way they talked about their bodies.

Gillianne is currently completing her Associates Degree and intends to pursue her B.A. and possibly a teaching career.

ALL WEEK LONG I HAVE BEEN hearing women complain about their bodies when I asked them how much *they* liked themselves. One of my co-workers I believe had noticed a flaw in every part of her body just about, and then got mad when my co-workers and I told her she was beautiful but she just did not notice it. It was scary and sad to see a beautiful young woman say and act the way she did, but we all understood, to some degree, because we were all her. Everybody had a flaw that he or she wanted changed but when asked why they wanted the change they said so that they could look better. When I asked better than who or what nobody had an answer they just wanted to look better. So I asked if they hated their bodies and all said no, but after sitting and listening I heard all my co-workers talking about going to the gym, dieting, surgeries they would have if they had money, and even starvation. But they all claim not to hate their bodies. How can you love something you treat so badly? If your body and you were married, you would go to jail for domestic violence.

In the article "Why Don't We Like the Human Body" by Barbara Ehrenreich, she tries to explain or bring to light the love-hate relationship with the horror movies and the human body. She compares our addiction to exercise and dieting to some crazy serial killer that hacks people up and eats them or plays with their rotting bodies. Ehrenreich also points out our fascination or need to see this kind of violence toward the human body. But I wonder what her thoughts would be if she ever saw the show *Nip/Tuck*; to me that is worse than any horror flick. Then there is the makeover show *Extreme Makeover*, where every week they pick two friends that feel that they are homely; they then take them away from their families for months and give them all the plastic surgeries they want and then when it is over a big party to show off their new look. They give them complete makeovers, changing their hair, teeth, bodies and of course attitude. Everything is done with surgery. They give the people liposuction, tummy tucks, breast implants, collagen injection, Botox, porcelain veneers, face lifts, and whatever else they feel they need, or that the show feels that the person needs to have done.

For the people at home the producers have decided that it would be more interesting if we saw every step of the transformation from hating the old body to loving the new and improved one that was built. We get to see every procedure, all implants and injections and removals, all dental work and every chemical peel, we at home get to see what the friends cannot see because there are no mirrors allowed until the very end of the show.

It is a horror show. They pull two victims in, then they beat them with images of how they could look, then they cut them up and add foreign objects to them. Then they abuse them some more, because now that they are healing from the many surgeries, they are starved, made to "work out" (a torture technique very popular nowadays), and then dressed up and put on parade like a circus monkey. It is horrible. And no body is free from ridicule. Last week (October 20, 2006), they had on the show a deaf man and his best friend, who was a burn victim with scars all over her body, and both of them got what some would call "the works." (Yes, the handicapped are not safe from the power of mass media.) Between the two of them they had everything nipped and/or tucked. At the end of the show not only do they recap the surgeries but, they also tell you the price, just to say you can look like this for only fifteen thousand dollars or monthly installments of two hundred and fifty dollars (and yes we do take Discover).

Extreme Makeover is like the show *This Old House* with Bob Vila. The same concept, take out some walls and add some paint, a few nails, drywall, a little plaster and perfect old into new. It might not be completely fair to compare a plastic surgery show to a fix it yourself show, mainly because they did not do it themselves, but it is a horror show, and I blame the media for its creation. Without the media's constant need to make people feel bad about themselves shows like *Nip/Tuck*, *Extreme Makeover*, and *Dr. 90210* would not exist. But they do, as a reminder that we are not perfect, these shows reinforce the ideas and beliefs of hatred towards the body. Mostly and without concern for the female body. Why must the media attack women so much? My answer, the world is run by men and a small amount of over achieving women with low self-esteem. Okay, so women are supposed to be weak and helpless making them easy prey, but what about men? Would not a man make a good victim? They are stronger, faster and considered to be more rational, making for a better hunt. So if guys make better prey would they also not make better subjects for shows about makeovers? The producers of the show. *The Swan* should make a male version where they take fifteen average looking guys and give them implants and liposuction, torture them mentally, starve them, place them on a crazy exercise plan and then place them on parade to be judged to see which of the men are the most handsome. But that will never happen, there will be episodes where men will get surgery and there will be episodes where men will be subjected to horrible treatments in order to obtain better ratings or to show that some shows are equal in their selection of victims, but there will never be an entire show or season where men are treated the same way as women.

I am not a big fan of horror movies nor am I a fan of makeover shows. I believe both to be sick and demeaning towards human life, but the only difference is that a horror movie is not real. They are only there to scare and shake you; they are a form of entertainment for those who like to be scared. Makeover shows are based around real people that think very little of themselves, generally people that are not very beautiful but are far from being absolutely horrible looking. These shows like many other forms of media never address the real issues or point people into a positive direction that will lead them away from self hate. If we thought of our bodies as a loved one, we would take care of them better. Like any great relationship it takes work and compromise. If we stopped trying to look like Barbie and Ken dolls and stopped listening and allowing the media to tell us that we are fat, ugly and our bodies are our enemies, maybe we will make a new friend or find a lover in the body we were given. If we cannot we will always just be prey for the crazy sicko murderer that wants to see us hacked up or that greasy plastic surgeon that only wants to dissect our bodies and transform us into something not human.

INTERPRETATIONS

1. At the end of her first paragraph, Duncan writes, "If your body and you were married, you would go to jail for domestic violence." What do you think she means by this statement? Why do you agree or disagree with it?

2. According to Duncan, why do people hate their bodies? To what extent do you agree with her perceptions?

3. In paragraph 5, Duncan addresses gender in the selection of sub-jects for the television shows that she has described. Why do you think that females, rather than males, are most often chosen for these shows? What does Duncan believe?

CORRESPONDENCES

1. How are the television shows that Duncan discusses similar to horror movies? How does what Duncan describes relate to what Stephen King presents in his essay "Why We Crave Horror Movies" (page 496)?

2. Duncan writes about how gender is the primary consideration in the selection of subjects for television shows like *Nip/Tuck* and *Extreme Makeover* and that these shows contribute to the problems that women face. What expectations, according to Theroux, must men live with? Given what society expects of them, which gender has a tougher time of it?

APPLICATIONS

1. What qualities would your dream partner possess?
    Create an equation that takes into account such aspects as per-sonality, emotional make-up, and physical characteristics. Try to compute a mathematical formula such as $a + b + c + \ldots = x$ where *a*, *b*, and *c* stand for personal qualities and characteristics (e.g., *patience, understanding, generosity, intellect, curiosity, musical ability, physical strength, adventurousness* . . .) and *x* equals "*the perfect part-ner.*" Where is physical beauty in your equation? What does its location tell you about the value you place upon it?

2. Scan the covers of several popular magazines. What general con-clusions can you make about the physical traits of those people who appear in the photographs? Write an analysis essay that examines the meaning of beauty in America.

3. Most likely, you have heard someone say, "Beauty is only skin deep." In view of Duncan's essay, do you think that we have gone too far as a society in what we will do to acquire beauty? Write an essay that articulates your response to this question. Like Duncan, provide plenty of specific examples to back up your views. In addition, in a second draft of your work, pay careful attention to the exact words you use to maximize your impact. Apply images and connotative (charged) language to increase the appeal your essay will have for a reader.

The Gravity of Mark Buehrle

JASON BARONE

Jason Barone (b. 1982) was born in Queens, New York and at age four moved to Canada. He lived in Oakville for fifteen years before returning to New York. He is currently pursuing his B.A. in Media Studies at Hunter College and hopes to become a sportswriter for a major publication or for the Anaheim Angels. As you read about Barone's expectations of his father, compare them with your idea about what a father should be.

I LIVE IN PARADISE as well as Pandemonium. I grew up in a beautiful town of Oakville, which lies only a 30-minute car ride west of Toronto. During my elementary years my life was a much younger version of *Everybody Loves Raymond*. In fact, when you look closely, you will find a great deal of similarities between the fictional Barone's on that show and the real life Barone's in my family. During high school I attended Appleby College, which was a private high school that backs onto Lake Ontario. The old red brick school buildings that spread throughout the campus and our quaint little chapel complete with stained glass windows could make you believe that life just could not get any better. My house was part of a collection of houses in the "Fairway Hills" community that slowly crept onto the Glen Abby golf course. For those of you who watch the PGA, you have probably seen my house in the background when the Canadian Open is played.

Over the years my friends have more or less stayed the same. The only real change with them has been the setting for where we hung out: from the portable steps to the dining hall and now at the downtown pub, The King's Arm's. It would all sound like paradise if not for the fact that five years ago my parents got divorced.

This heart crushing news was delivered to family and friends in January 1998. I found out in December 1997, just as Christmas Eve passed into Christmas. To no surprise, Christmas has turned from an exciting time into nothing. I overcompensate for this by always wanting to have the tree, the lights, and our *Alvin and the Chipmunks Christmas* CD all roaring at full force a few weeks before Christmas. My guess is that I do this so that my mother, younger brother, and sister are too distracted to see how empty my eyes are.

We had come down from Canada to visit my Mom's side of the family and were staying with an Uncle in New Jersey. It was on the ride back to Jersey when my brother, sister, and I had all fallen asleep in the back of my Dad's Jeep. I had awakened, but my eyes for some reason had not opened; it had never happened before, and it's never happened since. To be truthful, I don't know how long I was up, I just remember the fighting. Everything was "discussed." Have you ever cried while frantically trying to keep motionless and expressionless? It's like a shiver that doesn't end. My parents still think I was asleep the whole time.

After that, I found myself praying every day, sometimes even multiple times. A sense of doom had overcome me and I was reaching out to the one person who might be able to help save my family. This went on for about a month until one Saturday afternoon while I was talking on the phone with my friend Patrick. I've heard how when bad news is delivered, the recipient seems to know what is going to be said before a word is spoken. Personally, I never bought into that. However, when my mother—in a calm and monotonous tone—said "Tell your friend you'll call him back, I need to tell you something," I immediately knew.

I have never received the Eucharist since.

• • •

"Did you talk to your mother?"
"Yes."
"OK, well."
"Did you cheat on her?"
"Yes."

I still wish that I had slammed the phone down at that moment; something to put him in his place. After my mom had told me, we sat there in silence for what felt like ten minutes (in truth it was closer to ten seconds). It was during that time that I was screaming at myself to keep composed, for Mommy. Eventually, I broke down. I had not even been on the job for two minutes and already I broke down; how was I going to do this for years after?

After a divorce most children and their fathers are not able to maintain a close relationship as the years pass. By the time most of these children are young adults, they often have little or no emotional intimacy left with their father. When they do talk, write, or get together—which is not often—too many of these fathers and their young adult children feel uncomfortable and emotionally distant. Their relationship has often dwindled into a fairly superficial one—more like a distant uncle who knows as little about the children's present lives as they know about his. Usually there is not animosity or resentment as much as indifference, awkwardness, and an underlying anxiety about what to say or do around each other. But for other young adults and their fathers, the lingering animosity and pain related to the parents' divorce continues to drive a wedge between them (Nielsen).

It was then that I decided I needed a new role model because I could no longer look at my dad in awe. I now shake my head while I let out a big sigh. Before the divorce, my dad and I used to really have something special. He came to all my baseball games and the majority of my practices. He himself had been all state in baseball and he was able to teach me things about the game that many kids didn't know. When we went to Blue Jays games, he always pointed out things like positioning, stance, and vision. Whenever I had a question about anything, he always had the answer. Now to most this may seem boring, but I couldn't get enough of it. I gorged myself on baseball, and he was my chef. In the years since, it became a big deal if we had a conversation that was longer than a few syllables. Some days I could go through a whole conversation with little more than a few low hums of acknowledgment to whatever he said. It became apparent that unless we were talking about sports, we would end up fighting. Yet whenever he called, there was a private joy inside of me. Knives were flying at my mother's back from all directions.

My father has since moved to Cleveland, and while we are now able to get along it's more of a friendly relationship than that of a father and son. His words no longer carry any weight.

There are times when I miss my dad. I remember once I was at my best friend's house, and he, his dad, and I were standing around the kitchen talking and joking around. My friend told his dad "You're not so tough now that I'm as tall as you." So as one could imagine, this had to be proved, and a friendly wrestling match ensued. As I watched my friend embarrass himself, I found myself envious because it was things like this that I realized I was unable to experience. Every once in a while, one of my friends would tell a funny story that they remember about my dad. I would nod and give a half-hearted smile, but it didn't matter any more. It had all been tarnished.

Last summer I visited him in Cleveland, and we had decided to take a little road trip to Detroit to see the Tigers play the White Sox. In the bottom of the first, we saw the White Sox pitcher take the mound. A few of his season's statistics flashed on the scoreboard under his name, Mark Buehrle. "Is he any good?." The question took me by surprise, more so when I looked over to see my dad looking up at me the way I used to do to him when I was younger. I rattled out an answer, but I could not get over the question. Wasn't *I* supposed to be asking *him* that? For five years before that, we rarely spoke. Silence had reversed our roles.

• • •

WORKS CITED:

Nielsen, Linda. "College Aged Students With Divorced Parents: Facts And Fiction." *College Student Journal* 33.4 (1999): 543–73.

INTERPRETATIONS

1. What associations do you have with the words "paradise" and "pandemonium"? What effect does Barone achieve by juxtaposing them in the first sentence?

2. Why does Barone focus on his responses to at least six Christmases after the divorce of his parents?

3. Throughout the essay Barone inserts short, objective, declarative statements such as "I have never received the Eucharist since" to reflect his subjective states. Find at least two others and discuss what they reveal about his emotional responses to the divorce.

4. What is the effect of including Nielsen's citation in his essay? Which of the possible responses that Nielsen cites best parallels Barones's?

5. Characterize Barone's relationship with his father before the divorce. How does it change? Does he judge his father too harshly? Why or why not?

CORRESPONDENCES

1. According to Yevtushenko's perspective, "not people die but worlds die in them." Discuss its relevance to the texts by Barone and Norris (page 129). In what sense did their "worlds die"? Explain.

2. Barone and Norris portray the emotional impact of disruptions in gender relations through the point of view of a child. How do you respond emotionally to the conclusion of each text? What insights did you gain?

Blackberries

LESLIE NORRIS

Leslie Norris (1921–2006), a poet, novelist, and critic, was born in Merthyr Tydfil, Wales. Educated at Coventry College and the University of Southampton, Norris taught in several English schools and colleges and finally at Brigham Young University in Utah. He published twenty-four collections of poetry, three collections of short fiction, translations, critical biography, and literary criticism. His books include The Loud Winter *(1967),* Ransoms *(1970),* Sliding and Other Stories *(1974),* Finding Gold *(1976), and* The Girl from Cardigan *(1988). Most recently, Norris published* Kershisnik: Painting from Life *(2002) and the children's book* Albert and the Angels *(2000). One critic noted that Norris "continually reinvented himself and transformed his art—crossing countries, cultures, and genres throughout his long life and career." In a sense the boy in the following selection has begun reinventing himself. In preparation for reading "Blackberries," try to remember the first time you felt a need for privacy, even from your own family.*

Merthyr Tydfil, located in the north side of the Taff Valley in Wales, often served as the subject of Norris's poetry. These poems often depict a town of boxing, whippet racing, pigeon breeding, rugby, and comic gossip by inhabitants of the Valleys. The early eighteenth century saw the establishment of iron-works complexes, which made Merthyr the Iron Capital of the World. In the past twenty years, there has been a remarkable transformation in both the working practices and topography of the area, with considerable land reclamation creating environmental improvements.

MR. FRENSHAM OPENED HIS SHOP at eight-thirty, but it was past nine when the woman and the child went in. The shop was empty and there were no footmarks on the fresh sawdust shaken onto the floor. The child listened to the melancholy sound of the bell as the door closed behind him and he scuffed his feet in the yellow sawdust. Underneath, the boards were brown and worn, and dark knots stood up in them. He had never been in this shop before. He was going to have his hair cut for the first time in his life, except for the times when his mother had trimmed it gently behind his neck.

Mr. Frensham was sitting in a large chair, reading a newspaper. He could make the chair turn around, and he spun twice about in it before he put down his paper, smiled, and said, "Good morning."

He was an old man, thin, with flat white hair. He wore a white coat.

"One gentleman," he said, "to have his locks shorn."

He put a board across the two arms of his chair, lifted the child, and sat him on it.

"How are you, my dear? And your father, is he well?" he said to the child's mother.

He took a sheet from a cupboard on the wall and wrapped it about the child's neck, tucking it into his collar. The sheet covered the child completely and hung almost to the floor. Cautiously the boy moved his hidden feet. He could see the bumps they made in the cloth. He moved his finger against the inner surface of the sheet and made a six with it, and then an eight. He liked those shapes.

"Snip, snip," said Mr. Frensham, "and how much does the gentleman want off? All of it? All his lovely curls? I think not."

"Just an ordinary cut, please, Mr. Frensham," said the child's mother, "not too much off. I, my husband and I, we thought it was time for him to look like a little boy. His hair grows so quickly."

Mr. Frensham's hands were very cold. His hard fingers turned the boy's head first to one side and then to the other and the boy could hear the long scissors snapping away behind him, and above his ears. He was quite frightened, but he liked watching the small tufts of his hair drop lightly on the sheet which covered him, and then roll an inch or two before they stopped. Some of the hair fell to the floor and by moving his hand surreptitiously he could make nearly all of it fall down. The hair fell without a sound. Tilting his head slightly, he could see the little bunches on the floor, not belonging to him any more.

"Easy to see who this boy is," Mr. Frensham said to the child's mother. "I won't get redder hair in the shop today. Your father had hair like this when he was young, very much this color. I've cut your father's hair for fifty years. He's keeping well, you say? There, I think that's enough. We don't want him to dislike coming to see me."

He took the sheet off the child and flourished it hard before folding it and putting it on a shelf. He swept the back of the child's neck with a small brush. Nodding his own old head in admiration, he looked at the child's hair for flaws in the cutting.

"Very handsome," he said.

The child saw his face in a mirror. It looked pale and large, but also much the same as always. When he felt the back of his neck, the new short hairs stood up sharp against his hand.

"We're off to do some shopping," his mother said to Mr. Frensham as she handed him the money.

They were going to buy the boy a cap, a round cap with a little button on top and a peak over his eyes, like his cousin Harry's cap. The boy wanted the cap very much. He walked seriously beside his mother and he was not impatient even when she met Mrs. Lewis and talked to her, and then took a long time at the fruiterer's buying apples and potatoes.

"This is the smallest size we have," the man in the clothes shop said. "It may be too large for him."

"He's just had his hair cut," said his mother. "That should make a difference."

The man put the cap on the boy's head and stood back to look. It was a beautiful cap. The badge in front was shaped like a shield and it was red and blue. It was not too big, although the man could put two fingers under it, at the side of the boy's head.

"On the other hand, we don't want it too tight," the man said. "We want something he can grow into, something that will last him a long time."

"Oh, I hope so," his mother said. "It's expensive enough."

The boy carried the cap himself, in a brown paper bag that had "Price, Clothiers, High Street" on it. He could read it all except "Clothiers" and his mother told him that. They put his cap, still in its bag, in a drawer when they got home.

His father came home late in the afternoon. The boy heard the firm clap of the closing door and his father's long step down the hall. He leaned against his father's knee while the man ate his dinner. The meal had been keeping warm in the oven and the plate was very hot. A small steam was rising from the potatoes, and the gravy had dried to a thin crust where it was shallow at the side of the plate. The man lifted the dry gravy with his knife and fed it to his son, very carefully lifting it into the boy's mouth, as if he were feeding a small bird. The boy loved this. He loved the hot savor of his father's dinner, the way his father cut away small delicacies for him and fed them to him slowly. He leaned drowsily against his father's leg.

Afterwards he put on his cap and stood before his father, certain of the man's approval. The man put his hand on the boy's head and looked at him without smiling.

"On Sunday," he said, "we'll go for a walk. Just you and I. We'll be men together."

Although it was late in September, the sun was warm and the paths dry. The man and his boy walked beside the disused canal and powdery white dust covered their shoes. The boy thought of the days before he had been born, when the canal had been busy. He thought of the long boats pulled by solid horses, gliding through the water. In his head he listened to the hushed, wet noises they would have made, the soft waves slapping the banks, and green tench looking up as the barges moved above them, their water suddenly darkened. His grandfather had told him about that. But now the channel was filled with mud and tall reeds. Bullrush and watergrass grew in the damp passages. He borrowed his father's walking stick and knocked the heads off a company of seeding dandelions, watching the tiny parachutes carry away their minute dark burdens.

"There they go," he said to himself. "There they go, sailing away to China."

"Come on," said his father, "or we'll never reach Fletcher's Woods."

The boy hurried after his father. He had never been to Fletcher's Woods. Once his father had heard a nightingale there. It had been in the summer, long ago, and his father had gone with his friends, to hear the singing bird. They had stood under a tree and listened. Then the moon went down and his father, stumbling home, had fallen into a blackberry bush.

"Will there be blackberries?" he asked.

"There should be," his father said. "I'll pick some for you."

In Fletcher's Woods there was shade beneath the trees, and sunlight, thrown in yellow patches on to the grass, seemed to grow out of the ground rather than come from the sky. The boy stepped from sunlight to sunlight, in and out of shadow. His father showed him a tangle of bramble, hard with thorns, its leaves just beginning to color into autumn, its long runners dry and brittle on the grass. Clusters of purple fruit hung in the branches. His father reached up and chose a blackberry for him. Its skin was plump and shining, each of its purple globes held a point of reflected light.

"You can eat it," his father said.

The boy put the blackberry in his mouth. He rolled it with his tongue, feeling its irregularity, and crushed it against the roof of his mouth. Released juice, sweet and warm as summer, ran down his throat, hard seeds cracked between his teeth. When he laughed his father saw that his mouth was deeply stained. Together they picked and ate the dark berries, until their lips were purple and their hands marked and scratched.

"We should take some for your mother," the man said.

He reached with his stick and pulled down high canes where the choicest berries grew, picking them to take home. They had nothing to carry them in, so the boy put his new cap on the grass and they filled its hollow with berries. He held the cap by its edges and they went home.

"It was a stupid thing to do," his mother said, "utterly stupid. What were you thinking of?"

The young man did not answer.

"If we had the money, it would be different," his mother said, "Where do you think the money comes from?"

"I know where the money comes from," his father said. "I work hard enough for it."

"His new cap," his mother said. "How am I to get him another?"

The cap lay on the table and by standing on tiptoe the boy could see it. Inside it was wet with the sticky juice of blackberries. Small pieces of blackberry skins were stuck to it. The stains were dark and irregular.

"It will probably dry out all right," his father said.

His mother's face was red and distorted, her voice shrill.

"If you had anything like a job," she shouted, "and could buy caps by the dozen, then—"

She stopped and shook her head. His father turned away, his mouth hard.

"I do what I can," he said.

"That's not much!" his mother said. She was tight with scorn. "You don't do much!"

Appalled, the child watched the quarrel mount and spread. He began to cry quietly, to himself, knowing that it was a different weeping to any he had experienced before, that he was crying for a different pain. And the child began to understand that they were different people; his father, his mother, himself, and that he must learn sometimes to be alone.

INTERPRETATIONS

1. What is meant by the final paragraph of the story? To what extent has Norris led up to these ideas? What examples in the text can you locate to support your answers?

2. What gender issues are presented by Norris? What specific examples can you provide to illustrate these issues?

3. Mr. Frensham is the first character presented in the story. What is his relation to the other major characters?

4. Where does this story take place? To what extent does this setting influence the tensions presented? What tensions do you find to exist in this story?

5. On page 131, the boy's father says: "On Sunday . . . we'll go for a walk. Just you and I. We'll be men together." How accurately does this statement summarize the gender issues of this story? Explain your answer fully.

CORRESPONDENCES

1. What is your perception of the father in "Blackberries"? To what extent does he represent the type of man Theroux describes in "The Male Myth"?
2. Analyze with your group the thematic and symbolic significance of the title of Barone's and Norris's texts.

APPLICATIONS

1. Of the characters in this story, which of them have names? Which do not? Why would Norris choose to make this decision? Write a description of an object without actually naming the object. If you were to read this description to your classmates, would they be able to guess the object? What writing techniques must you use to create an accurate description without naming the object or giving away its identity too easily?
2. Notice the details that Norris uses to depict the events occurring in the story from the perspective of the child. Which specific details stand out in your mind that best capture the boy's perspective? Write a story that depicts an event from a child's viewpoint. What must you do with your choice of words, sentence structures, and selection of details to present this perspective effectively?
3. Assume the role of Barone's father and write an essay imagining how he would explain his unfaithfulness, his emotional reactions to the changes in their relationship, and the reversal of roles that occurs at the end of the essay.
4. If you *really* wanted to get to know someone, what questions would you ask of that person to learn about him or her?

   Think carefully about questions that would provide little information and those that would yield essential facts and insights. Now, make up a list of the five questions you think are most important to ask. Next, pair up with a classmate who you do not know very well and ask that person your five questions. Be sure to take notes as your questions are answered! After you have asked your questions, reverse the process.

   After all five questions have been asked and answered by both you and your classmate, separate from each other and use your notes to create a "character sketch." (Perhaps the first thing you might do is change the name of the person you interviewed to preserve his or her privacy!) When creating your sketch, what information will you include and what will you leave out? What information might you manipulate to make your "character" more interesting? While working on this sketch, reflect on the characters that Norris has invented and presented in "Blackberries." How has Norris helped you to get to know his characters? What techniques has he used that you might use in creating your character?

The Knowing Eye

Michelle V. Agins/*The New York Times*

READING IMAGES

1. How does each photograph address "gender issues"? What message about gender and identity is being given by each photographer?

2. One theory about art is that at its center is ambiguity. What does the word ambiguous mean? How does each photograph embrace ambiguity? How are these treatments of ambiguity similar or different?

MAKING CONNECTIONS

1. How does the photograph of the women boxers relate to the essays by Paul Theroux and Jerry Rockwood?

2. What is the tone or mood presented in the photograph of the faces? Which essays do you think best correspond to this feeling?

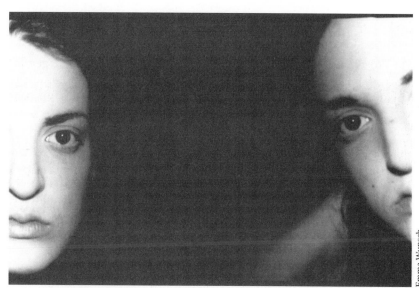

Emma Wunsch

WORDS AND IMAGES

1. What would the people from the first and second photographs say to each other? Create a dialogue that captures this conversation.

2. The photograph of the women boxers directly confronts the issue of gender roles. Are there certain jobs that you think are gender specific? If so, what are they? Why do you think they should be available only to men or to women? After thinking and writing about these questions, compare your responses with those from the members of your peer group. How are your ideas similar to and different from those of your classmates? What consensus opinion has been formed?

Additional Writing Topics

1. To what extent have your concepts of gender roles and gender relationships changed during the last five years? Write an essay that analyzes the factors that contributed to your modifying your point of view on these issues.

2. Write an essay discussing whether it is realistic to expect marriage to last a lifetime today. What expectations do most people have about marriage? What expectations should they have?

3. Debates in the United States often include religious and moral arguments against same-sex marriage. By including several references to religion, has Brooks increased or decreased support for his argument for gay marriage? Write an essay supporting or refuting Brook's point of view.

4. Societal and cultural attitudes toward masculinity are the focus of the essays by Theroux, Rockwood, and Soto. How does your attitude toward this emotionally charged subject compare to theirs? Write an essay defining your concept of masculinity and analyzing your emotional reactions to it.

5. Assume the role of Barone's father and write an essay imagining how he would explain his unfaithfulness, his emotional reactions to the changes in their relationship, and the reversal of roles that occurs at the end of the essay.

6. Bring to class four advertisements from current magazines featuring dress styles for men and women. Analyze with your group the images they intend to communicate. To what extent are they based on gender stereotypes? What do they "promise" the consumer?

7. From the perspective of a parent, write a letter explaining to your daughter what it means to be a woman or to your son explaining what it means to be a man.

8. Brainstorm with your group on your concepts of fatherhood. What images and emotions does the word evoke? What responsibilities are fathers expected to assume in the family? How has the role of father changed in the last decade?

9. Societal and familial attitudes toward homosexuality are explored by Altman and Quindlen. Write an essay analyzing your emotional associations with this topic.

CHAPTER

4

Education

HUMAN BEINGS SHOW A WONDERFUL CAPACITY to learn and unlearn—if it were not so you would not see such diversity in this and other chapters of this book. "The greatest happiness of man as a thinking being," said Goethe, "is to know what is knowable and quietly to revere what is unknowable." Several cross-cultural texts in this chapter clearly support Goethe's notion of the joy of learning, including "Poets in the Kitchen," "The Mistress of Make Believe, "Dwellings," and "A View from the Bridge."

In "A View from the Bridge," Cherokee Paul McDonald recounts an "epiphany"—a chance encounter with a remarkable young boy with whom he established a relationship, however brief. Through this experience, he is able to revive a sense of wonder about what we can learn if we maintain our curiosity and are open to new experiences. Tom Montgomery-Fate in "Dancing Geckos," recalls an equally important lesson he relearned while teaching English in Laoag, a small town in the Iloco regions of the Philippines, namely the high cost of being too busy. While reading Masao Takenaka's *God is Rice*, he discovered that the meaning of the character for "busy" in several Asian writings, is "to destroy one's heart."

Education is also an important issue to politicians, educators, and parents, and the pendulum swings back and forth constantly as to what aspects of the educational system should be reevaluated. Currently, the national spotlight is on assessment and measuring students' performance through a series of standardized tests beginning in third grade and continuing through college.

Another "hot" issue is bilingual education, a matter of controversy in several states despite the large numbers of students in public schools for whom English is not a first language. Critics of bilingual education claim that this approach delays the acquisition of English and a student's ability to achieve proficiency in the language of public discourse. The more extreme groups view bilingualism as a threat to national unity, and that has prompted the formation of English-only movements.

Defenders of bilingualism argue that forcing students to abandon their private language is pedagogically unsound, and often psychologically debilitating. For example, Eva Hoffman, forced to leave her native Poland in 1959 at age thirteen, describes in her memoir *Lost in Translation*, the trauma of linguistic dispossession as she struggled to learn English in school in Vancouver, Canada. "Blind rage, helpless rage is rage that has no words—rage that overwhelms one with darkness."

Several texts in this chapter focus on the crucial and controversial implications of the connections between language and culture. Is it desirable and possible for public schools to perform this mission without robbing students of their natal language and culture? Is it possible to achieve biculturalism, as well as bilingualism? Is it possible to tolerate—even respect—other religions, systems of law, forms of art, and languages without losing respect for one's own? Is our idea of culture clear and distinct enough to speak of absolute boundaries between cultures? If we accept the concept of cultural differences, even cultural boundaries, is cultural exclusiveness the goal we want to pursue?

In "Always Living in Spanish," Marjorie Agosin talks about the "solitude of exile" that she has experienced since leaving her native Chile (then under the dictatorship of the Pinochet regime), and her years at a high school in Georgia where her "poor English and accent were the cause of ridicule and insult." José Torres emphasizes the importance of education and the link between language and power, and Chang-Rae Lee recalls his mother's powerlessness expressed by her silence as a Korean immigrant in the United States.

Is a person educated who knows only his own culture as it is at that moment? Carlos Fuentes, the eminent contemporary Mexican writer would respond negatively as he is convinced that "cultures only flourish in contact with others; they perish in isolation." Anyone who knows the history of his or her own culture expects change. But at what price? By what vehicle? Preparation for the global culture of the twenty-first century surely requires your generation to forge new definitions of an educated person.

Perspectives

Only the curious have, if they live, a tale worth telling at all.

—Alastair Reid

Not to transmit an experience is to betray it.

—Elie Wiesel

I hear and I forget. I see and I remember. I do and I understand.

—Chinese proverb

Education is what survives when what has been learnt has been forgotten.

—B. F. Skinner

Sexist language, racist language, theistic language—all are typical of the policing languages of mastery, and cannot, do not, permit new knowledge or encourage the mutual exchange of ideas.

—Toni Morrison

Learning to read books—or pictures, or films—is not just a matter of acquiring information from texts, it is a matter of learning to read and write the texts of our lives.

—Robert Scholes

What I wish for all students is some release from the clammy grip of the future. I wish them a chance to savor each segment of their education as an experience in itself and not as a grim preparation for the next step. I wish them the right to experiment, to trip and fall, to learn that defeat is as instructive as victory and is not the end of the world.

—William Zinsser

Education is not a product: mark, diploma, job, money—in that order: it is a process, a never-ending one.

—Bel Kaufman

Education is hanging around until you've caught on.

—Robert Frost

Put yourself in a different room, that's what the mind is for.

—Margaret Atwood

Teachers are the door. You enter yourself.

—Chinese proverb

141

Shall I teach you what knowledge is? When you know a thing, to recognize that you know it, and when you do not know a thing, to recognize that you do not know it. That is knowledge.

—*Confucius*

Education! Which of the various me's do you propose to educate, and which do you propose to suppress?

—*D. H. Lawrence*

By doubting we are led to enquire: By enquiry we perceive the truth.

—*Abelard*

The greatest difficulty in education is to get experience from ideas.

—*George Santayana*

It is above all by the imagination that we achieve perception, and compassion, and hope.

—*Ursula K. Le Guin*

I have always come to life after coming to books.

—*Jorge Luis Borges*

Power is the ability to take one's place in whatever discourse is essential to action and the right to have one's part matter.

—*Carolyn Heilbrun*

. . . That is what learning is. You suddenly understand something you've understood all your life, but in a new way.

—*Doris Lessing*

Knowledge is power.

—*Francis Bacon*

The mind is an enchanting thing.

—*Marianne Moore*

But it is not hard work which is dreary; it is superficial work. That is always boring in the long run, and it has always seemed strange to me that in our endless discussions about education so little stress is ever laid on the pleasure of becoming an educated person, the enormous interest it adds to life. To be able to be caught up into the world of thought—that is to be educated.

—*Edith Hamilton*

It ought to be embarrassing, in this age of celebration of America's diversity, that the schools have been so slow to move toward teaching about our nation's diverse religious traditions. . . . After all, if the material is well taught, many children will be intrigued by what will be for many their first exposure to religious traditions different from their own—or, in some instances, to any religious tradition at all.

—*Stephen L. Carter*

APPLICATIONS

1. Discuss Hamilton's description of an educated person. To what extent has your education been pleasurable? How has it made your life more interesting? What does it mean to you "to be caught up in the world of thought"?

2. Abelard and Reid focus on the importance of curiosity in acquiring knowledge and becoming an interesting person. Have you been encouraged by your teachers to ask questions? Do you consider yourself curious? Has curiosity played a positive role in your education? Cite one or two examples.

3. Discuss Zinsser's perspective on education. To what extent do you agree that it is important "to trip and fall" and that defeat or failure may be used constructively? How can these views be reconciled with the pressures facing today's college students? Write a summary of your group's discussion.

The Creation of the Crow World

CROW LEGEND

The Crow, who were one of the most powerful tribes in Montana, are members of the second largest Indian language group north of Mexico (the Siouan; the largest is the Algonquian). They lived along the Yellowstone River and its tributaries and hunted across the plains and into the Rocky Mountains. Their reservation is in Montana near Billings. The name "Crow" is thought to be a mistranslation of their name for themselves, Apsaruke.

From the several versions of the Crow creation myth that have been recorded, this one has been selected because it is the most revealing of the material culture of the tribe and because it has less similarity with creation myths of other tribes.

LONG BEFORE THERE WAS ANY LAND and before there was any living thing except four little ducks, the Creator, whom we call Old Man, came and said to the ducks, "Which one of you is brave?"

"I am the bravest," replied one duck.

"Dive into the water," Old Man said to the duck, "and get some dirt from the bottom. I will see what I can do with it."

The brave duck went down and was gone a long time. It came up again carrying on its beak some dirt that it gave to Old Man. He held it in his hand until it became dry. Then he blew the dirt in all directions and thus made the land and the mountains and the rivers.

Old Man, who was all-powerful, was asked by the ducks to make other living things. So he took more dirt in his hand and, after it had dried, he blew it off. And there stood a man and a woman, the first Crow Indians. Old Man explained to them how to increase their number. At first they were blind; when their eyes were opened and they saw their nakedness, they asked for something with which to clothe themselves.

So that they might have food and clothing, Old Man took the rest of the dirt brought up by Duck and made animals and plants. Then he killed one of the buffalo he had made, broke a rock, and with one of the pieces cut up the animal. Then he explained its parts and told the man and woman how to use them.

"To carry water," he said, "take the pouch from the inside of the buffalo and make a bucket. Make drinking cups from its horns and also from the horns of the mountain sheep. Use the best pieces of buffalo for food. When you have had enough to eat, make a robe from the hide."

Then he showed the woman how to dress the skin. He showed the man how to make arrowheads, axes, knives, and cooking vessels from hard stone. "To make a fire," said Old Man, "take two sticks and place a little sand on one of them and also some of the driest buffalo chips. Then take the other stick and roll it between your hands until fire comes."

Old Man told them to take a large stone and fasten to it a handle made from hide. "With it you can break animal bones to get the marrow for making soup," he said to the woman. He also showed her how to scrape skins with a bone from the foreleg of an animal, to remove the hair.

At first, Old Man gave the man and woman no horses; they had only dogs for carrying their things. Later he told them how to get horses. "When you go over that hill there, do not look back, no matter what you hear." For three days they walked without looking back, but on the third day they heard animals coming behind them. They turned around and saw horses, but the horses vanished.

Old Man told them how to build a sweat lodge and also explained its purpose. And he told the man how to get dreams and visions. "Go up in the mountains," he said, "cut a piece of flesh from yourself, and give it to me. Do not eat while you are there. Then you will have visions that will tell you what to do."

"This land is the best of the lands I have made," Old Man said to them. "Upon it you will find everything you need—pure water, vegetation, timber, game animals. I have put you in the center of it, and I have put people around you as your enemies. If I had made you in large numbers, you would be too powerful and would kill the other people I have created. You are few in number, but you are brave."

INTERPRETATIONS

1. How important is Old Man's role as a teacher?
2. How apt are the Crows as students? What is the point of Old Man's lesson on how to get horses?
3. Old Man's last lesson is about the Crows' relations with other peoples—foreign affairs. How do you interpret this lesson? What does this lesson indicate about Old Man's nature, character, or qualities?

CORRESPONDENCES

1. Compare "The Creation of the Crow World" with the creation stories in Chapter 6 and discuss the significance of differences in their emphases.

2. Review the Abelard perspective on education. What role does enquiry play in "The Creation of the Crow World"? In your educational experiences?

APPLICATIONS

1. "The Creation of the Crow World" is part of the oral tradition of the Crow Indians. What cultural and educational functions does the oral tradition perform? Write a journal entry on what the Crow legend communicates about teaching and learning.

2. Review the Chinese proverb and discuss its application to "The Creation of the Crow World." Do you agree that we learn by seeing and doing rather than by listening? Cite supporting examples.

3. "The Creation of the Crow World" links disobedience with punishment. Have you ever learned something valuable by breaking the rules? If so, write a journal entry on the experience.

Dwellings

LINDA HOGAN

*Linda Hogan (b. 1947 in Denver), a member of the Chickasaw nation, has published poetry, novels, short stories, plays, and a memoir—*The Woman Who Watches Over the World: A Native Memoir *(2001). This book, one critic has said, ". . . goes a long way toward explaining Native Americans today." In 2004 she edited, with Brenda Peterson,* Face to Face: Women Writers on Faith, Mysticism, and Awakening. *Her interest in narrative and the environment is shown in the following selection from her book of essays,* Dwellings: A Spiritual History of the Living World *(1995). She has received numerous awards. Hogan taught American Indian studies at the University of Minnesota, Minneapolis from 1984–1989 and until recently was professor of English at the University of Colorado, Boulder. What expectations does the title "Dwellings" (rather than, say, "Housing" or "Lodging") set up?*

NOT FAR FROM where I live is a hill that was cut into by the moving water of a creek. Eroded this way, all that's left of it is a broken wall of earth that contains old roots and pebbles woven together and exposed. Seen from a distance, it is only a rise of raw earth. But up close it is something wonderful, a small cliff dwelling that looks almost as intricate and well made as those the Anasazi left behind when they vanished mysteriously centuries ago. This hill is a place that could be the starry skies at night turned inward into the thousand round holes where solitary bees have lived and died. It is a hill of tunneling rooms. At the mouths of some of the excavations, half-circles of clay beetle out like awnings shading a doorway. It is earth that was turned to clay in the mouths of the bees and spit out as they mined deeper into their dwelling places.

This place is where the bees reside at an angle safe from rain. It faces the southern sun. It is a warm and intelligent architecture of memory, learned by whatever memory lives in the blood. Many of the holes still contain gold husks of dead bees, their faces dry and gone, their flat eyes gazing out from death's land toward the other uninhabited half of the hill that is across the creek from the catacombs.

The first time I found the residence of the bees, it was dusty summer. The sun was hot, and land was the dry color of rust. Now and then a car rumbled along the dirt road and dust rose up behind it before

147

settling back down on older dust. In the silence, the bees made a soft droning hum. They were alive then, and working the hill, going out and returning with pollen, in and out through the holes, back and forth between daylight and the cooler, darker regions of the inner earth. They were flying an invisible map through air, a map charted by landmarks, the slant of light, and a circling story they told one another about the direction of food held inside the center of yellow flowers.

Sitting in the hot sun, watching the small bees fly in and out around the hill, hearing the summer birds, the light breeze, I felt right in the world. I belonged there. I thought of my own dwelling places, those real and those imagined. Once I lived in a town called Manitou, which means "Great Spirit," and where hot mineral springwater gurgled beneath the streets and rose into open wells. I felt safe there. With the underground movement of water and heat a constant reminder of other life, of what lives beneath us, it seemed to be the center of the world.

A few years after that, I wanted silence. My daydreams were full of places I longed to be, shelters and solitudes. I wanted a room apart from others, a hidden cabin to rest in. I wanted to be in a redwood forest with trees so tall the owls called out in the daytime. I daydreamed of living in a vapor cave a few hours away from here. Underground, warm, and moist, I thought it would be the perfect world for staying out of cold winter, for escaping the noise of living.

And how often I've wanted to escape to a wilderness where a human hand has not been in everything. But those were only dreams of peace, of comfort, of a nest inside stone or woods, a sanctuary where a dream or life wouldn't be invaded.

Years ago, in the next canyon west of here, there was a man who followed one of those dreams and moved into a cave that could only be reached by climbing down a rope. For years he lived there in comfort, like a troglodite. The inner weather was stable, never too hot, too cold, too wet, or too dry. But then he felt lonely. His utopia needed a woman. He went to town until he found a wife. For a while after the marriage, his wife climbed down the rope along with him, but before long she didn't want the mice scurrying about in the cave, or the untidy bats that wanted to hang from the stones of the ceiling. So they built a door. Because of the closed entryway, the temperature changed. They had to put in heat. Then the inner moisture of earth warped the door, so they had to have airconditioning, and after that the earth wanted to go about life in its own way and it didn't give in to the people.

In other days and places, people paid more attention to the strong-headed will of earth. Once homes were built of wood that had been felled from a single region in a forest. That way, it was thought, the house would hold together more harmoniously, and the family of walls would not fall or lend themselves to the unhappiness or arguments of the inhabitants.

An Italian immigrant to Chicago, Aldo Piacenzi, built birdhouses that were dwellings of harmony and peace. They were the incredible spired shapes of cathedrals in Italy. They housed not only the birds, but also his memories, his own past. He painted them the watery blue of his Mediterranean, the wild rose of flowers in a summer field. Inside them was straw and the droppings of lives that layed eggs, fledglings who grew there. What places to inhabit, the bright and sunny birdhouses in dreary alleyways of the city.

One beautiful afternoon, cool and moist, with the kind of yellow light that falls on earth in these arid regions, I waited for barn swallows to return from their daily work of food gathering. Inside the tunnel where they live, hundreds of swallows had mixed their saliva with mud and clay, much like the solitary bees, and formed nests that were perfect as a potter's bowl. At five in the evening, they returned all at once, a dark, flying shadow. Despite their enormous numbers and the crowding together of nests, they didn't pause for even a moment before entering the nests, nor did they crowd one another. Instantly they vanished into the nests. The tunnel went silent. It held no outward signs of life.

But I knew they were there, filled with the fire of living. And what a marriage of elements was in those nests. Not only mud's earth and water, the fire of sun and dry air, but even the elements contained one another. The bodies of prophets and crazy men were broken down in that soil.

I've noticed often how when a house is abandoned, it begins to sag. Without a tenant, it has no need to go on. If it were a person, we'd say it is depressed or lonely. The roof settles in, the paint cracks, the walls and floorboards warp and slope downward in their own natural ways, telling us that life must stay in everything as the world whirls and tilts and moves through boundless space.

One summer day, cleaning up after long-eared owls where I work at a rehabilitation facility for birds of prey, I was raking the gravel floor of a flight cage. Down on the ground, something looked like it was moving. I bent over to look into the pile of bones and pellets I'd just raked together. There, close to the ground, were two fetal mice. They were new to the planet, pink and hairless. They were so tenderly young. Their faces had swollen blue-veined eyes. They were nestled in a mound of feathers, soft as velvet, each one curled up smaller than an infant's ear, listening to the first sounds of earth. But the ants were biting them. They turned in agony, unable to pull away, not yet having the arms or legs to move, but feeling, twisting away from, the pain of the bites. I was horrified to see them bitten out of life that way. I dipped them in water, as if to take away the sting, and let the ants fall in the bucket. Then I held the tiny mice in the palm of my hand. Some of the ants were drowning in the water. I was trading one life for another, exchanging the lives of the ants for those of mice, but I hated their suffering, and hated even more that they had not yet grown to a life, and already they inhabited the miserable world of pain. Death and life feed each other. I know that.

Inside these rooms where birds are healed, there are other lives besides those of mice. There are fine gray globes the wasps have woven together, the white cocoons of spiders in a corner, the downward tunneling anthills. All these dwellings are inside one small walled space, but I think most about the mice. Sometimes the downy nests fall out of the walls where their mothers have placed them out of the way of their enemies. When one of the nests falls, they are so well made and soft, woven mostly from the chest feathers of birds. Sometimes the leg of a small quail holds the nest together like a slender cornerstone with dry, bent claws. The mice have adapted to life in the presence of their enemies, adapted to living in the thin wall between beak and beak, claw and claw. They move their nests often, as if a new rafter or wall will protect them from the inevitable fate of all our returns home to the deeper, wider nests of earth that houses us all.

One August at Zia Pueblo during the corn dance I noticed tourists picking up shards of all the old pottery that had been made and broken there. The residents of Zia know not to take the bowls and pots left behind by the older ones. They know that the fragments of those earlier lives need to be smoothed back to earth, but younger nations, travelers from continents across the world who have come to inhabit this land, have little of their own to grow on. The pieces of earth that were formed into bowls, even on their way home to dust, provide the new people a lifeline to an unknown land, help them remember that they live in the old nest of earth.

It was in early February, during the mating season of the great horned owl. It was dusk, and I hiked up the back of a mountain to where I'd heard the owls a year before. I wanted to hear them again, the voices so tender, so deep, like a memory of comfort. I was halfway up the trail when I found a soft, round nest. It had fallen from one of the bare-branched trees. It was a delicate nest, woven together of feathers, sage, and strands of wild grass. Holding it in my hand in the rosy twilight, I noticed that a blue thread was entwined with the other gatherings there. I pulled at the thread a little, and then I recognized it. It was a thread from one of my skirts. It was blue cotton. It was the unmistakable color and shape of a pattern I knew. I liked it, that a thread of my life was in an abandoned nest, one that had held eggs and new life. I took the nest home. At home, I held it to the light and looked more closely. There, to my surprise, nestled into the gray-green sage, was a gnarl of black hair. It was also unmistakable. It was my daughter's hair, cleaned from a brush and picked up out in the sun beneath the maple tree, or the pit cherry where the birds eat from the overladen, fertile branches until only the seeds remain on the trees.

I didn't know what kind of nest it was, or who had lived there. It didn't matter. I thought of the remnants of our lives carried up the hill that way and turned into shelter. That night, resting inside the walls of our home, the world outside weighed so heavily against the thin wood of the house. The sloped roof was the only thing between us and the universe. Everything outside of our wooden boundaries seemed so large. Filled with the night's citizens, it all came alive. The world opened in the thickets of the dark. The wild grapes would soon ripen on the vines. The burrowing ones were emerging. Horned owls sat in treetops. Mice scurried here and there. Skunks, fox, the slow and holy porcupine, all were passing by this way. The young of the solitary bees were feeding on the pollen in the dark. The whole world was a nest on its humble tilt, in the maze of the universe, holding us.

INTERPRETATIONS

1. What meaning does Hogan give to the word dwelling? How do the different descriptions she provides contribute to an overall definition of the word? Provide specific examples from the essay.

2. What do you notice about how this essay is written? How does this structure help to convey Hogan's meaning?

3. How has Hogan learned about dwellings? What tools has she employed to gain this understanding?

CORRESPONDENCES

1. To an extent, Hogan describes physical dwellings, actual places where people or animals reside. In his essay, "A Letter to a Child Like Me," Torres (page 161) describes dwellings of the *mind*. What physical places does Hogan write about? What psychological dwellings does Torres address?

2. Compare the kinds of dwellings Hogan describes with those that appear in Bambara's "The Lesson" (page 181).

3. How does Alastair Reid's perspective apply to Hogan?

APPLICATIONS

1. Reread Hogan's essay, paying attention to her use of imagery. In addition to the visual images that are created, you might also notice the sound of her words. Next, create a list of five images that you like. Now, carefully arrange this list into a sequence that seems to work for you. Read this new creation aloud. How does it make you feel? How does it relate to Hogan's original essay?

2. Go to a dwelling that is new to you. (In seeking out such a place, keep in mind those dwellings that Hogan has included in her essay.) Observe the place, and, if present, the inhabitants. In an essay that emulates Hogan's style, try to provide a vivid description of this dwelling. You might address such questions as: What does this dwelling look like? Who lives there? What is the purpose of the dwelling? Who has lived in this dwelling prior to the current residents? Who will live there next?

3. Write a descriptive essay of a place that is meaningful to you. Rather than describe the whole place, think of the exact spot that is most important. For example, if you like to go to a relative's house or a cottage in the country, rather than describe the entire structure, find that exact place that holds the most meaning. As you describe this specific spot (a single room, place on the porch, particular step on a stoop) explain why this place is important to you. Remember to use your senses to create images that will help your reader to experience this place and to know its significance.

A View From the Bridge

CHEROKEE PAUL MCDONALD

Cherokee Paul McDonald (b. 1949) is a fiction writer and journalist. In his most recent book, Into the Green *(2001), he records his tour of duty as an Army lieutenant during the Vietnam War. He later joined the police department in Fort Lauderdale where he served for ten years and in 1991 published* Blue Truth, *a memoir of his years in the police force that includes graphic descriptions of crimes he had to deal with. "A View from the Bridge" was published in* Sunshine *(1990), a Florida sporting magazine.*

I WAS COMING UP ON THE LITTLE BRIDGE in the Rio Vista neighborhood of Fort Lauderdale, deepening my stride and my breathing to negotiate the slight incline without altering my pace. And then, as I neared the crest, I saw the kid.

He was a lumpy little guy with baggy shorts, a faded T-shirt and heavy sweat socks falling down over old sneakers.

Partially covering his shaggy blond hair was one of those blue base-ball caps with gold braid on the bill and a sailfish patch sewn onto the peak. Covering his eyes and part of his face was a pair of those stupid-looking '50s-style wrap-around sunglasses.

He was fumbling with a beat-up rod and reel, and he had a little bait bucket by his feet. I puffed on by, glancing down into the empty bucket as I passed.

"Hey, mister! Would you help me, please?"

The shrill voice penetrated my jogger's concentration, and I was determined to ignore it. But for some reason, I stopped.

With my hands on my hips and the sweat dripping from my nose I asked, "What do you want, kid?"

"Would you please help me find my shrimp? It's my last one and I've been getting bites and I know I can catch a fish if I can just find that shrimp. He jumped outta my hand as I was getting him from the bucket."

Exasperated, I walked slowly back to the kid, and pointed.

"There's the damn shrimp by your left foot. You stopped me for *that*?"

As I said it, the kid reached down and trapped the shrimp.

"Thanks a lot, mister," he said.

I watched as the kid dropped the baited hook down into the canal. Then I turned to start back down the bridge.

153

That's when the kid let out a "Hey! Hey!" and the prettiest tarpon I'd ever seen came almost six feet out of the water, twisting and turning as he fell through the air.

"I got one!" the kid yelled as the fish hit the water with a loud splash and took off down the canal.

I watched the line being burned off the reel at an alarming rate. The kid's left hand held the crank while the extended fingers felt for the drag setting.

"No, kid!" I shouted, "Leave the drag alone . . . just keep that damn rod tip up!"

Then I glanced at the reel and saw there were just a few loops of line left on the spool.

"Why don't you get yourself some decent equipment?" I said, but before the kid could answer I saw the line go slack.

"Ohhh, I lost him," the kid said. I saw the flash of silver as the fish turned.

"Crank, kid, crank! You didn't lose him. He's coming back toward you. Bring in the slack!"

The kid cranked like mad, and a beautiful grin spread across his face.

"He's heading in for the pilings," I said. "Keep him out of those pilings!"

The kid played it perfectly. When the fish made its play for the pilings, he kept just enough pressure on to force the fish out. When the water exploded and the silver missile hurled into the air, the kid kept the rod tip up and the line tight.

As the fish came to the surface and began a slow circle in the middle of the canal, I said, "Whooee, is that a nice fish or what?"

The kid didn't say anything, so I said, "Okay, move to the edge of the bridge and I'll climb down to the seawall and pull him out."

When I reached the seawall I pulled in the leader, leaving the fish lying on its side in the water.

"How's that?" I said.

"Hey, mister, tell me what it looks like."

"Look down here and check him out," I said. "He's beautiful."

But then I looked up into those stupid-looking sunglasses and it hit me. The kid was blind.

"Could you tell me what he looks like, mister?" he said again.

"Well, he's just under three, uh, he's about as long as one of your arms," I said. "I'd guess he goes about 15, 20 pounds. He's mostly silver, but the silver is somehow made up of *all* the colors, if you know what I mean." I stopped. "Do you know what I mean by colors?"

The kid nodded.

"Okay. He has all these big scales, like armor all over his body. They're silver too, and when he moves they sparkle. He has a strong body and a large powerful tail. He has big round eyes, bigger than a quarter, and a lower jaw that sticks out past the upper one and is very tough. His belly is almost white and his back is a gunmetal gray. When he jumped he came out of the water about six feet, and his scales caught the sun and flashed it all over the place."

By now the fish had righted itself, and I could see the bright-red gills as the gill plates opened and closed. I explained this to the kid, and then said, more to myself, "He's a beauty."

"Can you get him off the hook?" the kid asked. "I don't want to kill him."

I watched as the tarpon began to slowly swim away, tired but still alive.

By the time I got back up to the top of the bridge the kid had his line secured and his bait bucket in one hand.

He grinned and said, "Just in time. My mom drops me off here, and she'll be back to pick me up any minute."

He used the back of one hand to wipe his nose.

"Thanks for helping me catch that tarpon," he said, "and for helping me to see it."

I looked at him, shook my head, and said, "No, my friend, thank you for letting *me* see that fish."

I took off, but before I got far the kid yelled again.

"Hey, mister!"

I stopped.

"Someday I'm gonna catch a sailfish and a blue marlin and a giant tuna and *all* those big sportfish!"

As I looked into those sunglasses I knew he probably would. I wished I could be there when it happened.

INTERPRETATIONS

1. McDonald uses foreshadowing to convey to the reader that the boy is blind. What clues did he provide and at what point did you realize that he could not see? Why does it take the narrator so long to realize this? How does his attitude change toward the boy after this knowledge?

2. Identify the sensory language that the author uses to describe the tarpon to the boy. What changes does he make in his language in the process? What does the boy know about fishing?

3. McDonald uses dialogue throughout the essay. Why is this effective for this situation? Be specific.

4. What did you find most interesting about the boy by the end of his encounter with the narrator? Do you believe that he will achieve his goal of catching "all those big sportfish"? Why or why not?

5. Why does the narrator thank the boy for allowing him to see the fish? How has the narrator changed as a result of their meeting?

CORRESPONDENCES

1. The typical learning situations in the texts by McDonald and Montgomery-Fate (page 174) are reversed. What do the adults learn from the children? Be specific.

2. Review Kaufman's perspective and discuss its relevance to "A View from the Bridge."

APPLICATIONS

1. Consult your thesaurus on "view" and "bridge" and write an essay on the multiple meanings of the title. Is irony implicit in the title? Explain.

2. Experiment with your group in describing an object or a bird, flower, butterfly, or goldfish to someone who cannot see. Use sensory language—smell, touch, texture, and color—to create a vivid verbal picture. What did you learn about language through this exercise?

3. The jogger and the young boy are strangers to each other but share a passion for fishing. Write an essay on the various roles that the tarpon plays in their encounter.

Mute in an English-Only World

CHANG-RAE LEE

Chang-Rae Lee (b. 1965, in Seoul, Korea) teaches at Hunter College in New York where he is a member of the Hunter Creative Writing Community. His father was a psychiatrist practicing in Westchester County, New York, and Lee attended Phillips Exeter Academy and Yale (B.A. 1987). Lee earned a master of fine arts degree from the University of Oregon in 1993. He is the author of the novels Native Speaker *(1994), which earned the Hemingway Foundation/PEN and more than six other major awards in 1995,* A Gesture Life *(1999), and* Aloft *(2004). All of these novels have received high critical praise. They all show his interest in language and identity, as does this Op-Ed essay, originally published in* The New York Times *in April 1996.*

WHEN I READ OF THE TROUBLES in Palisades Park, New Jersey, over the proliferation of Korean language signs along its main commercial strip, I unexpectedly sympathized with the frustrations, resentments and fears of the longtime residents. They clearly felt alienated and even unwelcome in a vital part of their community. The town, like seven others in New Jersey, has passed laws requiring that half of any commercial sign in a foreign language be in English.

Now I certainly would never tolerate any exclusionary ideas about who could rightfully settle and belong in the town. But having been raised in a Korean immigrant family, I saw every day the exacting price and power of language, especially with my mother, who was an outsider in an English-only world.

In the first years we lived in America, my mother could speak only the most basic English, and she often encountered great difficulty whenever she went out.

We lived in New Rochelle, New York in the early 70s, and most of the local businesses were run by the descendants of immigrants who, generations ago, had come to the suburbs from New York City. Proudly dotting Main Street and North Avenue were Italian pastry and cheese shops, Jewish tailors and cleaners and Polish and German butchers and bakers. If my mother's marketing couldn't wait until the weekend, when my father had free time, she would often hold off until I came home from school to buy the groceries.

Though I was only six or seven years old, she insisted that I go out shopping with her and my younger sister. I mostly loathed the task, partly because it meant I couldn't spend the afternoon playing catch with my friends but also because I knew our errands would inevitably lead to an awkward scene, and that I would have to speak up to help my mother.

I was just learning the language myself, but I was a quick study, as children are with new tongues. I had spent kindergarten in almost complete silence, hearing only the high nasality of my teacher and comprehending little but the cranky wails and cries of my classmates. But soon, seemingly mere months later, I had already become a terrible ham and mimic, and I would crack up my father with impressions of teachers, his friends and even himself. My mother scolded me for aping his speech, and the one time I attempted to make light of hers I rated a roundhouse smack on my bottom.

For her, the English language was not very funny. It usually meant trouble and a good dose of shame, and sometimes real hurt. Although she had a good reading knowledge of the language from university classes in South Korea, she had never practiced actual conversation. So in America, she used English flashcards and phrase books and watched television with us kids. And she faithfully carried a pocket workbook illustrated with stick-figure people and compound sentences to be filled in.

But none of it seemed to do her much good. Staying mostly at home to care for us, she didn't have many chances to try out sundry words and phrases. When she did, say, at the window of the post office, her readied speech would stall, freeze, sometimes altogether collapse.

One day was unusually harrowing. We ventured downtown in the new Ford Country Squire my father had bought her, an enormous station wagon that seemed as long—and deft—as an ocean liner. We were shopping for a special meal for guests visiting that weekend, and my mother had heard that a particular butcher carried fresh oxtails, which she needed for a traditional soup.

We'd never been inside the shop, but my mother would pause before its window, which was always lined with whole hams, crown roasts and ropes of plump handmade sausages. She greatly esteemed the bounty with her eyes, and my sister and I did also, but despite our desirous cries she'd turn us away and instead buy the packaged links at the Finast supermarket, where she felt comfortable looking them over and could easily spot the price. And, of course, not have to talk.

But that day she was resolved. The butcher store was crowded, and as we stepped inside the door jingled a welcome. No one seemed to notice. We waited for some time, and people who entered after us were now being served. Finally, an old woman nudged my mother and waved a little ticket, which we hadn't taken. We patiently waited again, until one of the beefy men behind the glass display hollered our number.

My mother pulled us forward and began searching the cases, but the oxtails were nowhere to be found. The man, his big arms crossed, sharply said, "Come on, lady, whaddya want?" This unnerved her, and she somehow blurted the Korean word for oxtail, soggori.

The butcher looked as if my mother had put something sour in his mouth, and he glanced back at the lighted board and called the next number.

Before I knew it, she had rushed us outside and back in the wagon, which she had double-parked because of the crowd. She was furious, almost vibrating with fear and grief, and I could see she was about to cry.

She wanted to go back inside, but now the driver of the car we were blocking wanted to pull out. She was shooing us away. My mother, who had just earned her driver's license, started furiously working the pedals. But in her haste she must have flooded the engine, for it wouldn't turn over. The driver started honking and then another car began honking as well, and soon the entire street was shrieking at us.

In the following years, my mother grew steadily more comfortable with English. In Korean, she could be fiery, stern, deeply funny and ironic; in English, just slightly less so. If she was never quite fluent, she gained enough confidence to make herself clearly known to anyone, and particularly to me.

Five years ago, she died of cancer, and some months after we buried her I found myself in the driveway of my father's house, washing her sedan. I liked taking care of her things; it made me feel close to her. While I was cleaning out the glove compartment, I found her pocket English workbook, the one with the silly illustrations. I hadn't seen it in nearly twenty years. The yellowed pages were brittle and dog-eared. She had fashioned a plain-paper wrapping for it, and I wondered whether she meant to protect the book or hide it.

I don't doubt that she would have appreciated doing the family shopping on the new Broad Avenue of Palisades Park. But I like to think, too, that she would have understood those who now complain about the Korean-only signs.

I wonder what these same people would have done if they had seen my mother studying her English workbook—or lost in a store. Would they have nodded gently at her? Would they have lent a kind word?

INTERPRETATIONS

1. What issues does Lee raise in the first paragraph?
2. What is his purpose in this essay? Is he seeking to inform or persuade his readers on the English-only debate? Cite evidence for your point of view.
3. How effectively does Lee's mother's workbook function literally and symbolically in the text?

A Letter to a Child Like Me

JOSÉ TORRES

José Torres (b. 1936) was raised in poverty in Puerto Rico. After winning a
silver medal in the 1956 Olympic Games, he became a professional boxer and
had a successful career that culminated in his winning the light-heavyweight
boxing championship in 1965. In 1969 he retired, and now frequently writes
about boxing and his life experiences. He is the author of In this Corner, Fire
and Fear: The Inside Story of Mike Tyson *(1989). In the following essay*
he offers advice to young people of his ethnic background.

DEAR PEDRITO:

You're thirteen now, and you must certainly be aware that there are
some people in this country who refer to you as "Hispanic." That is,
you're a member of a minority group. You read newspapers and magazines, you watch television, so you know that the world is moving into
the twenty-first century faced with big problems, enormous possibilities, huge mysteries. I worry that you might not be fully prepared for
the journey.

The statistics are scary. They show us Hispanics facing a sea of
trouble. The United States has 250 million people, a little more than
20 million of whom are of Hispanic descent. That's only 8 percent of
this nation's total population. We're also the youngest ethnic group in
the nation. We earn the lowest salaries, and, in cities where we have a
large concentration of Hispanics, we have the highest school dropout
rate. In New York City, for example, we comprise 25.7 percent of the
high school dropouts, 42.7 percent of pregnant teenagers and 8.9 percent of the unemployed.

It should not be too hard for you to understand, my friend, that these
statistics hurt us a lot. That means that many of our young people end up
badly, as both victims and perpetrators. Some blame us for these conditions, despite our minuscule stock in this country and the fact the overwhelming majority of us are hardworking, decent, law-abiding citizens.

Still, you should realize that the world is not made up of statistics
but of individuals. By the year 2030, you'll be my age, and what you do
now is going to determine what you'll be doing then.

I've had my defeats; I've made my share of mistakes. But I've
also learned something along the way. Let me tell you about a few of

them. You didn't ask for this advice, but I'm going to give it to you anyway.

Let's start with a fundamental human problem, and I don't mean race or religion or origin. I mean fear. Fright, my young friend, may be the first serious enemy you have to face in our society. It's the most destructive emotional bogeyman there is. Cold feet, panic, depression, and violence are all symptoms of fear—when it's out of control. But this feeling, ironically, can also trigger courage, alertness, objectivity. You must learn not to try to rid yourself of this basic human emotion but to manipulate it for your own advantage. You cannot surrender to fear, but you *can* use it as a kind of fuel. Once you learn to control fear—to make it work for you—it will become one of your best friends.

I learned this the hard way. I was a boxer. I became a world champion, but on my way up the ladder I found Frankie Kid Anslem, a tough young Philadelphian made of steel. The match proceeded, to my increasing dismay, with me hitting and Anslem smiling. At one point, I remember, I let go a particularly left hook-right cross combination. The punches landed flush on his jaw, but he simply riposted with a smile—and some hard leather of his own.

Suddenly, I found myself struggling for my life. I was afraid. For two rounds—the eighth and ninth—Anslem and I seemed contestants in an evil struggle. My punches seemed to give him energy and pleasure! Unexpectedly, my chest began to burn, my legs weakened, my lungs gasped for air. I felt exhausted. I was dying! Thoughts of defeat and humiliation assailed me. I was grappling with these facts when I saw Anslem's jaw exposed and, reaching from somewhere beyond my terror, I threw a straight right with all my might. And Anslem lost his smile and dropped like an old shoe.

My fatigue disappeared. I felt good, happy, invigorated. Fear had overtaken me, been recognized, then resolved and manipulated for a positive result.

I was obliged to learn about handling fear through the brutal trade of boxing. I didn't have the option now open to you, my young friend. I was one of seven poor kids who lived under many layers of an underdeveloped subculture. I chose a tough profession because two black boxers—a heavyweight champion named Joe Louis, and a middleweight marvel called Sugar Ray Robinson—showed me the way. They lived far away from my hometown in Puerto Rico. But I knew them. I wanted to be like them.

Looking back, I wonder what my choice would have been if real alternatives had been available when I was your age. Don't get me wrong. I'm very proud of my first profession. To be recognized as the best in the world at what you do, even if only for a moment, is a wonderful experience. Still, I was very much aware that boxing was a temporary activity intended only for the young. And so I had a pretty good idea of what your choice should not be if you're given a chance to become an artist, a corporate executive, a doctor, a lawyer, an engineer, a writer, or a prizefighter—though it should be *my* choice.

Whatever your ambition, you must educate yourself. School is a great gift our society offers you. It provides the key for your future. You must accept this gift, not disdain it. School is where you'll learn about your country and your world and your life in both. You also discover the conflicts and contradictions of history. You'll unlock the treasure chest of the world's literature and begin to sense the beauty of music and art. You'll acquire the tools of abstract thinking, of science and mathematics—and the computer, perhaps the primary instrument of the world you'll inherit.

At home, you should learn about compassion and dignity and care. You should realize that the workings of an individual's heart and soul can be as important as the histories of the great battles, military generals, dictators and kings. Most of all, you should learn that it's *you* who are responsible for your future.

There is a basic principle you should never forget: Don't be ruled by other people's low expectation of you! It almost happened to me. I grew up in Playa de Ponce, a small *barrio* in the southern part of Puerto Rico, an island 100 miles long and 35 miles wide, with a dense population today of more than 3.3 million—1,000 human beings per square mile. I was only five when I first noticed the American military men—many of them tall, blond, and blue-eyed—wearing a variety of uniforms, roaming the streets of my neighborhood and picking up the prettiest girls. They seemed to own Playa de Ponce. Their attitude in the streets and their country's constant military victories, which we witnessed at the movie houses, became symbols of these young men's "obvious superiority." By comparison, we Puerto Ricans felt limited, inadequate.

To catch up, I volunteered to serve in the U.S. Army as soon as I became of age. And, for some mysterious reason, I joined its boxing team. My first four opponents were two compatriots and two black men from the Virgin Islands, all of whom I had no trouble disposing of. But just before my fifth fight—against one of those tall, blond, blue-eyed "superior" American soldiers, doubt started to creep into my mind. Yet, despite my worries, after three rounds of tough boxing, I overcame. I won! I had discovered the equality of the human race.

Your best defense against the ignorance of bigots and haters is pride in your own heritage. That's why you must learn your own history. Do it now. Don't wait until you are in college. You don't need teachers. Go to the library. Ask your parents and relatives and friends.

Be proud of your ethnicity and language. Don't be afraid to use it. Don't give up to the stupidity of those know-nothings who insist one language is better than two or three. You should know, and be proud, that in the Western Hemisphere more people speak Spanish than English; that Español was the language of the Hemisphere's first university—the Santo Tomás de Aquino University in the Dominican Republic, founded in 1538—and of the books in its first library. When you discover the long and honorable tradition to which you belong, your pride will soar.

So do not lose the language of your parents, which is also yours. Instead, refine your skill in it. If you're having trouble with grammar or writing, take courses in Spanish. Go to the library and read Cervantes' *Don Quixote*, the first full-fledged novel, or the works of the hundreds of great modern Hispanic authors, such as Gabriel García Márquez, Lola Rodriguez de Tió, Carlos Fuentes, Mario Vargas Llosa, Octavio Paz, Jorge Luis Borges, and Oscar Hijuelos, the 1990 Pulitzer Prize winner in fiction (who writes in English). Read them in both languages; know the strength of both. This is the treasure that no one can ever beat.

Puerto Rico is a nearly imperceptible dot on the map, my friend. Still, this small island recently had five boxing champions at the same time. And consider this: Baseball star Reggie Jackson; the great entertainer Sammy Davis, Jr.; Dr. Joaquín Balaguer, poet, writer and six-time president of the Dominican Republic; the renowned cellist Pablo Casals all had one thing in common—one of their parents was Puerto Rican. The film and stage star Rita Moreno, a Puerto Rican, is one of the few performers ever to win an Oscar, a Tony, a Grammy, and an Emmy award. José Ferrer, a proud Puerto Rican, was once selected as the American citizen with the finest English diction in the United States. Ferrer also won an Oscar for his brilliant performance in the classic film *Cyrano de Bergerac*. Dr. Raul García Rinaidi, a physician of world prominence and a native Puerto Rican, helped invent six instruments now used in cardiovascular surgery. Arturo Alfonso Schomburg, a native Puerto Rican, made extensive investigation into Black history. In his honor, the New York Public Library system erected the Schomburg Center for Research in Black Culture.

The contribution of Hispanics to the development of the United States of America has been vast and unquestionable. But much more remains to be done, my friend. Every member of society must work together in order to survive together.

We live in a country where more than 27 million people can't read or write well enough to take a driving test, and many can't recognize "danger," or "poison." Every eight seconds of the school day a student drops out; every sixty seconds a teenager has a baby; every six minutes a child is arrested for drugs; every year, the schools graduate 700,000 who cannot read their diplomas.

Most of them are *not* Hispanics. Yet, many of these victims are the same people who, day after day, throw themselves in front of a TV set and become passive, docile ghosts, allowing their lives to be easily controlled by others. Television, with its emphasis on package images and quick bites, discourages thought and imagination. Studies indicate that chronic televiewers develop problems with their thinking processes and articulation. Excessive viewing dulls the most indispensable muscle—the brain.

Instead of watching TV, read and write. Words are the symbols of reality, and a well-read person, skilled at decoding those symbols, is better able to comprehend and think about the real world.

Many years ago, the great Japanese artist, Katsushika Hokusai lay on his deathbed at age 89. Experts say no one could paint better than Hokusai during his prime, and many are convinced that his work is as good as—or better than—today's top artists. But Hokusai was never satisfied with his triumphs and successes. "If I could live one more year," he said, "I could learn how to draw."

You, my young friend, would do well to become like Hokusai—a person who can lead a humble but useful and productive life, free of harm and, most important, free of the influences that generate hate, murder, suicide, and death. If you choose to spend your time not reading, thinking, and creating, but watching TV and learning how to deceive, cheat, and lie, then you become another person out there perpetuating the cycle of ignorance that leads to poverty, suffering, and despair. But if you commit yourself to a lifetime of honest work—if you assure yourself that a day in which you are unable to produce anything positive is a tragically misspent day—then, my friend, the twenty-first century is yours.

Go and get it!

INTERPRETATIONS

1. Why does Torres begin his letter by citing mainly negative statistics about Hispanics and then go on to say "that the world is not made up of statistics but of individuals"?

2. Torres tells his young friend that fear may be his greatest enemy. How did Torres overcome his own fear? To what extent do you agree or disagree about the negative power of fear?

3. "School is a great gift our society offers you." What evidence does he cite to support his thesis? How do your experiences with school correspond to Torres's expectation?

4. "Be proud of your ethnicity and language." What evidence did you find most convincing regarding this advice?

5. Respond to Torres's views on watching television, particularly to his comment about television's dulling the brain.

CORRESPONDENCES

1. Lee focuses on the connection between language and powerlessness while Torres emphasizes the relation between language and power. What factors account for differences in their points of view?

2. What conversation can you imagine Lee and Torres sharing on the issue of bilingualism? What would you add to the debate?

APPLICATIONS

1. Write a journal entry responding to Lee's title. Can you imagine being mute in a culture whose native language is not English? How might you respond in a situation similar to the one in the butcher's shop?

2. Listen to the sounds of a language that you do not understand. Listen for rhythms and melodies. How would you describe this language as a song?

3. According to Torres, "television, with its emphasis on packaged images and quick bites, discourages thought and imagination." Debate this issue with your group, citing examples from your own experience that support or refute Torres. What consensus did you reach?

4. Create a concept map of the types of learning or education that Torres presents in his essay. To learn more about concept mapping, check the following Web sites:

http://www.cotf.edu/ete/pb12.html

http://users.edte.utwente.nl/lanzing/cm_home.htm

Always Living in Spanish

MARJORIE AGOSÍN

Margorie Agosín (b. 1955) spent her childhood in Chile. She is a prolific writer in many forms: poetry, short fiction, autobiographies, essays, longer works of nonfiction, as well as collections of other writers' work. Just before Salvador Allende's government was overthrown by the dictatorship of Augusto Pinochet, she immigrated with her family to the United States. She earned a B.A. from the University of Georgia in 1976 and a Ph.D. from Indiana University–Bloomington in 1982 and teaches in the Department of Spanish at Wellesley College. A Cross and a Star: Memoirs of a Jewish Girl in Chile *(1995) illustrates her cross-cultural and human rights interests: it is about her family's life in a small Chilean town from the perspective of her mother, who was excluded from all except the Indian school. Two other books, both published in 1996, also explore human rights issues:* Tapestries of Hope. Threads of Love: The Arpillera Movement in Chile, 1974–1994 *and* Ashes of Revolt: Essays on Human Rights. *Agosín is the winner of the 1995 Letros de Oro Award, the Latino Literature Prize, and the Good Neighbor Award. Examine your feelings about your own native language before you read how Agosín has been "tormented" by a change from Spanish to English.*

Chile is a republic lying along the Pacific coast of South America. To the east are Argentina and Bolivia; to the north is Peru. The population, which is 95 percent European and Mestizo and 3 percent Indian, is largely urban. Salvador Allende, a Marxist, was elected president in 1970, but three years later General Augusto Pinochet seized power and ruled until 1990. Under his military dictatorship nearly three thousand people were executed, "disappeared," or died as a result of torture and other kinds of political violence.

IN THE EVENINGS in the northern hemisphere, I repeat the ancient ritual that I observed as a child in the southern hemisphere: going out while the night is still warm and trying to recognize the stars as it begins to grow dark silently. In the sky of my country, Chile, that long and wide stretch of land that the poets blessed and dictators abused, I could easily name the stars: the three Marias, the Southern Cross, and the three Lilies, names of beloved and courageous women.

But here in the United States, where I have lived since I was a young girl, the solitude of exile makes me feel that so little is mine, that

167

not even the sky has the same constellations, the trees and the fauna the same names or sounds, or the rubbish the same smell. How does one recover the familiar? How does one name the unfamiliar? How can one be another or live in a foreign language? These are the dilemmas of one who writes in Spanish and lives in translation.

Since my earliest childhood in Chile I lived with the tempos and the melodies of a multiplicity of tongues: German, Yiddish, Russian, Turkish, and many Latin songs. Because everyone was from somewhere else, my relatives laughed, sang, and fought in a Babylon of languages. Spanish was reserved for matters of extreme seriousness, for commercial transactions, or for illnesses, but everyone's mother tongue was always associated with the memory of spaces inhabited in the past: the shtetl, the flowering and vast Vienna avenues, the minarets of Turkey, and the Ladino whispers of Toledo. When my paternal grandmother sang old songs in Turkish, her voice and body assumed the passion of one who was there in the city of Istanbul, gazing by turns toward the west and the east.

Destiny and the always ambiguous nature of history continued my family's enforced migration, and because of it I, too, became one who had to live and speak in translation. The disappearances, torture, and clandestine deaths in my country in the early seventies drove us to the United States, that other America that looked with suspicion at those who did not speak English and especially those who came from the supposedly uncivilized regions of Latin America. I had left a dangerous place that was my home, only to arrive in a dangerous place that was not: a high school in the small town of Athens, Georgia, where my poor English and my accent were the cause of ridicule and insult. The only way I could recover my usurped country and my Chilean childhood was by continuing to write in Spanish, the same way my grandparents had sung in their own tongues in diasporic sites.

The new and learned English language did not fit with the visceral emotions and themes that my poetry contained, but by writing in Spanish I could recover fragrances, spoken rhythms, and the passion of my own identity. Daily I felt the need to translate myself for the strangers living all around me, to tell them why we were in Georgia, why we are differently, why we had fled, why my accent was so thick, and why I did not look Hispanic. Only at night, writing poems in Spanish, could I return to my senses, and soothe my own sorrow over what I had left behind.

This is how I became a Chilean poet who wrote in Spanish and lived in the southern United States. And then, one day, a poem of mine was translated and published in the English language. Finally, for the first time since I had left Chile, I felt I didn't have to explain myself. My poem, expressed in another language, spoke for itself . . . and for me.

Sometimes the austere sounds of English help me bear the solitude of knowing that I am foreign and so far away from those about whom I write. I must admit I would like more opportunities to read in Spanish to people whose language and culture is also mine, to join in our common heritage and in the feast of our sounds. I would also like readers of English to understand the beauty of the spoken word in Spanish, that constant flow of oxytonic and paraoxytonic syllables (*Verde que te quiero verdo*), the joy of writing—of dancing—in another language. I believe that many exiles share the unresolvable torment of not being able to live in the language of their childhood.

I miss that undulating and sensuous language of mine, those baroque descriptions, the sense of being and feeling that Spanish gives me. It is perhaps for this reason that I have chosen and will always choose to write in Spanish. Nothing else from my childhood world remains. My country seems to be frozen in gestures of silence and oblivion. My relatives have died, and I have grown up not knowing a young generation of cousins and nieces and nephews. Many of my friends disappeared, others were tortured, and the most fortunate, like me, became guardians of memory. For us, to write in Spanish is to always be in active pursuit of memory. I seek to recapture a world lost to me on that sorrowful afternoon when the blue electric sky and the Andean cordillera bade me farewell. On that, my last Chilean day, I carried under my arm my innocence recorded in a little blue notebook I kept even then. Gradually that diary filled with memoranda, poems written in free verse, descriptions of dreams and of the thresholds of my house surrounded by cherry trees and gardenias. To write in Spanish is for me a gesture of survival. And because of translation, my memory has now become a part of the memory of many others.

Translators are not traitors, as the proverb says, but rather splendid friends in this great human community of language.

INTERPRETATIONS

1. Brainstorm on the multiple meanings in Agosín's title.

2. What evidence does she provide to support her statement that she "left a place that was my home, only to arrive in a dangerous place that was not."

3. Agosín offers several reasons as to why she will always write in Spanish. Which do you find most convincing?

4. Explain the conclusion of her essay.

CORRESPONDENCES

1. What conversation can you imagine Torres and Agosín sharing on the issue of biculturalism? What would you add to the debate?

2. Compare and contrast the tone of Agosín's and Lee's texts. How is purpose related to tone in each essay?

APPLICATIONS

1. Discuss with your group Agosín's statement that she believes "that many exiles share the unresolvable torment of not being able to live in the language of their childhood." If this is also your experience, what would you add to the examples Agosín offers?

2. Agosín discloses much about herself as a result of her family's "forced migration" from Chile to the United States. If you have had a similar experience, write an essay about what you learned about yourself.

3. Write a journal entry on the relationship between language and identity according to Agosín.

Thinking

ROLANDO JORIF

Rolando Jorif was born in Panama, and was raised in Queens, New York. After attending Catholic parochial school in the 1950s, he graduated from the Bronx High School of Science and continued on to Lehman College–City University of New York (CUNY). A true 1960s dropout, Jorif left college to become a dancer. He has a Ph.D. from CUNY Graduate Center and teaches writing and literature at Borough of Manhattan Community College (CUNY). In addition to his literary interests in Herman Melville and Frederick Douglass, he is also an accomplished painter.

Panama is a Republic on the Isthmus of Panama that connects Central and South America. The capital is Panama City. Christopher Columbus landed in Panama in 1502. In 1510, Vasco Nunez de Balboa was the first European to cross Panama and see the Pacific Ocean. The indigenous population was soon wiped out and Spain established control. In 1821, Panama became a province of Colombia. After a revolt in 1903, Panama declared independence from Colombia. In 1904, the United States began construction of the Panama Canal and established the Panama Canal Zone. Since it was opened in 1914, the status of the Canal has been a feature of Panamanian politics. United States forces intervened in 1908, 1912, and 1918 to protect U.S. interests. Panama was politically unstable throughout the twentieth century, with a series of dictatorial regimes and military coups. Civil strife during the 1950s and 1960s led to negotiations with the United States for the transfer of the Canal Zone. In 1977, a treaty confirmed Panama's sovereignty over the canal, while providing for U.S. bases in the Canal Zone. The United States agreed to hand over control of the Canal on December 31, 1999. In 1983, General Noriega took control of the National Guard and ruled Panama through a succession of puppet governments. In 1987, the U.S. withdrew its support for Noriega after he was accused of murder, electoral fraud, and aiding drug smuggling. In December 1989, he made himself president and declared war on the U.S. On December 20, 1989, 25,000 U.S. troops invaded Panama. Noriega was captured in January 1990 and taken to the United States for trial. Pere Balladares was elected president in 1994.

THINKING IS A VERY NICE EXERCISE when you are young. I used to think a great deal about freedom when I was a child. My ideas developed slowly. No matter what I thought, though, I would try my ideas out to see what would happen. I didn't do this deliberately. It's just how things worked out. I can easily recall three experiences.

My first or second winter in school, I reached over and took a handful of snow off the windowsill and ate it—cold, delicious snow. I was newly arrived in this country and snow was still a marvel. I should tell you that I had waited until the nun had left the room and that she had chosen my greatest enemy to be the monitor. I'm not making excuses, I'm only setting the scene. If the fool hadn't been left in charge, someone else who took his work seriously would have been left to watch us. Someone else, though, might have understood why I did what I did and might have left me alone. In any case, I was reported for my "bad behavior." I was sent down to the principal's office where that formidable woman told me that eating snow off windowsills would not do; my attempt at an explanation only made more trouble for me.

I learnt my first lesson about freedom that day: you had better be discreet in your expression of it.

My second lesson happened because I had lost a button from my school shirt. We wore uniforms, and the dress code included the proper maintenance of our clothes. I spent my childhood in terror of not being properly dressed in school, or any place else, for that matter. In any case, I had lost a button from my shirt and it needed to be replaced. I approached my very tired mother (she worked to support us) for help. The good woman got up, left the room and returned with needle and thread. She taught me to sew.

My second lesson about freedom was that you had better be able to take care of your own needs.

My third lesson was a bit more painful to learn.

I was an immigrant and I had entered the school system a cultural virgin. Very quickly, I learned about prejudice and "truth, justice, and the American way." Despite what my parents did to encourage me by telling me that we had not come to America to be anyone's friend, or that I was as good as anyone (I did not tell them very much of what really happened to me), I felt that things were hopeless. One day we were told to read the Declaration of Independence. I was thunderstruck; these people knew all the stuff about freedom that I had learned. I memorized the first paragraph and repeated it to myself every chance I had. One day, we were asked to recite it; I was the only one who knew it. Not only that, but when I recited it, the audience of blank faces meant that I was the only one who understood it. Freedom, I learned, was a secret and it meant being all alone in the crowd.

Thinking is a very nice exercise when you are young. What I had thought was freedom was something else, and I had to examine myself and the world around me to correct my error. It spared me a great deal of trouble, even if it gave me some anxious moments. I don't get very much time to think, now that I am older. I also don't get spared much trouble.

INTERPRETATIONS

1. Jorif recalls three experiences from elementary school that taught him about freedom. What did he learn not only about freedom but about himself?
2. Characterize the tone of his essay. Is it humorous, angry, ironic, or sarcastic? Cite evidence for your point of view.
3. How does Jorif use his introduction and conclusion to unify his essay? Why does he think less as an adult?

CORRESPONDENCES

1. Review Frost's perspective on education and discuss its relevance to Jorif's essay. To what did Jorif "catch on"?
2. According to Bacon's perspective, "knowledge is power." Did Jorif's experiences in school make him feel powerful? Explain.

APPLICATIONS

1. Jorif, an immigrant student from Panama, had to grapple with prejudice in a parochial school in New York City. If you have felt alienated for a similar reason, write a journal entry focusing on your reactions to the experience.
2. Imagine inviting Jorif to join your group discussion on thinking and freedom. What points would you raise with him? What questions would you ask?
3. Jorif's experiences in elementary school took place in the 1950s. To what extent would a Panamanian student today encounter a more friendly environment? What factors would you cite to support your point of view?

Dancing Geckos

TOM MONTGOMERY-FATE

Tom Montgomery-Fate (b. 1960) grew up in a small town in Iowa. Currently a professor of English at College of DuPage in Glen Ellyn, Illinois, he is the author of four books of nonfiction. The most recent is Steady and Trembling *(2005). His work has appeared in* The Boston Globe, The Chicago Tribune, *in many literary journals and magazines, and has aired on National Public Radio. This essay comes from the year he spent teaching English in Laoag, a rice-farming community in the Ilocos region of the Philippines.*

The Malay peoples of the Philippine Islands, whose ancestors probably migrated from Southeast Asia, were mostly hunters, fishermen, and farmers. The archipelago was visited by Magellan in 1521. The Spanish founded Manila in 1571. The Islands, named for King Philip II of Spain, were ceded by Spain to the United States for $20 million in 1898 following the Spanish-American War.

Japan attacked the Philippines on December 8, 1941, and occupied the Islands during World War II. On July 4, 1946, independence was proclaimed in accordance with an act of Congress and a republic was established. In 1972, President Ferdinand Marcos declared martial law. He then instituted a new constitution. In 1983, after bitter elections and demonstrations, Marcos and his wife fled the country. Corazon Aquino, widow of an opponent of the Marcos', was elected president. Her government was plagued by economic problems and widespread poverty, Communist and Muslim insurgents, and ineffective military support. An attempted coup in 1989 was thwarted, and in 1992 Fidel Ramos was elected president. The United States vacated the Subic Bay Naval Station in 1992, ending its long military presence in the Philippines. An autonomous Muslim region was established in 1996, formally ending a rebellion that had lasted for 25 years and cost 120,000 lives.

Attentiveness without aim is the supreme form of prayer.

—Simone Weil

THE SLOW PACE OF MY ACCULTURATION in Laoag resulted in a daily life full of misperception and miscommunication. I laughed when I should have been looking serious and concerned. I looked serious and concerned when I should have been laughing. I closed doors that should have been left open. I had answers to questions that no one asked. In my naiveté, I was often painfully (for others) direct and honest. I was drowning in a sea of languages. Some were verbal. I was disappointed that people didn't use the phrases or pronunciations I had learned in language school, or that they wanted to practice their broken English with a native speaker, rather than struggle with our broken Ilokano. The college had furnished an overly large, dark, cement and wood house, with little furniture and bars over all of the windows. When we suggested that it was too big for two people, we were hushed with knowing smiles. But as was so often the case, we didn't know what they knew. A few days later our respective deans, with big, understanding smiles, gave us each what seemed like a heavy teaching load (five classes, five preparations). There were few books or audiovisual aids. Much of the time there was no electricity. You had to bring your own chalk and eraser. The classrooms were large and noisy. It was hot.

Eventually another teacher and four students moved in with us and we realized that the house was not too big, but just right. We also discovered that we *did* have a light teaching load, as many of our colleagues taught seven or even eight classes. We learned how to teach with few books and occasional electricity. We learned more about language, the non-verbal kind. And we became more patient spectacles, less flustered by our undeserved and undesired celebrity status.

The clusters of children that buzzed around me on the way to school still made me uneasy, but only because their perpetual pointing, laughing, and staring reminded me that I was a permanent outsider. The ironic thing was that while I wanted to be an "insider," to be accepted and included, to get beyond cordiality, I simultaneously longed for a U.S. brand of privacy, for a place to hide. As I became more consumed by these competing desires, I tried to slow down and quietly wade into the culture. I tried to talk with *bibingka* (sweet rice treats) vendors in my mangled Ilokano. I asked a rice farmer to show me how to plant seedlings. Though underqualified, I agreed to teach a guitar class at the college. There were eleven students and three guitars. One stayed in tune. We still made music. I stopped avoiding the gawking children. My frustration evolved into curiosity. What did they think of the lanky *puraw* ("*white*") who walked twice as fast as everyone else? Could they tell that I didn't always know where I was going or what I would say or do when I arrived? What did they suspect? What did they see? We watched each other, and we both wondered what *the other* saw.

I watched a sea of black-haired kids suck mango seeds white, stick-tease rats and chickens, fall asleep in the *jeepney*, rock-flatten bottle caps, float sandals in the sewer, lay down on the backs of enormous *carabao*, dangle from the *balete* tree, play basketball barefoot on the hot, cracked cement, buy warm, brown paper sacks of *pan de sal* at dawn at the bakery, and hug them all the way home to their mothers.

I began to understand their curiosity as an invitation to participate in their culture, as a reminder that my curiosity had dried up. I knew that if I was going to make it here I would need to become more like them: to ask more questions, to live in the present tense, to depend whole-heartedly on others. Like so many of my other Filipino mentors, the children reminded me that I would best adapt to Ilokano culture not by trying to "help," but by sharing my cross-cultural ignorance. The children were teaching me a central tenet of cross-cultural work: *vulnerability is not weakness*.

• • •

One morning I went over to the college for my usual 10:00 class and discovered that a.m. classes were canceled. This had happened before. Sometimes I knew why, sometimes I didn't. With the gift of a free morning, and a bit frustrated by the seeming randomness of our daily lives, I decided to make a list of things to accomplish that day. Overly intent on my blank notepad, I didn't notice a battalion of red ants which had rerouted its march across my desk in search of a cracker and smear of peanut butter beneath my papers. A sharp bite brought me back to the present moment. I cleaned the mess up and wiped off the ants, but then noticed more on the window sill. Dozens of disordered ant platoons obsessively marching toward who knows what. They constantly bumped into each other and knocked each other out of the way without apology or pause. Many literally walked on the backs of others in order to get to wherever they were going more quickly. They frequently reversed direction without reason or warning—movement without meaning—busyness as virtue. I decided these ants were from Chicago, my home. They belonged on Michigan Avenue at rush hour—thousands of arms and legs propelling determined, yet oblivious bodies toward unknown destinations.

I stopped my list of "things to do" and looked beyond the ants out the window. A scraggly, tailless, yellow cat had crawled on an adjacent window sill, apparently stalking something on the roof just below us. I looked closer. The cat was watching a large lizard, which was watching a large cockroach, which sensing the lizard suddenly set off in a menacing waddle and disappeared over the edge of the roof. The lizard followed. The cat didn't. At that moment I turned to see if anyone was watching me. Convinced that no one was, I started on my list: write cross-cult education report, scrub out water tank, pick up gas tank for stove, Xerox articles for classes, shopping at market.

Satisfied that my list was long enough, I dutifully started in. The first item was to write an essay analyzing the "challenges of a cross-cultural educator" for an education journal in the U.S. I plugged in the typewriter. There was no electricity. There was the first challenge. I dug out a legal pad and pencil and began to scratch out some ideas.

Initially, the central challenge of teaching in a radically different culture is accepting the fact that you are much more student than teacher. The challenge is not to "teach the material" but to learn how to open yourself to the ways the students can teach you about their culture and about how to teach in their culture. This requires paying compassionate attention. Let go of the future tense. Trust the possibility of the present.

Too vague. The editors wanted concrete anecdotes that could serve as cross-cultural parables about teaching. I started over. Another attempt:

Many of my students arrive in Laoag after a day or two of jeepney and bus travel from their tribal communities in the mountains. They bring hundred pound sacks of rice on their backs to sustain them for the fifteen week term. Some bring chickens and cabbages and coconuts. One student told me he was living on rice, marunggay fruit (they had a tree behind his boarding house) and two cans of sardines a week. He wasn't complaining though. He had invited me for lunch and wanted to "warn" me about what we'd be having. This student, like some others I knew, viewed each class, each hour in school, as a gift, as a possibility. He had to assume this present tense orientation because he was never sure how long he would be in college—another week, another month, another quarter? It depended on his aunt, who was a domestic worker in Hong Kong. She sent the tuition for the first term, but not for the second. He left for Manila to try and find work. He couldn't, so returned to his home province, to subsistence farming with his father—an increasingly difficult life.
At the college where I teach in the states my students are mostly middle class. Most always knew they would go to college. It's a given, a necessary hoop. Campus issues often concern parking policies and computer accessibility. Many students struggle financially, but few with day to day survival. Most find the cost of a community college affordable. They can think more long term.

I wasn't satisfied with this either. It's oversimplified. My students in the U.S. struggle too, but in different ways. Many have been recently downsized out of jobs. What's "middle class" anymore? I haven't the slightest idea. I was getting frustrated.

I looked up to see two geckos shaking the screen in their endless frenzies to go nowhere. Like the ants their movement seemed pointless, accomplishing nothing, a life reduced to a few thousand push button scrambles. They'd dart to the rusty perimeter then return to non-rest, to nervous pause. They'd flypaper-tongue a mosquito, contemplate a patched hole, fail to squeeze through a crack, then return to nervous pause.

Sometimes I felt like a gecko in Laoag. I had tremendous energy and desire to move, and I did. I was busy, or at least tried to look busy, but it all seemed meaningless. During one of these frustrating periods I remember reading Masao Takenaka's *God is Rice*. He helped me better understand the limits of modern "western" culture.

> We live an increasingly hectic life and we are busy with much busyness. The character for "busy" in Chinese writing, which Koreans and Japanese also use, literally means "to destroy one's heart." If we are too busy we forget what is most important. It is interesting that the same components of the character for busy are used to indicate forgetfulness. Both mean the destruction of ones heart.[1]

When we are "busy" completing our list of tasks, we forget to pay attention to things that matter. Our heart may be destroyed by our preoccupation, our inner drive to control time and life.

Ironically, I had perceived the opportunity to go to the Philippines in part as a chance to live "out of control" or with someone else in control, who wouldn't and couldn't expect too much from me, precisely because I didn't fit in. It was my way of losing my life in order to find it. But when I arrived, adapting to Ilokano culture often seemed less difficult than the simultaneous process of coming to terms with ingrained U.S. culture. Despite my best intentions, when I arrived in Laoag I immediately sought responsibility, a role, a means of self definition—tasks to keep me busy, which I could somehow use to measure my success or failure.

Takenaka reminded me that the cross-cultural education process continues whether we want it to or not, whether we are "busy" or not. "Meaning" is not easily measured, and it may come most readily in the

[1]Masao Takenaka, *God is Rice: Asian Culture and Faith* (Geneva: World Council of Churches, 1986), p. 8.

times when we are least busy. "Being" may be more important than "doing" in the new culture. Some doing might come later, or it might not. The meaning of the cross-cultural education might reveal itself in the future tense, but only if we pay attention and risk vulnerability in the now, in the present.

What am I supposed to do here? What is my role? How will my skills fit in? What will I accomplish? How will I know if I'm successful? These were the questions that cluttered my mind during the first few months in Laoag.

I later found a different set of questions to be more helpful: Am I listening? What do I hear? How can I listen more carefully? Am I watching? What do I see? I kept watching the geckos, their entropic dashing, their delicate chaos. I blocked out the lure of the notepad, my list of potential accomplishments, and focused. Slowly, over the next hour, I began to notice redundant movements and pauses. These evolved into several patterns which slowly became clear, even obvious. By noon, a crawling intricacy, a prehistoric choreography, a short-circuited waltz, had revealed itself in an unending string of cold-blooded encores. They continued despite my silent ovations, and long after I left for my 1:00 class.

INTERPRETATIONS

1. The author experiences several cross-cultural dilemmas including privacy and community, being and doing. How does he resolve them? Can you think of other strategies that might have helped him to adapt more readily?

2. Montgomery-Fate says he sometimes "feels like a gecko." What does he mean? Is this an accurate comparison in light of the rest of the essay? Explain.

3. Characterize the author's relationship with his students. To what extent does it change during his stay?

4. Review the author's second attempt to encapsulate his experience for the education journal in the United States. To what extent does his description of American students apply to you? Explain.

CORRESPONDENCES

1. Review Reid's perspective on curiosity and discuss its relevance to Montgomery-Fate's essay.

2. Review Atwood's perspective and apply it to the author's experiences in "Dancing Geckos."

APPLICATIONS

1. Write a journal entry on the relevance of the idea that "vulnerability is not weakness" in your life and/or in the wider world.

2. Discuss with your group what the author learned from reading *God is Rice*. What role does being busy play in your lives? How do you respond to the Asian concept that busyness means "to destroy the heart."

3. The author's struggle is not adapting to the new culture, but accepting his new understanding of his culture of origin—ingrained U.S. culture. Write a short essay reflecting on this irony in light of your own experience in other cultures, and/or the perspective of other cross-cultural writers in this text.

The Lesson

TONI CADE BAMBARA

Toni Cade Bambara (1939–1995) grew up in New York City, deeply conscious of the inequities of race and class. She graduated from Queens College in 1959 and received her M.A. from City College of New York. Her publications include Gorilla, My Love *(1972),* The Sea Birds Are Still Alive *(1977), and* The Salt Eaters *(1980). This is how she perceived her role as a writer:*

> *Stories are important. They keep us alive. In the ships, in the camps, in the quarters, fields, prisons, on the road, on the run, underground, under siege, in the throes, on the verge—the storyteller snatches us back from the edge to hear the next chapter in which we are the subjects. We, the hero of the tales. Our lives preserved. How it was, how it be. Passing it along in the relay. That is what I work to do, to produce stories that save our lives.*

As you read "The Lesson," set in New York City, pay particular attention to Bambara's use of dialogue.

BACK IN THE DAYS when everyone was old and stupid or young and foolish and me and Sugar were the only ones just right, this lady moved on our block with nappy hair and proper speech and no makeup. And quite naturally we laughed at her, laughed the way we did at the junk man who went about his business like he was some big-time president and his sorry-ass horse his secretary. And we kinda hated her too, hated the way we did the winos who cluttered up our parks and pissed on our handball walls and stank up our hallways and stairs so you couldn't halfway play hide-and-seek without a goddamn gas mask. Miss Moore was her name. The only woman on the block with no first name. And she was black as hell, cept for her feet, which were fish-white and spooky. And she was always planning these boring-ass things for us to do, us being my cousin, mostly, who lived on the block cause we all moved North the same time and to the same apartment then spread out gradual to breathe. And our parents would yank our heads into some kinda shape and crisp up our clothes so we'd be presentable for travel with Miss Moore, who always looked like she was going to church, though she never did. Which is just one of things the grownups talked about when they talked behind her back like a dog. But when she came calling with some sachet she'd sewed up or some gingerbread she'd made or some book, why then they'd all be too embarrassed to turn her down and we'd get handed over all spruced up. She'd been to college and said it was only right that she should take responsibility for the young ones' education, and she not even related by marriage or blood. So they'd go for it. Specially Aunt Gretchen. She was the main gofer in the family. You got some old dumb shit foolishness you want somebody to go for, you send for Aunt Gretchen. She been screwed into the go-along for so long, it's a blood-deep natural thing with her. Which is how she got saddled with me and Sugar and Junior in the first place while our mothers were in a la-de-da apartment up the block having a good ole time.

So this one day Miss Moore rounds us all up at the mailbox and it's puredee hot and she's knockin herself out about arithmetic. And school suppose to let up in the summer I heard, but she don't never let up. And the starch in my pinafore scratching the shit outta me and I'm really hating this nappy-head bitch and her goddamn college degree. I'd much rather go to the pool or to the show where it's cool. So me and Sugar leaning on the mailbox being surly, which is a Miss Moore word. And Flyboy checking out what everybody brought for lunch. And Fat Butt already wasting his peanut-butter-and-jelly sandwich like the pig he is. And Junebug punchin on Q. T.'s arm for potato chips. And Rosie Giraffe shifting from one hip to the other waiting for somebody to step on her foot or ask if she from Georgia so she can kick ass, preferably Mercedes'. And Miss Moore asking us do we know what money is, like we a bunch of retards. I mean real money, she say, like it's only poker chips or monopoly papers we lay on the grocer. So right away I'm tired of this and say so. And would much rather snatch Sugar and go to the Sunset and terrorize the West Indian kids and take their hair ribbons and their money too. And Miss Moore files that remark away for next week's lesson on brotherhood, I can tell. And finally I say we oughta get to the subway cause it's cooler and besides we might meet some cute boys. Sugar done swiped her mama's lipstick, so we ready.

So we heading down the street and she's boring us silly about what things cost and what our parents make and how much goes for rent and how money ain't divided up right in this country. And then she get to the part about we all poor and live in the slums, which I don't feature. And I'm ready to speak on that, but she steps out in the street and hails two cabs just like that. Then she hustles half the crew in with her and hands me a five-dollar bill and tells me to calculate 10 percent tip for the driver. And we're off. Me and Sugar and Junebug and Flyboy hanging out the window and hollering to everybody, putting lipstick on each other cause Flyboy a faggot anyway, and making farts with our sweaty armpits. But I'm mostly trying to figure how to spend this money. But they all fascinated with the meter ticking and Junebug starts laying bets as to how much it'll read when Flyboy can't hold his breath no more. Then Sugar lay bets as to how much it'll be when we get there. So I'm stuck. Don't nobody want to go for my plan, which is to jump out at the next light and run off to the first bar-b-que we can find. Then the driver tells us to get the hell out cause we there already. And the meter reads eight-five cents. And I'm stalling to figure out the tip and Sugar say give him a dime. And I decided he don't need it bad as I do, so later for him. But then he tries to take off with Junebug foot still in the door so we talk about his mama something ferocious. Then we check out that we on Fifth Avenue and everybody dressed up in stockings. One lady in a fur coat, hot as it is. White folks crazy.

"This is the place," Miss Moore say, presenting it to us in the voice she uses at the museum. "Let's look in the windows before we go in."

"Can we steal?" Sugar asks very serious like she's getting the ground rules squared away before she plays. "I beg your pardon," say Miss Moore, and we fall out. So she leads us around the windows of the toy store and me and Sugar screamin, "This is mine, that's mine, I gotta have that, that was made for me, I was born for that," till Big Butt drowns us out.

"Hey, I'm goin to buy that there."

"That there? You don't even know what it is, stupid."

"I do so," he say punchin on Rosie Giraffe. "It's a microscope."

"Whatcha gonna do with a microscope, fool?"

"Look at things."

"Like what, Ronald?" ask Miss Moore. And Big Butt ain't got the first notion. So here go Miss Moore gabbing about the thousands of bacteria in a drop of water and the somethinorother in a speck of blood and the million and one living things in the air around us is invisible to the naked eye. And what she say that for? Junebug go to town on that "naked" and we rolling. Then Miss Moore ask what it cost. So we all jam into the window smudgin it up and the price tag say $300. So then she ask how long'd take for Big Butt and Junebug to save up their allowances. "Too long," I say. "Yeh," adds Sugar, "outgrown it by that time." And Miss Moore say no, you never outgrow learning instruments. "Why, even medical students and interns and," blah, blah, blah. And we ready to choke Big Butt for bringing it up in the first damn place.

"This here costs four hundred eighty dollars," say Rosie Giraffe. So we pile up all over her to see what she pointin out. My eyes tell me it's a chunk of glass cracked with something heavy, and different-color inks dripped into the splits, then the whole thing put into a oven or something. But for $480 it don't make sense.

"That's a paperweight made of semi-precious stones fused together under tremendous pressure," she explains slowly, with her hands doing the mining and all the factory work.

"So what's a paperweight?" asks Rosie Giraffe.

"To weigh paper with, dumbbell," say Flyboy, the wise man from the East.

"Not exactly," say Miss Moore, which is what she say when you warm or way off too. "It's to weigh paper down so it won't scatter and make your desk untidy." So right away me and Sugar curtsy to each other and then to Mercedes who is more the tidy type.

"We don't keep paper on top of the desk in my class," say Junebug, figuring Miss Moore crazy or lyin one.

"At home, then," she say. "Don't you have a calendar and a pencil case and a blotter and a letter-opener on your desk at home where you do your homework?" And she know damn well what our homes look like cause she nosys around in them every chance she gets.

"I don't even have a desk," say Junebug. "Do we?"

"No. And I don't get no homework neither," says Big Butt.

"And I don't even have a home," say Flyboy like he do at school to keep the white folks off his back and sorry for him. Send this poor kid to camp posters, is his specialty.

"I do," says Mercedes. "I have a box of stationery on my desk and a picture of my cat. My godmother bought the stationery and the desk. There's a big rose on each sheet and the envelopes smell like roses."

"Who wants to know about your smelly-ass stationery," say Rosie Giraffe fore I can get my two cents in.

"It's important to have a work area all your own so that . . ."

"Will you look at this sailboat, please," say Flyboy, cuttin her off and pointin to the thing like it was his. So once again we tumble all over each other to gaze at this magnificent thing in the toy store which is just big enough to maybe sail two kittens across the pond if you strap them to the posts tight. We all start reciting the price tag like we in assembly. "Handcrafted sailboat of fiberglass at one thousand one hundred ninety-five dollars."

"Unbelievable," I hear myself say and am really stunned. I read it again for myself just in case the group recitation put me in a trance. Same thing. For some reason this pisses me off. We look at Miss Moore and she lookin at us, waiting for I dunno what.

"Who'd pay all that when you can buy a sailboat set for a quarter at Pop's, a tube of glue for a dime, and a ball of string for eight cents? It must have a motor and a whole lot else besides," I say. "My sailboat cost me about fifty cents."

"But will it take water?" say Mercedes with her smart ass.

"Took mine to Alley Pond Park once," say Flyboy. "String broke. Lost it. Pity."

"Sailed mine in Central Park and it keeled over and sank. Had to ask my father for another dollar."

"And you got the strap," laugh Big Butt. "The jerk didn't even have a string on it. My old man wailed on his behind."

Little Q. T. was staring hard at the sailboat and you could see he wanted it bad. But he too little and somebody'd just take it from him. So what the hell. "This boat for kids, Miss Moore?"

"Parents silly to buy something like that just to get all broke up," say Rosie Giraffe.

"That much money it should last forever," I figure.

"My father'd buy it for me if I wanted it."

"Your father, my ass," say Rosie Giraffe getting a chance to finally push Mercedes.

"Must be rich people shop here," say Q. T.

"You are a very bright boy," say Flyboy. "What was your first clue?" And he rap him on the head with the back of his knuckles, since Q. T. the only one he could get away with. Though Q. T. liable to come up behind you years later and get his licks in when you half expect it.

"What I want to know is," I says to Miss Moore though I never talk to her, I wouldn't give the bitch that satisfaction, "is how much a real boat costs? I figure a thousand'd get you a yacht any day?"

"Why don't you check that out," she says, "and report back to the group?" Which really pains my ass. If you gonna mess up a perfectly good swim day least you could do is have some answers. "Let's go in," she say like she got something up her sleeve. Only she don't lead the way. So me and Sugar turn the corner to where the entrance is, but when we get there I kinda hang back. Not that I'm scared, what's there to be afraid of, just a toy store. But I feel funny, shame. But what I got to be shamed about? Got as much right to go in as anybody. But somehow I can't seem to get hold of the door, so I step away for Sugar to lead. But she hangs back too. And I look at her and she looks at me and this is ridiculous. I mean, damn, I have never ever been shy about doing nothing or going nowhere. But then Mercedes steps up and then Rosie Giraffe and Big Butt crowd in behind and shove, and next thing we all stuffed into the door-way with only Mercedes squeezing past us, smoothing out her jumper and walking right down the aisle. Then the rest of us tumble in like a glued-together jigsaw done all wrong. And people lookin at us. And it's like the time me and Sugar crashed into the Catholic church on a dare. But once we got in there and everything so hushed and holy and the candles and the bowin and the handkerchiefs on all the drooping heads, I just couldn't go through with the plan. Which was for me to run up to

the altar and do a tap dance while Sugar played the nose flute and
messed around in the holy waters. And Sugar kept givin me the elbow.
Then later teased me so bad I tied her up in the shower and turned it on
and locked her in. And she'd be there till this day if Aunt Gretchen hadn't
finally figured I was lyin about the boarder takin a shower.

Same thing in the store. We all walkin on tiptoe and hardly touchin
the games and puzzles and things. And I watched Miss Moore who is
steady watchin us like she waiting for a sign. Like Mama Drewery
watches the sky and sniffs the air and takes note of just how much slant
is in the bird formation. Then me and Sugar bump smack into each
other, so busy gazing at the toys, 'specially the sailboat. But we don't
laugh and go into our fat-lady bump-stomach routine. We just stare at
that price tag. Then Sugar run a finger over the whole boat. And I'm
jealous and want to hit her. Maybe not her, but I sure want to punch
somebody in the mouth.

"Watcha bring us here for, Miss Moore?"

"You sound angry, Sylvia. Are you mad about something?" Givin
me one of them grins like she tellin a grown-up joke that never turns out
to be funny. And she's lookin very closely at me like maybe she plannin
to do my portrait from memory. I'm mad, but I won't give her that satisfaction. So I slouch around the store bein very bored and say, "Let's go."

Me and Sugar at the back of the train watchin the tracks whizzin by
large then small then gettin gobbled up in the dark. I'm thinkin about
this tricky toy I saw in the store. A clown that somersaults on a bar then
does chin-ups just cause you yank lightly at his leg. Cost $35. I could see
me askin my mother for a $35 birthday clown. "You wanna who that
costs what?" she'd say, cocking her head to the side to get a better view
of the hole in my head. Thirty-five dollars and the whole household
could go visit Grandaddy Nelson in the country. Thirty-five dollars
would pay for the rent and the piano bill too. Who are these people that
spend that much for performing clowns and $1000 for toy sailboats?
What kinda work they do and how they live and how come we ain't in
on it? Where we are is who we are, Miss Moore always pointin out. But it
don't necessarily have to be that way, she always adds then waits for
somebody to say that poor people have to wake up and demand their
share of the pie and don't none of us know what kind of pie she talkin
about in the first damn place. But she ain't so smart cause I still got her
four dollars from the taxi and she sure ain't gettin it. Messin up my day
with this shit. Sugar nudges me in my pocket and winks.

Miss Moore lines us up in front of the mailbox where we started
from, seem like years ago, and I got a headache for thinkin so hard. And
we lean all over each other so we can hold up under the draggy-ass lecture she always finishes us off with at the end before we thank her for

borin us to tears. But she just looks at us like she readin tea leaves. Finally she say, "Well, what did you think of F. A. O. Schwartz?"

Rosie Giraffe mumbles, "White folks crazy."

"I'd like to go there again when I get my birthday money," says Mercedes, and we shove her out the pack so she has to lean on the mailbox by herself.

"I'd like a shower. Tiring day," say Flyboy.

Then Sugar surprises me by saying, "You know, Miss Moore, I don't think all of us here put together eat in a year what that sailboat costs." And Miss Moore lights up like somebody goosed her. "And?" she say, urging Sugar on. Only I'm standin on her foot so she don't continue.

"Imagine for a minute what kind of society it is in which some people can spend on a toy what it would cost to feed a family of six or seven. What do you think?"

"I think," say Sugar pushing me off her feet like she never done before, cause I whip her ass in a minute, "that this is not much of a democracy if you ask me. Equal chance to pursue happiness means an equal crack at the dough, don't it?" Miss Moore is besides herself and I am disgusted with Sugar's treachery. So I stand on her foot one more time to see if she'll shove me. She shuts up, and Miss Moore looks at me, sorrowfully I'm thinkin. And somethin weird is goin on. I can feel it in my chest.

"Anybody else learn anything today?" lookin dead at me. I walk away and Sugar has to run to catch up and don't even seem to notice when I shrug her arm off my shoulder.

"Well, we got four dollars anyway," she says.

"Uh hunh."

"We could go to Hascombs and get half a chocolate layer and then to the Sunset and still have plenty of money for potato chips and ice cream sodas."

"Uh hunh."

"Race you to Hascombs," she say.

We start down the block and she gets ahead which is O.K. by me cause I'm goin to the West End and then over the Drive to think this day through. She can run if she want to and even run faster. But ain't nobody gonna beat me at nuthin.

INTERPRETATIONS

1. What does Miss Moore hope to accomplish during the class outing? What lesson does she want to teach? Do you agree that the lesson needs teaching? Why? Has Miss Moore chosen an effective method of teaching?

2. What evidence is there that this outing is only the latest in a series of attempts to teach a lesson and that the children already know what they are expected to "learn"? How does that repetition affect your reaction to Sylvia's irritation at Sugar's "treachery" in saying what Sugar believes to be the lesson: "Equal chance to pursue happiness means an equal crack at the dough, don't it?" Has Sylvia failed to understand the lesson or is she irritated at the repetition?

3. Although Sylvia says "I'm mad," she will not admit her anger to Miss Moore. Why not? Does Sylvia know what has made her angry? Do we know?

4. Why do you think Miss Moore never demands change due her from the narrator?

5. What do you consider the more important element of this story, the lesson itself or the personalities and/or attitudes of the three or four main characters? Why?

CORRESPONDENCES

1. Review the Frost perspective on education and discuss its relevance to "The Lesson."

2. McDonald and Bambara focus on learning experiences that occur outside of the classroom. Discuss with your group what you learned about the relation between education and experiences.

APPLICATIONS

1. Working with your group, create a short profile of Sylvia's current life. What is she doing? What has she achieved? To what extent did she benefit from or rebel against Miss Moore?

2. According to fiction writer Grace Paley, "If you say what's on your mind in the language that comes to you from your parents and your street and friends you'll probably say something beautiful." Write an essay showing the extent to which "The Lesson" supports Paley's point of view.

3. According to Miss Moore, "where we are is who we are." To what extent do you agree? Do you consider yourself the product of your social class? What other factors have contributed to who you are?

4. When you are with your friends, listen carefully to their conversation. Pay attention to the words they use and the rhythms of their sentences. What kind of vocabulary is used? How does the

conversation flow? Does one person always wait for another to cease speaking? Do your friends stick to one topic? If possible, take notes of what is being said and how it is being said. Next, take your notes and memories and use them to create a dialogue between two characters that you have invented. How does the conversation that you have created compare with the dialogue presented in Bambara's story?

The Mistress of Make Believe

DORIS VILORIA

Doris Viloria (b. 1972) was brought up and educated in Queens, New York, and is a graduate of Queens College–City University of New York (CUNY). As you read Viloria's essay, find evidence to support her introductory paragraph.

SHE WAS HUGE, but in a majestic awe-inspiring way like a mountain that only added to her enigma. The word fat never came to mind.

"Good morning class," she'd briskly salute each day, as she marched in on stiletto heels. Her hair would be piled high on her head, in a fountain of honey blond and gray tendrils that was most undoubtedly dyed. The heady scent of lilacs drenched the room as she entered; a tornado of fragrances, heavy make-up, and shopping bags, her gaudy jewelry sending out smart metallic clinks. She always squeezed herself into tight "form fitting" cashmere turtlenecks, which emphasized her rather copious stomach and voluptuous bosom and created the illusion of a kind of fanciful, woman-caterpillar hybrid. Then shifting her bulk considerably, she would sit atop her tall, rickety wooden swivel chair, crossing her legs jauntily, and bringing one polished long red fingernail to her lips. As her meaty arms settled on her lectern, one perfectly tweezed eyebrow languidly drifted up like a cobra, contemplating the class.

"Aaah," she'd purr in her thick coppery, baritone New England accent, as she towered over us, her mouth curling up in a sly grin. "How many of you are ready to let your imagination take you off to distant mystical lands?"

Together we explored the unbridled savagery of William Golding's *The Lord of the Flies*, the silent yearnings and personal betrayals of John Knowles' *A Separate Peace*, and the coming of age in the heart of injustice of a young girl in Harper Lee's *To Kill a Mockingbird*. Golding's desolate, desperate island sprang to life as she needled us with questions.

"Is man simply a beast temporarily tamed by years of affecting proper etiquette, whose mask might drop if taken out of his 'civilized' environment?" she'd fire at us. "How would any of you react if placed in a jungle where your actions were accountable to no one? Would you aspire to rule as a belligerent dictator, or would you struggle to maintain your moralistic humanity and preserve democracy?"

Having thus spat out these challenges she would take a long draught of steaming black coffee from her styrofoam cup, leaving a sharp stain of fuschia lipstick on the rim. Then in a smokey, hypnotic tone she would read a passage from the book. The mood became trance-like as we followed her into the story. Afterwards, those characters would linger about the room like inspirational phantoms as I slaved over my writing assignment.

Creating solely on pure instinct and guided by the illuminations of those benevolent daimons, I wrote a short story based on a gripping terrifying nightmare I'd had. It was as though I had exorcised all the horrors of my dream from myself, and they had metamorphosized into a story that had a life of its own. With a feeling of deep-seated pride and accomplishment, I turned it in.

Walking out of class one day, I heard that unmistakable voice ask for a moment of my time. I was brimming with curiosity as I approached her desk. Those penetrating blue eyes gazed at me with a mixture of respect and mischief. Tapping my story gently on her desk, she inclined that lion's mane of a head to the side and whispered in a close and confidential way, "Where did it come from?"

My eyes darted about the room as I searched for some response. Finally, I turned to her levelly and said honestly, "It just sort of wove itself."

Nodding her head in understanding after what seemed like an hour, she handed me the paper. "It really is very special," she said with a sigh. "You have a way with words that is a talent, a gift. I expect you to be a woman of great individual distinction."

Those words have bolstered me like iron saviors through countless fits of self-doubt and introspection over the past few years. I walked out of the room that day with charmed visions of exquisitely soaring dragonflies before me. The spell has never waned.

INTERPRETATIONS

1. What scene and what group of people do you assume the author to be describing? How effective is that description? What purpose does the description seem intended to serve?

2. How do you interpret the question "Where did it [the story] come from?" How important to the meaning of the essay is this question?

3. How would this essay be affected if the story itself were included or appended here?

4.   The last paragraph is perhaps the most important in terms of the meaning of the essay. Comment on the effectiveness of saving this information until the end.

CORRESPONDENCES

1.   Review Moore's perspective. How does it apply to Viloria's educational experience? How many "enchanting" minds are there in her essay?

2.   Review Borges's perspective on books. To what extent does it apply to Viloria's essay? To your own experiences with reading?

APPLICATIONS

1.   Viloria is excited by using language effectively. You may be creative in another medium, such as photography, music, art, or dance. Write an essay describing your creative process and the emotions it evokes.

2.   Write a journal entry describing the teacher from whom you learned most. Recreate the classroom environment. How was it conducive to learning? Describe a learning activity that excited you.

3.   Write a journal entry comparing and contrasting an experience with reading or writing that took place outside of the classroom. How was it different from reading or writing in school?

4.   Notice Viloria's use of details in this essay. From her description, create a drawing of "The Mistress of Make Believe." Which details in the text have you focused upon in your artwork?

From Dropout to Graduate

LAURA KUEHN

Laura Kuehn (b. 1976) was raised in Ellisville, Illinois and graduated from high school in 1994. She moved to New York City in 2000 and two years later enrolled in Queensborough Community College (CUNY). After a two-year break in her studies, she graduated with an Associate in Arts degree with honors from Queensborough and will continue her studies for the B.A. degree at Queens College (CUNY). She hopes that her essay will encourage students returning to college after a break in their studies.

WHEN I WAS FOURTEEN AND A FRESHMAN in high school, I, like many of my classmates, began thinking of college. Of course, back then my expectations weren't so much on academics as they were on other things. College was all about experiencing the first taste of parental freedom, meeting new and interesting people, late night cram sessions, and most importantly . . . partying! Or so that's how my girlfriends and I imagined it to be. However, many years would pass, long after graduating high school, before I would get my chance at college. And when I finally got there, the last thing on my mind was partying.

Soon after high school, even before I was eighteen, I moved out of my family's home to live with my boyfriend. A couple of years later he and I would be married with a mortgage. I suppose I could have gone to college then, but between taking care of a husband, a home, and maintaining my two part-time jobs I was exhausted. But that's what happens. Looking back, it seems to me that the longer I waited to attend college the bigger the obstacles were to get there. Before I knew it I was in my mid-twenties, divorced, bankrupt, and uneducated. I had been through a slew of dead-end jobs and was all out frustrated. That's when I packed up and moved to New York City. Luck was on my side though, and within several months I was managing a successful yet small club in Manhattan, so I decided to consider college again.

After years of being out of high school I was terrified of the thought of college. It no longer was about the social aspect, but rather the academics. I can still recall vividly the day a good friend went with me to check out a college campus. I became so consumed with self doubt that I had a full blown anxiety attack. My friend sat with me in the parking lot as my tears flowed and listened to me profess my ineptitude. But

I mustarded up the courage and a month later took the entrance exam to my local community college. To my own amazement I scored quite well on portions of the exam.

In the spring of 2001, almost seven years after high school, I began attending my first college courses at Queensborough Community College. I was exempted from English 101 and allowed to immediately take English 102 Honors. I also took a simple math course. I was thrilled! And I was overwhelmed! My first semester of college only seemed to prove what I had feared all along. My full-time job that paid the bills was a priority and it left virtually no time for my studies. I endured that first semester and barely scraped by one more. Consequently, I finished out my second semester and begrudgingly left my newfound college life behind.

So, for a while, I accepted things as they were. And at first things were good. I had a good paying job and could afford a better life. But as the years went by I realized that I had peaked. I saw no advancement. No ladder of success to climb higher and higher. I managed that club for over three and a half years and never once requested vacation time. I was never late and sometimes worked twelve hour shifts. Why? Because I was scared. Without an education to back me up I was afraid to lose the job. I was trapped. And miserable. Once again I found myself thinking of college, but this time things would be different. Nothing was going to get in my way. I prepared myself for a rough road ahead.

I registered for two courses in the spring of 2004. I studied hard and did well. Yet I knew I needed to make some drastic changes if I was going to make my second attempt at college work. So that fall I quit my job and focused all my energy on school. By the end of the fall 2004 semester I was on the dean's list and accepted back into the Honor's program. To pay the bills I did whatever odd job would fit into my school schedule. One day I'd be tending bar or waiting tables and the next I'd be doing makeup or hair for a photo shoot. It didn't matter as long as I could study.

The further I got into my school career the more excited I became. Sure I was poorer, lonelier, and more frustrated than ever! But I was happier than ever. In the spring of 2006 I graduated with honors from Queensborough Community College with an associate's degree in liberal arts and sciences. To some it may seem minuscule, but to me it was empowering.

Soon I will be starting classes at Queens College and I plan on continuing my academic success. Things are much different than when I first began QCC. Now I know my own strength and determination, and I have confidence in myself. I agreed to write this essay about my journey because I know that I'm not alone. There are countless others like myself who deprive themselves of an education because they think it's too late. As adults, we have jobs, spouses, children, bills, and many other responsibilities that we can't simply overlook. However, we also have a responsibility to ourselves. I can't say where I'll be in five years (who can?), but I do know that my chances of having a better life are greater with an education. My college experience thus far has had a positive effect. I know, without any doubt, that every sacrifice I've made or will make has been worth it. My education is priceless to me. It is something that no one can take away.

INTERPRETATIONS

1. Why did Kuehn drop out of college? Why did she return?
2. How did Kuehn approach college the first time she enrolled? How about the second time? What similarities and/or differences do you notice?
3. How does Kuehn feel after completing her associate's degree?

CORRESPONDENCES

1. What might Kuehn have learned from reading Torres's "A Letter to a Child Like Me"?
2. Kuehn's essay is in certain ways a literacy narrative. How does her story compare with those of Marshall (page 196) and Cremona (page 206)?

APPLICATIONS

1. How did you decide to enroll in college? Write your story!
    Try to clarify in your narrative your motives and motivations for attending college, your expectations of it, and the realities you encountered in your first semester. How does your story compare with Kuehn's?
2. What must a student have to succeed in college?
    Make a list of five characteristics that you think are most important. Compare these items with those on the lists of the members of your peer group. What three characteristics can you all agree on? Be prepared to explain to your whole class why these three qualities are essential.
3. Some people think it best that all students take a year off before attending college. What do you think of this idea? As you present your reasons in an essay, explain what you might have done in that year between high school and college.

Literacy Narratives

The literacy narratives of Paule Marshall and Vincent Cremona involve metaphor—a figure of speech that makes an implicit comparison between two dissimilar things. Metaphor is complex, inventive, subtle, and powerful. It can transform people, places, objects, and ideas into whatever the writer imagines them to be. Successful metaphors make it possible for us as readers to "see" things in new ways. What is your response, for example, to the metaphor that "the heart is a lonely hunter"? In Paule Marshall's narrative, her poets inform us that "the sea ain' got no back door," while Vincent Cremona transforms a familiar metaphor from the workplace into one that describes his writing style. As you read their narratives, think of a metaphor that you might use to describe your writing.

---

from Poets in the Kitchen

PAULE MARSHALL

Paule Marshall (b. 1929 in Brooklyn, New York) learned storytelling from her mother, a native of Barbados, whose West Indian friends used to gather in Marshall's home after a hard day of "scrubbing floor." She graduated from Brooklyn College in 1953 and received a Guggenheim fellowship in 1960. She was a librarian in New York City public libraries before working for Our World, *a popular 1950s African-American magazine. In 1959, Marshall's first novel* Brown Girl, Brownstones *was published. The novel is set in what Marshall calls "Bajan [Barbadian] Brooklyn" and according to one reader, expresses "in a lyrical, powerful language a culturally distinct and expansive world." Marshall's other novels include* Soul Clap Hands and Sing *(1961),* The Chosen Place, The Timeless People *(1969),* Praisesong for the Widow *(1983), and* Daughters *(1991). Her most recent novel,* The Fisher King, *for which she received the Dos Passos Prize for Literature, was published in 2000. In 1992 she became a MacArthur Fellow. She has been a lecturer on black literature and a teacher of creative writing at numerous universities, and is currently a professor of English at New York University.*

The history of Barbados, the most easterly of the West Indies, begins with the arrival of an English ship in 1605 and with British settlers at the uninhabited island in 1627. Slavery was abolished in 1834. The island, eighty percent of whose population of 256,000 is of African descent, declared its independence from Britain in 1966 but remains within the Commonwealth.

Some years ago, when I was teaching a graduate seminar in fiction at Columbia University, a well-known male novelist visited my class to speak on his development as a writer. In discussing his formative years, he didn't realize it but he seriously endangered his life by remarking that women writers are luckier than those of his sex because they usually spend so much time as children around their mothers and their mothers' friends in the kitchen.

What did he say that for? The women students immediately forgot about being in awe of him and began readying their attack for the question and answer period later on. Even I bristled. There again was that awful image of women locked away from the world in the kitchen with only each other to talk to, and their daughters locked in with them.

But my guest wasn't really being sexist or trying to be provocative or even spoiling for a fight. What he meant—when he got around to examining himself more fully—was that, given the way children are (or were) raised in our society, with little girls kept closer to home and their mothers, the women writer stands a better chance of being exposed, while growing up, to the kind of talk that goes on among women, more often than not in the kitchen; and that this experience gives her an edge over her male counterpart by instilling in her an appreciation for ordinary speech.

It was clear that my guest lecturer attached great importance to this, which is understandable. Common speech and the plain, workaday words that make it up are, after all, the stock in trade of some of the best fiction writers. They are the principal means by which a character in a novel or story reveals himself and gives voice sometimes to profound feelings and complex ideas about himself and the world. Perhaps the proper measure of a writer's talent is his skill in rendering everyday speech—when it is appropriate to his story—as well as his ability to tap, to exploit, the beauty, poetry and wisdom it often contains.

"If you say what's on your mind in the language that comes to you from your parents and your street and friends you'll probably say something beautiful." Grace Paley[1] tells this, she says, to her students at the beginning of every writing course.

It's all a matter of exposure and a training of the ear for the would-be writer in those early years of his or her apprenticeship. And, according to

[1]Contemporary American fiction writer.

my guest lecturer, this training, the best of it, often takes place in as unglamorous a setting as the kitchen.

He didn't know it, but he was essentially describing my experience as a little girl. I grew up among poets. Now they didn't look like poets—whatever that breed is supposed to look like. Nothing about them suggested that poetry was their calling. They were just a group of ordinary housewives and mothers, my mother included, who dressed in a way (shapeless housedresses, dowdy felt hats and long, dark, solemn coats) that made it impossible for me to imagine they had ever been young.

Nor did they do what poets were supposed to do—spend their days in an attic room writing verses. They never put pen to paper except to write occasionally to their relatives in Barbados. "I take my pen in hand hoping these few lines will find you in health as they leave me fair for the time being," was the way their letters invariably began. Rather, their day was spent "scrubbing floor," as they described the work they did.

Several mornings a week these unknown bards would put an apron and a pair of old house shoes in a shopping bag and take the train or streetcar from our section of Brooklyn out to Flatbush. There, those who didn't have steady jobs would wait on certain designated corners for the white housewives in the neighborhood to come along and bargain with them over pay for a day's work cleaning their houses. This was the ritual even in the winter.

Later, armed with the few dollars they had earned, which in their vocabulary became "a few raw-mouth pennies," they made their way back to our neighborhood, where they would sometimes stop off to have a cup of tea or cocoa together before going home to cook dinner for their husbands and children.

The basement kitchen of the brownstone house where my family lived was the usual gathering place. Once inside the warm safety of its walls the women threw off the drab coats and hats, seated themselves at the large center table, drank their cups of tea or cocoa, and talked. While my sister and I sat at a smaller table over in a corner doing our homework, they talked—endlessly, passionately, poetically, and with impressive range. No subject was beyond them. True, they would indulge in the usual gossip: whose husband was running with whom, whose daughter looked slightly "in the way" (pregnant) under her bridal gown as she walked down the aisle. That sort of thing. But they also tackled the great issues of the time. They were always, for example, discussing the state of the economy. It was the mid and late 30s then, and the aftershock of the Depression, with its soup lines and suicides on Wall Street, was still being felt.

Some people, they declared, didn't know how to deal with adversity. They didn't know that you had to "tie up your belly" (hold in the pain, that is) when things got rough and go on with life. They took their image from the bellyband that is tied around the stomach of a newborn baby to keep the navel pressed in.

They talked politics. Roosevelt was their hero. He had come along and rescued the country with relief and jobs, and in gratitude they christened their sons Franklin and Delano and hoped they would live up to the names.

If F. D. R. was their hero, Marcus Garvey was their God. The name of the fiery, Jamaican-born black nationalist of the '20s was constantly invoked around the table. For he had been their leader when they first came to the United States from the West Indies shortly after World War I. They had contributed to his organization, the United Negro Improvement Association (UNIA), out of their meager salaries, bought shares in his ill-fated Black Star Shipping Line, and at the height of the movement they had marched as members of his "nurses' brigade" in their white uniforms on Seventh Avenue in Harlem during the great Garvey Day parades. Garvey: He lived on through the power of their memories.

And their talk was of war and rumors of wars. They raged against World War II when it broke out in Europe, blaming it on the politicians. "It's these politicians. They're the ones always starting up all this lot of war. But what they care? It's the poor people got to suffer and mothers with their sons." If it was *their* sons, they swore they would keep them out of the Army by giving them soap to eat each day to make their hearts sound defective. Hitler? He was for them "the devil incarnate."

Then there was home. They reminisced often and at length about home. The old country, Barbados—or Bimshire, as they affectionately called it. The little Caribbean island in the sun they loved but had to leave. "Poor—poor but sweet" was the way they remembered it.

And naturally they discussed their adopted home. America came in for both good and bad marks. They lashed out at it for the racism they encountered. They took to task some of the people they worked for, especially those who gave them only a hard-boiled egg and a few spoonfuls of cottage cheese for lunch. "As if anybody can scrub floor on an egg and some cheese that don't have no taste to it!"

Yet although they caught H in "this man country," as they called America, it was nonetheless a place where "you could at least see your way to make a dollar." That much they acknowledged. They might even one day accumulate enough dollars, with both them and their husbands working, to buy the brownstone houses which, like my family, they were only leasing at that period. This was their consuming ambition: to "buy house" and to see the children through.

There was no way for me to understand it at the time, but the talk that filled the kitchen those afternoons was highly functional. It served as therapy, the cheapest kind available to my mother and her friends. Not only did it help them recover from the long wait on the corner that morning and the bargaining over their labor, it restored them to a sense of themselves and reaffirmed their self-worth. Through language they were able to overcome the humiliations of the work-day.

But more than therapy, that freewheeling, wide-ranging, exuberant talk functioned as an outlet for the tremendous creative energy they possessed. They were women in whom the need for self-expression was strong, and since language was the only vehicle readily available to them they made of it an art form that—in keeping with the African tradition in which art and life are one—was an integral part of their lives.

And their talk was a refuge. They never really ceased being baffled and overwhelmed by America—its vastness, complexity and power. Its strange customs and laws. At a level beyond words they remained fearful and in awe. Their uneasiness and fear were even reflected in their attitude toward the children they had given birth to in this country. They referred to those like myself, the little Brooklyn-born Bajans (Barbadians), as "these New York children" and complained that they couldn't discipline us properly because of the laws here. "You can't beat these children as you would like, you know, because the authorities in this place will dash you in jail for them. After all, these is New York children." Not only were we different, American, we had, as they saw it, escaped their ultimate authority.

Confronted therefore by a world they could not encompass, which even limited their rights as parents, and at the same time finding themselves permanently separated from the world they had known, they took refuge in language. "Language is the only homeland," Czeslaw Milosz, the emigré Polish writer and Nobel Laureate, has said. This is what it became for the women at the kitchen table.

It served another purpose also, I suspect. My mother and her friends were after all the female counterpart of Ralph Ellison's invisible man.[2] Indeed, you might say they suffered a triple invisibility, being black, female and foreigners. They really didn't count in American society except as a source of cheap labor. But given the kind of women they were, they couldn't tolerate the fact of their invisibility, their powerlessness. And they fought back, using the only weapon at their command: the spoken word.

---

[2]Title of novel published in 1947 that has become the seminal metaphor for African-Americans.

Those late afternoon conversations on a wide range of topics were a way for them to feel they exercised some measure of control over their lives and the events that shaped them. "Soully-gal, talk yuh talk!" they were always exhorting each other. "In this man world you got to take yuh mouth and make a gun!" They were in control, if only verbally and if only for the two hours or so that they remained in our house.

For me, sitting over in the corner, being seen but not heard, which was the rule for children in those days, it wasn't only what the women talked about—the content—but the way they put things—their style. The insight, irony, wit, and humor they brought to their stories and discussions and their poet's inventiveness and daring with language—which of course I could only sense but not define back then.

They had taken the standard English taught them in the primary schools of Barbados and transformed it into an idiom, an instrument that more adequately described them—changing around the syntax and imposing their own rhythm and accent so that the sentences were more pleasing to their ears. They added the few African sounds and words that had survived, such as the derisive suck-teeth sound and the word "yam," meaning to eat. And to make it more vivid, more in keeping with their expressive quality, they brought to bear a raft of metaphors, parables, Biblical quotations, sayings and the like:

"The sea ain' got no back door," they would say, meaning that it wasn't like a house where if there was a fire you could run out the back. Meaning that it was not to be trifled with. And meaning perhaps in a larger sense that man should treat all of nature with caution and respect.

"I has read hell by heart and called every generation blessed!" They sometimes went in for hyperbole.

A woman expecting a baby was never said to be pregnant. They never used that word. Rather, she was "in the way" or, better yet, "tumbling big." "Guess who I butt up on in the market the other day tumbling big again!"

And a woman with a reputation of being too free with her sexual favors was known in their book as a "thoroughfare"—the sense of men like a steady stream of cars moving up and down the road of her life. Or she might be dubbed "a free-bee," which was my favorite of the two. I liked the image it conjured up of a woman scandalous perhaps but independent, who flitted from one flower to another in a garden of male beauties, sampling their nectar, taking her pleasure at will, the roles reversed.

And nothing, no matter how beautiful, was ever described as simply beautiful. It was always "beautiful-ugly": the beautiful-ugly dress, the beautiful-ugly house, the beautiful-ugly car. Why the word "ugly," I used to wonder, when the thing they were referring to was beautiful, and they knew it. Why the antonym, the contradiction, the linking of opposites? It used to puzzle me greatly as a child.

There is the theory in linguistics which states that the idiom of a people, the way they use language, reflects not only the most fundamental views they hold of themselves and the world but their very conception of reality. Perhaps in using the term "beautiful-ugly" to describe nearly everything, my mother and her friends were expressing what they believed to be a fundamental dualism in life: the idea that a thing is at the same time its opposite, and that these opposites, these contradictions make up the whole. But theirs was not a Manichaean brand of dualism[3] that sees matter, flesh, the body, as inherently evil, because they constantly addressed each other as "soully-gal"—soul: spirit; gal: the body, flesh, the visible self. And it was clear from their tone that they gave one as much weight and importance as the other. They had never heard of the mind/body split.

As for God, they summed up His essential attitude in a phrase, "God," they would say, "don' love ugly and He ain' stuck on pretty."

Using everyday speech, the simple commonplace words—but always with imagination and skill—they gave voice to the most complex ideas. Flannery O'Connor[4] would have approved of how they made ordinary language work, as she put it, "double-time," stretching, shading, deepening its meaning. Like Joseph Conrad[5] they were always trying to infuse new life in the "old old words worn thin . . . by . . . careless usage." And the goals of their oral art were the same as his: "to make you hear, to make you feel . . . to make you *see*." This was their guiding esthetic.

By the time I was eight or nine, I graduated from the corner of the kitchen to the neighborhood library, and thus from the spoken to the written word. The Macon Street Branch of the Brooklyn Public Library was an imposing half block long edifice of heavy gray masonry, with glass-paneled doors at the front and two tall metal torches symbolizing the light that comes of learning flanking the wide steps outside.

The inside was just as impressive. More steps—of pale marble with gleaming brass railings at the center and sides—led up to the circulation desk, and a great pendulum clock gazed down from the balcony stacks that faced the entrance. Usually stationed at the top of the steps like the guards outside Buckingham Palace was the custodian, a stern-faced West Indian type who for years, until I was old enough to obtain an adult card, would immediately shoo me with one hand into the Children's Room

---

[3]Religious sect founded in 276 A.D. in Persia, which teaches the release of the spirit from matter through asceticism.
[4]American writer (1925–1964).
[5]British fiction writer (1857–1924).

and with the other threaten me into silence, a finger to his lips. You would have thought he was the chief librarian and not just someone whose job it was to keep the brass polished and the clock wound. I put him in a story called "Barbados" years later and had terrible things happen to him at the end.

I was sheltered from the storm of adolescence in the Macon Street library, reading voraciously, indiscriminately, everything from Jane Austen to Zane Grey, but with a special passion for the long, full-blown, richly detailed eighteenth- and nineteenth-century picaresque tales: *Tom Jones, Great Expectations, Vanity Fair*.

But although I loved nearly everything I read and would enter fully into the lives of the characters—indeed, would cease being myself and become them—I sensed a lack after a time. Something I couldn't quite define was missing. And then one day, browsing in the poetry section, I came across a book by someone called Paul Laurence Dunbar, and opening it I found the photograph of a wistful, sad-eyed poet who to my surprise was black. I turned to a poem at random. "Little brown-baby wif spa'klin'/eyes/Come to yo' pappy an' set on his knee." Although I had a little difficulty at first with the words in dialect, the poem spoke to me as nothing I had read before of the closeness, the special relationship I had had with my father, who by then had become an ardent believer in Father Divine and gone to live in Father's "kingdom" in Harlem. Reading it helped to ease somewhat the tight knot of sorrow and longing I carried around in my chest that refused to go away. I read another poem, "Lias! Lias! Bless de Lawd!/Don' you know de day's/erbroad?/Ef you don' get up, you scamp/Dey'll be trouble in dis camp." I laughed. It reminded me of the way my mother sometimes yelled at my sister and me to get out of bed in the mornings.

And another: "Seen my lady home las' night/Jump back, honey, jump back./Hel'/huh han'/an'/sque'z it tight . . ." About love between a black man and a black woman. I had never seen that written about before and it roused in me all kinds of delicious feelings and hopes.

And I began to search then for books and stories and poems about "The Race" (as it was put back then), about my people. While not abandoning Thackeray, Fielding, Dickens and the others, I started asking the reference librarian, who was white, for books by Negro writers, although I must admit I did so at first with a feeling of shame—the shame I and many others used to experience in those days whenever the word "Negro" or "colored" came up.

No grade school literature teacher of mine had ever mentioned Dunbar or James Weldon Johnson or Langston Hughes.[6] I didn't know

---

[6]Paul Laurence Dunbar (1870–1906), James Weldon Johnson (1871–1938), Langston Hughes (1902–1967)—African-American poets of the Harlem Renaissance.

that Zora Neale Hurston[7] existed and was busy writing and being published during those years. Nor was I made aware of people like Frederick Douglass and Harriet Tubman[8]—their spirit and example—or the great 19th-century abolitionist and feminist Sojourner Truth. There wasn't even Negro History Week when I attended P.S. 35 on Decatur Street!

What I needed, what all the kids—West Indian and native black American alike—with whom I grew up needed, was an equivalent of the Jewish shul, someplace where we could go after school—the schools that were shortchanging us—and read works by those like ourselves and learn about our history.

It was around that time also that I began harboring the dangerous thought of someday trying to write myself. Perhaps a poem about an apple tree, although I had never seen one. Or the story of a girl who could magically transplant herself to wherever she wanted to be in the world—such as Father Divine's kingdom in Harlem. Dunbar—his dark, eloquent face, his large volume of poems—permitted me to dream that I might someday write, and with something of the power with words my mother and her friends possessed.

When people at readings and writers' conferences ask me who my major influences were, they are sometimes a little disappointed when I don't immediately name the usual literary giants. True, I am indebted to those writers, white and black, whom I read during my formative years and still read for instruction and pleasure. But they were preceded in my life by another set of giants whom I always acknowledge before all others: the group of women around the table long ago. They taught me my first lesson in the narrative art. They trained my ear. They set a standard of excellence. This is why the best of my work must be attributed to them; it stands as testimony to the rich legacy of language and culture they so freely passed on to me in the wordshop of the kitchen.

INTERPRETATIONS

1. Were the "poets in the kitchen" as interesting on paper as in their conversations? What does Marshall think their orality revealed about them? Cite two or three examples.

2. Marshall's "unknown bards" use language to combat their powerlessness in a culture in which they experienced the "triple invisibility

---

[7] African-American novelist (1901–1961).
[8] Frederick Douglass (1817–1895), Harriet Tubman (1820–1913)—African-American abolitionists.

of being black, female and foreigners." Which expressions best reflect this?

APPLICATIONS

1. In what contexts do Marshall's poets view language as a refuge? How do you respond to this concept?

2. What kind of literacy is Marshall writing about when she speaks of her early upbringing? What must a participant in kitchen conversation be aware of? What other kinds of literacy might be invoked by "these unknown bards"?

3. Later on in her life, Marshall comes to understand and value another kind of literacy that she has discovered in the "Macon Street Branch of the Brooklyn Public Library." What kind of literacy is this? How is it related to the kinds of literacies that she has described earlier?

4. "It was around that time also that I began harboring the dangerous thought of someday trying to write myself." Why does Marshall use the word "dangerous"? How does her consideration of becoming a writer affect her perceptions of literacy? What happens to your sense of literacy when you engage in a writing task?

My Pen Writes in Blue and White

VINCENT CREMONA

Vincent Cremona grew up in a middle-class neighborhood on Long Island, New York. He is currently working full-time while pursuing his education in the evening at Queensborough Community College, CUNY.

SOME PEOPLE SAY THAT THEY SEE THINGS in black and white. I tend to view things a little bit differently. I like to say that I see things in blue and white. Certain things that I will see, or hear, or read, and I will say, "This is blue." Other times I will come to the conclusion, "That is white." Sometimes I can even view things as blue and white at the same time. I have been taught, though unintentionally, to view things in this manner since I first learned to read and write.

The manner in which I now write, and communicate for that matter, has been directly affected by the two major influences in my life, my parents. Even though my parents communicate in two completely different ways, I have borrowed from both of them. I am reminded of the words of Richard Rodriguez when he lamented, "I now speak in the chromium accents of my grammar school classmates . . ." I, myself, have taken the plain, frank, honest words of my father and joined them with the proper and formal words of my mother to form the dialect that I now speak. This combination has given me the ability to communicate in many different ways.

When I say that I see things as blue, I mean that I view them as basic, bold, and workman-like. I see things from a blue-collar point of view. I have learned to view things in this manner from my father. A truck driver by trade, my father was a card-carrying member of the International Brotherhood of Teamsters, Local 851. My father was cut in the Jimmy Hoffa mold, in that Jimmy Hoffa believed that most Americans are basically hard working individuals, who have respect for one another, as they face the trials and tribulations of providing a good home life for their families. As a union man, there is a lot of pride and patriotism in his words. He would say things like, "A day's work for a day's pay." It was said by Barbara Brandt that, "For many Americans today, paid work is not just a way to make money but is a crucial source of their self-worth." These words could easily be used to describe my father's attitude towards work. Work was a way of life for my father.

The most interesting thing to me was not his work, but rather my father's relationship with his co-workers. I would go to union meetings with my father and listen to the men talk about politics, finances, and all aspects of life. I was amazed that at such a young age, I could understand everything that they were saying. They spoke in a plain, although loud and brash, English. When I read their union-oriented propaganda, I noticed that it too was easy to understand. These were not complicated men. No one was out to impress or upstage anyone else. These men were union brothers, unmistakably blue-collared, and proud of it.

While I was listening to my father with one ear, my other was always pointed towards my mother. Although my mother also spoke English, like my father, they hardly sounded similar. My mother speaks what I like to call white-collar English. My mother is an office manager at a law firm. She goes to work all cleaned and pressed, briefcase in hand. When I listen to her talk about work, all I would hear was legalese. My mother uses words with many syllables and plenty of letters. She speaks in a very proper and clear voice. When she writes, she does so in a manner that makes the most ordinary things seem complicated. I remember she once wrote me a note for school that read, "Vincent will be unable to attend the upcoming academic function due to a prior commitment." I think she was trying to tell my teacher that I couldn't go on a class trip because we were going on vacation, but I am not really sure.

My mother aligned herself more with Emily Post because she believed the manner in which you talk, or write, or act in a certain situation would determine whether you have acted with class and dignity. My mother is all about being proper, no matter what the situation. Her I's are always dotted and her T's are always crossed. In my mother's white-collared world, the manner in which you conduct yourself has a direct influence on your career.

Learning to see things from these two different points of view has had a dramatic effect on the way I communicate. It is also very evident in my writing. I recently had to write a letter to an airline that had canceled my flight home from vacation, causing me to miss work on Monday. Needless to say, this cancellation was a tremendous inconvenience to me. I conveyed those feelings to the airline, in the bold, brash words of my father, in the beginning of the letter. Then, I used the poignant and legal sounding terms of my mother to convince them that they had better make restitution to me. I received a check from the airline only a few weeks later.

Since most of my writing is now done at work, I can see examples of my dual dialects all over my desk. I am a foreman at a construction company. The people who work directly under me are union construction workers. When I write their work orders, I do it in plain, ordinary, lay-men's terms. I do this not because I think they will not understand, but because I know this is the way they choose to communicate.

When I write the same work orders for my supervisors, I write them completely differently. My supervisors are made up of account-ants, architects, and other assorted managers and executives. When I communicate with them, whether it is via e-mail, fax, memo, or report, I do it in a very professional manner. The terms I use are very technical and official sounding. I know this is the way it has to be in the corporate world.

Even the writings that I do for school have the traces of these two viewpoints. When I am asked to do a serious business paper, for instance, I tend to write very professionally. I use the long-winded terms used by my professors and textbooks. On the other hand, when I am asked to write about more common ideas, like my experiences, or about myself, I write differently. I prefer to write in a more basic, every-day English. I like to write to the point and from the heart. When it is appropriate, I can even write from both perspectives at the same time. Some people may have to work at this, but to me it comes naturally.

All of my writing, now, I can see as either blue, or white, or some shade thereof. I used to think this made me write like two different people, with different personalities. Now I feel that I have the voice of one author, with a broadened horizon.

INTERPRETATIONS

1. How effective is Cremona's metaphor for describing his writing process? Try to create one to describe yours.

2. How do his parents' prose styles differ? Which do you prefer? How has he used both to his advantage?

APPLICATIONS

1. Review Cremona's last paragraph. What point does he make about language and identity?

2. What view of literacy does each of Cremona's parents represent? What evidence do you find to support your analysis?

3. In the fourth paragraph of the essay, Cremona recounts going to his father's union meetings. What kind of literacy did he observe at those times?

4. Who is Emily Post (mentioned in paragraph 6)? What kind of literacy does she represent? Who is an "Emily Post" in your life?

5. How does Cremona ultimately integrate the literacies that he presents in the essay? How well do you relate to what the author has written about? In what situations do you find yourself navigating among seemingly conflicting definitions of literacy?

The Knowing Eye

U.S. State Department/USAID

READING IMAGES

1. When you hear the word "education," what *image* comes to mind? How do these photographs illustrate your visual definition of the word?

2. Which part of each photograph captures your attention? Why do you think the photographer has chosen to make this person/object the focus of the image?

MAKING CONNECTIONS

1. There are many ways to learn, and people generally favor a few methods. How do these photographs and the kinds of learning they convey relate to the essays you have read in this chapter? Which essays seem to address the kind of learning implied by the first, second, and third photograph respectively?

Arnold Asrelsky

2. Which photograph do you think best illustrates a reading from this chapter? Which reading does it recall? What connections do you make between the written text and the visual one?

WORDS AND IMAGES

1. How do you relate to the classroom experience depicted in the first photograph? Write a comparison and contrast essay that examines your early education and that takes into account some of the following criteria: the number of students in the class, classroom architecture and decoration, student posture, student attentiveness, teaching methods, and class composition (in terms of gender, clothing worn). Remember to state a clear thesis!

2. Examine the photograph of the museum-goers. What does the body posture of the people in the photograph tell you about the

Bianca Henriquez

physical aspects of learning in this environment? Now, visit an art museum or gallery and concentrate on one work of your choice. Look at this work from one position for a few minutes. Then, take five steps back and reexamine the work. Repeat this procedure from another physical location. Write an essay about what you have learned about viewing art (and about learning in general) from this experience.

3. These photographs depict different ways that people learn. Which photograph is closer to depicting the way that *you* learn? If you have not already written a "Literacy Narrative" (see pages 10–13), write an essay that describes how you learn things best.

Additional Writing Topics

1. Write an essay discussing Agosín's concept that one's first language is the most vivid and crucial key to identity as it links memories, emotions, and a sense of place. Include in your essay specific examples from your own experience.

2. "Words themselves are innocuous; it is the consensus that gives them true power." Using a word that has powerful emotional connotations for you, write an essay defining that word as common usage has defined it and analyzing your emotional reactions to it.

3. Review the Kaufman perspective. What are the ramifications of viewing education as a process rather than a product? To what extent do the selections in this chapter support or refute Kaufman? Write an essay responding to these questions, concluding with your views on this issue.

4. Discuss with your group an educational experience that occurred outside of school. What did you learn from it? From the experience of group members?

5. Should a teacher serve as a role model for students? How important is it that he or she be a member of the students' ethnic group? Do teachers have too much or too little influence on their students? Write an essay that answers these questions.

6. Review Reid's perspective on curiosity and write an essay on the role of curiosity in the learning process described by Viloria and Torres. Is it possible to learn without being curious? Why or why not?

7. Review the introduction to Bambara's story. Why does she think stories are important? How have stories that you were told and that you have read contributed to your knowledge of your cultural heritage and to your education? Write a speech for your local school board in which you argue for the inclusion of a storytelling component in each of the elementary grades.

8. Some educational theorists argue that because students have grown up with television they prefer the visual to the linear—the image to the word. For such learners, "a picture is worth a thousand words." To what extent do you agree? How has the visual affected information processing? Should more visual techniques of communication be incorporated into the classroom? Write an essay responding to these questions.

CHAPTER

5

Work

ATTITUDES TOWARD WORK and the workplace are constantly changing. Traditionally, work was viewed as something to endure to support one's family, an effort rewarded by a pension and social security. Younger people have different expectations. Some desire economic success and job satisfaction; others prefer to shun the pressures of the corporate world and work for themselves.

We spend a great deal of our lives choosing, preparing for, and doing our work. "What do you do?" is perhaps the first question we want to ask of a new acquaintance. "Talking shop" is supposed to be taboo everywhere except at the office, factory, or construction site, yet no taboo is more frequently, and more gladly broken. For many people, the workplace is life. Talk about it ranges from the personal to the particular to the abstract, whatever one's culture.

The workplace is also changing rapidly. Technological expertise is in demand and will be rewarded by economic gains for those with innovative ideas and appropriate education. The increasing presence of women poses a challenge to traditional career choices and criteria for promotion, and attitudes toward work itself vary widely. For some, the workplace is a vital community, while others regard it as a location in which to perform a service. The notion of staying with one company for a lifetime or even making only one career choice is alien to many, and the concept of loyalty between employer and employee and vice versa is no longer assumed.

As you will discover, attitudes toward work and its value differ among cultures and exist in a matrix of customs, traditions, education, and class. In the Genesis account, work is viewed as a punishment for human disobedience, while in the Nez Percé selection, work is portrayed as interfering with dreams.

Few people seem to think of work as a vocation or a passion despite the fact that they will spend a great part of their lives making a living. Michael Dorris in "Life Stories" places work in the context of the former. In Native American culture, a young man leaving his village for the first time was expected to benefit from his solitary journey, and "through this unique prism, abstractly preserved in a vivid memory or song, a boy caught foresight of both his adult persona and of his vocation, the two inextricably linked."

In "Measuring Success," Renee Loth contrasts the limitations of her definition of success as a college student with the important discoveries she later makes in the workplace, namely, her failure to take "into account the joy of creation; the approbation of one's peers; the energy of collaboration; or the sheer satisfaction of a job well done." On the other hand, Andrew Curry, in "Why We Work," concedes that although some people work because they enjoy it, or want to make money, most people work because they "have no other choice."

The most negative treatment of work in the United States is Gary Soto's "Living Up the Street Black Hair"—a grueling account of a summer job at Valley Tire Factory that made him keenly aware of the effects of the destructive power of hopelessness that caused his co-workers to no longer value themselves. Ellen Ullman explains and explodes the stereotypical behavior associated with computer programmers by demonstrating from personal experience how their complex relationship to computers is determined by the nature of programming. Fiction writer R. K. Narayan examines the personal and professional commitment expected by employers in his native India.

The issue of affirmative action in the workplace is discussed from a multicultural perspective in the story by Lalita Gandbhir, while Michael Gnolfo presents his reasons for opposing affirmative action programs in the United States.

As you explore the complexities, even controversies, and changes in the workplace and in attitudes toward work, you may decide that now is a good time to join the conversation on these issues.

Perspectives

Work spares us from three great evils: boredom, vice and need.

—Voltaire

The ability to take pride in your own work is one of the hallmarks of sanity. Take away the ability to both work and be proud of it and you can drive anyone insane.

—Nikki Giovanni

If people are highly successful in their professions they lose their senses. Sound goes. They have no time to listen to music. Speech goes. They have no time for conversation. They lose their sense of proportion—the relations between one thing and another. Humanity goes.

—Virginia Woolf

Work is a necessity for man. Man invented the alarm clock.

—Pablo Picasso

Life is a continual distraction which does not allow us to reflect on that from which we are distracted.

—Franz Kafka

Each of you has a call, a vocation, which beckons you from the deepest places of your soul.

—David Hilfiker

He that maketh haste to be rich shall not be innocent.

—Proverbs 28:20

A job as a human right is a principle that applies to men as well as women. But women have more cause to fight for it.

—Gloria Steinem

The workplace performs the function of community.

—Robert Schrank

This book, being about work, is, by its very nature, about violence—to the spirit as well as the body.

—Studs Terkel

In fact, there is perhaps only one human being in a thousand who is passionately interested in his job for the job's sake.

—Dorothy Sayers

More and more, we take for granted that work must be destitute of pleasure. More and more, we assume that if we want to be pleased we must wait until evening, or the weekend, or vacation, or retirement. More and more, our farms and forests resemble our factories and offices, which in turn more and more resemble prisons—why else should we be so eager to escape them? We recognize defeated landscapes by the absence of pleasure from them. We are defeated at work because our work gives us no pleasure.

—Wendell Berry

Increased means and increased leisure are the two civilizers of man.

—Benjamin Disraeli

We are not far from the time when a man after a hard weekend of leisure will thankfully go back to work.

—Russell Baker

APPLICATIONS

1. According to Schrank, "the workplace performs the function of community." To what extent do you agree or disagree? Is it possible to establish community in competitive environments? What factors contribute to your feeling at home in the workplace?

2. Discuss Picasso's perspective with your group. Do you think there is a connection between work and time? What is your attitude toward time? Are you punctual for school, work, and leisure activities? Does lateness in others bother you? Summarize your discussion.

3. According to Berry, "we are defeated at work because work gives us no pleasure." To what kind of work is Berry referring? What factors account for boredom in the workplace? What is the difference between a job and a vocation? How would you diminish drudgery in the workplace?

The Fall

GENESIS 3:1–9

The Genesis account of the Fall explains, among other things, the origin of work, painful childbirth, and death. This seminal story following immediately after the Genesis account of Creation continues to exert an influence on Western culture out of proportion to its modest length.

THE SERPENT WAS MORE CRAFTY than any wild creature that the Lord God had made. He said to the woman, "Is it true that God has forbidden you to eat from any tree in the garden?" The woman answered the serpent, "We may eat the fruit of any tree in the garden, except for the tree in the middle of the garden; God has forbidden us either to eat or to touch the fruit of that; if we do, we shall die." The serpent said, "Of course you will not die. God knows that as soon as you eat it, your eyes will be opened and you will be like gods knowing both good and evil." When the woman saw that the fruit of the tree was good to eat, and that it was pleasing to the eye and tempting to contemplate, she took some and ate it. She also gave her husband some and he ate it. Then the eyes of both of them were opened and they discovered that they were naked; so they stitched fig-leaves together and made themselves loincloths.

The man and his wife heard the sound of the Lord God walking in the garden at the time of the evening breeze and hid from the Lord God among the trees of the garden. But the Lord God called to the man and said to him, "Where are you?" He replied, "I heard the sound as you were walking in the garden, and I was afraid because I was naked, and I hid myself." God answered, "Who told you that you were naked? Have you eaten from the tree which I forbade you?" The man said, "The woman you gave me for a companion, she gave me fruit from the tree and I ate it." Then the Lord God said to the woman, "What is this that you have done?" The woman said, "The serpent tricked me, and I ate." Then the Lord God said to the serpent:

Because you have done this you are accursed
more than all cattle and all wild creatures.
On your belly you shall crawl, and dust you shall eat
all the days of your life.
I will put enmity between you and the woman,

between your brood and hers.
They shall strike at your head,
and you shall strike at their heel.

To the woman he said:

I will increase your labour and your groaning,
and in labour you shall bear children.
You shall be eager for your husband,
and he shall be your master.

And to the man he said:

Because you have listened to your wife
and have eaten from the tree which I forbade you,
accursed shall be the ground on your account.
With labour you shall win your food from it
all the days of your life.
It will grow thorns and thistles for you,
none but wild plants for you to eat.
You shall gain your bread by the sweat of your brow
until you return to the ground;
for from it you were taken.
Dust you are, to dust you shall return.

INTERPRETATIONS

1. What attitude toward work does the passage reveal?
2. What attitude toward woman does the story reveal? Does the story explain why the serpent chose to speak to the woman, not the man? Of what significance is this choice?
3. What attributes of God does this story reveal? Does God's ban on the knowledge of good and evil (morality?) play into the serpent's evil designs, making the man and woman unnecessarily vulnerable? Is obedience God's main objective, and is this simply a test case to see whether the new man and woman can obey orders, no matter what the orders?

My Young Men Shall Never Work

CHIEF SMOHALLA
AS TOLD BY HERBERT J. SPINDEN

The Nez Percé are a tribe of American Indians, formerly occupying much of the Pacific Northwest, whose reservation is in Idaho.

Because Native Americans resisted giving up their homes and nomadic way of life to become farmers, white people have often called them lazy, stubborn, and impractical. But to Indians, whose homes, land, and hunting were sacred, anything that threatened any one of these threatened their whole system of beliefs and values, in short, their very lives.

MY YOUNG MEN SHALL NEVER WORK. Men who work cannot dream and wisdom comes in dreams.

You ask me to plow the ground. Shall I take a knife and tear my mother's breast? Then when I die she will not take me to her bosom to rest.

You ask me to dig for stone. Shall I dig under her skin for bones? Then when I die I cannot enter her body to be born again.

You ask me to cut grass and make hay and sell it and be rich like white men. But how dare I cut off my mother's hair?

It is a bad law and my people cannot obey it. I want my people to stay with me here. All the dead men will come to life again. We must wait here in the house of our fathers and be ready to meet them in the body of our mother.

INTERPRETATIONS

1. Are the Nez Percé objecting to all work? Would you define work to include hunting?

2. What is the Nez Percé's reason for rejecting what they call "work"? What do they value more than work? How common is it for a culture to place the highest value on something other than work? Is work the highest value of American culture? What's the evidence?

3. To what extent is the misunderstanding between the Nez Percé and the whites a matter of language (definition)? Of tradition?

What is the Nez Percé attitude toward the earth? What metaphor extends through and is elaborated within the whole passage?

CORRESPONDENCES

1. Review the Voltaire perspective. How does it apply to the Genesis account of the origins of work? Which attitude toward work best reflects your own?
2. Review the Kafka perspective. What does it mean? To what extent does it reflect the sentiments about work expressed by Smohalla of the Nez Percé?

APPLICATIONS

1. "The Fall" portrays work as punishment for disobedience. Can work also be rewarding? Can you imagine living a fulfilled life without work? Write a journal entry on these questions.
2. "Men who work cannot dream and wisdom comes in dreams." Write a journal entry responding to Chief Smohalla. To what extent does involvement in work affect time for dreams?
3. Many college students work at least 20 hours per week. If this is true of you, write a short essay on how you juggle your schedule to meet these responsibilities.

Life Stories

MICHAEL DORRIS

Michael Dorris (1945–1997) wrote fiction and essays about Native American life and social issues. He was educated at Georgetown University and Yale University, and was a professor of Native American studies at Dartmouth College. His several publications, many of them co-authored with his wife, Louise Erdrich, include The Broken Cord *(1990), an account of his adopted son's struggle with fetal alcohol syndrome. Other publications include* Working Men *(1993),* Paper Trail *(1994) from which "Life Stories" is taken. His last novel,* Cloud Chamber *was published in 1997.*

IN MOST CULTURES, adulthood is equated with self-reliance and responsibility, yet often Americans do not achieve this status until we are in our late twenties or early thirties—virtually the entire average lifespan of a person in a traditional non-Western society. We tend to treat prolonged adolescence as a warm-up for real life, as a wobbly suspension bridge between childhood and legal maturity. Whereas a nineteenth-century Cheyenne or Lakota teenager was expected to alter self-conception in a split-second vision, we often meander through an analogous rite of passage for more than a decade—through high school, college, graduate school.

Though he had never before traveled alone outside his village, the Plains Indian male was expected at puberty to venture solo into the wilderness. There he had to fend for and sustain himself while avoiding the menace of unknown dangers, and there he had absolutely to remain until something happened that would transform him. Every human being, these tribes believed, was entitled to at least one moment of personal, enabling insight.

Anthropology proposes feasible psychological explanations for why this flash was eventually triggered: Fear, fatigue, reliance on strange foods, the anguish of loneliness, stress, and the expectation of ultimate success all contributed to a state of receptivity. Every sense was quickened, alerted to perceive deep meaning, until at last the interpretation of an unusual event—a dream, a chance encounter, or an unexpected vista—reverberated with metaphor. Through this unique prism, abstractly preserved in a vivid memory or song, a boy caught foresight of both his adult persona and of his vocation, the two inextricably entwined.

Today the best approximations that many of us get to such a heady sense of eventuality come in the performance of our school vacation jobs. Summers are intermissions, and once we hit our teens it is during these breaks in our structured regimen that we initially taste the satisfaction of remuneration that is earned, not merely doled. Tasks defined as *work* are not only graded, they are compensated; they have a worth that is unarguable because it translates into hard currency. Wage labor—and in the beginning, this generally means a confining, repetitive chore for which we are quickly over-qualified—paradoxically brings a sense of blooming freedom. At the outset, the complaint to a peer that business supersedes fun is oddly liberating—no matter what drudgery requires your attention, it is by its very required nature serious and adult.

At least that's how it seemed to me. I come from a line of people hard hit by the Great Depression. My mother and her sisters went to work early in their teens—my mother operated a kind of calculator known as a comptometer while her sisters spent their days, respectively, at a peanut factory and at Western Union. My grandmother did piecework sewing. Their efforts, and the Democratic Party, saw them through, and to this day they never look back without appreciation for their later solvency. They take nothing for granted. Accomplishments are celebrated, possessions are valuable, in direct proportion to the labor entailed to acquire them; anything easily won or bought on credit is suspect. When I was growing up we were far from wealthy, but what money we had was correlated to the hours some one of us had logged. My eagerness to contribute to, or at least not diminish, the coffer was countered by the arguments of those whose salaries kept me in school: My higher education was a sound group investment. The whole family was adamant that I have the opportunities they had missed and, no matter how much I objected, they stinted themselves to provide for me.

Summer jobs were therefore a relief, an opportunity to pull a share of the load. As soon as the days turned warm I began to peruse the classifieds, and when the spring semester was done, I was ready to punch a clock. It even felt right. Work in June, July, and August had an almost Biblical aspect: In the hot, canicular weather your brow sweated, just as God had ordained. Moreover, summer jobs had the luxury of being temporary. No matter how bizarre, how onerous, how off my supposed track, employment terminated with the falling leaves and I was back on neutral ground. So, during each annual three-month leave from secondary school and later from the university, I compiled an eclectic résumé: lawn cutter, hair sweeper in a barber shop, lifeguard, delivery boy, temporary mail carrier, file clerk, youth program coordinator on my Montana reservation, ballroom dance instructor, theater party promoter, night-shift hospital records keeper, human adding machine in a Paris bank, encyclopedia salesman, newspaper stringer, recreation bus manager, salmon fisherman.

The reasonable titles disguise the madness of some of these occupations. For instance, I seemed inevitably to be hired to trim the yards of the unconventional. One woman followed beside me, step by step, as I traversed her yard in ever tighter squares, and called my attention to each missed blade of grass. Another client never had the "change" to pay me, and so reimbursed my weekly pruning with an offering culled from his library. I could have done without the *Guide to Artificial Respiration* (1942) or the many well-worn copies of Reader's Digest Condensed Books, but sometimes the selection merited the wait. Like a rat lured repeatedly back to the danger of mild electric shock by the mystique of intermittent reen-forcement, I kept mowing by day in hopes of turning pages all night.

The summer I was eighteen a possibility arose for a rotation at the post office, and I grabbed it. There was something casually sophisticated about work that required a uniform, about having a federal ranking, even if it was GS-1 (Temp/Sub), and it was flattering to be entrusted with a leather bag containing who knew what important correspondence. Every day I was assigned a new beat, usually in a rough neighborhood avoided whenever possible by regular carriers, and I proved quite capable of complicating what would normally be fairly routine missions. The low point came on the first of August when I diligently delivered four blocks' worth of welfare checks to the right numbers on the wrong streets. It is no fun to snatch unexpected wealth from the hands of those who have but moments previously opened their mailboxes and received a bonus.

After my first year of college, I lived with relatives on an Indian reservation in eastern Montana and filled the only post available: Coordinator of Tribal Youth Programs. I was seduced by the language of the announcement into assuming that there existed Youth Programs to be coordinated. In fact, the Youth consisted of a dozen bored, disgruntled kids—most of them my cousins—who had nothing better to do each day than to show up at what was euphemistically called "the gym" and hate whatever Program I had planned for them. The Youth ranged in age from fifteen to five and seemed to have as their sole common ambition the determination to smoke cigarettes. This put them at immediate and on-going odds with the Coordinator, who on his first day naively encouraged them to sing the "Doe, a deer, a female deer" song from

The Sound of Music. They looked at me, that bleak morning, and I looked at them, each boy and girl equipped with a Pall Mall behind an ear, and we all knew it would be a long, struggle-charged battle. It was to be a contest of wills, the hearty and wholesome vs. prohibited vice. I stood for dodge ball, for collecting bugs in glass jars, for arts and crafts; they had pledged a preternatural allegiance to sloth. The odds were not in my favor and each waking dawn I experienced the light-headedness of anticipated exhaustion, that thrill of giddy dissociation in which nothing seems real or of great significance. I went with the flow and learned to inhale.

The next summer, I decided to find work in an urban setting for a change, and was hired as a general office assistant in the Elsa Hoppenfeld Theatre Party Agency, located above Sardi's restaurant in New York City. The Agency consisted of Elsa Hoppenfeld herself, Rita Frank, her regular deputy, and me. Elsa was a gregarious Viennese woman who established contacts through personal charm, and she spent much of the time courting trade away from the building. Rita was therefore both my immediate supervisor and constant companion; she had the most incredible fingernails I had ever seen—long, carefully shaped pegs lacquered in cruel primary colors and hard as stone—and an attitude about her that could only be described as zeal.

The goal of a theater party agent is to sell blocks of tickets to imminent Broadway productions, and the likely buyers are charities, B'nai Briths, Hadassahs, and assorted other fund-raising organizations. We received commissions on volume, and so it was necessary to convince a prospect that a play—preferably an expensive musical—for which we had reserved the rights to seats would be a boffo smash hit.

The object of our greatest expectation that season was an extravaganza called *Chu Chem*, a saga that aspired to ride the coattails of *Fiddler on the Roof* into entertainment history. It starred the estimable Molly Picon and told the story of a family who had centuries ago gone from Israel to China during the diaspora, yet had, despite isolation in an alien environment, retained orthodox culture and habits. The crux of the plot revolved around a man with several marriageable daughters and nary a kosher suitor within 5,000 miles. For three months Rita and I waxed eloquent in singing the show's praises. We sat in our little office, behind facing desks, and every noon while she redid her nails I ordered out from a deli that offered such exotic (to me) delicacies as fried egg sandwiches, lox and cream cheese, pastrami, *tongue*. I developed of necessity and habit a telephone voice laced with a distinctly Yiddish accent. It could have been a great career. However, come November, *Chu Chem* bombed. Its closing was such a financial catastrophe for all concerned that when the following January one Monsieur Dupont advertised on the Placement Board at my college. I decided to put an ocean between me and my former trusting clientele.

M. Dupont came to campus with the stated purpose of interviewing candidates for teller positions in a French bank. Successful applicants, required to be fluent in *français*, would be rewarded with three well-paid months and a rent-free apartment in Paris. I headed for the language lab and registered for an appointment.

The only French in the interview was *Bonjour, ça va?*, after which M. Dupont switched into English and described the wonderful deal on charter air flights that would be available to those who got the nod. Round-trip to Amsterdam, via Reykjavik, leaving the day after exams and returning in mid-September, no changes or substitutions. I signed up on the spot. I was to be a *banquier*, with *pied-à-terre* in Montparnasse!

Unfortunately, when I arrived with only $50 in travelers checks in my pocket—the flight had cleaned me out, but who needed money since my paycheck started right away—no one in Paris had ever heard of M. Dupont.

Alors.

I stood in the Gare du Nord and considered my options. There weren't any. I scanned a listing of Paris hotels and headed for the cheapest one: the Hotel Villedo, $10 a night. The place had an ambiance that I persuaded myself was antique, despite the red light above the sign. The only accommodation available was "the bridal suite," a steal at $20. The glass door to my room didn't lock and there was a rather continual floor show, but at some point I must have dozed off. When I awoke the church bells were ringing, the sky was pink, and I felt renewed. No little setback was going to spoil my adventure. I stood and stretched, then walked to a mirror that hung above the sink next to the bed. I leaned forward to punctuate my resolve with a confident look in the eye.

The sink disengaged and fell to the floor. Water gushed. In panic I rummaged through my open suitcase, stuffed two pair of underwear into the pipe to quell the flow, and before the dam broke, I was out the door. I barreled through the lobby of the first bank *I passed, asked to see the director*, and told the startled man my sad story. For some reason, whether from shock or pity, he hired me at $1.27 an hour to be a cross-checker of foreign currency transactions, and with two phone calls found me lodgings at a commercial school's dormitory.

From eight to five each weekday my duty was to sit in a window-less room with six impeccably dressed people, all of whom were total-ing identical additions and subtractions. We were highly dignified with each other, very professional, no *tutoyering*. Monsieur Saint presided, but the formidable Mademoiselle was the true power: she oversaw each of our columns and shook her head sadly at my American-shaped numbers.

My legacy from that summer, however, was more than an enduring penchant for crossed 7s. After I had worked for six weeks, M. Saint asked me during a coffee break why I didn't follow the example of other foreign students he had known and depart the office at noon in order to spend the afternoon touring the sights of Paris with the *Alliance Française.*

"Because," I replied in my halting French, "that costs money. I depend upon my full salary the same as any of you." M. Saint nodded gravely and said no more, but then on the next Friday he presented me with a white envelope along with my check.

"Do not open this until you have left the Société Générale," he said ominously. I thought I was fired for the time I had mixed up krøners and guilders, and, once on the sidewalk, I steeled myself to read the worst. I felt the quiet panic of blankness.

"Dear Sir," I translated the perfectly formed script. "You are a person of value. It is not correct that you should be in our beautiful city and not see it. Therefore we have amassed a modest sum to pay the tuition for a two-week afternoon program for you at the *Alliance Française.* Your wages will not suffer, for it is your assignment to appear each morning in this bureau and reacquaint us with the places you have visited. We shall see them afresh through your eyes." The letter had thirty signatures, from the Director to the janitor, and stuffed inside the envelope was a sheaf of franc notes in various denominations.

I rushed back to the tiny office. M. Saint and Mademoiselle had waited, and accepted my gratitude with their usual controlled smiles and precise handshakes. But they had blown their Gallic cover, and for the next ten days and then through all the days until I went home in September, our branch was awash with sightseeing paraphernalia. Everyone had advice, favorite haunts, criticisms of the *Alliance*'s choices or explanations. Paris passed through the bank's granite walls as sweetly as a June breeze through a window screen, and ever afterward the lilt of overheard French, a photograph of *Sacré Coeur* or the Louvre, even a monthly bank statement, recalls to me that best of all summers.

I didn't wind up in an occupation with any obvious connection to the careers I sampled during my school breaks, but I never altogether abandoned those brief professions either. They were jobs not so much to be held as to be weighed, absorbed, and incorporated, and, collectively, they carried me forward into adult life like overlapping stairs, unfolding a particular pattern at once haphazard and inevitable.

INTERPRETATIONS

1. Dorris begins an essay on summer jobs by contrasting how Native Americans and white cultures measure maturity. What examples in the first three paragraphs do you find particularly interesting? With what points, if any, did you disagree?
2. Dorris cites several personal experiences with summer jobs. How does he rate them? Did they contribute positively to his transitions from adolescence to adulthood? Cite specific examples to support your point of view.
3. Dorris changes tone several times in the essay. Cite at least three instances and show how he uses tone to enhance meaning.
4. What factors contributed to making his French experience "the best of all summers."
5. Explain Dorris's concluding paragraph. How does it relate to his introduction? To the unity of his essay?

CORRESPONDENCES

1. How did Dorris's and Soto's experiences with summer jobs contribute to their maturity? Was there a particular summer job that despite its negative aspects had a positive effect on your personal growth? Explain.
2. Review Hilfiker's perspective on work and discuss its relevance to Dorris's essay. What relevance does it have for you? How would you differentiate between a job as opposed to a calling or vocation?

APPLICATIONS

1. Review paragraph 5 of Dorris's essay. To what economic class did his family belong? Characterize their attitudes toward work. To Dorris's education? To what extent is your family's economic situation and attitudes toward work and education similar to or different from his? Discuss these issues with your group and write a summary of your conversations.
2. Describe someone with whom you work who obviously likes or dislikes his or her job. How much does that person communicate this in performance and attitude? How do such attitudes affect the workplace? Be specific.

3. Review paragraphs 8 and 9 in which Dorris recalls his summer jobs as a temporary postal worker and as Coordinator of Tribal Youth Programs. Evaluate the effectiveness of using humor to describe two difficult experiences. What does Dorris communicate about himself through his account of both positions? Write a journal entry responding to these questions.

4. Using Dorris's title, "Life Stories," write an essay on one or two summer jobs that you would characterize as "rites of passage."

Why We Work

ANDREW CURRY

Andrew Curry is currently a general editor of Smithsonian *magazine. He writes regularly on contemporary issues for a variety of publications including the* Christian Science Monitor, *the* Miami Herald, *and the* Guardian. *"Why We Work" was first published in* U.S. News and World Report *in 2003, when Curry held the position of associate editor*

SOME DO IT FOR LOVE. Others do it for money. But most of us do it because we have no other choice.

In 1930, W. K. Kellogg made what he thought was a sensible decision, grounded in the best economic, social, and management theories of the time. Workers at his cereal plant in Battle Creek, Michigan, were told to go home two hours early. Every day. For good.

The Depression-era move was hailed in *Factory and Industrial Management* magazine as the "biggest piece of industrial news since [Henry] Ford announced his five-dollar-a-day policy." President Herbert Hoover summoned the eccentric cereal magnate to the White House and said the plan was "very worthwhile." The belief: Industry and machines would lead to a workers' paradise where all would have less work, more free time, and yet still produce enough to meet their needs.

So what happened? Today, work dominates Americans' lives as never before, as workers pile on hours at a rate not seen since the Industrial Revolution. Technology has offered increasing productivity and a higher standard of living while bank tellers and typists are replaced by machines. The mismatch between available work and those available to do it continues, as jobs go begging while people beg for jobs. Though Kellogg's six-hour day lasted until 1985, Battle Creek's grand industrial experiment has been nearly forgotten. Instead of working less, our hours have stayed steady or risen—and today many more women work so that families can afford the trappings of suburbia. In effect, workers chose the path of consumption over leisure.

But as today's job market shows so starkly, that road is full of potholes. With unemployment at a nine-year high and many workers worried about losing their jobs—or forced to accept cutbacks in pay and benefits—work is hardly the paradise economists once envisioned.

231

Instead, the job market is as precarious today as it was in the early 1980s, when business began a wave of restructurings and layoffs to maintain its competitiveness. Many workers are left feeling insecure, unfulfilled, and under-appreciated. It's no wonder surveys of today's workers show a steady decline in job satisfaction. "People are very emotional about work, and they're very negative about it," says David Rhodes, a principal at human resource consultants Towers Perrin. "The biggest issue is clearly workload. People are feeling crushed."

The backlash comes after years of people boasting about how hard they work and tying their identities to how indispensable they are. Ringing cell phones, whirring faxes, and ever-present e-mail have blurred the lines between work and home. The job penetrates every aspect of life. Americans don't exercise, they work out. We manage our time and work on our relationships. "In reaching the affluent society, we're working longer and harder than anyone could have imagined," says Rutgers University historian John Gillis. "The work ethic and identifying ourselves with work and through work is not only alive and well but more present now than at any time in history."

It's all beginning to take a toll. Fully one third of American workers—who work longer hours than their counterparts in any industrialized country—felt overwhelmed by the amount of work they had to do, according to a 2001 Families and Work Institute survey. "Both men and women wish they were working about 11 hours [a week] less," says Ellen Galinsky, the institute's president. "A lot of people believe if they do work less they'll be seen as less committed, and in a shaky economy no one wants that."

The modern environment would seem alien to pre-industrial laborers. For centuries, the household—from farms to "cottage" craftsmen—was the unit of production. The whole family was part of the enterprise, be it farming, blacksmithing, or baking. "In pre-industrial society, work and family were practically the same thing," says Gillis.

The Industrial Revolution changed all that. Mills and massive iron smelters required ample labor and constant attendance. "The factory took men, women and children out of the workshops and homes and put them under one roof and timed their movements to machines," writes Sebastian de Grazia in *Of Time, Work and Leisure*. For the first time, work and family were split. Instead of selling what they produced, workers sold their time. With more people leaving farms to move to cities and factories, labor became a commodity, placed on the market like any other.

Innovation gave rise to an industrial process based on machinery and mass production. This new age called for a new worker. "The only safeguard of order and discipline in the modern world is a standardized worker with interchangeable parts," mused one turn-of-the-century writer.

Business couldn't have that, so instead it came up with the science of management. The theories of Frederick Taylor, a Philadelphia factory foreman with deep Puritan roots, led to work being broken down into component parts, with each step timed to coldly quantify jobs that skilled craftsmen had worked a lifetime to learn. Workers resented Taylor and his stopwatch, complaining that his focus on process stripped their jobs of creativity and pride, making them irritable. Long before anyone knew what "stress" was, Taylor brought it to the workplace—and without sympathy. "I have you for your strength and mechanical ability, and we have other men paid for thinking," he told workers.

The division of work into components that could be measured and easily taught reached its apex in Ford's River Rouge plant in Dearborn, Michigan, where the assembly line came of age. "It was this combination of a simplification of tasks . . . with moving assembly that created a manufacturing revolution while at the same time laying waste human potential on a massive scale," author Richard Donkin writes in *Blood, Sweat and Tears*.

To maximize the production lines, businesses needed long hours from their workers. But it was no easy sell. "Convincing people to work 9 to 5 took a tremendous amount of propaganda and discipline," says the University of Richmond's Joanne Ciulla, author of *The Working Life: The Promise and Betrayal of Modern Work*. Entrepreneurs, religious leaders, and writers like Horatio Alger created whole bodies of literature to glorify the work ethic.

The first labor unions were organized in response to the threat of technology, as skilled workers sought to protect their jobs from mechanization. Later, semi- and unskilled workers began to organize as well, agitating successfully for reduced hours, higher wages, and better work conditions. Unions enjoyed great influence in the early 20th century, and at their height in the 1950s, 35 percent of U.S. workers belonged to one.

Union persistence and the mechanization of factories gradually made shorter hours more realistic. Between 1830 and 1930, work hours were cut nearly in half, with economist John Maynard Keynes famously predicting in 1930 that by 2030 a 15-hour workweek would be standard. The Great Depression pressed the issue, with job sharing proposed as a serious solution to widespread unemployment. Despite business and religious opposition over worries of an idle populace, the Senate passed a bill that would have mandated a 30-hour week in 1933; it was narrowly defeated in the House.

Franklin Delano Roosevelt struck back with a new gospel that lives to this very day: consumption. "The aim . . . is to restore our rich domestic market by raising its vast consuming capacity," he said. "Our first purpose is to create employment as fast as we can." And so began the modern work world. "Instead of accepting work's continuing decline and imminent fall from its dominant social position, businessmen, economists, advertisers, and politicians preached that there would never be 'enough,'" says University of Iowa Professor Benjamin Hunnicutt, author of *Work Without End: Abandoning Shorter Hours for the Right to Work.* "The entrepreneur and industry could invent new things for advertising to sell and for people to want and work for indefinitely."

The New Deal dumped government money into job creation, in turn encouraging consumption. World War II fueled the fire, and American workers soon found themselves in a "golden age"—40-hour workweeks, plenty of jobs, and plenty to buy. Leisure was the road not taken, a path quickly forgotten in the postwar boom of the 1950s and 1960s.

Decades of abundance, however, did not bring satisfaction. "A significant number of Americans are dissatisfied with the quality of their working lives," said the 1973 report "Work in America" from the Department of Health, Education and Welfare. "Dull, repetitive, seemingly meaningless tasks, offering little challenge or autonomy, are causing discontent among workers at all occupational levels." Underlying the dissatisfaction was a very gradual change in what the "Protestant work ethic" meant. Always a source of pride, the idea that hard work was a calling from God dated to the Reformation and the teachings of Martin Luther. While work had once been a means to serve God, two centuries of choices and industrialization had turned work into an end in itself, stripped of the spiritual meaning that sustained the Puritans who came ready to tame the wilderness.

By the end of the '70s, companies were reaching out to spiritually drained workers by offering more engagement while withdrawing the promise of a job for life, as the American economy faced a stiff challenge from cheaper workers abroad. "Employees were given more control over their work and schedules, and "human relations" consultants and motivational speakers did a booming business. By the 1990s, technology made working from home possible for a growing number of people. Seen as a boon at first, telecommuting and the rapidly proliferating "electronic leash" of cellphones made work inescapable, as employees found themselves on call 24/7. Today, almost half of American workers use computers, cellphones, e-mail, and faxes for work during what is supposed to be non-work time, according to the Families and Work Institute. Home is no longer a refuge but a cozier extension of the office.

The shift coincided with a shortage of highly skilled and educated workers, some of whom were induced with such benefits as stock options in exchange for their putting the company first all the time. But some see a different explanation for the rise in the amount of time devoted to work. "Hours have crept up partly as a consequence of the declining power of the trade-union movement," says Cornell University labor historian Clete Daniel. "Many employers find it more economical to require mandatory overtime than hire new workers and pay their benefits." Indeed, the trend has coincided with the steady decline in the percentage of workers represented by unions, as the labor movement failed to keep pace with the increasing rise of white-collar jobs in the economy. Today fewer than 15 percent of American workers belong to unions.

In a study of Silicon Valley culture over the past decade, San Jose State University anthropologist Jan English-Lueck found that skills learned on the job were often brought home. Researchers talked to families with mission statements, mothers used conflict-resolution buzzwords with their squabbling kids, and engineers used flowcharts to organize Thanksgiving dinner. Said one participant: "I don't live life; I manage it."

In some ways, we have come full circle. "Now we're seeing the return of work to the home in terms of telecommuting," says Gillis. "We may be seeing the return of households where work is the central element again."

But there's still the question of fulfillment. In a recent study, human resources consultants Towers Perrin tried to measure workers' emotions about their jobs. More than half of the emotion was negative, with the biggest single factor being workload but also a sense that work doesn't satisfy their deeper needs. "We expect more and more out of our jobs," says Hunnicutt. "We expect to find wonderful people and experiences all around us. What we find is Dilbert."

INTERPRETATIONS

1. Curry's research indicates that although increasingly American workers have chosen material prosperity rather than personal time, they are still dissatisfied with their jobs. What explanations does he offer to explain this apparent contradiction?

2. How has technology (cell phones, e-mail, faxes) contributed to the concept of being on the job "at home as well as in the workplace"? To what extent do you agree with Curry that "we manage our time and work on our relationships"?

3. How has the role of trade unions changed over the decades? To what extent has their decline resulted in an increase in the number of hours Americans work each week?

4. Review paragraph 22 that focuses on Silicon Valley culture and the changes of the last decade. To what extent have they affected personal and family life adversely in your opinion?

CORRESPONDENCES

1. Review Terkel's perspective on work and discuss its relevance to Curry's essay. What evidence is there of "violence to the spirit as well as the body"? Explain.

2. Review Baker's perspective and discuss how Curry's essay contradicts Baker's prediction. To what extent do you balance work and leisure?

APPLICATIONS

1. Write a journal entry on your criteria for choosing a profession. Is it part of a dream that you would like to fulfill or do you view your choice as mainly pragmatic? How important is personal satisfaction?

2. Economic success has long been associated with the American dream. Discuss with your group your concepts of the American dream. How are they similar or different? How do they compare to those of your parents' generation?

3. A recent survey estimates that 20 percent of high earners in the United States are working more than sixty hours per week at tasks that include meeting tight deadlines, frequent travel, increased flow of work, and work-related social events on evenings and even weekends. Can you imagine being one of these people involved in what is now termed an "extreme job"? Discuss this issue with your group and summarize your findings.

Measuring Success

RENÉE LOTH

Renee Loth has been editor of the editorial page of The Boston Globe *since May 2000, after serving for six years as deputy editor. In this position, she sets policy for the* Globe *editorial board and is responsible for oversight of the Op-Ed page and letters to the editors. Her career at* Globe *for the past nineteen years in various important positions included political editor, State House correspondent, and magazine writer. Loth has a degree in journalism from Boston University's School of Public Communication, where she was editor of the college newspaper. Does Loth, in "Measuring Success," consider her position at the* Globe *a job or a vocation?*

BACK WHEN I WAS A CALLOW COLLEGE STUDENT, I devised a neat grid system for what I hoped would be my life's achievements. I could count my life a good one, I thought, if I could attain both success and happiness. So I set about analyzing the component parts of each: Happiness I subdivided into sections labeled health and love; success, I determined, was composed of wealth and fame.

Once I actually entered the world of work, however, I learned that success is not so easy to define. For one thing, when I made my simple calculation, I never took into account the joy of creation; the approbation of one's peers; the energy of collaboration; or the sheer satisfaction of a job well done. These are real qualities of success that live outside of wealth or fame.

Also, I found that definitions of success are mutable, shifting along with our changing values. If we stick with our chosen fields long enough, we sometimes have an opportunity to meet our heroes, people we thought wildly successful when we were young. A musician friend told me that he spent most of his youth wanting to play like the greats, until he started getting to know some of them. To his surprise, many turned out to be embittered, dulled by drink or boredom, unable to hold together a marriage, or wantonly jealous of others. That's when he realized he wanted to play like himself.

Success is defined differently by different people. For some, it is symbolized by the number of buttons on the office phone. For others, it is having only one button—and a secretary to field the calls. Some think the more nights and weekends they spend at the office, the more successful they must be. For others, success is directly proportional to time off.

And what about those qualities I did include in my handy grid system? Wealth—beyond what is needed to provide for oneself and one's family, with a little left over for airfare to someplace subtropical in January—turned out to be superfluous. And the little experience I had with fame turned out to be downright scary.

Several years ago, I had occasion to appear on a dull but respected national evening television news show. My performance lasted exactly six minutes, and my name flashed only twice. But when I got home from the live broadcast, my answering machine had maxed-out on messages.

I heard from a woman I had last seen in Brownie Scouts. I heard from former boyfriends, conspiracy theorists, and celebrity agents. I even got an obscene phone call—what kind of pervert watches PBS?—from someone who might have been an old friend pulling my leg. At least, I hope so.

For weeks afterward, I received tons of what an optimist might call fan mail. One fellow insisted that if I froze a particular frame of a political campaign ad I had been discussing, I could see the face of Bill Clinton in the American flag. Somebody sent me a chapter of a novel in progress with a main character disturbingly like me. Several people sent me chain letters.

I was relieved when the fickle finger of fame moved on to someone else.

When I was young and romanticizing about success, I liked a particular Joni Mitchell lyric: "My struggle for higher achievement and my search for love don't seem to cease." Ah, but the trouble with struggling and searching is that it keeps us in a permanent state of wanting—always reaching for more. The drive to succeed keeps us focused on the future, to the detriment of life in the moment. And the moment is all we ever really have.

When I look back at my simplistic little value system, I am a bit chagrined at how absolute I thought life was. But I am also happy to report that the achievements that have come my way are the ones that count. After 20 years of supercharged ambition, I have stumbled upon this bit of wisdom. Who needs wealth and fame? Two out of four ain't bad.

INTERPRETATIONS

1.   What point is Loth making regarding definitions of happiness or success? What causes her to reevaluate her earlier concepts of both?

2. Why does she include the short episode on the national evening television news show?

3. Review paragraph 10. To what extent do you agree with Loth that constantly searching for success or love detracts one from enjoying the present moment? How can you preserve the balance between present successes and future goals?

CORRESPONDENCES

1. What conversation about work can you imagine Curry and Loth sharing? Does Loth work because she must or because she enjoys what she does? What evidence would you cite to support your point of view?

2. Review the perspective on wealth from Proverbs 28:2. What does it mean? How does it apply to paragraphs 8 and 11 of Loth's essay?

APPLICATIONS

1. Working with your group, conduct a survey of friends, family members, or co-workers as to how their definitions of happiness and/or success changed over time. Write a summary of your findings.

2. Several sociological surveys indicate that job satisfaction is difficult to attain. Discuss with your group the implications of choosing a major in college based on job market trends or a major based on talents and interests.

3. Review paragraph 2 of Loth's essay and write a journal entry supporting or disagreeing with her "real qualities of success that live outside wealth or fame."

Black Hair

GARY SOTO

Gary Soto (b. 1952) was raised in Fresno, California and is the author of ten poetry collections. New and Selected Poems *(1995) was a finalist for the Los Angeles Book Award and the National Book Award.* Living Up The Street, *Soto's memoir, received a Before Columbus Foundation American Book Award in 1985. In addition to writing, Soto has produced a film and wrote a libretto for the Los Angeles Opera. Soto also serves as Young People's Ambassador for the California Rural Legal Assistance and the United Farm Workers of America. Before reading Soto's essay, write a journal entry on the summer job you most hated. What did you learn from the experience?*

THERE ARE TWO KINDS OF WORK: One uses the mind and the other uses muscle. As a kid I found out about the latter. I'm thinking of the summer of 1969 when I was a seventeen-year-old runaway who ended up in Glendale, California, to work for Valley Tire Factory. To answer an ad in the newspaper I walked miles in the afternoon sun, my stomach slowly knotting on a doughnut that was breakfast, my teeth like bright candles gone yellow.

I walked in the door sweating and feeling ugly because my hair was still stiff from a swim at the Santa Monica beach the day before. Jules, the accountant and part owner, looked droopily through his bifocals at my application and then at me. He tipped his cigar in the ashtray, asked my age as if he didn't believe I was seventeen, but finally after a moment of silence, said, "Come back tomorrow. Eight-thirty."

I thanked him, left the office, and went around to the chain link fence to watch the workers heave tires into a bin; others carted uneven stacks of tires on hand trucks. Their faces were black from tire dust and when they talked—or cussed—their mouths showed a bright pink.

From there I walked up a commercial street, past a cleaners, a motorcycle shop, and a gas station where I washed my face and hands; before leaving I took a bottle that hung on the side of the Coke machine, filled it with water, and stopped it with a scrap of paper and a rubber band.

The next morning I arrived early at work. The assistant foreman, a potbellied Hungarian, showed me a timecard and how to punch in. He showed me the Coke machine, the locker room with its slimy shower, and also pointed out the places where I shouldn't go: The ovens where the tires were recapped and the customer service area, which had a slashed couch, a coffee table with greasy magazines, and an ashtray. He introduced me to Tully, a fat man with one ear, who worked the buffers that resurfaced the white walls. I was handed an apron and a face mask and shown how to use the buffer: Lift the tire and center, inflate it with a footpedal, press the buffer against the white band until cleaned, and then deflate and blow off the tire with an air hose.

With a paint brush he stirred a can of industrial preserver. "Then slap this blue stuff on." While he was talking a co-worker came up quietly from behind him and goosed him with the air hose. Tully jumped as if he had been struck by a bullet and then turned around cussing and cupping his genitals in his hands as the other worker walked away calling out foul names. When Tully turned to me smiling his gray teeth, I lifted my mouth into a smile because I wanted to get along. He has to be on my side, I thought. He's the one who'll tell the foreman how I'm doing.

I worked carefully that day, setting the tires on the machine as if they were babies, since it was easy to catch a finger in the rim that expanded to inflate the tire. At the day's end we swept up the tire dust and emptied the trash into bins.

At five the workers scattered for their cars and motorcycles while I crossed the street to wash at a burger stand. My hair was stiff with dust and my mouth showed pink against the backdrop of my dirty face. I then ordered a hotdog and walked slowly in the direction of the abandoned house where I had stayed the night before. I lay under the trees and within minutes was asleep. When I woke my shoulders were sore and my eyes burned when I squeezed the lids together.

From the backyard I walked dully through a residential street, and as evening came on, the TV glare in the living rooms and the headlights of passing cars showed against the blue drift of dusk. I saw two children coming up the street with snow cones, their tongues darting at the packed ice. I saw a boy with a peach and wanted to stop him, but felt embarrassed by my hunger. I walked for an hour only to return and discover the house lit brightly. Behind the fence I heard voices and saw a flashlight poking at the garage door. A man on the back steps mumbled something about the refrigerator to the one with the flashlight.

I waited for them to leave, but had the feeling they wouldn't because there was the commotion of furniture being moved. Tired, even more desperate, I started walking again with a great urge to kick things and tear the day from my life. I felt weak and my mind kept drifting because of hunger. I crossed the street to a gas station where I sipped at the water fountain and searched the Coke machine for change. I started walking again, first up a commercial street, then into a residential area where I lay down on someone's lawn and replayed a scene at home—my Mother crying at the kitchen table, my step-father yelling with food in his mouth. They're cruel, I thought, and warned myself that I should never forgive them. How could they do this to me.

When I got up from the lawn it was late. I searched out a place to sleep and found an unlocked car that seemed safe. In the back seat, with my shoes off, I fell asleep but woke up startled about four in the morning when the owner, a nurse on her way to work, opened the door. She got in and was about to start the engine when I raised my head up from the backseat to explain my presence. She screamed so loudly when I said "I'm sorry" that I sprinted from the car with my shoes in hand. Her screams faded, then stopped altogether, as I ran down the block where I hid behind a trash bin and waited for a police siren to sound. Nothing. I crossed the street to a church where I slept stiffly on cardboard in the balcony.

I woke up feeling tired and greasy. It was early and a few street lights were still lit, the east growing pink with dawn. I washed myself from a garden hose and returned to the church to break into what looked like a kitchen. Paper cups, plastic spoons, a coffee pot littered on a table. I found a box of Nabisco crackers which I ate until I was full.

At work I spent the morning at the buffer, but was then told to help Iggy, an old Mexican, who was responsible for choosing tires that could be recapped without the risk of exploding at high speeds. Every morning a truck would deliver used tires, and after I unloaded them Iggy would step among the tires to inspect them for punctures and rips on the sidewalls.

With a yellow chalk he marked circles and Xs to indicate damage and called out "junk." For those tires that could be recapped, he said "goody" and I placed them on my hand truck.

When I had a stack of eight I kicked the truck at an angle and balanced them to another work area where Iggy again inspected the tires, scratching Xs and calling out "junk."

Iggy worked only until three in the afternoon, at which time he went to the locker room to wash and shave and to dress in a two-piece suit. When he came out he glowed with a bracelet, watch, rings, and a shiny fountain pen in his breast pocket. His shoes sounded against the asphalt. He was the image of a banker stepping into sunlight with millions on his mind. He said a few low words to workers with whom he was friendly and none to people like me.

I was seventeen, stupid because I couldn't figure out the difference between an F 78 14 and 750 14 at sight. Iggy shook his head when I brought him the wrong tires, especially since I had expressed interest in being his understudy. "Mexican, how can you be so stupid?" he would yell at me, slapping a tire from my hands. But within weeks I learned a lot about tires, from sizes and makes to how they are molded in iron forms to how Valley stole from other companies. Now and then we received a truckload of tires, most of them new or nearly new, and they were taken to our warehouse in the back where the serial numbers were ground off with a sander. On those days the foreman handed out Cokes and joked with us as we worked to get the numbers off.

Most of the workers were Mexican or black, though a few redneck whites worked there. The base pay was a dollar sixty-five, but the average was three dollars. Of the black workers, I knew Sugar Daddy the best. His body carried two hundred and fifty pounds, armfuls of scars, and a long knife that made me jump when he brought it out from his boot without warning. At one time he had been a singer, and had cut a record in 1967 called *Love's Chance*, which broke into the R and B charts. But nothing came of it. No big contract, no club dates, no tours. He made very little from the sales, only enough for an operation to pull a steering wheel from his gut when, drunk and mad at a lady friend, he slammed his Mustang into a row of parked cars.

"Touch it," he smiled at me one afternoon as he raised his shirt, his black belly kinked with hair. Scared, I traced the scar that ran from his chest to the left of his belly button, and I was repelled but hid my disgust.

Among the Mexicans I had few friends because I was different, a *pocho*[1] who spoke bad Spanish. At lunch they sat in tires and laughed over burritos, looking up at me to laugh even harder. I also sat in tires while nursing a Coke and felt dirty and sticky because I was still living on the street and had not had a real bath in over a week. Nevertheless, when the border patrol came to round up the nationals, I ran with them as they scrambled for the fence or hid among the tires behind the warehouse. The foreman, who thought I was an undocumented worker, yelled at me to run, to get away. I did just that. At the time it seemed fun because there was no risk, only a goodhearted feeling of hide-and-seek, and besides it meant an hour away from work on company time. When the police left we came back and some of the nationals made up stories of how they were almost caught—how they out-raced the police. Some of the stories were so convoluted and unconvincing that everyone

[1]A derogatory term for Mexicans living in the United States who have forgotten their cultural heritage.

laughed *mentiras*,[2] especially when one described how he overpowered
a policeman, took his gun away, and sold the patrol car. We laughed
and he laughed, happy to be there to make up a story.

If work was difficult, so were the nights. I still had not gathered
enough money to rent a room, so I spent the nights sleeping in parked
cars or in the balcony of a church. After a week I found a newspaper ad
for room for rent, phoned, and was given directions. Finished with
work, I walked the five miles down Mission Road looking back into the
traffic with my thumb out. No rides. After eight hours of handling tires,
I was frightening, I suppose, to drivers since they seldom looked at me;
if they did, it was a quick glance. For the next six weeks I would try to
hitchhike, but the only person to stop was a Mexican woman who gave
me two dollars to take the bus. I told her it was too much and that no
bus ran from Mission Road to where I lived, but she insisted that
I keep the money and trotted back to her idling car. It must have hurt
her to see me day after day walking in the heat and looking very much
the dirty Mexican to the many minds that didn't know what it meant
to work at hard labor. That woman knew. Her eyes met mine as she
opened the car door, and there was a tenderness that was surprisingly true—one for which you wait for years but when it comes it
doesn't help. Nothing changes. You continue on in rags, with the sun
still above you.

I rented a room from a middle-aged couple whose lives were a
mess. She was a school teacher and he was a fireman. A perfect set up,
I thought. But during my stay there they would argue with one another
for hours in their bedroom.

When I rang at the front door both Mr. and Mrs. Van Deusen
answered and didn't bother to disguise their shock at how awful
I looked. But they let me in all the same. Mrs. Van Deusen showed me
around the house, from the kitchen and bathroom to the living room with
its grand piano. On her fingers she counted out the house rules as she
walked me to my room. It was a girl's room with lace curtains, scenic
wallpaper of a Victorian couple enjoying a stroll, canopied bed, and
stuffed animals in a corner. Leaving, she turned and asked if she could do
laundry for me and, feeling shy and hurt, I told her no; perhaps the next
day. She left and I undressed to take a bath, exhausted as I sat on the edge
of the bed probing my aches and my bruised places. With a towel around
my waist I hurried down the hallway to the bathroom where Mrs. Van
Deusen had set out an additional towel with a tube of shampoo. I ran
the water in the tub and sat on the toilet, lid down, watching the steam
curl toward the ceiling. When I lowered myself into the tub I felt my

[2]Lies.

body sting. I soaped a wash cloth and scrubbed my arms until they lightened, even glowed pink, but still I looked unwashed around my neck and face no matter how hard I rubbed. Back in the room I sat in bed reading a magazine, happy and thinking of no better luxury than a girl's sheets, especially after nearly two weeks of sleeping on cardboard at the church.

I was too tired to sleep, so I sat at the window watching the neighbors move about in pajamas, and, curious about the room, looked through the bureau drawers to search out personal things—snapshots, a messy diary, and a high school yearbook. I looked up the Van Deusen's daughter, Barbara, and studied her face as if I recognized her from my own school—a face that said "promise," "college," "nice clothes in the closet." She was a skater and a member of the German Club; her greatest ambition was to sing at the Hollywood Bowl.

After awhile I got into bed and as I drifted toward sleep I thought about her. In my mind I played a love scene again and again and altered it slightly each time. She comes home from college and at first is indifferent to my presence in her home, but finally I overwhelm her with deep pity when I come home hurt from work, with blood on my shirt. Then there was another version: Home from college she is immediately taken with me, in spite of my work-darkened face, and invites me into the family car for a milkshake across town. Later, back at the house, we sit in the living room talking about school until we're so close I'm holding her hand. The truth of the matter was that Barbara did come home for a week, but was bitter toward her parents for taking in boarders (two others besides me). During that time she spoke to me only twice: Once, while searching the refrigerator, she asked if we had any mustard; the other time she asked if I had seen her car keys.

But it was a place to stay. Work had become more and more difficult. I not only worked with Iggy, but also with the assistant foreman who was in charge of unloading trucks. After they backed in I hopped on top to pass the tires down by bouncing them on the tailgate to give them an extra spring so they would be less difficult to handle on the other end. Each truck was weighed down with more than two hundred tires, each averaging twenty pounds, so that by the time the truck was emptied and swept clean I glistened with sweat and my T-shirt stuck to my body. I blew snot threaded with tire dust onto the asphalt, indifferent to the customers who watched from the waiting room.

The days were dull. I did what there was to do from morning until the bell sounded at five; I tugged, pulled, and cussed at tires until I was listless and my mind drifted and caught on small things, from cold sodas to shoes to stupid talk about what we would do with a million dollars. I remember unloading a truck with Hamp, a black man.

"What's better than a sharp lady?" he asked me as I stood sweaty on a pile of junked tires. "Water. With ice," I said.

He laughed with his mouth open wide. With his fingers he pinched the sweat from his chin and flicked at me. "You be too young, boy. A woman can make you a god."

As a kid I had chopped cotton and picked grapes, so I knew work. I knew the fatigue and the boredom and the feeling that there was a good possibility you might have to do such work for years, if not for a lifetime. In fact, as a kid I imagined a dark fate: To marry Mexican poor, work Mexican hours, and in the end die a Mexican death, broke and in despair.

But this job at Valley Tire Company confirmed that there was something worse than field work, and I was doing it. We were all doing it, from foreman to the newcomers like me, and what I felt heaving tires for eight hours a day was felt by everyone—black, Mexican, redneck. We all despised those hours but didn't know what else to do. The workers were unskilled, some undocumented and fearful of deportation, and all struck with an uncertainty at what to do with their lives. Although everyone bitched about work, no one left. Some had worked there for as long as twelve years; some had sons working there. Few quit; no one was ever fired. It amazed me that no one gave up when the border patrol jumped from their vans, baton in hand, because I couldn't imagine any work that could be worse—or any life. What was out there, in the world, that made men run for the fence in fear?

How we arrived at such a place is a mystery to me. Why anyone would stay for years is even a deeper concern. You showed up, but from where? What broken life? What ugly past? The foreman showed you the Coke machine, the washroom, and the yard where you'd work. When you picked up a tire, you were amazed at the black it could give off.

INTERPRETATIONS

1.   "There are two kinds of work: one uses the mind and the other uses muscles." How effectively does Soto support this thesis in his essay? Cite evidence.

2.   Soto catalogs his first day at work in great detail. How do his sensory and visual descriptions not only enhance his essay but also serve his purpose?

3.   What role does Iggy play in Soto's summer work experience? How is Iggy different from his co-workers? Does Soto ever resolve his doubts about Iggy's "dignity"? Explain.

4. Why does Soto include the Van Duesens? Is it digressive or does it add another dimension to his narrative? Explain.

5. In paragraphs 29 and 30, Soto contrasts being a field worker with his summer in the tire factory. Although field work pays less, why is it better in his view than the tire factory?

6. Most writers use their conclusions to summarize their essays. Why does Soto conclude his essay with a series of questions? To what effect?

Getting Close to the Machine

ELLEN ULLMAN

Ellen Ullman (b. 1950) earned a B.A. in English from Cornell University and was a software engineer for twenty years when she began writing about her profession. Her writing has appeared in Harper's, Salon, Wired, The Washington Post, *and* The New York Times. *Ullman is the author of the memoir* Close to the Machine: Technophilia and Its Discontents *(1997) and* The Bug, *a novel published in 2003. The Bug's principal character is a Silicon Valley software tester who discovers a bug in one of her company's programs. To what extent is your workplace dependent on your relationship to machines? Explain.*

PEOPLE IMAGINE that computer programming is logical, a process like fixing a clock. Nothing could be further from the truth. Programming is more like an illness, a fever, an obsession. It's like riding a train and never being able to get off.

The problem with programming is not that the computer is illogical—the computer is terribly logical, relentlessly literal. It demands that the programmer explain the world on its terms; that is, as an algorithm that must be written down in order, in a specific syntax, in a strange language that is only partially readable by regular human beings. To program is to translate between the chaos of human life and the rational, line-by-line world of computer language.

When you program, reality presents itself as thousands of details, millions of bits of knowledge. This knowledge comes at you from one perspective and then another, then comes a random thought, then you remember something else important, then you reconsider that idea with a what-if attached. For example, try to think of everything you know about something as simple as an invoice. Now try to tell an idiot how to prepare one. That is programming.

I used to have dreams in which I was overhearing conversations I had to program. Once I dreamed I had to program two people making love. In my dream they sweated and tumbled while I sat looking for the algorithm. The couple went from gentle caresses to ever-deepening passion, and I tried desperately to find a way to express the act of love in the C computer language.

When you are programming, you must not let your mind wander. As the human-world knowledge tumbles about in your head, you must keep typing, typing. You must not be interrupted. Any break in your concentration causes you to lose a line here or there. Some bit comes, then— oh no, it's leaving, please come back. But it may not come back. You may lose it. You will create a bug and there's nothing you can do about it.

People imagine that programmers don't like to talk because they prefer machines to people. This is not completely true. Programmers don't talk because they must not be interrupted.

This need to be uninterrupted leads to a life that is strangely asynchronous to the one lived by other human beings. It's better to send e-mail to a programmer than to call. It's better to leave a note on the chair than to expect the programmer to come to a meeting. This is because the programmer must work in mind time while the phone rings and the meetings happen in real time. It's not just ego that prevents programmers from working in groups—it's the synchronicity problem. Synchronizing with other people (or their representations in telephones, buzzers, and doorbells) can only mean interrupting the thought train. Interruptions mean bugs. You must not get off the train.

I once had a job in which I didn't talk to anyone for two years. Here was the arrangement: I was the first engineer to be hired by a start-up software company. In exchange for large quantities of stock that might be worth something someday, I was supposed to give up my life.

I sat in a large room with two other engineers and three workstations. The fans in the machines whirred, the keys on the keyboards clicked. Occasionally one of us would grunt or mutter. Otherwise we did not speak. Now and then I would have an outburst in which I pounded the keyboard with my fists, setting off a barrage of beeps. My colleagues might have looked up, but they never said anything.

Real time was no longer compelling to me. Days, weeks, months, and years came and went without much change in my surroundings. Surely I was aging. My hair must have grown, I must have cut it, it must have slowly become grayer. Gravity must have been working on my late-thirties body, but I didn't pay attention.

What was compelling was the software. I was making something out of nothing, I thought, and I admit that the software had more life for me during those years than a brief love affair, my friends, my cat, my house, or my neighbor who was stabbed and nearly killed by her husband. One day I sat in a room by myself, surrounded by computer monitors. I remember looking at the screens and saying, "Speak to me."

I was creating something called a device-independent interface library. ("Creating"—that is the word we used, each of us a genius in the attic.) I completed the library in two years and left the company. Five years later, the company's stock went public, and the original arrangement was made good: the engineers who stayed—the ones who had given seven years of their lives to the machine—became very, very wealthy.

If you want money and prestige, you need to write code that only machines or other programmers understand. Such code is called "low." In regular life, "low" usually signifies something bad. In programming, "low" is good. Low means that you are close to the machine.

If the code creates programs that do useful work for regular human beings, it is called "high." Higher-level programs are called "applications." Applications are things that people use. Although it would seem that usefulness is a good thing, direct people-use is bad from a programmer's point of view. If regular people, called "users," can understand the task accomplished by your program, you will be paid less and held in lower esteem.

A real programmer wants to stay close to the machine. The machine means midnight dinners of Diet Coke. It means unwashed clothes and bare feet on the desk. It means anxious rides through mind time that have nothing to do with the clock. To work on things used only by machines or other programmers—that's the key. Programmers and machines don't care how you live. They don't care when you live. You can stay, come, go, sleep—or not. At the end of the project looms a deadline, the terrible place where you must get off the train. But in between, for years at a stretch, you are free: free from the obligations of time.

I once designed a graphical user interface with a man who wouldn't speak to me. My boss hired him without letting anyone else sit in on the interview. My boss lived to regret it.

I was asked to brief my new colleague with the help of the third member of our team. We went into a conference room, where my co-worker and I filled two white boards with lines, boxes, circles, and arrows while the new hire watched. After about a half hour, I noticed that he had become very agitated.

"Are we going too fast?" I asked him.

"Too much for the first day?" asked my colleague.

"No," said our new man, "I just can't do it like this."

"Do what?" I asked. "Like what?"

His hands were deep in his pockets. He gestured with his elbows. "Like this," he said.

"You mean design?" I asked.

"You mean in a meeting?" asked my colleague.

No answer from the new guy. A shrug. Another elbow motion.

Something terrible was beginning to occur to me. "You mean talking?" I asked.

"Yeah, talking," he said, "I can't do it by talking."

By this time in my career, I had met many strange software engineers. But here was the first one who wouldn't talk at all. We had a lot of design work to do. No talking was certainly going to make things difficult.

"So how *can* you do it?" I asked.

"Mail," he said. "Send me e-mail."

Given no choice, we designed a graphical user interface by e-mail. Corporations across North America and Europe are still using a system designed by three people in the same office who communicated via computer, one of whom barely spoke at all.

Pretty graphical interfaces are commonly called "user-friendly." But they are not really your friends. Underlying every user-friendly interface is terrific contempt for the humans who will use it.

The basic idea of a graphical interface is that it will not allow anything alarming to happen. You can pound on the mouse button, your cat can run across it, your baby can punch it, but the system should not crash.

To build a crash-proof system, the designer must be able to imagine—and disallow—the dumbest action possible. He or she has to think of every single stupid thing a human being could do. Gradually, over months and years, the designer's mind creates a construct of the user as an imbecile. This image is necessary. No crash-proof system can be built unless it is made for an idiot.

The designer's contempt for your intelligence is mostly hidden deep in the code. But now and then the disdain surfaces. Here's a small example: You're trying to do something simple such as copying files onto a diskette on your Mac. The program proceeds for a while, then encounters an error. Your disk is defective, says a message, and below the message is a single button. You absolutely must click this button. If you don't click it, the program will hang there indefinitely. Your disk is defective, your files may be bollixed up, but the designer leaves you only one possible reply. You must say, "OK."

The prettier the user interface, and the fewer replies the system allows you to make, the dumber you once appeared in the mind of the designer. Soon, everywhere we look, we will see pretty, idiot-proof interfaces designed to make us say, "OK." Telephones, televisions, sales kiosks will all be wired for "interactive," on-demand services. What power—demand! See a movie, order seats to a basketball game, make hotel reservations, send a card to mother—all of these services will be waiting for us on our televisions or computers whenever we want them, midnight, dawn, or day. Sleep or order a pizza: it no longer matters exactly what we do when. We don't need to involve anyone else in the satisfaction of our needs. We don't even have to talk. We get our services when we want them, free from the obligations of regularly scheduled time. We can all live, like programmers, close to the machine. "Interactivity" is misnamed. It should be called "asynchrony": the engineering culture come to everyday life.

The very word "interactivity" implies something good and wonderful. Surely a response, a reply, an answer is a positive thing. Surely it signifies an advance over something else, something bad, something that doesn't respond. There is only one problem: what we will be interacting with is a machine. We will be "talking" to programs that are beginning to look surprisingly alike; each has little animated pictures we are supposed to choose from, like push buttons on a toddler's toy. The toy is meant to please us. Somehow it is supposed to replace the rewards of fumbling for meaning with a mature human being, in the confusion of a natural language, together, in a room, within touching distance.

As the computer's pretty, helpful face (and contemptuous underlying code) penetrates deeper into daily life, the cult of the engineer comes with it. The engineer's assumptions and presumptions are in the code. That's the purpose of the program, after all: to sum up the intelligence and intentions of all the engineers who worked on the system over time—tens and hundreds of people who have learned an odd and highly specific way of doing things. The system reproduces and re-enacts life as engineers know it: alone, out of time, disdainful of anyone far from the machine.

INTERPRETATIONS

1. "To program is to translate between the chaos of human life and the rational line-by-line world of computer language." What talents does a potential computer programmer need in addition to absolute concentration? Does Ullman make the job appealing? Why or why not?

2. Ullman distinguishes between "mind time" and "real time." How would you define both kinds of time? What activities do you associate with "mind time"? Is there a connection between creativity and "mind time"? Explain.

3. "I once had a job in which I didn't talk to anyone for two years." Review paragraphs 8 through 15 carefully and list the psychological costs of Ullman's isolation.

4. Why does she include paragraphs 16 through 31? What new element does she introduce? How might you respond in her situation?

5. "We can all live, like programmers, close to the machine." What predictions does Ullman make regarding human communication? Is she exaggerating? Explain.

CORRESPONDENCES

1. Review Soto's and Ullman's introductions. What makes them effective? Are they equally provocative? Explain.

2. According to Shrank's perspective, the workplace performs the function of community. To what extent do Soto and Ullman refute this concept?

APPLICATIONS

1. If you involve yourself with hard labor, the kind that Soto has described in his essay, what kind of literacy is acquired? For a few minutes, do an activity that requires the use of your muscles. For example, you might run a few sprints, lift weights, work vigorously in the garden, or split firewood. As you engage in this activity, pay attention to the physical sensations you experience. Write a few paragraphs about what you felt and came to understand about your body and physical activity.

2. Conduct an experiment with your group by logging for a week your use of communications technology including e-mail, faxes, ATMs, and the Web. What possibilities for human interactions did you eliminate? At what personal cost?

3. In the context of describing his summer job, Soto also focuses on the destructive effects of poverty. Write an analysis of the connections he makes between poverty and despair. How does poverty also contribute to emotional and intellectual paralysis?

4. Compare with your group your various experiences with summer jobs. Then focus on one that was particularly pleasant or unpleasant. What did you learn about yourself from this experience? Was it an effective rite of passage? Explain.

Forty-Five a Month

R. K. NARAYAN

R. K. Narayan (1906–2001) was one of India's most prolific writers. During his lifetime Narayan wrote 34 novels, which include: Swami and Friends *(1935),* The English Teacher *(1953),* The Printer of Malgudi *(1957),* The Guide *(1958),* The Man-Eater of Malgudi *(1961),* The Vendor of Sweets *(1967),* The Painter of Signs *(1976), and* A Tiger for Malgudi *(1983). Narayan's short-story collections include:* Malgudi Days *(1982) and* The Grandmother's Tale and Selected Stories *(1994). As you read Narayan's story, think about how you would have reacted in Rao's situation.*

In 1947, India declared its independence from the British, who had controlled most of that country for about 300 years. Colonial India had at the same time been partitioned into Pakistan and India, creating in the same year about 12 million Hindu and Muslim refugees, of whom about 200,000 were killed. Mohandas K. Gandhi (known as the Mahatma), the leader of Indian independence who had advocated nonviolent civil disobedience and abolition of the Untouchable caste, was assassinated the year after independence. The Congress Party dominated Indian politics for forty years (from Independence until late 1989) under Prime Ministers Jawaharlal Nehru, his daughter Indira Gandhi (no relation to Mohandas), and her son Rajiv Gandhi. The Nehru-Gandhi dynasty ended when Rajiv Gandhi lost the November 1989 election and was assassinated while campaigning two years later. His successors have faced an electorate that is more assertive and more impatient, a new divergence between state and society, increasing clashes between Hindus, Sikhs, and Muslims, and ongoing tensions between India and its neighbors, particularly Pakistan.

Indian history, one of the oldest in the world, can be traced to at least 5,000 B.C. The founder of Buddhism lived in fifth-century India. In the third century B.C. Buddhism became the established religion; the native Hinduism revived, however, and eventually prevailed, and now claims well over three-quarters of the Indian population of 800 million.

SHANTA COULD NOT STAY IN HER CLASS any longer. She had done clay-modeling, music, drill, a bit of alphabets and numbers and was now cutting coloured paper. She would have to cut till the bell rang and the teacher said, "Now you may all go home," or "Put away the scissors and take up your alphabets—" Shanta was impatient to know the time. She asked her friend sitting next to her, "Is it five now?"

"Maybe," she replied.

"Or is it six?"

"I don't think so," her friend replied, "because night comes at six."

"Do you think it is five?"

"Yes."

"Oh, I must go. My father will be back at home now. He has asked me to be ready at five. He is taking me to the cinema this evening. I must go home." She threw down her scissors and ran up to the teacher. "Madam, I must go home."

"Why, Shanta Bai?"

"Because it is five o'clock now."

"Who told you it was five?"

"Kamala."

"It is not five now. It is—do you see the clock there? Tell me what the time is. I taught you to read the clock the other day." Shanta stood gazing at the clock in the hall, counted the figures laboriously and declared, "It is nine o'clock."

The teacher called the other girls and said, "Who will tell me the time from that clock?" Several of them concurred with Shanta and said it was nine o'clock, till the teacher said, "You are seeing only the long hand. See the short one, where is it?"

"Two and a half."

"So what is the time?"

"Two and a half."

"It is two forty-five, understand? Now you may all go to your seats—" Shanta returned to the teacher in about ten minutes and asked, "Is it five, madam, because I have to be ready at five. Otherwise my father will be very angry with me. He asked me to return home early."

"At what time?"

"Now." The teacher gave her permission to leave, and Shanta picked up her books and dashed out of the class with a cry of joy. She ran home, threw her books on the floor and shouted, "Mother, Mother," and Mother came running from the next house, where she had gone to chat with her friends.

Mother asked, "Why are you back so early?"

"Has Father come home?" Shanta asked. She would not take her coffee or *tiffin*[1] but insisted on being dressed first. She opened the trunk and insisted on wearing the thinnest frock and knickers, while her mother wanted to dress her in a long skirt and thick coat for the evening. Shanta picked out a gorgeous ribbon from a cardboard soap box in which she kept pencils, ribbons and chalk bits. There was a heated argument

---

[1]Midday snack.

between mother and daughter over the dress, and finally Mother had to give in. Shanta put on her favourite pink frock, braided her hair and flaunted a green ribbon on her pigtail. She powdered her face and pressed a vermilion mark on her forehead. She said, "Now Father will say what a nice girl I am because I'm ready. Aren't you also coming, Mother?"

"Not today."

Shanta stood at the little gate looking down the street.

Mother said, "Father will come only after five; don't stand in the sun. It is only four o'clock."

The sun was disappearing behind the house on the opposite row, and Shanta knew that presently it would be dark. She ran in to her mother and asked, "Why hasn't Father come home yet, Mother?"

"How can I know? He is perhaps held up in the office."

Shanta made a wry face. "I don't like these people in the office. They are bad people—"

She went back to the gate and stood looking out. Her mother shouted from inside, "Come in, Shanta. It is getting dark, don't stand there." But Shanta would not go in. She stood at the gate and a wild idea came into her head. Why should she not go to the office and call out Father and then go to the cinema? She wondered where his office might be. She had no notion. She had seen her father take the turn at the end of the street every day. If one went there, perhaps one went automatically to Father's office. She threw a glance about to see if Mother was anywhere and moved down the street.

It was twilight. Everyone going about looked gigantic, walls of houses appeared very high and cycles and carriages looked as though they would bear down on her. She walked on the very edge of the road. Soon the lamps were twinkling, and the passersby looked like shadows. She had taken two turns and did not know where she was. She sat down on the edge of the road biting her nails. She wondered how she was to reach home. A servant employed in the next house was passing along, and she picked herself up and stood before him.

"Oh, what are you doing here all alone?" he asked. She replied, "I don't know. I came here. Will you take me to our house?" She followed him and was soon back in her house.

Venkat Rao, Shanta's father, was about to start for his office that morning when a *jutka*[2] passed along the street distributing cinema handbills. Shanta dashed to the street and picked up a handbill. She held it up and asked, "Father, will you take me to the cinema today?" He felt unhappy at the question. Here was the child growing up without

[2]A two-wheeled horse-drawn carriage.

having any of the amenities and the simple pleasures of life. He had hardly taken her twice to the cinema. He had no time for the child. While children of her age in other houses had all the dolls, dresses and outings that they wanted, this child was growing up all alone and like a barbarian more or less. He felt furious with his office. For forty rupees[3] a month they seemed to have purchased him outright.

He reproached himself for neglecting his wife and child—even the wife could have her own circle of friends and so on: she was after all a grown-up, but what about the child? What a drab, colourless existence was hers! Every day they kept him at the office till seven or eight in the evening, and when he came home the child was asleep. Even on Sundays they wanted him at the office. Why did they think he had no personal life, a life of his own? They gave him hardly any time to take the child to the park or the pictures. He was going to show them that they weren't to toy with him. Yes, he was prepared even to quarrel with his manager if necessary.

He said with resolve, "I will take you to the cinema this evening. Be ready at five."

"Really! Mother!" Shanta shouted. Mother came out of the kitchen. "Father is taking me to a cinema in the evening."

Shanta's mother smiled cynically. "Don't make false promises to the child—" Venkat Rao glared at her. "Don't talk nonsense. You think you are the only person who keeps promises—"

He told Shanta, "Be ready at five, and I will come and take you positively. If you are not ready, I will be very angry with you."

He walked to his office full of resolve. He would do his normal work and get out at five. If they started any old tricks of theirs, he was going to tell the boss, "Here is my resignation. My child's happiness is more important to me than these horrible papers of yours."

All day the usual stream of papers flowed onto his table and off it. He scrutinized, signed and drafted. He was corrected, admonished and insulted. He had a break of only five minutes in the afternoon for his coffee.

When the office clock struck five and the other clerks were leaving, he went up to the manager and said, "May I go, sir?" The manager looked up from his paper. "You!" It was unthinkable that the cash and account section should be closing at five. "How can you go?"

"I have some urgent private business, sir," he said, smothering the lines he had been rehearsing since the morning: "Herewith my resignation." He visualized Shanta standing at the door, dressed and palpitating with eagerness.

[3]The rupee is an Indian unit of money.

"There shouldn't be anything more urgent than the office work; go back to your seat. You know how many hours I work?" asked the manager. The manager came to the office three hours before opening time and stayed nearly three hours after closing, even on Sundays. The clerks commented among themselves, "His wife must be whipping him whenever he is seen at home; that is why the old owl seems so fond of his office."

"Did you trace the source of that ten-eight difference?" asked the manager.

"I shall have to examine two hundred vouchers. I thought we might do it tomorrow."

"No, no, this won't do. You must rectify it immediately."

Venkat Rao mumbled, "Yes, sir," and slunk back to his seat. The clock showed 5:30. Now it meant two hours of excruciating search among vouchers. All the rest of the office had gone. Only he and another clerk in his section were working, and of course, the manager was there. Venkat Rao was furious. His mind was made up. He wasn't a slave who had sold himself for forty rupees outright. He could make that money easily; and if he couldn't, it would be more honourable to die of starvation.

He took a sheet of paper and wrote: "Herewith my resignation. If you people think you have bought me body and soul for forty rupees, you are mistaken. I think it would be far better for me and my family to die of starvation than slave for this petty forty rupees on which you have kept me for years and years. I suppose you have not the slightest notion of giving me an increment. You give yourselves heavy slices frequently, and I don't see why you shouldn't think of us occasionally. In any case it doesn't interest me now, since this is my resignation. If I and my family perish of starvation, may our ghosts come and haunt you all your life—" He folded the letter, put it in an envelope, sealed the flap and addressed it to the manager. He left his seat and stood before the manager. The manager mechanically received the letter and put it on his pad.

"Venkat Rao," said the manager, "I'm sure you will be glad to hear this news. Our officer discussed the question of increments today, and I've recommended you for an increment of five rupees. Orders are not yet passed, so keep this to yourself for the present." Venkat Rao put out his hand, snatched the envelope from the pad and hastily slipped it in his pocket.

"What is that letter?"

"I have applied for a little casual leave, sir, but I think . . ."

"You can't get any leave for at least a fortnight to come."

"Yes, sir, I realize that. That is why I am withdrawing my application, sir."

"Very well. Have you traced that mistake?"

"I'm scrutinizing the vouchers, sir. I will find it out within an hour . . ."

It was nine o'clock when he went home. Shanta was already asleep. Her mother said. "She wouldn't even change her frock, thinking that any moment you might be coming and taking her out. She hardly ate any food; and wouldn't lie down for fear of crumpling her dress. . . ."

Venkat Rao's heart bled when he saw his child sleeping in her pink frock, hair combed and face powdered, dressed and ready to be taken out. "Why should I not take her to the night show?" He shook her gently and called, "Shanta, Shanta." Shanta kicked her legs and cried, irritated at being disturbed. Mother whispered, "Don't wake her," and patted her back to sleep.

Venkat Rao watched the child for a moment. "I don't know if it is going to be possible for me to take her out at all—you see, they are giving me an increment—" he wailed.

INTERPRETATIONS

1. Why do you think Narayan focuses on the daughter at the outset of the story?

2. "For forty rupees a month they seemed to have purchased him outright." Is this an accurate portrayal of Rao's situation? How does his personality contribute to his dissatisfaction at work?

3. Analyze the mother's role in the story. Does she share her husband's antipathy toward his job? How do you know?

CORRESPONDENCES

1. Dorris and Narayan focus on rights in the workplace from different vantage points and cultural perspectives. What conversation can you imagine them sharing?

2. Review Terkel's perspective on work and discuss its relevance to the texts by Narayan and Soto.

APPLICATIONS

1. Imagine yourself in Shanta's position and write a journal entry on your emotional responses to your father's broken promise.

2. Narayan's stories often reflect the conflict between tradition and individuality. How are both reflected in "Forty-Five a Month"? Analyze the elements of the conflict.

3. Brainstorm with your group on images of power. Do you associate power with the workplace? In what context? Is it possible to have power within the constraints of the employee–employer relationship? Summarize the group's discussion.

4. In the story "Forty-Five a Month," the plot seems to follow directly from the beginning to the end. Despite the hopes and expectations of both Shanta and a reader, Venkat Rao will not attend the cinema that evening. What, however, do you think would have happened if Rao had said his piece and left his resignation with his manager? How would this twist in plot affect not only what happens in the story but characterization, setting, and theme? After considering the possibilities, write your version of a section of the story that takes into account the twist in plot offered above. Try as best you can to match Nayaran's style and literary technique (e.g., attention to detail, use of dialogue, involvement of the narrator).

Free and Equal

LALITA GANDBHIR

Lalita Gandbhir (b. 1938) works as a physician in the Boston area, where she has lived since coming to the United States in 1963. She has published stories in the Toronto South Asian Review, *the* Massachusetts Review, Spotlight, *and other journals, as well as two collections of short stories in India. Before reading her short story, freewrite about your association with its title.*

RAMESH CAREFULLY STUDIED his reflection in the mirror hung in the hallway. His hair, shirt, tie, suit, nothing escaped his scrutiny. His tie seemed a little crooked, so he undid it and fixed it with slow deliberate movements. Then he reexamined the tie. A conservative shade of maroon, not too wide, not too narrow, just right for the occasion, for the image he wanted to project.

All of a sudden he was aware of two eyes staring at him. He turned to Jay, his little son. Jay sat on the steps leading to the second floor, his eyes focused on his father.

"Why are you staring at me?" Ramesh inquired.

"Going to work now?" Jay intimated the reason for the surprised stare.

Ramesh understood the reason behind Jay's confusion. He used to go to work dressed like this in the mornings. Jay had not seen him dressed in a suit in the evening.

For a moment Ramesh was proud of his son. "What a keen observer Jay is!" Ramesh thought to himself. "For six months I have not worked, yet he noticed a change in my old routine."

However, the implications behind the question bothered Ramesh.

"I am going to a job fair," he answered irritably and again attempted to focus on his tie.

"Can I come?" Jay promptly hurled a question in Ramesh's direction. To him a fair was a fun event. He had been to fairs with his mother before and did not wish to miss this one.

"Jay, this is not the kind of fair you are thinking of. This is a job fair."

"Do they sell jobs at job fairs?"

"Yes." Jay's question struck a sensitive spot. "No, they don't sell jobs. They are buyers. They shop for skills. It's me who is selling my skills. Unfortunately, it's a buyer's market."

The question stimulated Ramesh's chain of thought. "Is my skill for sale?" Ramesh wondered. "If that is true, then why did I dress so carefully? Why did I rehearse answers to imaginary questions from interviewers?"

"No, this job hunting is no longer a simple straightforward business transaction like it used to be when engineers were in demand. I am desperate. I am selling my soul. The job market is no longer a two-way street. I have no negotiating power. I just have to accept what I can get."

Ramesh pulled on his socks mechanically and longingly thought of the good old days like a sick old man thinking of his healthful youth.

Just ten years ago he had hopped from job to job at will. Money, interesting work, more responsibility, benefits, a whim for any reason that appealed to him, and he had switched jobs. Responding to advertisements was his hobby. Head hunters called him offering better and better situations. He went to job fairs casually dressed and never gave a second thought to his attire.

He had job offers, not one or two, but six or seven. The industry needed him then. It was so nice to be coveted!

Ramesh wiped his polished, spotless shoes with a soft cloth.

How carefree he used to be! He dressed like this every morning in five minutes and, yes, Jay remembers.

He never polished his shoes then. His hand moving the cloth on his shoes stood still for a minute. Yes, Rani, his wife, did it for him. Nowadays she seemed to do less and less for him. Why? He asked himself.

Rani had found a part-time job on her own when companies in the area had started to lay off engineers. She had not bothered to discuss the matter with him, just informed him of her decision. In a year she accepted a full-time slot. "How did she manage to receive promotions so soon?" Ramesh wondered.

Rani still ran the home and cared for their young children. Ramesh had seen her busy at all kinds of tasks from early morning until late at night.

Over the last three months she did less and less for Ramesh. She no longer did his laundry or ironing. She had stopped polishing his shoes and did not wait up for him when he returned late from job fairs.

"She is often tired," Ramesh tried to understand, but he felt that she had let him down, wronged him just when his spirit was sinking and he needed her most.

"She should have made an effort for the sake of appearance. It was her duty toward a jobless, incomeless husband."

He pushed all thoughts out of his mind.

He tied his polished shoes, dragged his heavy winter coat out of the closet, and picked up his keys.

"Tell your Ma that I have left," he ordered Jay, and closed the door without saying good-bye to Rani.

In the car, thoughts flooded his mind again.

Perhaps he made a mistake in coming to study abroad for his Master's in engineering. No! That was not the error. He should not have stayed on after he received his Master's. He should have returned home as he originally planned.

He intended to return, but unfortunately he attended a job fair after graduation just for fun and ended up accepting a job offer. A high salary in dollars converted into a small fortune in rupees, proved impossible to resist. He always converted dollars into rupees then, before buying or selling. He offered himself an excuse of short-term American experience and stayed on. The company that hired him sponsored him for a green card.

He still wanted to return home, but he postponed it, went for a visit instead and picked Rani from several prospective brides, married her and returned to the United States.

The trip left bitter memories, especially for Rani. He could not talk his mother out of accepting a dowry.

"Mother, Rani will earn the entire sum of a dowry in a month in the United States. A dowry is a hardship for her middle-class family. Let us not insist on it. Just accept what her family offers."

But Mother, with Father's tacit support, insisted. "You are my only son. I have waited for this occasion all my life. I want a proper wedding, the kind of wedding our friends and relatives will remember forever."

Ramesh gave in to her wishes and had a wedding with pomp and special traditional honors for his family. His mother was only partially gratified because she felt that their family did not get what was due them with her foreign returned son! The dowry, however, succeeded in upsetting Rani, who looked miserable throughout the ceremony.

"We will refund all the money once you come to the United States," Ramesh promised her. "It's a minor sum when dollars are converted to rupees."

Instead of talking in his conciliatory tone, Rani demanded, too harshly for a bride, "If it's a minor sum, why did you let your family insist on a dowry? You know my parents' savings are wiped out."

Over a few years they refunded the money, but Rani's wounds never healed and during fights she referred to the dowry spitefully.

Her caustic remarks did not bother Ramesh before, but now with her income supporting the family, they were beginning to hurt. "Write your mother that your wife works and makes up for part of the dowry her father failed to provide!" she had remarked once.

"Don't women ever forgive?" he had wondered.

"I am extra sensitive." He brushed off the pain that Rani's words caused.

The job fair was at a big hotel. He followed the directions and turned into a full parking lot. As he pulled into the tight space close to the exit, he glanced at the hotel lobby. Through the glass exterior wall, underneath a brightly lit chandelier, he could see a huge crowd milling in the lobby.

Panic struck him. He was late. So many people had made it there ahead of him. All applicants with his experience and background might be turned away.

Another car approached and pulled into the last parking space in the lot. The engine noise died and a man roughly his height and build stepped out, just as Ramesh shut his car door. Out on the walkway Ramesh heard a greeting.

"Hello, how are you?"

Ramesh looked up.

In the fluorescent lights his eyes met friendly blue eyes. He noticed a slightly wrinkled forehead and receding hairline, like his own.

"Hello," Ramesh responded.

The stranger smiled. "Sometimes I wonder why I come to these fairs. In the last six months I must have been to at least ten."

"Really? So have I!" He must have been laid off at the same time, Ramesh thought.

"We must have attended the same ones. I don't remember seeing you," the newcomer said.

"Too many engineers looking for a job—you know," Ramesh offered as explanation.

The pair had approached the revolving lobby doors. Ramesh had a strong urge to turn back and return home.

"Come on, we must try." The newcomer apparently had sensed the urge. "My name is Bruce. Would you like to meet me at the door in an hour? We will have a drink before we go home. It will—kind of lift my spirits."

"All right," Ramesh agreed without thinking and added, "I am Ramesh."

Bruce waited for Ramesh to step into the revolving door.

Ramesh mechanically pushed into the lobby. His heart sagged even further. "With persons like Bruce looking for a job, who will hire a foreigner like me?" he wondered. He looked around. Bruce had vanished into the crowd.

Ramesh looked at a row of booths set up by the side wall. He approached one looking for engineers with his qualifications. A few

Americans had already lined up to talk to the woman screening the applicants.

She looked at him and repeated the same questions she had asked applicants before him. "Your name, sir?"

He had to spell it. She made a mistake in noting it down. He had to correct her.

"Please fill out this application." He sensed a slight irritation in her voice.

"Thank you," he said. His accent seemed to have intensified. He took the application and retreated to a long table.

He visited six or seven booths of companies who might need—directly, indirectly, or remotely—someone of his experience and education; challenge, benefit package, location, salary, nothing mattered to him anymore. He had to find a job.

An hour and a half later, as he approached the revolving door, he noticed Bruce waiting for him.

During the discussion over drinks, he discovered that Bruce had the same qualifications as himself. However, Bruce had spent several years wandering around the world, so he had only four years of experience. Ramesh had guessed right. Bruce had been laid off the same time as himself.

"It's been very hard," Bruce said. "What little savings we had are wiped out and my wife is fed up with me. She thinks I don't try hard. This role reversal is not good for a man's ego."

"Yes," Ramesh agreed.

"I may have to move but my wife doesn't want to. Her family is here."

"I understand."

"I figure you don't have that problem."

"No. You must have guessed I'm from India."

After a couple of drinks they walked out into an empty lobby and empty parking lot.

Two days later Bruce called. "Want to go to a job fair? It's in Woodland, two hundred miles from here. I hate to drive out alone." Ramesh agreed.

"Who will hire me when Americans are available?" he complained to Rani afterward.

"You must not think like that. You are as good as any of them," Rani snapped. "Remember what Alexander said."

Ramesh remembered. Alexander was a crazy history student with whom he had shared an apartment. Rani always referred to Alexander's message.

Ramesh had responded to an advertisement on his university's bulletin board and Alexander had answered the phone.

"You have to be crazy to share an apartment with me. My last roommate left because he could not live with me."

"What did you do? I mean, why did he leave?" Ramesh asked.

"I like to talk. You see, I wake up people and tell them about my ideas at night. They call me crazy Alexander . . ."

"I will get back to you." Ramesh put the receiver down and talked to the student who had moved out.

"You see, Alexander's a nut. He sleeps during the day and studies at night. He's a history buff. He studies revolutions. He wakes up people just to talk to them, about theories, others and his own! He will offer to discount the rent if you put up with him."

Short of funds, Ramesh moved in with Alexander.

Much of Alexander's oratory bounced off Ramesh's half-asleep brain, but off and on a few sentences made an impression and stuck in his memory.

"You must first view yourself as free and equal," Alexander had said.

"Equal to whom?"

"To those around you who consider you less than equal . . ."

"Me? Less than equal?"

"No! Not you, stupid. The oppressed person. Oppression could be social, religious, foreign, traditional."

"Who oppressed me?"

"No! No! Not you! An imaginary oppressed person who must first see himself as the equal of his oppressors. The idea of equality will ultimately sow seeds of freedom and revolution in his mind. That idea is the first step. You see . . . stop snoring . . . That's the first step toward liberation."

Soon Ramesh walked like a zombie.

In another month, he too moved out.

After his marriage he told Rani some of his conversations with Alexander.

"Makes sense," she said, looking very earnest.

"Really! You mean you understand?" Rani's reaction amazed Ramesh.

"Yes, I do. I am an oppressed person, socially and traditionally. That's why my parents had to come up with a dowry."

A month went by and Ramesh was called for an interview.

Bruce telephoned the same night. He and some other engineers he knew had also been called. Had Ramesh received a call, too?

Ramesh swallowed hard. "No, I didn't." He felt guilty and ashamed. He had lied to Bruce, who was so open, friendly, and supportive, despite his own difficulties.

Ramesh's ego had already suffered a major trauma. He was convinced that he would not get a job if Americans were available and he did not wish to admit to Bruce later on, "I had an interview, but they didn't hire me." It was easier to lie now.

The interview over, Ramesh decided to put the job out of his mind. His confidence at a low ebb, he dared not hope.

Three weeks went by and he received a phone call from the company that interviewed him. He had the job.

"They must have hired several engineers," Ramesh thought, elated.

Bruce called again. "I didn't get the job. The other guys I know have also received negative replies."

The news stunned Ramesh. He could not believe that he had the job and the others did not. As he pondered this, he realized he owed an embarrassing explanation to Bruce. How was he going to tell him that he had the job?

As Bruce jabbered about something, Ramesh collected his courage.

"I have an offer from them," he stated in a flat tone and strained his ear for a response.

After a few unbearable seconds of silence, Bruce exclaimed, "Congratulations! At least one of us made it. Now we can all hope. I know you have better qualifications."

Ramesh knew that the voice was sincere, without a touch of the envy he had anticipated.

They agreed to meet Saturday for a drink, a small celebration, Bruce suggested.

"Rani, I got the job. The others didn't." Ramesh hung up the receiver and bounded up to Rani.

"I told you you are as good as any of them," Rani responded nonchalantly and continued to fold laundry.

"Maybe . . . possibly . . . they needed a minority candidate," Ramesh muttered.

Rani stopped folding. "Ramesh," she said as her eyes scanned Ramesh's face, "You may have the job and the knowledge and the qualifications, but you are not free and equal."

"What do you mean?" Ramesh asked.

INTERPRETATIONS

1. Alexander, for all his eccentricities, is portrayed as the voice of wisdom. How does his "message" of free and equal relate to the problems of job seeking? To the problems of competition between foreign and native-born job seekers? To the problem of dowries?

2. How realistic is Bruce's lack of resentment that Ramesh got a job? How well does the story make us believe in Ramesh's "better qualifications"?

3. From your own experience, what is the usual relationship between two candidates competing in a limited job market? Do they confide in each other or share tips? Does the first one to get a job feel guilty?

CORRESPONDENCES

1. Soto and Gandbhir discuss how one's job affects self-respect. Which examples did you find most convincing?

2. What was Gandbhir's purpose in writing this story? Is she trying to show human nature in action, or to entertain, or to persuade? How does her purpose compare with Narayan's?

APPLICATIONS

1. "You may have the job and the knowledge and the qualifications, but you are not free and equal." Discuss Rani's assessment of her husband. Is it possible for Ramesh to be "free and equal" in the United States? Why or why not?

2. Discuss with your group your images of success. To what extent do they involve economic prosperity? Your self-image? Is it possible for everyone to be successful? Do individual strivings for success affect communal values? How?

3. Discuss with your group issues of discrimination in the workplace involving race, gender, disabilities, and/or seniority. What suggestions would you make to cope with these situations?

A View of Affirmative Action in the Workplace

MICHAEL GNOLFO

Michael Gnolfo was born in Brooklyn, New York, in 1951. He grew up in Queens, and lives in Nassau County on Long Island with his wife and son. He works for a major utility company as a customer-service supervisor. He returned to college after a sixteen-year absence and is now a graduate of Queensborough Community College. Before reading Gnolfo's essay, write a journal entry on your views on affirmative action.

AFFIRMATIVE ACTION IS BY DEFINITION any plan or program that promotes the employment of women and members of minority groups. This has come about to right all the wrongs suffered by these groups in the past. It is intended to be a positive force for civil rights.

Directly or indirectly, because of Affirmative Action women and minorities have increasingly found more opportunity where none existed for them. Traditional role separation is disappearing. Society is realizing an untapped wealth of talent, and business is reaping a whirlwind of benefits from this new diversity.

Jobs that were traditionally male-dominated have had major inroads by women. Bus drivers, construction workers, telephone technicians and pilots now count women among their numbers as do the management staffs of many corporations. The reverse is also true. Men have increasingly entered such fields as nursing, secretarial sciences and flight attendants, which have been traditionally female occupations. It seems that no barriers exist to an individual with the skills to perform a job.

While all of this is good and the proper course to pursue, there are problems. We can all agree that the protection and promotion of one group in society is wrong. So, when does a program designed to promote fairness become discriminatory? When capable people are neglected at the expense of less capable or similarly capable politically correct/connected candidates. A glaring example of this is the New York City Police exam and requirements. A comparison of physical requirements from today versus thirty years ago reveals a less demanding test of strength and physique. The requirements were relaxed to allow lesser physical candidates to pass. Minority candidates with lower written test marks are also taken over other candidates if a certain percentage of those minorities are not represented on the force. We are legislating mediocrity at best. What is more desirable, a competent organization or a gender/racially correct structure?

Private business is doing just the same. It is especially true in any large company that is contractually obligated to the government or is regulated by it. Those not included in Affirmative Action become less likely to be successful despite qualification. They are fast becoming a new oppressed minority. Companies are zealous in their adherence to Affirmative Action not out of altruism but of fear of loss of contract or stiffer regulation. Remember that while there has been much progress by minorities in business there is a dearth of minority CEOs in the major corporations, and that says so much about the reality of Affirmative Action.

The time is right for another step in the evolution of American society. We all realize the positive contributions of the groups protected by Affirmative Action. They have been valuable additions to our society. But abuses have now surfaced. Let's not make the same mistakes we made before. We need a Positive Fairness principle to replace Affirmative Action. Qualification and achievement should be the deciding factors in society and business. Quotas are abhorrent. Discrimination is bad, be it directed toward a race, gender, religion or anyone for any reason. Affirmative Action is becoming a racist, sexist instrument that is quickly turning into a tool of those who would replace one form of dominance with another. Contrary to the belief of feminists, the best man for the job is not a WOMAN but the most qualified individual.

INTERPRETATIONS

1. Gnolfo says that the purpose of Affirmative Action has been "to right all the wrongs suffered by these groups in the past." If this was once a worthwhile goal, has the goal been met? Are there perhaps other reasons for Affirmative Action (such as diversification) that make it still worthwhile?

2. What is the relationship between economic hard times and Affirmative Action in the workplace?

3. What is the legal status of Affirmative Action? Gnolfo says that companies don't practice Affirmative Action out of "altruism." What difference would it make if it were voluntary? Would it still accomplish its goal without the "abuses" Gnolfo attributes to it?

4. Comment on the relationship between Gnolfo's first three paragraphs and the rest of the essay. How effective is this two-part organization?

CORRESPONDENCES

1. Gnolfo examines the effects of Affirmative Action in the workplace. What conversation can you imagine him having with Ramesh in "Free and Equal"?
2. "Affirmative Action is becoming a racist, sexist instrument that is quickly turning into a tool of those who would replace one form of dominance with another." To what extent do you agree or disagree? Compare Gnolfo's assessment of Affirmative Action with that expressed in Steinem's perspective on work.

APPLICATIONS

1. Affirmative Action is a controversial issue. If you are a member of a minority group who could benefit from Affirmative Action, write an essay citing reasons why your choice to do so is ethical. If you are in a position to be hurt by Affirmative Action, write an essay citing reasons why Affirmative Action programs offer unfair opportunities to minorities. Be as specific as you can.
2. Discuss Gnolfo's thesis that, "Contrary to the belief of feminists, the best man for the job is not a WOMAN but the most qualified individual."
3. Write an essay analyzing the causes and effects of women's entry into the workplace in the 1990s. You might focus on *one* of the following issues: the responsibility of the employer or the state to provide adequate child care, or the impact of working mothers playing multiple roles.
4. In his third paragraph Gnolfo states, "Jobs that were traditionally male dominated have had major inroads by women." Do you agree with this statement? Check these sites to support your opinions.

   http://www.gendercenter.org/genderwork.htm

   http://www.census.gov/population/pop-profile/2000/
     chap20.pdf

   ftp://ftp.bls.gov/pub/special.requests/lf/aat10.txt

The Knowing Eye

Ridley Gunderson

READING IMAGES

1. What kinds of work are the people in the photographs doing? In general, are cultural values placed upon the work that people do? Explain your answers to these questions.

2. In the future, would you like to work by yourself or with people? What are the advantages and disadvantages of each work situation? How may you use each photograph to reinforce what you have stated?

MAKING CONNECTIONS

1. What relationship can you find between these two photographs? What connection can you establish between the people in them?

2. In "Living Up the Street Black Hair," Gary Soto writes about his observations and feelings when working in a tire shop. How do you think the workers in the fish market would relate to Soto's essay?

Zack Rutkin

WORDS AND IMAGES

1. Places where people do their marketing are often filled with commotion and social activity. Taking your cues from the photograph of the fish market, create a conversation that one might hear in this setting. Try to generate at least twenty lines of dialogue, and include no less than four speakers.

2. There is a saying that a picture is worth a thousand words. Pick one photograph and write an essay that expresses your thoughts about it. Be sure to create a focused essay, using a clear thesis statement and body paragraphs to support it.

Additional Writing Topics

1. Loth talks about the importance of fulfilling work. How would you characterize your goals with regard to work? Do you think being ambitious is more important than enjoying work? How can you imagine doing both? Write an essay defining your attitudes toward work, including the factors that influence them.

2. Gnolfo and Gandbhir note attitudes toward Affirmative Action in the workplace. Review their comments. Then conduct an informal survey by interviewing several people affected by Affirmative Action programs. Summarize your findings.

3. Have you, like Dorris, had experiences that resembled his wilderness quest? How did they help you better understand yourself and your talents? Write an essay describing these experiences and how they helped shape your identity and vocational goals.

4. Review Sayers's perspective on work and test its validity by interviewing people you know in various occupations on their attitudes toward working and the workplace. What conclusions did you reach? Write an analysis based on their responses.

5. Recent sociological surveys indicate that overworked parents in the United States are unable to provide a sense of family and community for their children. Discuss this with your group. How is it pertinent to the concept of latchkey children? How would you classify that lifestyle and its effects on family life? What solutions can you think of?

6. Working with your group, construct your own Bill of Rights for a changing workplace. You might consider such issues as:

   Drug testing

   Health benefits

   Retirement plans

   Child care

   Flexible hours

   Promotional opportunities

   Tuition reimbursement for upgrading skills

   Write a brief rationale for the inclusion of each item in your "Bill."

7. Is there a career that has captured your imagination that you would like to pursue? Do you dream of being a musician, talk show host, archeologist, or lawyer? Write an essay explaining

what draws you to this career. How do you intend to make it a reality?

8. Reflect on your reasons for pursuing your education. To what extent are they related to your professional goals? Are your goals market driven or based on personal preference? Write a journal entry on these issues.

CHAPTER

6

Traditions

THE IDEA OF TRADITION or heritage is inherent in most definitions of culture. A culture incorporates the shared knowledge, expectations, and beliefs of a group of people. The human imagination has always been captivated by the idea of the past and its connections to the present. Stories from the oral traditions of ancient cultures as well as our own evoke the powers and mysteries of the past by recreating a time in which myths, fables, legends, and archetypes dictated the values of human actions within the community. The ritual of orality—of storytelling—was an integral part of communal life, as tribe members from the oldest to the youngest listened to, recalled, or retold stories about creation, good and evil, war and peace, life and death.

Folklore also helps explain human relationships, hopes, fears, and dreams. Folktales and myths are not culturally or ethnically bound as people from all over the world use them to explain their cultures, religions, traditions, and social customs. Many Native American writers cherish their roots. N. Scott Momaday, for example, in "The Way to Rainy Mountain," celebrates his tribal heritage by creating a tapestry in which he interweaves myth, history, and family stories. He unites these elements through the traditional journey motif that links the actual journey of his tribe the Kiowas, and his own quest to discover his roots and identity, which he describes as "many journeys in one."

In the United States we tend to value the new over the old; to seek solutions to problems that often involve breaking with the past. Thus it should be no surprise that our attitude toward roots and traditions is ambivalent: We want it, but we want to be free of it; we love part of the tradition but hate part of it. Tradition is both past and future, both history and destiny. Thus it is essential that we engage in conversations with one another about our own traditions and those of other, older cultures.

It is no accident that several texts in this chapter come out of a very old culture: Bantu, Mayan, Native American, Northern European, Chinese, and Indian. Our purpose is to explore the significance of these traditions—both our own and those of others. These opening texts demonstrate the universal importance of traditions but also celebrate their diversity. They show how essential it is to converse about an astonishing variety of traditions including rituals, ceremonies, and customs, as well as symbols, ideals, and emotions. Consequently, intracultural and intercultural conversations often end in argument. You can see such arguments variously in progress in Yael Yarimi's reflections on the importance of cultural mourning and in Salman Rushdie's meditation on Bombay, his "lost city."

When dialogue stops—when tradition is unquestioningly accepted or revered—it can stifle, maim, or even kill. So, at least, suggests John King Fairbank as he looks at footbinding, a thousand-year-old custom that only ended in the last century. In "The Lottery," a cautionary tale set in a New England village in the 1940s, Shirley Jackson also suggests that blind adherence to custom can be destructive, even deadly. A similar point is made by Mark Fineman in his factual account of a tradition obsessed in his 1970s essay "Stone-Throwing in India: An Annual Bash."

Participation in conversations about your own traditions and those of other cultures can be challenging, even disturbing, since it may involve new ways of listening and seeing. It invites you to suspend judgment and avoid making unfavorable comparisons by looking at the value of a people and their culture through a different lens. Although it is impossible to be totally free of ethnocentrism, we hope that the overheard conversations in this chapter will deepen your appreciation of cultural pluralities.

Perspectives

History has a way of intruding upon the present.

—Louise Erdrich

Every man, every woman, carries in head and mind the image of the ideal place, the right place, the one true home, known or unknown, actual or visionary.

—Edward Abbey

Contemporary man has rationalized the myths, but he has not been able to destroy them.

—Octavio Paz

I was born a thousand years ago, born in the culture of bows and arrows . . . born in an age when people loved the things of nature, and spoke to it as though it had a soul.

—Chief Dan George

The past is a foreign country: they do things differently there.

—L. P. Hartley

I have found that life persists in the midst of destruction, and therefore, there must be a bigger law than that of destruction.

—Mohandas K. (Mahatma) Gandhi

The position of women in a society provides an exact measure of the development of that society.

—Gustav Geiger

Memory is the diary that we all carry about with us.

—Oscar Wilde

Tradition is a guide and not a jailor.

—W. Somerset Maugham

True places are not found on maps.

—Herman Melville

To everything there is a season, and a time to every purpose under the heaven: a time to be born, and a time to die; a time to plant, and a time to pluck up that which is planted; a time to kill, and a time to heal; a time to break down, and a time to build up; a time to weep, and a time to laugh; a time to mourn, and a time to dance; a time to cast away stones, and a time to gather stones together; a time to embrace, and a time to refrain from embracing; a time to get, and a time to lose; a time to keep, and a time to cast away; a time to rend, and a time to sew; a time to keep silence, and a time to speak; a time to love, and a time to hate; a time of war, and a time of peace. What profit hath he that worketh in that wherein he laboreth?

—Ecclesiastes 3:1–10

History is the present. That's why every generation writes it anew. But what most people think of as history is its end product, myth.

—E. L. Doctorow

We do not remember days, we remember moments.

—Cesare Pavese

We have to do with the past only as we can make it useful to the present and the future.

—Frederick Douglass

We want to remain curious, startled, provoked, mystified, and uplifted. We want to glare, gaze, gawk, behold, and stare. We want to be given opportunities to change, and ultimately we want to be told that we can become kings and queens, or lords of our own destinies. We remember wonder tales and fairy tales to keep our sense of wonderment alive and to nurture our hope that we can seize possibilities and opportunities to transform ourselves and our worlds.

—Jack Zipes

Memory is something we reconstruct, something we create. Memory is a story we make up from snatches of the past.

—Lynne Sharon Schwartz

Myths are public dreams, dreams are private myths.

—Joseph Campbell

Each act of creation shall leave you humble, for it is never as great as your dream and always inferior to that most marvelous dream of God which is nature.

—Gabriela Mistral

Gratitude is the heart's memory.

—French Proverb

To be ourselves we must have ourselves—possess, if need be repossess, our life-stories. We must "recollect" ourselves, recollect the inner drama, the narrative, of ourselves. A man needs such a narrative, a continuous inner narrative, to maintain his identity, his self.

—*Oliver Sachs*

Where I come from, the words that are most highly valued are those which are spoken from the heart, unpremeditated and unrehearsed. Among the Pueblo people, a written speech or statement is highly suspect because the true feelings of the speaker remain hidden as he reads words that are detached from the occasion and the audience.

—*Leslie Marmon Silko*

APPLICATIONS

1. Wilde and Schwartz comment on the relationship between memory and identity as well as its importance in the rituals of story-telling. Discuss their perspectives with your group. To what extent is it true that we all have stories to tell?

2. Analyze the points of view expressed in three perspectives on aspects of traditions. On what functions of traditions do they focus? What do they suggest about the roles of traditions? Do you agree that our attitude toward tradition is ambivalent? Write an essay using these questions as a framework.

3. To what extent do stories help us to know who we are? Is there a story that made an impression on you as a child? Summarize this story for your group and analyze the reasons for its effect.

Here are two different stories about how the world was created. The first is a legend from the Bantu, a diverse black people inhabiting a large part of south-ern Africa south of the Congo and speaking many languages (including Zulu and Swahili) and dialects. The second is the opening of the Popol Vuh, the sacred saga of the Quiché, a branch of the great Mayan civilization. The Quiché Maya live in what is now western Guatemala.

In the Beginning:
Bantu Creation Story

AFRICAN LEGEND

IN THE BEGINNING, in the dark, there was nothing but water. And Bumba was alone.

One day Bumba was in terrible pain. He retched and strained and vomited up the sun. After that light spread over everything. The heat of the sun dried up the water until the black edges of the world began to show. Black sandbanks and reefs could be seen. But there were no living things.

Bumba vomited up the moon and then the stars, and after that the night had its light also.

Still Bumba was in pain. He strained again and nine living creatures came forth: the leopard named Koy Bumba, and Pongo Bumba the crested eagle, the crocodile, Ganda Bumba, and one little fish named Yo; next, old Kono Bumba, the tortoise, and Tsetse, the lightning, swift, deadly, beautiful like the leopard; then the white heron, Nyanyi Bumba, also one beetle, and the goat named Budi.

Last of all came forth men. There were many men, but only one was white like Bumba. His name was Loko Yima.

The creatures themselves then created all the creatures. The heron created all the birds of the air except the kite. He did not make the kite. The crocodile made serpents and the iguana. The goat produced every beast with horns. Yo, the small fish, brought forth all the fish of all the seas and waters. The beetle created insects.

Then the serpents in their turn made grasshoppers, and the iguana made the creatures without horns.

Then the three sons of Bumba said they would finish the world. The first, Nyonye Ngana, made the white ants; but he was not equal to the task, and died of it. The ants, however, thankful for life and being, went searching for black earth in the depths of the world and covered the barren sands to bury and honour their creator.

Chonganda, the second son, brought forth a marvellous living plant from which all the trees and grasses and flowers and plants in the world have sprung. The third son, Chedi Bumba, wanted something different, but for all his trying made only the bird called the kite.

Of all the creatures, Tsetse, lightning, was the only troublemaker. She stirred up so much trouble that Bumba chased her into the sky. Then mankind was without fire until Bumba showed the people how to draw fire out of trees. "There is fire in every tree," he told them, and showed them how to make the firedrill and liberate it. Sometimes today Tsetse still leaps down and strikes the earth and causes damage.

When at last the work of creation was finished, Bumba walked through the peaceful villages and said to the people, "Behold these wonders. They belong to you." Thus from Bumba, the Creator, the First Ancestor, came forth all the wonders that we see and hold and use, and all the brotherhood of beasts and man.

Quiché-Mayan Creation Story

QUICHÉ-MAYAN LEGEND

BEFORE THE WORLD WAS CREATED, Calm and Silence were the great kings that ruled. Nothing existed, there was nothing. Things had not yet been drawn together, the face of the earth was unseen. There was only motionless sea, and a great emptiness of sky. There were no men anywhere, or animals, no birds or fish, no crabs. Trees, stones, caves, grass, forests, none of these existed yet. There was nothing that could roar or run, nothing that could tremble or cry in the air. Flatness and emptiness, only the sea, alone and breathless. It was night; silence stood in the dark.

In this darkness the Creators waited, the Maker, Tepeu, Gucumatz, the Forefathers. They were there in this emptiness, hidden under green and blue feathers, alone and surrounded with light. They are the same as wisdom. They are the ones who can conceive and bring forth a child from nothingness. And the time had come. The Creators were bent deep around talk in the darkness. They argued, worried, sighed over what was to be. They planned the growth of the thickets, how things would crawl and jump, the birth of man. They planned the whole creation, arguing each point until their words and thoughts crystallized and became the same thing. Heart of Heaven was there, and in the darkness the creation was planned.

Then let the emptiness fill! they said. Let the water weave its way downward so the earth can show its face! Let the light break on the ridges, let the sky fill up with the yellow light of dawn! Let our glory be a man walking on a path through the trees! "Earth!" the Creators called. They called only once, and it was there, from a mist, from a cloud of dust, the mountains appeared instantly. At this single word the groves of cypresses and pines sent out shoots, rivulets ran freely between the round hills. The Creators were struck by the beauty and exclaimed, "It will be a creation that will mount the darkness!"

INTERPRETATIONS

1. In the Bantu story "The creatures themselves then created all the creatures": Fish produced fish, birds produced birds (except for the predatory kite), and so on. How "scientific" is this explanation?

2. Why is there almost no explanation of Bumba's identity (other than his being white and "the Creator, the First Ancestor") or of

his sickness? Are such details better omitted? Can you supply the missing explanation?

3. In the Bantu story what purpose does the retching incident serve? What tone does it set?

4. What is the purpose of the Bantu story?

5. How important in the Quiché creation story is language?

6. In the Quiché story what are the Creators' main attributes? How are they demonstrated in the story?

7. What seems to be the Creators' main motive in creating "a man" in the Quiché story?

8. Interpret the last sentence of the Quiché story. What explanation does it provide for the Creation?

CORRESPONDENCES

1. Review the perspective from Ecclesiastes. Compare the concepts in Ecclesiastes with those in the Bantu and Quiché stories. Which account do you prefer? How do they differ in implication?

2. Compare the tones and meanings of the two creation stories.

APPLICATIONS

1. Working in your group, discuss the roles and function of creation texts. Why is it important to become aware of different cultural explanations of the origins of the natural world? Analyze the significance of the motifs of light and darkness in both creation stories. What do they suggest about the nature of good and evil?

2. Review Zipes's perspective and write an essay in which you seek to persuade your audience of the importance of preserving a sense of wonder about yourself and the world. Be specific.

3. Write an essay discussing the importance of storytelling in your family. Have any of the stories become family traditions? What elements account for their popularity? How have the stories affected your sense of identity and that of your family?

Footbinding

JOHN KING FAIRBANK

John King Fairbank (1907–1991) was born in South Dakota and received degrees from Harvard and Oxford universities. He was the director emeritus of Harvard's East Asian Research Center and enjoyed a distinguished career in the field of Asian studies. His numerous books on China include Modern China: A Bibliographical Guide to Chinese Works, 1898–1937 *(1950);* The United States and China *(1971);* Chinabound: A Fifty-Year Memoir *(1983); and* China Watch *(1987). Before reading Fairbank's essay, consult a dictionary for a definition of footbinding.*

China, one of the world's oldest civilizations (dating at least to 5000 B.C.) with a fifth of the world's population (about a billion inhabitants), has had a tumultuous history, especially in the last two centuries. For thousands of years, beginning with the Shang Dynasty (about 1500–1000 B.C.), a succession of dynasties ruled China and expanded Chinese political and cultural domination of East Asia. In 1644 a foreign invader, the Manchus, established the Ch'ing Dynasty without destroying the underlying culture. The nineteenth century was a time of increasing stagnation and rebellion. European powers took advantage of internal strife to take control of large parts of the country. The country became a republic in 1912, but lost much of its territory to the Japanese, both before and during World War II. The People's Republic of China was declared in 1949 under the leadership of Mao Zedong, by which time footbinding—but not its effects—had vanished. In the excerpt that follows, Fairbank describes the rise of the custom of footbinding in the tenth century, details its mechanics and its influence on domestic life, and advances reasons for its longevity.

OF ALL THE MANY UNEXPLORED FACETS of China's ancient history, the subjection of women has been the least studied. Women were fitted into the social and cosmic order (which were a continuum) by invoking the principles of Yang and Yin. All things bright, warm, active, male, and dominant were Yang while all things dark, cold, passive, female, and yielding were Yin. This dualism, seen in the alternation of night and day or the contrast of the sun and moon, was a ready-made matrix in which women could be confined. The subjection of women was thus a sophisticated and perfected institution like the other Chinese achievements, not a mere accident of male biceps or female childbearing as might be more obviously the case in a primitive tribe. The inequality between the sexes was buttressed with philosophical underpinnings and long-continued social practices. Symbolic of woman's secondary status was her bridal night: she expected to be deflowered by a stranger, a husband selected by her family whom she had never seen before. Even though the facts may often have been less stark, the theory was hard-boiled.

Out of all this complex of theory and custom by which the Chinese world was given an enduring and stable order, the most neglected aspect is the institution of footbinding. This custom arose at court in the tenth century during the late T'ang and spread gradually among the upper class during the succeeding Sung period. By the Ming and Ch'ing eras after 1368 it had penetrated the mass of the Han Chinese population. It became so widespread that Western observers in the nineteenth century found it almost universal, not only among the upper class but throughout the farming population.

Footbinding spread as a mark of gentility and upper-class status. Small feet became a prestige item to such an extent that a girl without them could not achieve a good marriage arrangement and was subjected to the disrespect and taunts of the community. In short, bound feet became *de rigueur,* the only right-thinking thing to do for a daughter, an obligation on the part of a mother who cared about her daughter's eventual marriage and success in life. The bound foot was a must. Only tribal peoples and exceptional groups like the Manchu conquerors or the Hakka Chinese migrant groups in South China or finally the mean people, that lowest and rather small group who were below the social norms of civility, could avoid binding their daughters' feet.

The small foot was called a "golden lotus" or "golden lily" (*chin-lien*) and was much celebrated in poems and essays by male enthusiasts. Here is the early Sung poet Su Tung-p'o (1036–1101):

> Anointed with fragrance, she takes lotus steps;
> Though often sad, she steps with swift lightness.
> She dances like the wind, leaving no physical trace.
> Another stealthily but happily tries on the palace style,
> But feels such distress when she tries to walk!
> Look at them in the palms of your hands, so wondrously
> small that they defy description.

The Sung philosophers stressed women's inferiority as a basic element of the social order. The great Chu Hsi (1130–1200) codified the cosmology of China as magistrally as his near contemporary Thomas Aquinas (d. 1274) codified that of Western Christendom. When he was a magistrate in Fukien province, Chu Hsi promoted footbinding to preserve female chastity and as "a means of spreading Chinese culture and teaching the separation of men and women."

By the Ming period the overwhelming majority of Han Chinese women all over the country had artificially small feet. The Manchu emperors many times inveighed against it in hortatory edicts, but to no avail. Male romanticizing on the subject continued unabated as in this poem of the fourteenth century:

> Lotus blossoms in shoes most tight,
> As if she could stand on autumnal waters!
> Her shoe tips do not peek beyond the skirt,
> Fearful lest the tiny embroideries be seen.[1]

There can be no doubt that footbinding was powered by a sexual fetish. Chinese love manuals are very specific about the use of bound feet as erogenous areas. All the different ways of taking hold of the foot, rubbing it with the hands, and using the mouth, tongue, and lips are explicitly catalogued. Many cases are recorded with the verisimilitude of high-class pornography. Meanwhile, the aesthetic attractiveness of the small shoes with their bright embroidered colors was praised in literature, while the tottering gait of a bound-foot woman was considered very fetching as a symbol of feminine frailty, which indeed it was. In fact, of course, bound feet were a guarantee of chastity because they kept women within the household and unable to venture far abroad. Lily feet, once formed, could not be unlocked like a chastity belt. By leaving only men able-bodied, they ensured male domination in a very concrete way.

Thus the prevalence of footbinding down to the 1920s, while the movement against it began only in the 1890s, vividly index the speed and scope of China's modern social revolution. This may be less comprehensible to white American males than to white women, or especially to black Americans, for Chinese women within the present century have had an emancipation from veritable slavery.

While footbinding is mentioned in so many foreign books about China, it is usually passed by as a curious detail. I don't think it was. It was a major erotic invention, still another achievement in Chinese social engineering. Girls painfully deformed themselves throughout their adolescence in order to attract desirable husbands who, on their part, subscribed to a folklore of self-fulfilling beliefs: for example, that

---

[1]Howard Levy, *Chinese Footbinding: The History of a Curious Erotic Custom* (New York: Walton Rawls, 1966), p. 47.

footbinding made a vagina more narrow and muscular and that lotus feet were major foci of erotic sensitivity, true erogenous zones, a net addition of 50 percent to the female equipment. Normal feet, we are now told by purveyors of sexual comfort, are an underdeveloped area sensually, but one must admit they are a bit hard to handle—whereas small lotus feet could be grasped, rubbed, licked, sucked, nibbled, and bitten. The garrulous Jesuit Father Ripa, who spent a decade at the court of K'ang-hsi in the early 1700s, reported that "Their taste is perverted to such an extraordinary degree that I knew a physician who lived with a woman with whom he had no other intercourse but that of viewing and fondling her feet."[2] Having compacted all their nerve endings in a smaller area, golden lilies were far more sensitive than, for example, the back of the neck that used to bewitch Japanese samurai. After all, they had been created especially for male appreciation. When every proper girl did it, what bride would say that her sacrifice, suffering, and inconvenience were not worth it? A bride without small feet in the old China was like a new house in today's America without utilities— who would want it? Consequently in the 1930s and '40s one still saw women on farms stumping about on their heels as they worked, victims of this old custom.

A girl's foot was made small, preferably only three inches long, by pressing the four smaller toes under the sole or ball of the foot (plantar) in order to make it narrower. At the same time it was made shorter by forcing the big toe and heel closer together so that the arch rose in a bowed shape. As a result the arch was broken and the foot could bear no weight except on the heel. If this process was begun at age five, the experience was less severe than if a little girl, perhaps in a peasant household, had been left with normal feet until age eight or ten so that she could be of more use in the household.

> When I was seven [said one woman to Ida Pruitt], my mother . . . washed and placed alum on my feet and cut the toenails. She then bent my toes toward the plantar with a binding cloth ten feet long and two inches wide, doing the right foot first and then the left. She . . . ordered me to walk but when I did the pain proved unbearable. That night . . . my feet felt on fire and I couldn't sleep; mother struck me for crying. On the following days, I tried to hide but was forced to walk on my feet . . . after several months all toes but the big one were pressed against the inner surface . . . mother would remove the bindings and wipe the blood and pus which dripped from my feet. She told me that

[2]Fortunato Prandi, ed. and trans., *Memoirs of Father Ripa* (London: John Murray, 1855), p. 58.

only with removal of the flesh could my feet become slender . . .
every two weeks I changed to new shoes. Each new pair was
one-to-two-tenths of an inch smaller than the previous one . . . In
summer my feet smelled offensively because of pus and blood;
in winter my feet felt cold because of lack of circulation . . . four
of the toes were curled in like so many dead caterpillars . . . it
took two years to achieve the three-inch model . . . my shanks
were thin, my feet became humped, ugly and odoriferous.[3]

After the first two years the pain lessened. But constricting the feet
to a three-inch size was only the beginning of trouble. By this time they
were very private parts indeed and required daily care, washing and
manicuring at the same time that they had to be kept constantly bound
and shod night and day. Unmanicured nails could cut into the instep,
bindings could destroy circulation, blood poisoning or gangrene could
result. Massage and applications of hot and cold water were used to
palliate the discomfort, but walking any distance remained difficult. It
also produced corns on the bent-under toes, which had to be pared
with a knife. Once deformed to taste, bound feet were of little use to
stand on. Since weight was carried entirely on the heels, it had to be
constantly shifted back and forth. Since the bound foot lacked the
resilience of a normal foot, it was a tiring and unsteady support.

Footbinding, in short, had begun as an ostentatious luxury, which
made a girl less useful in family work and more dependent on help from
others. Yet, once the custom had spread among the populace, lotus feet
were considered essential in order to get a good husband. Marriages, of
course, were arranged between families and often by professional
matchmakers, in whose trade the length of the lily foot was rated more
important than beauty of face or person. When the anti-footbinding
movement began at the end of the nineteenth century, many mothers
and daughters, too, stubbornly clung to it to avoid the public shame of
having large feet. The smallness of the foot, in short, was a source of
social pride both to the family and to the victim. First and last one may
guess that at least a billion Chinese girls during the thousand-year currency of this social custom suffered the agony of footbinding and reaped
its rewards of pride and ecstasy, such as they were.

There are three remarkable things about footbinding. First, that it
should have been invented at all—it was such a feat of physio-psycho-
sociological engineering. Second, that once invented it should have
spread so pervasively and lasted so long among a generally humane

[3]Ida Pruitt, *A Daughter of Han: The Autobiography of a Chinese Working Woman* (New Haven: Yale University Press, 1945), p. 22.

and practical-minded farming population. We are just at the beginning of understanding this phenomenon. The fact that an upper-class erotic luxury permeated the peasantry of Old China, for whom it could only lower productivity, suggests that the old society was extraordinarily homogeneous.

Finally, it was certainly ingenious how men trapped women into mutilating themselves for an ostensibly sexual purpose that had the effect of perpetuating male domination. Brides left their own homes and entered their husband's family in the lowest status, servants of their mothers-in-law. Husbands were chosen for them sight unseen, and might find romance in extra-marital adventures or, if they could afford it, bring in secondary wives. But a woman once betrothed, if her husband-to-be died even as a child, was expected to remain a chaste widow thereafter. Mao remarked that "women hold up half the sky," but in the old China they were not supposed to lift their heads. The talent that one sees in Chinese women today had little chance to grow and express itself. This made a weak foundation for a modern society.

INTERPRETATIONS

1. What is Fairbank's purpose in describing "the principles of Yang and Yin"? How does this relate to the topic of footbinding? Does the intellectual theory (Yang-Yin) really explain any important aspects of Chinese behavior? Or is it a rationalization? A pretext? An emblem?

2. According to Fairbank, "there are three remarkable things about footbinding." What are they and why are they significant?

3. What examples can you give of elaborate psychological or other theories in contemporary America that have the aura of science or intellect but really explain very little? Do these theories affect our society for good or for ill, or do they simply remain in the realm of theory? If you find they have practical effects on people's behavior, what effects?

CORRESPONDENCES

1. Review the Douglass perspective on traditions. How does it apply to the selection by Fairbank? To what extent was footbinding "useful" in the culture of its day?

2. Review the Geiger perspective. How does it apply to "Footbinding"? To which other selections in this chapter is it also relevant? In what way?

APPLICATIONS

1. Fairbank estimates that "at least a billion Chinese girls during the thousand-year currency of this social custom suffered the agony of footbinding . . ." What does Fairbank's essay suggest about reevaluating the custom?

2. What is the general relationship between tradition and individual desires? For example, are the traditional ethnic or tribal costumes you are familiar with calculated to promote individual beauty (or sex appeal) or the beliefs and values of the tribe or collective? Write an essay responding to these questions with specific examples.

3. A fetish is an inanimate object or charm thought to possess magical powers such as good luck or protection from evil. In psychiatry, fetishism is associated with an abnormal sexual attraction to an inanimate object such as a shoe. What associations do you and your group have with fetishes or fetishism? Summarize your discussion.

4. In "Footbinding," Fairbank writes about the physical subjugation of women. Do you think that such practices continue to exist? Check the following Web sites for information that you might use to formulate an argument.

   http://www.towson.edu/%7Eloiselle/foot.html

   http://outlawtv.com/333/016.htm

   http://www.nefilim.de/addfiles/myth/nephilim/articles/cranial_deformation.htm

The Algonquin Cinderella

NATIVE AMERICAN MYTH

The small Algonquin tribe of Canada was one of the first with whom the French formed alliances. Because of their mingling with whites, little remains of Algonquin culture. Their name, however, came to be used to designate other nearby tribes, and their language family (known as Algonquian) is one of the most widespread of all North American Indian languages, extending from New Brunswick to the Rocky Mountains. Among Indian languages in the Algonquian stock are the Arapaho, the Cheyenne, the Blackfoot, the Potawatami, the Ottawa, the Passamaquoddy, the Penobscot, the Delaware, and the Cree. Record your memory of the first fairy tale that impressed you as a child.

THERE WAS ONCE A LARGE VILLAGE of the MicMac Indians of the Eastern Algonquins, built beside a lake. At the far end of the settlement stood a lodge, and in it lived a being who was always invisible. He had a sister who looked after him, and everyone knew that any girl who could see him might marry him. For that reason there were very few girls who did not try, but it was very long before anyone succeeded.

This is the way the test of sight was carried out: at evening-time, when the Invisible One was due to be returning home, his sister would walk with any girl who might come down to the lakeshore. She, of course, could see her brother, since he was always visible to her. As soon as she saw him, she would say to the girls:

"Do you see my brother?"

"Yes," they would generally reply—though some of them did say "No."

To those who said that they could indeed see him, the sister would say:

"Of what is his shoulder strap made?" Some people say that she would enquire:

"What is his moose-runner's haul?" or "With what does he draw his sled?"

And they would answer:

"A strip of rawhide" or "a green flexible branch," or something of that kind.

Then she, knowing that they had not told the truth, would say:

"Very well, let us return to the wigwam!"

When they had gone in, she would tell them not to sit in a certain place, because it belonged to the Invisible One. Then, after they had helped to cook the supper, they would wait with great curiosity, to see him eat. They could be sure that he was a real person, for when he took off his moccasins they became visible, and his sister hung them up. But beyond this they saw nothing of him, not even when they stayed in the place all the night, as many of them did.

Now there lived in the village an old man who was a widower, and his three daughters. The youngest girl was very small, weak and often ill: and yet her sisters, especially the elder, treated her cruelly. The second daughter was kinder, and sometimes took her side: but the wicked sister would burn her hands and feet with hot cinders, and she was covered with scars from this treatment. She was so marked that people called her *Oochigeaskw*, the Rough-Faced-Girl.

When her father came home and asked her why she had such burns, the bad sister would at once say that it was her own fault, for she had disobeyed orders and gone near the fire and fallen into it.

These two elder sisters decided one day to try their luck at seeing the Invisible One. So they dressed themselves in their finest clothes, and tried to look their prettiest. They found the Invisible One's sister and took the usual walk by the water.

When he came, and when they were asked if they could see him, they answered: "Of course." And when asked about the shoulder strap or sled cord, they answered: "A piece of rawhide."

But of course they were lying like the others, and they got nothing for their pains.

The next afternoon, when the father returned home, he brought with him many of the pretty little shells from which wampum was made, and they set to work to string them.

That day, poor Little Oochigeaskw, who had always gone barefoot, got a pair of her father's moccasins, old ones, and put them into water to soften them so that she could wear them. Then she begged her sisters for a few wampum shells. The elder called her a "little pest," but the younger one gave her some. Now, with no other clothes than her usual rags, the poor little thing went into the woods and got herself some sheets of birch bark, from which she made a dress, and put marks on it for decoration, in the style of long ago. She made a petticoat and a loose gown, a cap, leggings and a handkerchief. She put on her father's large old moccasins, which were far too big for her, and went forth to try her luck. She would try, she thought, to discover whether she could see the Invisible One.

She did not begin very well. As she set off, her sisters shouted and hooted, hissed and yelled, and tried to make her stay. And the loafers around the village, seeing the strange little creature, called out "Shame!"

The poor little girl in her strange clothes, with her face all scarred, was an awful sight, but she was kindly received by the sister of the Invisible One. And this was, of course, because this noble lady understood far more about things than simply the mere outside which all the rest of the world knows. As the brown of the evening sky turned to black, the lady took her down to the lake.

"Do you see him?" the Invisible One's sister asked.

"I do, indeed—and he is wonderful!" said Oochigeaskw.

The sister asked:

"And what is his sled-string?"

The little girl said:

"It is the Rainbow."

"And, my sister, what is his bow-string?"

"It is the Spirit's Road—the Milky Way."

"So you *have* seen him," said his sister. She took the girl home with her and bathed her. As she did so, all the scars disappeared from her body. Her hair grew again, as it was combed, long, like a blackbird's wing. Her eyes were like stars; in all the world there was no other such beauty. Then, from her treasures, the lady gave her a wedding garment, and adorned her.

Then she told Oochigeaskw to take the *wife's* seat in the wigwam; the one next to where the Invisible One sat, beside the entrance. And when he came in, terrible and beautiful, he smiled and said:

"So we are found out!"

"Yes," said his sister. And so Oochigeaskw became his wife.

INTERPRETATIONS

1. Why does Oochigeaskw succeed where her sisters failed?

2. What explanation does the story offer or imply for Oochigeaskw's ability to see the Invisible One? How is this ability related to Oochigeaskw's persecuted position in the family?

3. How do the clothes Oochigeaskw makes or assembles for herself indicate a reverence for tradition? What effect do you think this reverence might have on her success in winning the Invisible One?

4. What part do moccasins play in the story?

CORRESPONDENCES

1. Compare the Native American version of the Cinderella story with the standard version you read as a child. What motifs do they have in common? How do they differ?

2. Review Chief Dan George's perspective on nature and discuss its relevance to "The Algonquin Cinderella."

APPLICATIONS

1. Write a contemporary version of a favorite childhood fairy tale and analyze the significance of your changes. To what extent do they reflect your values?

2. Is there anything positive to be learned from the Cinderella story? What does it teach about sibling rivalry? How might identifying with Cinderella be helpful to some children?

3. From ancient times to the present, poets and lyricists have used nature as their subject. Share with your group a favorite poem or lyric about nature. What aspects of nature emerged in the various texts? To what extent were the writers' attitudes toward nature influenced by their cultural backgrounds?

Cinderella's Stepsisters

TONI MORRISON

Toni Morrison (b. 1931) received a B.A. in English from Howard University and an M.A. from Cornell University. Morrison made her debut as a novelist in 1970 with the acclaimed The Bluest Eye. *Her other novels include:* Sula *(1973),* Song of Solomon *(1977),* Tar Baby *(1981),* Beloved *(1987),* Jazz *(1992), and* Paradise *(1998).* Love, *Morrison's most recent novel, was published in 2003. Morrison's last four publications have been retellings for children, with her son Slade Morrison, of Aesop's fables, collected in 2005 into one volume* Who's Got Game? Three Fables *(2005). The following essay also shows Morrison's interest in fairy-tale characters, although she soon broadens the subject. Morrison has received the National Book Critics Circle Award, the American Academy and Institute of Arts and Letters Award, the Pulitzer Prize, and the Robert F. Kennedy Award. Morrison has taught at several universities, since 1989 as Professor of the Humanities at Princeton University. Before reading Morrison's remarks on the conflict between ambition and the nurturing sensibility, search your memory for times when these two drives competed in your own life.*

LET ME BEGIN BY TAKING YOU BACK A LITTLE. Back before the days at college. To nursery school, probably, to a once-upon-a-time time when you first heard or read, or, I suspect, even saw "Cinderella." Because it is Cinderella that I want to talk about; because it is Cinderella who causes me a feeling of urgency. What is unsettling about that fairy tale is that it is essentially the story of a household—a world, if you please—of women gathered together and held together in order to abuse another woman. There is, of course, a rather vague absent father and a nick-of-time prince with a foot fetish. But neither has much personality. And there are the surrogate "mothers," of course (god- and, step-), who contribute both to Cinderella's grief and to her release and happiness. But it is her stepsisters who interest me. How crippling it must have been for those young girls to grow up with a mother, to watch and imitate that mother, enslaving another girl.

I am curious about their fortunes after the story ends. For contrary to recent adaptations, the stepsisters were not ugly, clumsy, stupid girls with outsize feet. The Grimm collection describes them as "beautiful and fair in appearance." When we are introduced to them they are beautiful, elegant women of status, and clearly women of power. Having watched and participated in the violent dominion of another woman, will they be any less cruel when it comes their turn to enslave other children, or even when they are required to take care of their own mother?

It is not a wholly medieval problem. It is quite a contemporary one: feminine power when directed at other women has historically been wielded in what has been described as a "masculine" manner. Soon you will be in a position to do the very same thing. Whatever your background—rich or poor—whatever the history of education in your family—five generations or one—you have taken advantage of what has been available to you at Barnard and you will therefore leave both the economic and social status of the stepsisters *and* you will have their power.

I want not to *ask* you but to *tell* you not to participate in the oppression of your sisters. Mothers who abuse their children are women, and another woman, not an agency, has to be willing to stay their hands. Mothers who set fire to school buses are women, and another woman, not an agency, has to tell them to stay their hands. Women who stop the promotion of other women in careers are women, and another woman must come to the victim's aid. Social and welfare workers who humiliate their clients may be women, and other women colleagues have to deflect their anger.

I am alarmed by the violence that women do to each other: professional violence, competitive violence, emotional violence. I am alarmed by the willingness of women to enslave other women. I am alarmed by a growing absence of decency on the killing floor of professional women's worlds. You are the women who will take your place in the world where *you* can decide who shall flourish and who shall wither; you will make distinctions between the deserving poor and the undeserving poor; where you can yourself determine which life is expendable and which is indispensable. Since you will have the power to do it, you may also be persuaded that you have the right to do it. As educated women the distinction between the two is first-order business.

I am suggesting that we pay as much attention to our nurturing sensibilities as to our ambition. You are moving in the direction of freedom and the function of freedom is to free somebody else. You are moving toward self-fulfillment, and the consequences of that fulfillment should be to discover that there is something just as important as you are and that just-as-important thing may be Cinderella—or your stepsister.

In your rainbow journey toward the realization of personal goals, don't make choices based only on your security and your safety. Nothing is safe. That is not to say that anything ever was, or that anything worth achieving ever should be. Things of value seldom are. It is not safe to have a child. It is not safe to challenge the status quo. It is not safe to choose work that has not been done before. Or to do old work in a new way. There will always be someone there to stop you. But in pursuing your highest ambitions, don't let your personal safety diminish the safety of your stepsister. In wielding the power that is deservedly yours, don't permit it to enslave your stepsisters. Let your might and your power emanate from that place in you that is nurturing and caring.

Women's rights is not only an abstraction, a cause; it is also a personal affair. It is not only about "us"; it is also about me and you. Just the two of us.

INTERPRETATIONS

1. How much of the Cinderella fairy tale do you remember from childhood? Why is Morrison particularly interested in the stepsisters? What contemporary relevance does she find in their story?

2. "I am alarmed by the violence that women do to each other: professional violence, competitive violence, emotional violence." What examples does Morrison cite to support her statement? To what extent do you agree with her?

3. What distinction does Morrison make between "masculine" and "feminine" power? Do men and women think differently about competition, ambition, and success? Explain.

CORRESPONDENCES

1. Review Gandhi's perspective and discuss its application to Morrison's text.

2. Morrison's purpose is to persuade. How would you characterize her tone? How do her purpose and tone compare with that of "The Algonquin Cinderella"?

APPLICATIONS

1. Discuss with your group Morrison's comments in paragraph 7 about safety and security. How plausible is it that "power emanates from that place in you that is nurturing and caring"?

2. Write an essay analyzing the implications of Morrison's conclusion. Be specific.

3. Write an essay about a character in a fairy tale that you identified with, or rejected as a child. What factors determined your responses? In retrospect, was the experience negative or positive? Cite reasons.

4. What do you think Cinderella herself would reply to Toni Morrison? Write a letter from Cinderella to Morrison that addresses issues that are raised in "Cinderella's Stepsisters."

from The Way to Rainy Mountain

N. SCOTT MOMADAY

N. Scott Momaday (b. 1934 in Lawton, Oklahoma), half Kiowa, has lived among various Indians as well as whites: He spent his childhood living on Navajo reservations in New Mexico and Arizona and at Jemez Pueblo in New Mexico, and he spent his last year of high school at a military academy in Virginia in order to prepare for college. He graduated from the University of New Mexico in 1958, and taught for a year at an Apache reservation in the same state. After Momaday's first novel House Made of Dawn *(1968) was awarded the Pulitzer Prize for Fiction, he taught for a year at the University of California at Berkeley. At Stanford University he earned a master's degree (1960) and a doctorate (1963) and taught there from 1973 to 1982. Moma-day's additional books include:* Angle of Geese and Other Poems *(1974),* The Names: A Memoir *(1976),* The Ancient Child *(1989),* In the Presence of the Sun *(1992), and* Circle of Wonder: A Native American Christmas Story *(1994). Momaday has taught English and comparative literature at the University of Arizona, Tucson, since 1982. In the following excerpt from* The Way to Rainy Mountain *(1969), Momaday traces the migration of his tribe from their origins in Montana to Oklahoma. He chronicles alliances of the Kiowas with other tribes (the Comanches and the Crows) and their subjugation by the United States Army. Notice how Momaday uses the memories of his grandmother's death to evoke the importance of preserving tribal traditions.*

After 1840 the Kiowas, occupying the Arkansas River region of western Oklahoma, allied with the Comanches and others against eastern tribes that had moved west. This provoked the United States Army to move against both groups. By 1874, the Kiowa were devastated; their horses had been killed, and their leaders had been deported to Florida. They surrendered at Fort Sill. By 1879, most of the tribe had been moved to a reservation in southwest Oklahoma, between Fort Sill and the Washita River—the very landscape Momaday describes so dramatically here.

A SINGLE KNOLL rises out of the plain in Oklahoma, north and west of the Wichita Range. For my people, the Kiowas, it is an old landmark, and they gave it the name Rainy Mountain. The hardest weather in the world is there. Winter brings blizzards, hot tornadic winds arise in the spring, and in summer the prairie is an anvil's edge. The grass turns brittle and brown, and it cracks beneath your feet. There are green belts along the rivers and creeks, linear groves of hickory and pecan, willow and witch hazel. At a distance in July or August the steaming foliage seems almost to writhe in fire. Great green-and-yellow grasshoppers are everywhere in the tall grass, popping up like corn to sting the flesh, and tortoises crawl about on the red earth, going nowhere in the plenty of time. Loneliness is an aspect of the land. All things in the plain are isolate; there is no confusion of objects in the eye, but *one* hill or *one* tree or *one* man. To look upon that landscape in the early morning, with the sun at your back, is to lose the sense of proportion. Your imagination comes to life, and this, you think, is where Creation was begun.

I returned to Rainy Mountain in July. My grandmother had died in the spring, and I wanted to be at her grave. She had lived to be very old and at last infirm. Her only living daughter was with her when she died, and I was told that in death her face was that of a child.

I like to think of her as a child. When she was born, the Kiowas were living that last great moment of their history. For more than a hundred years they had controlled the open range from the Smoky Hill River to the Red, from the headwaters of the Canadian to the fork of the Arkansas and Cimarron. In alliance with the Comanches, they had ruled the whole of the southern Plains. War was their sacred business, and they were among the finest horsemen the world has ever known. But warfare for the Kiowas was preeminently a matter of disposition rather than of survival, and they never understood the grim, unrelenting advance of the U.S. Cavalry. When at last, divided and ill-provisioned, they were driven onto the Staked Plains in the cold rains of autumn, they fell into panic. In Palo Duro Canyon they abandoned their crucial stores to pillage and had nothing then but their lives. In order to save themselves, they surrendered to the soldiers at Fort Sill and were imprisoned in the old stone corral that now stands as a military museum. My grandmother was spared the humiliation of those high gray walls by eight or ten years, but she must have known from birth the affliction of defeat, the dark brooding of old warriors.

Her name was Aho, and she belonged to the last culture to evolve in North America. Her forebears came down from the high country in western Montana nearly three centuries ago. They were a mountain people, a mysterious tribe of hunters whose language has never been positively classified in any major group. In the late seventeenth century they began a long migration to the south and east. It was a long journey toward the dawn, and it led to a golden age. Along the way the Kiowas were befriended by the Crows, who gave them the culture and religion of the Plains. They acquired horses, and their ancient nomadic spirit was suddenly free of the ground. They acquired Tai-me, the sacred Sun

Dance doll, from that moment the object and symbol of their worship, and so shared in the divinity of the sun. Not least, they acquired the sense of destiny, therefore courage and pride. When they entered upon the southern Plains, they had been transformed. No longer were they slaves to the simple necessity of survival; they were a lordly and dangerous society of fighters and thieves, hunters and priests of the sun. According to their origin myth, they entered the world through a hollow log. From one point of view, their migration was the fruit of an old prophecy, for indeed they emerged from a sunless world.

Although my grandmother lived out her long life in the shadow of Rainy Mountain, the immense landscape of the continental interior lay like memory in her blood. She could tell of the Crows, whom she had never seen, and of the Black Hills, where she had never been. I wanted to see in reality what she had seen more perfectly in the mind's eye, and traveled fifteen hundred miles to begin my pilgrimage.

Yellowstone, it seemed to me, was the top of the world, a region of deep lakes and dark timber, canyons and waterfalls. But, beautiful as it is, one might have the sense of confinement there. The skyline in all directions is close at hand, the high wall of the woods and deep cleavages of shade. There is a perfect freedom in the mountains, but it belongs to the eagle and the elk, the badger and the bear. The Kiowas reckoned their stature by the distance they could see, and they were bent and blind in the wilderness.

Descending eastward, the highland meadows are a stairway to the plain. In July the inland slope of the Rockies is luxuriant with flax and buckwheat, stonecrop and larkspur. The earth unfolds and the limit of the land recedes. Clusters of trees and animals grazing far in the distance cause the vision to reach away and wonder to build upon the mind. The sun follows a longer course in the day, and the sky is immense beyond all comparison. The great billowing clouds that sail upon it are shadows that move upon the grain like water, dividing light. Farther down, in the land of the Crows and Blackfeet, the plain is yellow. Sweet clover takes hold of the hills and bends upon itself to cover and seal the soil. There the Kiowas paused on their way; they had come to the place where they must change their lives. The sun is at home on the plains. Precisely there does it have the certain character of a god. When the Kiowas came to the land of the Crows, they could see the dark lees of the hills at dawn across the Bighorn River, the profusion of light on the grain shelves, the oldest deity ranging after the solstices. Not yet would they veer southward to the caldron of the land that lay below; they must wean their blood from the northern winter and hold the mountains a while longer in their view. They bore Tai-me in procession to the east.

A dark mist lay over the Black Hills, and the land was like iron. At the top of a ridge I caught sight of Devil's Tower upthrust against the gray sky as if in the birth of time the core of the earth had broken through its crust and the motion of the world was begun. There are things in nature that engender an awful quiet in the heart of man; Devil's Tower is one of them. Two centuries ago, because they could not do otherwise, the Kiowas made a legend at the base of the rock. My grandmother said:

> Eight children were there at play, seven sisters and their brother. Suddenly the boy was struck dumb; he trembled and began to run upon his hands and feet. His fingers became claws, and his body was covered with fur. Directly there was a bear where the boy had been. The sisters were terrified; they ran, and the bear after them. They came to the stump of a great tree, and the tree spoke to them. It bade them climb upon it, and as they did so, it began to rise into the air. The bear came to kill them, but they were just beyond its reach. It reared against the tree and scored the bark all around with its claws. The seven sisters were borne into the sky, and they became the stars of the Big Dipper.

From that moment, and so long as the legend lives, the Kiowas have kinsmen in the night sky. Whatever they were in the mountains, they could be no more. However tenuous their well-being, however much they had suffered and would suffer again, they had found a way out of the wilderness.

My grandmother had a reverence for the sun, a holy regard that now is all but gone out of mankind. There was a wariness in her, and an ancient awe. She was a Christian in her later years, but she had come a long way about, and she never forgot her birthright. As a child she had been to the Sun Dances; she had taken part in those annual rites, and by them she had learned the restoration of her people in the presence of Tai-me. She was about seven when the last Kiowa Sun Dance was held in 1887 on the Washita River above Rainy Mountain Creek. The buffalo were gone. In order to consummate the ancient sacrifice—to impale the head of a buffalo bull upon the medicine tree—a delegation of old men journeyed into Texas, there to beg and barter for an animal from the Goodnight herd. She was ten when the Kiowas came together for the last time as a living Sun Dance culture. They could find no buffalo; they had to hang an old hide from the sacred tree. Before the dance could begin, a company of soldiers rode out from Fort Sill under orders to disperse the tribe. Forbidden without cause the essential act of their faith, having seen the wild herds slaughtered and left to rot upon the ground, the Kiowas backed away forever from the medicine tree. That was July 20, 1890, at the great bend of the Washita. My grandmother was there. Without bitterness, and for as long as she lived, she bore a vision of deicide.

Now that I can have her only in memory, I see my grandmother in the several postures that were peculiar to her: standing at the wood stove on a winter morning and turning meat in a great iron skillet; sitting at the south window, bent above her beadwork, and afterwards, when her vision had failed, looking down for a long time into the fold of her hands; going out upon a cane, very slowly as she did when the weight of age came upon her; praying. I remember her most often at prayer. She made long, rambling prayers out of suffering and hope, having seen many things. I was never sure that I had the right to hear, so exclusive were they of all mere custom and company. The last time I saw her she prayed standing by the side of her bed at night, naked to the waist, the light of a kerosene lamp moving upon her dark skin. Her long, black hair, always drawn and braided in the day, lay upon her shoulders and against her breasts like a shawl. I do not speak Kiowa, and I never understood her prayers, but there was something inherently sad in the sound, some merest hesitation upon the syllables of sorrow. She began in a high and descending pitch, exhausting her breath to silence; then again and again—and always the same intensity of effort, of something that is, and is not, like urgency in the human voice. Transported so in the dancing light among the shadows of her room, she seemed beyond the reach of time. But that was illusion; I think I knew then that I should not see her again.

INTERPRETATIONS

1. According to tribal myth, the Kiowa "entered the world through a hollow log." From what sort of world did they consider themselves to have emerged? How might this tradition have shaped the Kiowas' attitude toward life and death?

2. Momaday says his grandmother regarded the last Kiowa Sun Dance (1887) as "a vision of deicide," or god-killing. Do you agree? Was it the death of a god or of a people?

3. What portrait of Momaday's grandmother emerges from the essay? How would you describe his relationship to her?

4. What is the significance of Momaday's equating family with tribe?

5. How does Momaday use description of the setting (the mountains and plains, the great spaces of the West) to control the mood or tone of his essay?

CORRESPONDENCES

1. Review Sachs's perspective on the importance of life-stories and discuss its application to Momaday's essay. To what extent does Momaday's return to his grandmother's house help him to "recollect" himself?

2. Review Paz's perspective on myth. How does it apply to the history of Momaday's ancestors? What changes occur in the myth of the Kiowa tribe as a result of their migration from the mountains to the plains?

APPLICATIONS

1. Discuss with your group what you were taught about Native Americans. What did you learn about their traditions, culture, and values? Do you think you were made sufficiently aware of their history? Write a concise summary of your discussion.

2. Write an essay about a person you associate with a specific place. Try to convey through sensory and other details why the place and the person seem inseparable to you.

3. Brainstorm about your associations with nature. Try to recall an experience with nature that was negative or positive and recreate the event with as many details as you can.

4. If there were a soundtrack to the essay "The Way to Rainy Mountain," what would it be? Write an essay describing the music that you perceive. (Or, create and record a song that you hear.)

Seven Days of Mourning

YAEL YARIMI

Yael Yarimi was born in Qiryat Eqron, Israel, a daughter of Jews of Yemenite descent. Like the majority of the sabras (first generation who were born in the new land), Yael had a communication problem with the old generation, who tried to practice the culture they had brought with them. The gaps that were created among the generations were very common in the country in which they lacked identity. Naturally, Yael pursued the Western lifestyle, the dominant one in Israel, and deserted the one of her ancestors, since the latter seemed to her obsolete. Yael rediscovered the richness of her roots only after she arrived in the United States in the late 1980s, when she reexamined her heritage.

In this essay, she expresses both appreciation and regret for the ignorance she had toward her heritage. She dedicates this essay to her parents Shalom and Yona ("peace" and "dove"), who endured many great ordeals when they came to the Holy Land. Going through a similar experience in America, Yael can now profoundly realize the high price her parents paid for their passage from the familiar to the strange. This is her way of thanking them for raising her with pride and confidence in spite of all the difficulties.

Tuesday

Dear Diary,

It is eleven p.m. I hear unclear words coming from the next room. It is as if Mom and Dad entered an unfamiliar state and are speaking in a strange language . . . Among these odd words I can only understand one sentence Mom just said: "We must call everybody and inform them about the funeral time" . . . Now I hear my father crying. Oh my God! This is the first time in my life I have ever heard him crying just like us—the children.

I WAS TWELVE and too young to digest the significance of my grandfather's death. However, I was bothered with the notion that I would never see him again. I couldn't sleep. Constantly hiding my diary under the pillow, I remember trying to strangle my weeping under the blanket. Threatening pictures emerged and floated in my mind.

I cannot forget the scene: our front yard that was also our playground, turned overnight into a huge black tent made of strong, plastic canvas sheet and a great number of supporting rods. Strange people were unloading dozens of long tables and benches into the tent.

By the afternoon, all my relatives, neighbors and some other people had already arrived. Naturally, the men formed into a big rectangular pattern and began praying in loud voices, while the women were transferring large cooking pots from our house to the back of the tent. There, they installed a giant cooking stove which could be big enough for an army division. These volunteer ladies looked as if they were in a hurry. They worked so skillfully, that one might have thought that their lives depended on it.

We—the children—were running around between the legs and were scolded with blaming fingers. We were asked to be quiet. "This is not a time for joy" rebuked one of the ladies while holding my little brother by his ear. He was then sent away promising to keep quiet. Everything had happened very fast.

My father's eyes were an unforgettable sight. As the son of the deceased, my father was sitting on the ground, in one of the tent corners. Suddenly, he seemed so old, so infirm. My father, who was naturally a strong man, a towering figure, changed before my eyes into a helpless man with a saddened feeling of inner rage.

Not far from the men, in another corner, the mourning women were sitting on the ground as well. In the center of them, a woman I had never seen before was mourning in a heartbreaking wailing voice and caused all the other women to cry with her. I still remember her holding a square handkerchief with one hand on her forehead in a way that covered her entire face. Accompanying her sad songs, she then moved her upper body from side to side in a steady rhythm. Her mourning songs were interrupted by her outcries after every two stanzas that described my grandfather. I could see my grandmother's pleading facial expression as if she was trying to stop these words from being said.

I then was wondering how the mourning woman could cry and sob in such an honest way as if she knew my grandfather. I also could not understand why she had to add more agony to the already sad situation.

Dear Diary,
    I hate Aunt Rina, I hate her so much. She had no right to push me and ask me to help the working ladies . . . I feel so sad today . . . I couldn't enter the cemetery this afternoon; Mom says that women with periods are not clean; therefore I couldn't be present when my grandfather was buried. It is so corny . . .

Grandpa, I know you hear me. I know you are watching me from heaven . . . This is a mad house. Mom says its going to be like that every day for the next seven days . . . My friend Sara, remember her?, the one you used to call "The Russian"?, she says they never cooked for funerals . . . She says our funeral is like camping. You would have been proud of me if you heard what a lecture I gave her about us, about our dream that came true; to be in the land of the Jews, about all the things you used to tell me.

I am still astonished each time I recall the dedication of the Yemenite Jewish Community during the Shiva—the seven days of mourning in Jewish tradition in which all the community has to console and help the family to get over the loss.

All men rose at dawn and were praying three times a day. After each prayer, meals were served, in a religious ceremony, first to the men, then to the mourning women and last to the congregation. Deep, stiff, plastic dishes were filled with soup and meat in the Yemenite style. Scattered pita breads were laid along the tables by the side of small round dishes that contained a spicy dip called *hilba*—made of herbs. Hilba is used to flavor the soup. People then were eating with their hands, and there were no conversations during the eating time.

Dear Diary,

It has been a couple days that people are sleeping in my house. Everywhere I turn I encounter people, it's as if my house has turned into a hostel . . . Today it is an important day that's why I marked it in red ink. Today I have received my very first kiss.

Eddie, my cousin and I climbed the lemon tree in our back yard and kissed . . . I love him so much . . . Dad must not know; he will kill me, like the time he beat me when I played with Eric.

I closed the diary, which had aged with the years. I held it to my bosom and allowed myself to cry. I can still feel the pain and the insult of the blows I received from my father. It was eighteen years ago, but I still remember him saying outrageously "Kiss is a half intercourse," then came a second round of blows.

Knocking on the door, my husband woke me up from the journey to my past. "Everybody is leaving," he shouted. "Hurry up." I wore a black dress with a black scarf as is customary at mourning in my family.

By the time we arrived at the cemetery, my grandmother had already been buried. Women were spread out on the grave, yelling and pulling their hair. Grandmother was eighty-nine years old when she died. I was so sorry that distance did not enable me to see her before.

Living in the Diaspora, I find myself torn apart between the home I am trying to establish with my American husband, and the great, rich and embracing tradition I have left in my land of birth. I miss the togetherness, the caring and the warmth among my people so much that I sometimes contemplate leaving everything I have accomplished here and just returning to my roots, to the familiar, and run away from the ambiguous coldness I feel in America.

Entering the tent, my husband and I were sitting on the benches, in front of the same old tables, listening to the same heartbreaking weeping but this time from a different lady.

New generation of kids in our family were laughing and running around happy for the opportunity that brought them all together. Some of the traditional rituals will probably vanish among the new generation of Yemenite Jews in Israel, but in appearance only. I believe the essential tradition will remain forever.

INTERPRETATIONS

1. How do you feel about the custom of a leader causing "all the other women to cry with her" even though the leader didn't know Yarimi's grandfather? What purpose does it serve?

2. Why do you think food has such an important place in these ceremonies? How common in other traditions is this attention to food?

3. Does moving away from one's home or native land strengthen or weaken the importance of tradition? What examples can you provide from your own experience?

4. What is added to this narrative by seeing most of it from the point of view of a twelve-year-old?

CORRESPONDENCES

1. Review Schwartz's perspective on memory and discuss its application to "Seven Days of Mourning." What do the journal entries reveal about the narrator's memories? What is Yarimi's purpose in linking her grandfather's death to the present?

2. The Algonquin Cinderella and Yarimi both focus on the importance of ritual and the preservation of traditions. To what extent do you agree that preserving both adds dimension to individual and communal living? What examples can you cite?

APPLICATIONS

1. Discuss with your group Yarimi's ambivalence about living in the Diaspora. Should she run away from the "ambiguous coldness of America"? What consensus did you reach?

2. Are all of Yarimi's memories pleasant? What portrait of her father emerges in her journal? What do the entries reveal about the writer?

3. How important are mourning rituals in your culture? Are prescribed gender roles involved? Is the food served part of the rituals? Will you teach your children these customs? Why or why not?

4. On page 308, Yael Yarimi describes the scene at her house following her grandfather's funeral. What sights do you see? Make a drawing that takes into account your interpretation of Yarimi's work. Pay attention to color as well as content and composition.

from Imaginary Homelands

SALMAN RUSHDIE

Salman Rushdie (b. 1947), one of the best-known writers of our times, was born in Mumbai (formerly Bombay), India, and sent to Rugby School in England when he was fourteen. After graduating in 1968 from King's College, Cambridge, he worked in television in Pakistan. In 1975, Rushdie made his debut with the novel Grimus. *His next novel,* Midnight's Children *(1981), an allegory of the history of modern India, won the Booker Prize. In 1988 he won the Whitbread Award with his fourth novel,* The Satanic Verses, *whose narrator Saleem is mentioned in the following essay. Many Muslims regarded* The Satanic Verses *as an insult to their religion; Rushdie always denied the charge. The author went into hiding when Ayatollah Ruholla Khomeini called for Rushdie and his publishers to be killed. Although Rushdie lived in hiding under the protection of the British government for at least the next six years, he published* Imaginary Homelands: The Collected Essays *(1991) and three novels,* The Moor's Last Sigh *(1995),* The Ground Beneath Her Feet *(1999), and* Fury *(2002). Though other fundamentalist Muslims have continued to offer rewards for Rushdie's death, in 1998 the Iranian government announced that the state would not put the fatwa against him into effect, and Rushide decided to end his hiding.* Shalimar The Clown *was published in 2005. Before reading Rushdie's essay, try to remember occasions when you were suspicious of your own or others' memories.*

AN OLD PHOTOGRAPH in a cheap frame hangs on a wall of the room where I work. It's a picture dating from 1946 of a house into which, at the time of its taking, I had not yet been born. The house is rather peculiar—a three-storied gabled affair with tiled roofs and round towers in two corners, each wearing a pointy tiled hat. "The past is a foreign country," goes the famous opening sentence of L. P. Hartley's novel *The Go-Between*, "they do things differently there." But the photograph tells me to invert this idea; it reminds me that it's my present that is foreign, and that the past is home, albeit a lost home in a lost city in the mists of lost time.

A few years ago I revisited Bombay, which is my lost city, after an absence of something like half my life. Shortly after arriving, acting on an impulse, I opened the telephone directory and looked for my father's name. And, amazingly, there it was; his name, our old address, the unchanged telephone number, as if we had never gone away to the unmentionable country across the border. It was an eerie discovery. I felt as if I were being claimed, or informed that the facts of my faraway life were illusions, and that this continuity was the reality. Then I went to visit the house in the photograph and stood outside it, neither daring nor wishing to announce myself to its new owners. (I didn't want to see how they'd ruined the interior.) I was overwhelmed. The photograph had naturally been taken in black and white; and my memory, feeding on such images as this, had begun to see my childhood in the same way, monochromatically. The colors of my history had seeped out of my mind's eye; now my other two eyes were assaulted by colors, by the vividness of the red tiles, the yellow-edged green of cactus-leaves, the brilliance of bougainvillaea creeper. It is probably not too romantic to say that that was when my novel *Midnight's Children* was really born; when I realized how much I wanted to restore the past to myself, not in the faded grays of old family-album snapshots, but whole, in Cinema-Scope and glorious Technicolor.

Bombay is a city built by foreigners upon reclaimed land; I, who had been away so long that I almost qualified for the title, was gripped by the conviction that I, too, had a city and a history to reclaim.

It may be that writers in my position, exiles or emigrants or expatri-ates, are haunted by some sense of loss, some urge to reclaim, to look back, even at the risk of being mutated into pillars of salt. But if we do look back, we must also do so in the knowledge—which gives rise to profound uncertainties—that our physical alienation from India almost inevitably means that we will not be capable of reclaiming precisely the thing that was lost; that we will, in short, create fictions, not actual cities or villages, but invisible ones, imaginary homelands, Indias of the mind.

Writing my book in North London, looking out through my win-dow onto a city scene totally unlike the ones I was imagining onto paper, I was constantly plagued by this problem, until I felt obliged to face it in the text, to make clear that (in spite of my original and I sup-pose somewhat Proustian ambition to unlock the gates of lost time so that the past reappeared as it actually had been, unaffected by the dis-tortions of memory) what I was actually doing was a novel of memory and about memory, so that my India was just that: "my" India, a ver-sion and no more than one version of all the hundreds of millions of possible versions. I tried to make it as imaginatively true as I could, but imaginative truth is simultaneously honorable and suspect, and I knew that my India may only have been one to which I (who am no longer what I was, and who by quitting Bombay never became what perhaps I was meant to be) was, let us say, willing to admit I belonged.

This is why I made my narrator, Saleem, suspect in his narration; his mistakes are the mistakes of a fallible memory compounded by quirks of character and of circumstances and his vision is fragmentary. It may be that when the Indian writer who writes from outside India tries to reflect that world, he is obliged to deal in broken mirrors, some of whose fragments have been irretrievably lost.

But there is a paradox here. The broken mirror may actually be as valuable as the one which is supposedly unflawed. Let me again try and explain this from my own experience. Before beginning *Midnight's Children*, I spent many months trying simply to recall as much of the Bombay of the 1950s and 1960s as I could; and not only Bombay— Kashmir, too, and Delhi and Aligarh, which, in my book, I've moved to Agra to heighten a certain joke about the Taj Mahal. I was genuinely amazed by how much came back to me. I found myself remembering what clothes people had worn on certain days, and school scenes, and whole passages of Bombay dialogue verbatim, or so it seemed; I even remembered advertisements, film posters, the neon Jeep sign on Marine Drive, toothpaste ads for Binaca and for Kolynos, and a footbridge over the local railway line which bore, on one side, the legend "Esso puts a tiger in your tank" and, on the other, the curiously contradictory admonition: "Drive like Hell and you will get there." Old songs came back to me from nowhere. . . .

I knew that I had tapped a rich seam; but the point I want to make is that of course I'm not gifted with total recall, and it was precisely the partial nature of these memories, their fragmentation, that made them so evocative for me. The shards of memory acquired greater status, greater resonance, because they were *remains*; fragmentation made trivial things seem like symbols, and the mundane acquired numinous qualities. There is an obvious parallel here with archaeology. The broken pots of antiquity, from which the past can sometimes, but always provisionally, be reconstructed, are exciting to discover, even if they are pieces of the most quotidian objects.

It may be argued that the past is a country from which we have all emigrated, that its loss is part of our common humanity. Which seems to me self-evidently true; but I suggest that the writer who is out-of-country and even out-of-language may experience this loss in an intensified form. It is made more concrete for him by the physical fact of discontinuity, of his present being in a different place from his past, of his being "elsewhere." This may enable him to speak properly and concretely on a subject of universal significance and appeal.

But let me go further. The broken glass is not merely a mirror of nostalgia. It is also, I believe, a useful tool with which to work in the present.

John Fowles begins *Daniel Martin* with the words: "Whole sight: or all the rest is desolation." But human beings do not perceive things whole; we are not gods but wounded creatures, cracked lenses, capable only of fractured perceptions. Partial beings, in all the senses of that phrase. Meaning is a shaky edifice we build out of scraps, dogmas, childhood injuries, newspaper articles, chance remarks, old films, small victories, people hated, people loved; perhaps it is because our sense of what is the case is constricted from such inadequate materials that we defend it so fiercely, even to the death. The Fowles position seems to me a way of succumbing to the guru-illusion. Writers are no longer sages, dispensing the wisdom of the centuries. And those of us who have been forced by cultural displacement to accept the provisional nature of all truths, all certainties, have perhaps had modernism forced upon us. We can't lay claim to Olympus, and are thus released to describe our worlds in the way in which all of us, whether writers or not, perceive it from day to day. . . .

The Indian writer, looking back at India, does so through guilt-tinted spectacles. (I am of course, once more, talking about myself.) I am speaking now of those of us who emigrated . . . and I suspect that there are times when the move seems wrong to us all, when we seem, to ourselves, post-lapsarian men and women. We are Hindus who have crossed the black water; we are Muslims who eat pork. And as a result—as my use of the Christian notion of the Fall indicates—we are now partly of the West. Our identity is at once plural and partial. Sometimes we feel that we straddle two cultures; at other times, that we fall between two stools. But however ambiguous and shifting this ground may be, it is not an infertile territory for a writer to occupy. If literature is in part the business of finding new angles at which to enter reality, then once again our distance, our long geographical perspective, may provide us with such angles.

INTERPRETATIONS

1. Review the first paragraph of Rushdie's essay and explain what the mirror represents to him.

2. Paragraph 7 begins "But there is a paradox here. The broken mirror may actually be as valuable as the one which is supposedly unflawed." What is the meaning of the paradox to which Rushdie refers?

3. What points does Rushdie make concerning memory in paragraph 8? To what extent do you agree or disagree? Explain.

4. Rushdie's identity as a person and a writer has been shaped by his experiences in England and India. What does he cherish most about his Indian experiences? His Western identity?

CORRESPONDENCES

1. Review Schwartz's perspective on memory and discuss its applications to Rushdie's essay. Focus on paragraphs 8–12. What connections does Rushdie make between memory and the writer?

2. A sense of place is central to the selections by Fineman (page 329) and Rushdie. What techniques do they use to establish the relationship between places and traditions?

APPLICATIONS

1. Although Rushdie describes Bombay as "his lost city," he still retains a deep emotional attachment to it. Write a journal entry explaining why this is the case.

2. Discuss with your group Melville's perspective on places. Is there a "place" that you cherish that fits his description? How has this "place" affected your sense of identity? Write a summary of your responses.

3. Rushdie writes that all immigrants have an identity that is both "plural" and "partial." What does he mean? If you share his experience as an immigrant, write a journal entry on your own identity that supports or refutes Rushdie's thesis.

4. In the second paragraph of this essay, Rushdie writes: "The photograph had naturally been taken in black and white; and my memory, feeding on such images as this, had begun to see my childhood in the same way, monochromatically." Examine the photograph on page 334. What colors do you imagine to exist? Which one is dominant? What subtle shades are visible? How does the absence of color make you feel?

New (and Improved?) Delhi

GAUTAM BHATIA

Gautam Bhatia (b. 1952) graduated in fine arts and did his postgraduate work in architecture at the University of Pennsylvania. He is the recipient of several national and international awards for his architectural work. His first publication boasts the modest title A Short History of Everything *(1998). He published three books in 1994:* Laurie Baker: Life, Works, Writings *(about an English architect who came to India and wrote a book entitled "Laurie Baker's Mud" [1993]);* Silent Spaces and Other Stories of Architecture; *and* Punjabi Baroque and Other Memories of Architecture. *After that he wrote* Eternal Stone *(2000),* Comic Century: An Unreliable History of the 20th Century *(2004), and* MUD the House *(with Vishwajyoti Ghosh) (2006). He lives and practices architecture in New Delhi. What aspect of the place would you emphasize if you should write an essay called "New (and Improved?) York" or "New (and Improved?) Hampshire"?*

ONE EVENING A FEW YEARS AGO, I found myself on the road that heads south out of Delhi, in the city's fastest-developing suburb: Qutab Enclave. The area along the road was one big construction site. Many new structures sat between piles of rubble, and workers milled around concrete mixers on brown hot ground, half dug, half built. Pigs and stray dogs strolled near new plate-glass outlets for Reebok, Benetton and Levi's.

As the head of a small architecture practice in Delhi, I had just made a routine visit to the site of a house under construction nearby when I decided to take a look at the newly-erected head-quarters of a leading software company. This was one of the first so-called e-buildings in India—what its makers described as intelligent, user-friendly architecture. In my own practice, I try to conform to the ideals of hand craft, low cost and no maintenance, and having just examined the hand-applied mud plaster of the house I was working on, the idea of a peek into a high-tech extreme machine seemed all the more intriguing.

I parked in the vast lot and made my way toward a composition of polished stone and beveled glass. Built of Italian marble and erected with American and French technologies under South Korean supervision, it was truly global architecture. It was also perhaps eight times as expensive as the most expensive building in India. But a structure that has intelligence and the ability to interact with its user was one of a kind among the dumb, unfriendly buildings of old India.

Nearing the entrance, a sensor alerted a mechanism in the base of the glass door that it might soon have to open. I stood under a concealed camera for a few seconds, while my picture was beamed to an electronic control center somewhere inside, and it informed the circuit in the door that I should be allowed to pass. Sure enough, the door opened. A simple device worth probably 22 lakhs, now about 50,000 U.S. dollars, had eliminated the need for a human Haryanvi guard at $110 per month.

Inside the lobby I stood in virtual darkness, looking for a light switch and hoping that the command center would measure my distress and send down a light. For a long while nothing happened. I stepped cautiously, hoping that the floor was real and not an e-floor. Once I reached the elevators, light flooded in as if all the switches had been flicked on at once. Rubbing my eyes, I hoped again that the command center would sense my distress and turn off a few lights; but no. Still, this complicated light circuitry that I imagine cost $50,000 was worth it: it defrayed the cost of a 60-watt bulb left on throughout the night and paid for itself in a mere 120 years.

Before long, I heard the white noise of all six elevators racing down to pick me up. But after the lobby experience, I wasn't too keen on getting into an e-lift and opted to climb nine floors by an old-fashioned set of steps. Upstairs, I was met by the building representative, who narrated the benefits of technology as if memorized from a brochure, explaining that the double-glass wall had microlouvers and heat sensors inserted in the glass—at the cost of about $700,000. "During hot days, the entire south wall is protected without any expenditure of human energy."

I wanted to say that in my parents' time they used reed mats that could just be rolled down when it got too hot. Instead I said, "That's nice," and looked through the glass at all the virtually free human energy around the road below: the thousands of underpaid laborers who had helped erect the building. It was clear that the world had embarked on a new adventure. In India, like everywhere else, building had become a device to display forms of new abundance and make them available to a growing market of consumers. One client of mine, a farmer turned garment exporter, wanted me to recreate Thomas Jefferson's Monticello on a suburban lot. Another, the owner of a Mumbai shipping company, asked me to design a house he saw in a film.

Back outside, I began driving home across a landscape of multiplex cinemas and shimmering plate-glass malls. All around me, a younger breed of professionals were attacking projects with the impatience of lucrative business deals—seeking to align their work with the idea of India as an industrial power. I thought of the house I was working on, its mud walls and brick courtyard, the kind even Mahatma Gandhi would have approved of. According to Gandhi, the ideal Indian house is built of materials and skills harnessed nearby.

For my client, a banker who had spent a working life all over the world, this new home was a symbolic return to traditional India. For me, the important thing was simply to go to my study each day, pull out a 6B pencil and spend time at the drawing board, trying for something timeless.

INTERPRETATIONS

1. Why does Bhatia visit the building he describes? What does he discover about it?
2. How does Bhatia use comparison and contrast in his essay? What specific examples support your answer?
3. Explain the tone that Bhatia chooses for this essay. Why do you think that this choice is appropriate or inappropriate?
4. What do you think Bhatia's main point is? Where is it most clearly stated?

CORRESPONDENCES

1. In "The Way to Rainy Mountain," Momaday describes the physical and spiritual journey undertaken by his ancestors. How does what has happened to the Kiowas relate to what Bhatia writes about in his essay?
2. How does Bhatia's perception of India compare with Rushdie's? How might Bhatia's essay help to inform Rushdie?

APPLICATIONS

1. Imagine that you live in a cluster of houses that all have a similar structure or that share a related theme. Suddenly a developer decides to build a home that is radically different and that compromises the integrity of the neighborhood. Write a letter to your Zoning Commission that argues for or against the project. Select a tone appropriate to your purpose, topic, and audience, and articulate specific supporting arguments.

2. What is something that you are able to do both by hand and by using a machine? Write a comparison and contrast essay that not only explains the process of making the object using both methods, but that also explains the subtleties and/or implications of using each system.

3. Describe a typical home in a country that you either lived in or visited. Accompany this verbal description with architectural drawings or photographs.

   Share your description and drawings with the members of your group. What is the relation between form and function? What features of the house reflect the culture or traditions present in the place where it stands?

The Lottery

SHIRLEY JACKSON

*Shirley Jackson (1919–1965) was born and raised in California. In 1933, she
moved with her family to Rochester, New York, where she briefly attended the
University of Rochester. Notable publications include the novel* Hangsaman
(1951) and the play We Have Always Lived in the Castle *(1962). In "The
Lottery" (1948), a frequently anthologized piece, Jackson scrutinizes scapegoating. Record in your journal your associations with "scapegoating."*

THE MORNING OF JUNE 27TH was clear and sunny, with the fresh warmth
of a full-summer day; the flowers were blossoming profusely and the
grass was richly green. The people of the village began to gather in the
square, between the post office and the bank, around ten o'clock; in
some towns there were so many people that the lottery took two days
and had to be started on June 26th, but in this village, where there were
only about three hundred people, the whole lottery took less than two
hours, so it could begin at ten o'clock in the morning and still be
through in time to allow the villagers to get home for noon dinner.

The children assembled first, of course. School was recently over
for the summer, and the feeling of liberty sat uneasily on most of them;
they tended to gather together quietly for a while before they broke into
boisterous play, and their talk was still of the classroom and the teacher,
of books and reprimands. Bobby Martin had already stuffed his pockets full of stones, and the other boys soon followed his example, select-
ing the smoothest and roundest stones; Bobby and Harry Jones and
Dickie Delacroix—the villagers pronounced this name "Dellacroy"—
eventually made a great pile of stones in one corner of the square and
guarded it against the raids of the other boys. The girls stood aside,
talking among themselves, looking over their shoulders at the boys,
and the very small children rolled in the dust or clung to the hands of
their older brothers or sisters.

Soon the men began to gather, surveying their own children, speaking of planting and rain, tractors and taxes. They stood together, away
from the pile of stones in the corner, and their jokes were quiet and they
smiled rather than laughed. The women, wearing faded house dresses
and sweaters, came shortly after their menfolk. They greeted one another
and exchanged bits of gossip as they went to join their husbands. Soon

321

the women, standing by their husbands, began to call to their children, and the children came reluctantly, having to be called four or five times. Bobby Martin ducked under his mother's grasping hand and ran, laughing, back to the pile of stones. His father spoke up sharply, and Bobby came quickly and took his place between his father and his oldest brother.

The lottery was conducted—as were the square dances, the teenage club, the Halloween program—by Mr. Summers, who had time and energy to devote to civic activities. He was a round-faced, jovial man and he ran the coal business, and people were sorry for him, because he had no children and his wife was a scold. When he arrived in the square, carrying the black wooden box, there was a murmur of conversation among the villagers, and he waved and called, "Little late today, folks." The postmaster, Mr. Graves, followed him, carrying a three-legged stool, and the stool was put in the center of the square and Mr. Summers set the black box down on it. The villagers kept their distance, leaving a space between themselves and the stool, and when Mr. Summers said, "Some of you fellows want to give me a hand?" there was a hesitation before two men, Mr. Martin and his oldest son, Baxter, came forward to hold the box steady on the stool while Mr. Summers stirred up the papers inside it.

The original paraphernalia for the lottery had been lost long ago, and the black box now resting on the stool had been put into use even before Old Man Warner, the oldest man in town, was born. Mr. Summers spoke frequently to the villagers about making a new box, but no one liked to upset even as much tradition as was represented by the black box. There was a story that the present box had been made with some pieces of the box that had preceded it, the one that had been constructed when the first people settled down to make a village here. Every year, after the lottery, Mr. Summers began talking again about a new box, but every year the subject was allowed to fade off without anything's being done. The black box grew shabbier each year; by now it was no longer completely black but splintered badly along one side to show the original wood color, and in some places faded or stained.

Mr. Martin and his oldest son, Baxter, held the black box securely on the stool until Mr. Summers had stirred the papers thoroughly with his hand. Because so much of the ritual had been forgotten or discarded, Mr. Summers had been successful in having slips of paper substituted for the chips of wood that had been used for generations. Chips of wood, Mr. Summers had argued, had been all very well when the village was tiny, but now that the population was more than three hundred and likely to keep on growing, it was necessary to use something that would fit more easily into the black box. The night before the lottery, Mr. Summers and Mr. Graves made up the slips of paper and put them in the box, and it was then taken to the safe of Mr. Summers's coal company and locked up until Mr. Summers was ready to take it to the square next morning. The rest of the year, the box was put away, sometimes one place, sometimes another; it had spent one year in Mr. Graves's barn and another year underfoot in the post office, and sometimes it was set on a shelf in the Martin grocery and left there.

There was a great deal of fussing to be done before Mr. Summers declared the lottery open. There were the lists to make up—of heads of families, heads of households in each family, members of each household in each family. There was the proper swearing-in of Mr. Summers by the postmaster, as the official of the lottery; at one time, some people remembered, there had been a recital of some sort, performed by the official of the lottery, a perfunctory, tuneless chant that had been rattled off duly each year; some people believed that the official of the lottery used to stand just so when he said or sang it, others believed that he was supposed to walk among the people, but years and years ago this part of the ritual had been allowed to lapse. There had been, also, a ritual salute, which the official of the lottery had had to use in addressing each person who came up to draw from the box, but this also had changed with time, until now it was felt necessary only for the official to speak to each person approaching. Mr. Summers was very good at all this; in his clean white shirt and blue jeans, with one hand resting carelessly on the black box, he seemed very proper and important as he talked interminably to Mr. Graves and the Martins.

Just as Mr. Summers finally left off talking and turned to the assembled villagers, Mrs. Hutchinson came hurriedly along the path to the square, her sweater thrown over her shoulders, and slid into place in the back of the crowd. "Clean forgot what day it was," she said to Mrs. Delacroix, who stood next to her, and they both laughed softly. "Thought my old man was out back stacking wood," Mrs. Hutchinson went on, "and then I looked out the window and the kids was gone, and then I remembered it was the twenty-seventh and came a-running." She dried her hands on her apron, and Mrs. Delacroix said, "You're in time, though. They're still talking away up there."

Mrs. Hutchinson craned her neck to see through the crowd and found her husband and children standing near the front. She tapped Mrs. Delacroix on the arm as a farewell and began to make her way through the crowd. The people separated good-humoredly to let her through; two or three people said, in voices just loud enough to be heard across the crowd, "Here comes your Missus, Hutchinson," and "Bill, she made it after all." Mrs. Hutchinson reached her husband, and Mr. Summers, who had been waiting, said cheerfully, "Thought we were going to have to get on without you, Tessie." Mrs. Hutchinson said, grinning, "Wouldn't have me leave m'dishes in the sink, now, would you, Joe?" and soft laughter ran through the crowd as the people stirred back into position after Mrs. Hutchinson's arrival.

"Well, now," Mr. Summers said soberly, "guess we better get started, get this over with, so's we can go back to work. Anybody ain't here?"

"Dunbar," several people said. "Dunbar, Dunbar."

Mr. Summers consulted his list. "Clyde Dunbar," he said. "That's right. He's broke his leg, hasn't he? Who's drawing for him?"

"Me, I guess," a woman said, and Mr. Summers turned to look at her. "Wife draws for her husband," Mr. Summers said. "Don't you have a grown boy to do it for you, Janey?" Although Mr. Summers and everyone else in the village knew the answer perfectly well, it was the business of the official of the lottery to ask such questions formally. Mr. Summers waited with an expression of polite interest while Mrs. Dunbar answered.

"Horace's not but sixteen yet," Mrs. Dunbar said regretfully. "Guess I gotta fill in for the old man this year."

"Right," Mr. Summers said. He made a note on the list he was holding. Then he asked, "Watson boy drawing this year?"

A tall boy in the crowd raised his hand. "Here," he said. "I'm drawing for m'mother and me." He blinked his eyes nervously and ducked his head as several voices in the crowd said things like "Good fellow, Jack," and "Glad to see your mother's got a man to do it."

"Well," Mr. Summers said, "guess that's everyone. Old Man Warner make it?"

"Here," a voice said, and Mr. Summers nodded.

A sudden hush fell on the crowd as Mr. Summers cleared his throat and looked at the list. "All ready?" he called. "Now, I'll read the names—heads of families first—and the men come up and take a paper out of the box. Keep the paper folded in your hand without looking at it until everyone has had a turn. Everything clear?"

The people had done it so many times that they only half listened to the directions; most of them were quiet, wetting their lips, not looking around. Then Mr. Summers raised one hand high and said, "Adams." A man disengaged himself from the crowd and came forward. "Hi, Steve," Mr. Summers said, and Mr. Adams said, "Hi, Joe." They grinned at one another humorlessly and nervously. Then Mr. Adams reached into the black box and took out a folded paper. He held it firmly by one corner as he turned and went hastily back to his place in the crowd, where he stood a little apart from his family, not looking down at his hand.

"Allen," Mr. Summers said, "Anderson . . . Bentham."

"Seems like there's no time at all between lotteries any more," Mrs. Delacroix said to Mrs. Graves in the back row. "Seems like we got through with the last one only last week."

"Time sure goes fast," Mrs. Graves said.

"Clark . . . Delacroix."

"There goes my old man," Mrs. Delacroix said. She held her breath while her husband went forward.

"Dunbar," Mr. Summers said, and Mrs. Dunbar went steadily to the box while one of the women said, "Go on, Janey," and another said, "There she goes."

"We're next," Mrs. Graves said. She watched while Mr. Graves came around from the side of the box, greeted Mr. Summers gravely, and selected a slip of paper from the box. By now, all through the crowd there were men holding the small folded papers in their large hands, turning them over and over nervously. Mrs. Dunbar and her two sons stood together, Mrs. Dunbar holding the slip of paper.

"Harburt . . . Hutchinson."

"Get up there, Bill," Mrs. Hutchinson said, and the people near her laughed.

"Jones."

"They do say," Mr. Adams said to Old Man Warner, who stood next to him, "that over in the north village they're talking of giving up the lottery."

Old Man Warner snorted. "Pack of crazy fools," he said. "Listening to the young folks, nothing's good enough for *them*. Next thing you know, they'll be wanting to go back to living in caves, nobody work any more, live *that* way for a while. Used to be a saying about 'Lottery in June, corn be heavy soon.' First thing you know, we'd all be eating stewed chickweed and acorns. There's *always* been a lottery," he added petulantly. "Bad enough to see young Joe Summers up there joking with everybody."

"Some places have already quit lotteries," Mrs. Adams said.

"Nothing but trouble in *that*," Old Man Warner said stoutly. "Pack of young fools."

"Martin." And Bobby Martin watched his father go forward. "Overdyke . . . Percy."

"I wish they'd hurry," Mrs. Dunbar said to her oldest son. "I wish they'd hurry."

"They're almost through," her son said.

"You get ready to run tell Dad," Mrs. Dunbar said.

Mr. Summers called his own name and then stepped forward precisely and selected a slip from the box. Then he called, "Warner."

"Seventy-seventh year I been in the lottery," Old Man Warner said as he went through the crowd. "Seventy-seventh time."

"Watson." The tall boy came awkwardly through the crowd. Some-one said, "Don't be nervous, Jack," and Mr. Summers said, "Take your time, son."

"Zanini."

After that, there was a long pause, a breathless pause, until Mr. Summers, holding his slip of paper in the air, said, "All right, fel-lows." For a minute, no one moved, and then all the slips of paper were opened. Suddenly, all the women began to speak at once, saying, "Who is it?" "Who's got it?" "Is it the Dunbars?" "Is it the Watsons?" Then the voices began to say, "It's Hutchinson. It's Bill." "Bill Hutchin-son's got it."

"Go tell your father," Mrs. Dunbar said to her older son.

People began to look around to see the Hutchinsons. Bill Hutchinson was standing quiet, staring down at the paper in his hand. Suddenly, Tessie Hutchinson shouted to Mr. Summers, "You didn't give him time enough to take any paper he wanted. I saw you. It wasn't fair!"

"Be a good sport, Tessie," Mrs. Delacroix called, and Mrs. Graves said, "All of us took the same chance."

"Shut up, Tessie," Bill Hutchinson said.

"Well, everyone," Mr. Summers said, "that was done pretty fast, and now we've got to be hurrying a little more to get done in time." He consulted his next list. "Bill," he said, "you draw for the Hutchinson family. You got any other households in the Hutchinsons?"

"There's Don and Eva," Mrs. Hutchinson yelled. "Make *them* take their chance!"

"Daughters drew with their husbands' families, Tessie," Mr. Summers said gently. "You know that as well as anyone else."

"It wasn't *fair*," Tessie said.

"I guess not, Joe," Bill Hutchinson said regretfully. "My daughter draws with her husband's family, that's only fair, And I've got no other family except the kids."

"Then, as far as drawing for families is concerned, it's you," Mr. Summers said in explanation, "and as far as drawing for house-holds is concerned, that's you, too. Right?"

"Right," Bill Hutchinson said.

"How many kids, Bill?" Mr. Summers asked formally.

"Three," Bill Hutchinson said. "There's Bill, Jr., and Nancy, and little Dave. And Tessie and me."

"All right, then," Mr. Summers said. "Harry, you got their tickets back?"

Mr. Graves nodded and held up the slips of paper. "Put them in the box, then," Mr. Summers directed. "Take Bill's and put it in."

"I think we ought to start over," Mrs. Hutchinson said, as quietly as she could. "I tell you it wasn't *fair*. You didn't give him time enough to choose. *Every*body saw that."

Mr. Graves had selected the five slips and put them in the box, and he dropped all the papers but those onto the ground, where the breeze caught them and lifted them off.

"Listen, everybody," Mrs. Hutchinson was saying to the people around her.

"Ready, Bill?" Mr. Summers asked, and Bill Hutchinson, with one quick glance around at his wife and children, nodded.

"Remember," Mr. Summers said, "take the slips and keep them folded until each person has taken one. Harry, you help little Dave." Mr. Graves took the hand of the little boy, who came willingly with him up to the box. "Take a paper out of the box, Davy," Mr. Summers said. Davy put his hand into the box and laughed. "Take just *one* paper," Mr. Summers said. "Harry, you hold it for him." Mr. Graves took the child's hand and removed the folded paper from the tight fist and held it while little Dave stood next to him and looked up at him wonderingly.

"Nancy next," Mr. Summers said. Nancy was twelve, and her school friends breathed heavily as she went forward, switching her skirt, and took a slip daintily from the box. "Bill, Jr.," Mr. Summers said, and Billy, his face red and his feet overlarge, nearly knocked the box over as he got a paper out. "Tessie," Mr. Summers said. She hesitated for a minute, looking around defiantly, and then set her lips and went up to the box. She snatched a paper out and held it behind her.

"Bill," Mr. Summers said, and Bill Hutchinson reached into the box and felt around, bringing his hand out at last with the slip of paper in it.

The crowd was quiet. A girl whispered, "I hope it's not Nancy," and the sound of the whisper reached the edges of the crowd.

"It's not the way it used to be," Old Man Warner said clearly. "People ain't the way they used to be."

"All right," Mr. Summers said. "Open the papers. Harry, you open little Dave's."

Mr. Graves opened the slip of paper and there was a general sigh through the crowd as he held it up and everyone could see that it was blank. Nancy and Bill, Jr., opened theirs at the same time, and both beamed and laughed, turning around to the crowd and holding their slips of paper above their heads.

"Tessie," Mr. Summers said. There was a pause, and then Mr. Summers looked at Bill Hutchinson, and Bill unfolded his paper and showed it. It was blank.

"It's Tessie," Mr. Summers said, and his voice was hushed. "Show us her paper, Bill."

Bill Hutchinson went over to his wife and forced the slip of paper out of her hand. It had a black spot on it, the black spot Mr. Summers had made the night before with the heavy pencil in the coal-company office. Bill Hutchinson held it up and there was a stir in the crowd.

"All right, folks," Mr. Summers said. "Let's finish quickly."

Although the villagers had forgotten the ritual and lost the original black box, they still remembered to use stones. The pile of stones the boys had made earlier was ready; there were stones on the ground with the blowing scraps of paper that had come out of the box. Mrs. Delacroix selected a stone so large she had to pick it up with both hands and turned to Mrs. Dunbar. "Come on," she said. "Hurry up."

Mrs. Dunbar had small stones in both hands, and she said, gasping for breath, "I can't run at all. You'll have to go ahead and I'll catch up with you."

The children had stones already, and someone gave little Davy Hutchinson a few pebbles.

Tessie Hutchinson was in the center of a cleared space by now, and she held her hands out desperately as the villagers moved in on her. "It isn't fair," she said. A stone hit her on the side of the head.

Old Man Warner was saying, "Come on, come on, everyone." Steve Adams was in the front of the crowd of villagers, with Mrs. Graves beside him.

"It isn't fair, it isn't right," Mrs. Hutchinson screamed and then they were upon her.

INTERPRETATIONS

1. What do the villagers mean by "fairness"? What is implied by the fact that the only villager to complain about the lottery's consequences is Tessie Hutchinson?

2. Why does Jackson use a flat, reportorial style to describe an event that would normally be headline news? Consider the role of irony in this story.

3. How important is it that the story is set in roughly contemporary New England? How, for example, would its influence differ if the story were set in Aztec Mexico, a culture that routinely practiced human sacrifice?

4. The tradition here depicted brings summary execution or reprieve. What traditions do we participate in that have life-or-death consequences, in either the short or the long run?

Stone-Throwing in India: An Annual Bash

MARK FINEMAN

Mark Fineman (b. 1952) has had a varied career in journalism since receiving his degree from Syracuse University. He has worked for The Chicago Sun-Times; *the Allentown, Pennsylvania,* Call-Chronicle; *and* The Philadelphia Inquirer. *At present he is based in Miami as Caribbean bureau chief for* The Los Angeles Times. *To what extent do you find Fineman's title engaging? Is there anything unusual about it?*

PANDHURNA, INDIA—To most of the 45,000 seemingly normal residents of this sleepy little town on the banks of the River Jam, Anil Sambare is nothing more than a spoilsport.

To some, he is something worse. A troublemaker, some say. An idealistic radical, according to others. Some even think him a traitor to his hometown.

And all because the twenty-seven-year-old high school teacher has dedicated his life to stopping his entire town from going completely berserk once a year in a frenzied festival of destruction—a daylong event in which thousands of people try to stone each other to death in the name of fun, tradition and, now, stardom.

The annual event is called the Gotmaar Festival—literally, "stone-hitting"—and it is an ancient Pandhurna tradition, unique and brutal even by Indian standards.

No one here remembers exactly how ancient it is, although older people say that it dates back at least three centuries. And no one knows exactly why they do it every year, year after year, despite scores of deaths and thousands of injuries, although the myth behind it is a compelling one.

All the Pandhurnans really know for sure is that once a year, on the day of the new moon in the Hindu month of Sharawan, when the drums start beating along the River Jam, the time for the madness has begun again.

Within minutes, thousands of male Pandhurnans, ranging in age from six to sixty, many of them deeply scarred or limping from festivals of years past, divide into two groups, gather their huge piles of stones on opposite sides of the river and, for the next six-and-a-half hours, try to kill, maim and mangle as many fellow townsfolk as they can.

When sunset comes, and the drumbeat stops, the two sides drop their rocks, come together, shake hands, nurse each other's wounds and return to the peaceful monotony of rural Indian life.

This year, the Gotmaar carnage, which took place two weeks ago, left four dead and 612 injured. But there were a few new twists this year that speak volumes about India's struggle to enter the modern age.

First, there was Anil Sambare and his signature drive to end the carnage, which drew the ire of almost everyone. Second, this is an election year in India, which meant that Sambare's signature campaign was doomed to failure. And finally, there was the introduction of a new evil, videotape equipment, which is likely to ensure that Pandhurna's sado-masochistic ritual will continue for many years to come.

The story of the Pandhurnans and their bizarre, ancient rite of stoning is a living illustration of the paradoxes of a modern-day India, as well as a freeze-frame glimpse at the ironies and distortions resulting from Indian Prime Minister Rajiv Gandhi's five-year-old pledge to modernize rural India.

Pandhurna, in central Madhya Pradesh state, is hardly what one would call a backwater. In many ways it is a model of Rajiv Gandhi's rural modernization plan.

There are 10,000 television sets in Pandhurna, 340 telephones and even 100 videocassette players. More than ninety percent of the homes have electricity. Everyone has access to clean drinking water. Unemployment is under five percent, and there are even beauty parlors doing booming business.

"There is just this one little thing that sets us apart," said Bhargao Pandurang Bhagwatkar, who has taught in the local high school for the last forty-one years. "We all know it is barbaric. It is a kind of madness. And it has no reason at all. But it has been with us since Day 1, and, on that day every year, we just cannot help ourselves."

Day 1, as myth has it, was sometime in the 1600s, according to local historians, police and other local officials, who say they and their predecessors have been trying to stop it every year for the last half-century.

On Day 1, it seems, Pandhurna's brutal battle began as a love story.

"The way the old ones tell it," town official M. M. Singh explained, "a boy from the Pandhurna side of the river eloped with a girl from the village on the other side, which was then known as Sawargaon but since has merged into Pandhurna.

"As the amorous young couple was trying to flee across the river, the Sawargaon people began throwing stones at them. The Pandhurnans heard about this and quickly ran to the river bank, where they began stoning the Sawargaons.

"The couple, of course, died in the cross-fire. And it's on the spot where they died that the people now put the tree every year."

"The tree?" the stranger asked.

"Oh, the tree. The tree is the main object of the game."

The Pandhurnans who actually play "the game," which is what everyone here except Sambare calls the annual stoning battle, explained that the tree is cut the day before the festival from a special grove of flame trees beside a temple to the Hindu god of destruction, which is where legend states that the mythical young couple first met.

The tree is then "planted" in the middle of the River Jam, and the object of "the game" is to chop down the tree with an ax, without, of course, getting stoned to death in the process.

Enter the videotape.

Unlike previous years, in which an average of two or three Pandhurnans were stoned to death during the festival, the four deaths this year were from drowning.

"These boys had climbed the tree, and were posing for the camera," Sambare explained. "They were so preoccupied with the video camera, they didn't see the stones coming. They got hit in the head, fell into the river and drowned."

Sambare knows what he's talking about. He lives on Stone-hitting Road, in a riverfront house with a view of the battle zone. And he jumped into the river and saved four other "players" from the same fate this year, getting hit in the back with stones in the process.

But that's not why Sambare is so committed to ending the carnage of Gotmaar. It's not even because his uncle was stoned to death twenty-seven years ago, or because he cannot stop his own younger brother from joining in—"imagine, my own brother bought five different outfits and changed clothes five times during the stone-hitting this year because he wanted to look good for the camera."

"No, I am fighting this because it is a perversion, because it is barbaric and because it puts all of India in a very poor light," said Sambare, who has a masters degree in mathematics.

"This is not a game. This is madness. And now, with this videotape, there is all of a sudden a renewed interest in joining in. Everyone wants to show off their bravado."

Enter Rajiv Gandhi's high-tech revolution.

The videotape was the government's idea. And the local police actually paid 5,000 rupees (about $300) in government funds to a local video contractor to film the festival this year.

"The idea was to minimize the killing," said Krishna Kohle, the enterprising Pandhurnan who got the video contract. "It was, how do you call it, a compromise."

For decades, local officials said, the authorities have attempted to end the festival. Two years ago, the police even opened fire on the festival, killing two Pandhurnans, in an attempt to end it after a passing constable was accidentally stoned to death.

"I myself have seen too many deaths and very much want this madness to end," said Dr. Ratan Singhvi, a local physician who is Pandhurna's equivalent of mayor and the local head of Gandhi's ruling Congress-I party.

"I have seen people with eyes bulging out, ears sheared off, noses broken, teeth shattered, skulls and legs fractured to bits. But we've never been able to stop it. My God, the people like it.

"Of course, an additional problem is these people are all dead drunk when they're playing the game, and the game gives them a good excuse to get drunk. They look forward to it all year long."

Enter politics.

"The people of Pandhurna, you see, are very sentimental about this festival," Singhvi said. "And such things are very important to our local voters. Had we stopped the Gotmaar this year, for example, the Congress Party definitely would be sent away in the next elections. So what we did instead was try to cut down on the deaths—we banned the slingshot."

Called *gofans*, the handmade slingshots came into vogue two years ago and clearly escalated the conflict. They turned the stones into speeding bullets, tripling the death toll and ultimately forcing the police to step in. The *gofan* was outlawed. And, in an effort to enforce that ban, police hired the video man to film violators for prosecution.

"I guess it backfired," said Kohle, who conceded he is now making a tidy profit renting out copies of the Gotmaar video to townspeople who want to relive their moments of bravery and endurance.

INTERPRETATIONS

1. Explain the myth that serves as the catalyst for the town's annual stone-hitting event.

2. "This is not a game. This is madness. And now with this videotape, there is all of a sudden a renewed interest in joining in." To what extent do you agree with Sambare? How has the video camera affected the stone-hitting activities?

3. What are Sambare's reasons for protesting against his town's tradition? Do you think he will succeed? To what extent is he foolish to try?

CORRESPONDENCES

1. Review the Maugham perspective on traditions and explain its meaning. How does it apply to the texts by Jackson and Fineman?
2. Imagine a conversation between Anil Sambare and *one* of the characters depicted in Shirley Jackson's short story "The Lottery" (e.g., Old Man Warner, Mrs. Hutchinson, Mr. Summers). What would these two people say to each other? Write down the conversation that you think they would have. Try to extend this discourse for twenty lines.

APPLICATIONS

1. A symbol is something that stands for something else. In Jackson's story, a reader may look at the lottery, the black box, or Old Man Warner as signifying something more than a literal meaning.
2. Select a work that you have already written. How might you use a symbol to represent an idea that you are discussing? What modifications must you make in your piece to accommodate your use of this symbol? Once you consider these questions, revise your essay to include your symbolic treatment of your topic.
3. When Jackson's story was first published in *The New Yorker* in 1948, she received hundreds of letters from people "who wanted to know where these lotteries were held, and whether they could go there and watch." Discuss with your group what the responses to "The Lottery" reveal about human nature. What is your response?
4. By showing how familiar the process of each event is to the townspeople involved, what are the authors implying about traditions, mass psychology, and social pressure? To what extent does your group's response to this question compare with that of other groups in your class?
5. Review the titles of the texts by Jackson and Fineman. What are your associations with a lottery or an annual bash? What images do the words evoke? How do these underscore the ironies in both titles?

The Knowing Eye

FreeStockPhotos.com

READING IMAGES

1. What is happening in these photographs? What is familiar to you? What is unfamiliar? To what extent are you able to relate to what is depicted in each photograph?

2. What is the relationship between the setting of each photograph and the people in it? How has the photographer chosen to use backgrounds and foregrounds?

Lu Feng

MAKING CONNECTIONS

1. Which photograph do you think best applies to the Shirley Jackson story "The Lottery"? Explain your answer fully.

2. What kinds of traditions are depicted by these photographs? How are these types represented in the essays of this chapter?

WORDS AND IMAGES

1. What music do you think would be listened to by the dancer in the second photograph? What details in the image help you to make this determination? Try to locate an example of this music and listen to it. Next, write a description of this music that includes how it makes you feel and what it helps you to think about.

Thomas Lee

2. What is a sacred tradition that you or your family participate in? What is a secular tradition that you uphold? Write an essay about these traditions: How they are similar to and different from each other.

Additional Writing Topics

1. Many writers in this chapter recall aspects of their family's traditions—weddings, funerals, and religious customs. Focus on a ritual that you would like to record, and do so from a cross-generational or a cross-cultural perspective. Interview members of your family and extended family on their memories and associations. Write an account of these recollections that illustrates and explains their importance.

2. In the Cinderella tales and Fairbank's "Footbinding," various traditions (or magic powers) are used to confine women, to control them in some way(s). In every case, women escape the controls or turn them, at least in part, to their advantage. Discuss for these works the advantages and consolations that women in these cultures find even in their arduous and rigidly ordered lives. What qualities of human nature do they reveal, and are the qualities common to both men and women, or not?

3. All cultures observe holidays of national or international importance. What functions do these observances serve? Write an essay about the holidays your family celebrates and the rituals you observe. How "traditional" are these observances—and your role in them?

4. Write a journal entry on what you know about your own roots. What else would you like to discover about them? Which members of your immediate and extended family might you consult? What sources—letters, journals, family photographs—might be useful? After compiling information from these various sources, write a narrative essay on what you discovered about your origins.

5. Several writers in this chapter recall and describe a place at a moment when a major truth comes into focus for them. Recall some major awakening in your past life—love, death, religion, hatred—and then describe briefly but exactly the place where the awakening occurred so that your mood is also evident.

6. Review Erdrich's perspective on the relation between past and present. How do the texts in this chapter support her theory that "history has a way of intruding upon the present"? To what extent do you agree with her point of view?

7. According to Cesare Pavese, "We do not remember days, we remember moments." Freewrite about a moment of special significance for you. Then expand on the memory and its importance in

a fully developed essay. Why do you remember it so vividly? What do you remember? How might you best explain its effects on you?

8. Past experiences—their own or others—are important to Momaday, Yarimi, and Rushdie. Does the fact that each essay is about a particular culture and its traditions have any relevance to the writer's purpose? Have you had a similar experience that could be valuable to record? Before writing your essay, decide whether your purpose is to inform or persuade.

7

Cultural Encounters

PEACEFUL ENCOUNTERS AMONG CULTURES take many forms: treaties, trade, tourism, art exhibits, drama, movies, dance, student exchanges, exchange of scientific information, world fairs, conferring of awards and honors like the Nobel Prizes, sports events, musical events, conferences, emergency and other aid, cooperation in law enforcement, the United Nations. In general these encounters please, intrigue, or interest us. Variety enhances—in food, dress, language, religion, art, celebrations, government. However, as the Senegalese folktale that begins this chapter implies, there is another side to human nature, and it is bleak. People may be so fond of their vested arrangements, so afraid that change will be for the worse, that they prefer falsehood to truth. Exposure to other cultures, the sifting of truth, the juxtaposition of another's knowledge and our ignorance, for example, are sometimes more than we can stand: "Better the devil we know than the devil we don't" expresses an enduring attitude that quickly surfaces when cultures compete rather than complement. Such clashes exact a price and take various forms.

Are our encounters with people affected by our culture? Indeed they are. "The American Dream," for example, is more than a slogan adorning a T-shirt; it is a shorthand expression of a widespread belief among Americans that freedom, social justice, and improvement in material standards are desirable and possible for all. But lack of awareness of cultural differences or the assumptions of one cultural group that another is inferior often results in encounters that are patriotic power struggles. Although the United States continues to be a nation of immigrants (a recent survey reported that almost 80 percent of New York City's population is comprised of immigrants) in search of that dream, many groups have felt excluded from the right to equality promised in the Declaration of Independence of 1776. They are challenging the monocultural concept that was first expressed in Hector St. Jean de Crevecoeur's 1781 statement that "individuals of all nations are melted down in a new race of men" and which has shaped the collective consciousness of North America for almost two centuries.

In fact, several new metaphors have been offered to replace that of the melting pot. Asian American writer Bharti Mukherjee proposes that a "fusion chamber" in which elements interact but do not melt, has become more appropriate to describe the new multiracial democracy of the twenty-first century. African American novelist Toni Morrison concurs: "We have to acknowledge that the thing we call 'literature' is pluralistic now, just as society ought to be." Isabelle de Courtivron, professor of language and literature at the Massachusetts Institute of Technology goes further in a recent article. "I think one can surely belong to a gender, a country, a language, a culture, a religion, a race,— or to several of each—without having to make consistently unilateral identifications with any of them."

Several of the personal encounters in this chapter involve confronting ethnic and cultural stereotypes. Michael T. Kaufman reflects on losing contact with a former schoolfriend because of his own "prejudice and stupidity" and on a school system that tracked students even in elementary school. Alton Fitzgerald White, an African American actor, expresses outrage at being wrongfully arrested and detained in 1999 as he was leaving his apartment building in Harlem; in "Passion and the Dream," Linda Stanley records how a jury in Queens, New York, had to reexamine their concepts of the American dream.

Encounters also often involve personal and cultural reevaluations. Garrett Hongo, for example, in "Fraternity," struggles with the "punishment" and "exclusion" of racism inflicted by members of his own and another ethnic group, as well as the personal rejection of his Portuguese girlfriend. Taneisha Grant, in "To Speak Patois," contrasts her personal and communal experiences of living in Jamaica until early adolescence with the personal and cultural adjustments she had to make as a college student in New York City.

As you read the cultural encounters in this chapter, consider how factors such as race, ethnicity, and social class have contributed to or detracted from your own position in American society. You might also consider what changes you may have to make in your own presuppositions as you forge your individual identity in the multicultural world of the twenty-first century.

Perspectives

The United States, by its very nature, by its very development, is
the essence of diversity. It is diverse in its geography, population,
institutions, technology; its social, cultural, and intellectual modes. It
is a society that at its best does not consider quality to be monolithic
in form or finite in quantity, or to be inherent in class. Quality in our
society proceeds in large measure out of the stimulus of diverse modes
of thinking and acting; out of the creativity made possible by the
different ways in which we approach things; out of diversion from
paths or modes hallowed by tradition.

—Arturo Madrid

Culture is that which binds men together.

—Ruth Benedict

The greatest distance between people is not space but culture.

—Jamake Highwater

People and their cultures perish in isolation, but they are born or
reborn in contact with other men and women, with men and women
of another culture, another creed, another race. If we do not recognize
our humanity in others, we will not recognize it in ourselves.

—Carlos Fuentes

As long as you keep a person down, some part of you has to be down
there to hold him down, so it means you cannot soar as you otherwise
might.

—Marian Anderson

Man is an animal suspended in the webs of significance which he
himself has created. I take culture to be those webs.

—Clifford Geertz

I speak to the black experience, but I am always talking about the
human condition—about what we can endure, dream, fail at, and still
survive.

—Maya Angelou

No man is an island, intire of it selfe; every man is a peece of the
Continent, apart of the maine; if a Clod bee washed away by the Sea,
Europe is the lesse, as well as if a Promontorie were, as well as if
a Mannor of thy friends or of thine owne were; any man's death

diminishes me, because I am involved in Mankinde; And therefore never send to know for whom the bell tolls; It tolls for thee.

—John Donne

Americans are wedded by proximity to a common culture.

—Richard Rodriguez

Culture regulates our lives at every turn. From the moment we are born until we die there is, whether we are conscious of it or not, constant pressure upon us to follow certain types of behavior that other men have created for us.

—Clyde Kluckhohn

It is a terrible, an inexorable, law that one cannot deny the humanity of another without diminishing one's own; in the face of one's victim one sees oneself.

—James Baldwin

Where justice is denied, where poverty is enforced, where ignorance prevails and where any one class is made to feel that society is in an organized conspiracy to oppress, rob and degrade them, neither persons nor property will be safe.

—Frederick Douglass

There are two ways of spreading light: to be the candle or the mirror that receives it.

—Edith Wharton

There is wisdom in turning as often as possible from the familiar to the unfamiliar; it keeps the mind nimble, it kills prejudice, and it fosters humor.

—George Santayana

We travel, initially, to lose ourselves; and we travel, next, to find ourselves.

—Pico Iyer

It's that same old, same old story. We all have an immigrant ancestor, one who believed in America, and who, daring or duped, took sail.

—Fae Myeene Ng

The alien resident mourns even as she chooses to abandon. Her memory, like her guilt and early love, is involuntary but her choice of the United States is willful.

—Shirley Geok-lin Lim

As social equality spreads there are more and more people who, though neither rich nor powerful enough to have much hold over others, have gained or kept enough wealth and enough understanding to look after their own needs. Such folk owe no man anything and hardly expect anything from anybody. They form the habit of thinking of themselves in isolation and imagine that their whole destiny is in their own hands.

Thus, not only does democracy make men forget their ancestors, but it also clouds their view of their descendants and isolates them from their contemporaries. Each man is forever thrown back on himself alone, and there is danger that he may be shut in the solitude of his own heart.

—Alexis de Tocqueville

The only way to make sure people you agree with can speak is to support the rights of people you don't agree with.

—Eleanor Holmes Norton

APPLICATIONS

1. Discuss Madrid's perspective on the United States. To what extent do you agree with his point of view? Consider how aspects of other cultures including food, fashion, music, or movies influence your daily life. Is it possible to appreciate multiculturalism without losing cultural identity?

2. Select two perspectives with which you disagree and, in your journal, record and analyze the reasons for your point of view.

3. The perspectives of Ng and Lim focus on aspects of the immigrant experience. Review them with your group and summarize your discussion in your journal.

The Falsehood of Truth

SENEGALESE MYTH

Senegal is a republic in western Africa that gained independence from France in 1960. Explain the paradox in the title of the Sengalese myth.

Fene-Falsehood and Deug-Truth started out on a journey one day.

Fene-Falsehood said, "Everyone says that the Lord loves truth better than falsehood, so I think that you had better do all the talking for us."

Deug-Truth agreed, and when they came to a village, Deug-Truth greeted the first woman they met and asked if they could have a drink. She gave them a filthy bowl full of lukewarm water and then sat down in the doorway of her hut and began to eat a big meal of rice. While the two travelers were still there, the woman's husband came home and asked for his supper.

"It's not ready," replied the woman insolently.

The husband then turned to the two strangers who were watching and asked, "What would you say about a woman like that?"

"I would say that she is the worst wife I have seen in a long time. It's bad enough for her not to be hospitable to strangers, but it is really disgraceful when she doesn't feed her own husband," replied Deug-Truth. Fene-Falsehood didn't say a word.

The woman became furious and began to yell and scream louder than either of the two travelers had ever heard anyone scream before. "Are you going to stand by and let these strangers insult me!" she screamed to her husband. "If so, I will go home to my father and you will have to raise a bride-price for a new wife."

Then the husband, too, became angry and chased the two strangers out of town.

So Deug and Fene continued their travels and next came to a village where they found several children dividing up a bull that had just been slaughtered. They thought that this was rather strange, for it was the custom that meat was always divided by the head-man. While they were still watching, they saw the chief come up and take a very poor share of meat which the children handed him. The chief saw the two strangers and asked, "Who do you think is the leader in this village?"

Fene said nothing but Deug immediately answered, "It seems to me that these children must be the leaders of this village, for they are dividing the meat."

The chief immediately became angry and chased them out of that village.

As they continued to walk along, Fene said to Deug, "It is said that the Lord loves you the best, but I am beginning to wonder if man is not rather different from God. It seems to me that men do not like you very well. I think I will try my luck at the next village."

At the next village, they found that all the people were weeping because the favorite wife of the king had just died. Fene thought for a minute and then said, "Go tell the king that a man is here who can raise people from the dead."

Soon Fene was brought before the king and said, "I will raise your wife from the dead if you will give me half of your fortune."

The king immediately agreed and Fene had a hut built above the family grave. The king and all of the people waited outside and listened to the strange noises. First they heard huffing and panting and strange chants, but then they began to hear Fene talking loudly as if he were arguing. Finally he burst out of the door and slammed it shut—holding it tightly.

"Oh, dear," he said, "you did not tell me that your whole family was buried in there. When I woke your wife up, your father and your grandfather both came out too. I thought I had better check before I let them all out."

The king and his advisers began to look frightened, for the king's father had been a very cruel king and the new king and his friends had given his death a little assistance.

"I think you had better leave them all," said the king. "We would have a lot of trouble here with three kings."

"Well, it's not that easy," said Fene slyly. "Your father has offered me half of his property to let him out. I am certainly not going to send him back for nothing."

"I will still give you half of my property," said the desperate king. "Just get rid of them all."

So Fene received half of the king's fortune and concluded that while truth might have the favor of God, falsehood was the best way to get ahead with men.

INTERPRETATIONS

1. Are the incidents along the journey effective illustrations of the moral? To what institutions does falsehood apply? How do you respond to the choices made by the husband and the king?

2. The Senegalese myth is an allegory about abstractions like false-hood and truth. What associations do you have with myths or fables? What expectations do characters based on abstractions set up?

3. What does this fable teach about human attitudes toward absolutes like truth and falsehood? Are they relevant only to Senegalese culture? Explain.

The Wise Rogue

JEWISH FOLKTALE AS TOLD BY MOSES GASTER

The editor of A Harvest of World Folk Tales *describes the origins of*
"The Wise Rogue" as follows:

> *The keynotes of Jewish folk story are wisdom, humor, and piety,*
> *and its favorite form is the parable. It is plainly the product of a society*
> *that was in its early days priestly and in its later days persecuted. Rare*
> *are the mighty, muscular heroes (Samson was one, of course, but David*
> *against Goliath and Judith against Holofernes seem much more charac-*
> *teristic); nor are there any authentic fire-breathing dragons or broom-*
> *riding witches. The heroes of the Jews are wise kings, learned rabbis, or*
> *rogues who live by their wits; their dragons are the Devil and the Temp-*
> *tations; their witches are those who have historically oppressed them.*
> *Even their humor is of a wordly wise or satiric sort; and their sillies, the*
> *Wise Men of Helm, are not so much numskulls as absent-minded*
> *philosophers, men whose heads are filled with more than is commonly*
> *useful.*

A MAN WHO WAS ONCE CAUGHT stealing was ordered by the king to be
hanged. On the way to the gallows he said to the governor that he knew
a wonderful secret, and it would be a pity to allow it to die with him,
and he would like to disclose it to the king. He would put a seed of a
pomegranate in the ground, and through the secret taught to him by his
father he would make it grow and bear fruit overnight. The thief was
brought before the king, and on the morrow the king, accompanied by
the high officers of state, came to the place where the thief was waiting
for them. There the thief dug a hole and said, "This seed must be put in
the ground only by a man who has never stolen or taken anything
which did not belong to him. I being a thief cannot do it." So he turned
to the vizier who, frightened, said that in his younger days he had
retained something which did not belong to him. The treasurer said
that in dealing with large sums he might have entered too much or too
little, and even the king owned that he had kept a necklace of his
father's. The thief then said, "You are all mighty and powerful and
want nothing, and yet you cannot plant the seed, whilst I who have
stolen a little because I was starving am to be hanged." The king,
pleased with the ruse of the thief, pardoned him.

INTERPRETATIONS

1. "The king, pleased with the ruse of the thief, pardoned him." Usually people do not enjoy being tricked; what was different about this case? How would you have felt if the trick had been played on you?

2. What does this story imply about the relationship between justice and mercy?

3. What is the tone of this story? How does it affect the meaning?

CORRESPONDENCES

1. In folk literature, the trickster is the antithesis of the cultural hero, and his role is to destabilize the status quo by introducing the unexpected. How does the trickster function in both the Senegalese and the Jewish fables?

2. Review the Geertz perspective. What does it mean? How does it relate to "The Wise Rogue"? What does the story imply?

APPLICATIONS

1. The folktale, in contrast to literature, which is transmitted through written texts, is communicated orally primarily through memory and tradition. Create a folktale with your group members. Before beginning, decide on the moral you wish to communicate and think of humorous ways to include it.

2. Do you think of yourself as an idealist or a realist? An optimist or pessimist? Introvert or extrovert? Honest or dishonest? Are these categories adequate or too absolute to be accurate? Write a short essay on your attitude toward labeling.

3. What do the Senegalese and the Jewish stories suggest about success? Are rogues likely to achieve success? What examples can you think of? Discuss these questions in your group and record your conclusions.

Fraternity

GARRETT HONGO

Garrett Hongo (b. 1951) was born in Hawaii and received an M.F.A. at the University of California at Irvine. Hongo's publications include: Budding Bandits Down Highway 99, *with Lawson Inada and Alan Lau (1978);* The River of Heaven *(1988), which was the Lamont Poetry Selection of* The Academy of American Poets *and a finalist for the Pulitzer Prize, and* Yellow Light *(1982). His most recent book,* Volcano: A Memoir of Hawaii, *was published in 1995. Hongo has received fellowships from the Guggenheim Foundation, the National Endowment for the Arts, and the Rockefeller Foundation. He is currently Professor of Creative Writing at the University of Oregon at Eugene. Before reading Hongo's essay, record in your journal your definition of fraternity.*

IT WAS HIGH SCHOOL IN GARDENA. I was in classes mostly with Japanese American kids—*kotonks*. Mainland Japanese, their ethnic pet name originated, during the war, with derisive Hawaiian GIs who thought of the sound of a coconut being hit with a hammer. Sansei *kotonks* were sons and daughters of the Nisei *kotonks* who had been sent off to the concentration camps during World War II. School was tepid, boring. We wanted cars, we wanted clothes, we wanted everything whites and blacks wanted to know about sex but were afraid to tell us. We "bee-essed" with the black kids in the school parking lot full of coastal fog before classes. We beat the white kids in math, in science, in typing. We ran track and elected cheerleaders. We *ruled*, we said. We were dumb, teeming with attitude and prejudice.

Bored, I took a creative writing class with an "academically mixed" bunch of students. There were Chicanos, whites, a black woman, and a troika of Japanese women who sat together on the other side of the room from me. They said nothing—*ever*—and wrote naturalistically correct *haiku*. Suddenly among boisterous non-Japanese, I enjoyed the gabbing, the bright foam of free talk that the teacher encouraged. An aging man in baggy pants that he wore with suspenders, he announced he was retiring at the end of the year and that he wanted no trouble, that he was going to read "Eee-bee White" during our hour of class every day, that we were welcome to read whatever we wanted so long as we gave him a list ahead of time, and that we could talk as much as we wanted so long as we left him alone. We could read, we could write, we could jive each other all class long. It was freedom. And I took advantage.

I sat next to a Chicano my age named Pacheco and behind a white girl a class younger than me named Regina. Behind us was a curly-headed white guy who played saxophone in the marching band. He'd been in academic classes with me, the only Caucasian among Japanese, a Korean, and a few Chinese. He was a joker, and I liked him, but usually stayed away—we didn't fraternize much across the races, though our school was supposed to be an experiment in integration.

Gardena H. S. wasn't so much a mix or blend as a mosaic. Along with a few whites and blacks, Japanese were in the tough, college-prep, "advanced placement" scholastic track. Most whites and blacks were in the regular curriculum of shop, business skills, and a minimum of academic courses. The "dumb Japs" were in there with them. And the Chicanos filled up what were called the *remedial* classes, all taught imperiously only in English, with no provision for language acquisition. We were a student body of about three thousand, and we walked edgily around each other, swaggering when we could, sliding the steel taps on our big black shoes along the concrete outdoor walkways when we wanted to attract a little attention, making a jest of our strut, a music in the rhythm of our walking. Blacks were bused in from Compton; the whites, Japanese, and Chicanos came from around the town. Girls seemed to me an ethnic group of their own too, giggling and forming social clubs, sponsoring dances, teaching some of us the steps.

Crazes of dress moved through our populations—for Chicanos: woolen Pendletons over thin undershirts and a crucifix; big low-top oxfords; khaki work trousers, starched and pressed; for the *bloods*: rayon and satin shirts in metallic "fly-ass" colors; pegged gabardine slacks; cheap moccasin-toed shoes from downtown shops in L.A.; and for us *Buddhas:* high-collar Kensingtons of pastel cloths, A-tapered "Racer" slacks, and the same moccasin shoes as the bloods, who were our brothers. It was crazy. And *inviolable*. Dress and social behavior were a code one did not break for fear of ostracism and reprisal. Bad dressers were ridiculed. Offending speakers were beaten, tripped walking into the john, and set upon by gangs. They *wailed* on you if you fucked up. A girl was nothing except pride, an ornament of some guy's crude power and expertise in negotiating the intricacies of this inner-city semiotic of cultural display and hidden violence. I did not know girls.

I talked to Regina, saying "white girl" one time. She told me not to call her that, that she was *Portuguese* if anything, that I better *know* that white people were *always* something too. From vague memories of

Hawaii, I reached for the few words in *Portuguese* that I knew, I asked her about the sweet bread her mother baked, about heavy donuts fried in oil and rolled in sugar. I said *bon dea* for "good day" to her. I read the books she talked about—Steinbeck, Kesey, Salinger, and Baldwin. Her mother brought paperbacks home from the salon she worked in, putting up other women's hair—*rich* women's. We made up our reading list from books her mother knew. I wanted desperately to impress her, so I began to write poetry too, imitating some melancholy rock and country-and-western lyrics. She invited me to her house after school. It was on the way, so I walked her home. It became a practice.

Her father was a big, diabetic man from Texas. With his shirt off, he showed me how he shot himself with insulin, poking the needle under the hairy red skin on his stomach, working it over the bulge of fat around his belly. He laughed a lot and shared his beer. There were other guys over too—white guys from the football team, a Filipino, and one other Japanese guy who played left tackle. They were tough, raucous, and talked easily, excitedly. I stood alone in the front yard one day, holding a soft drink in my hand, the barbecue party going on around me. Regina and her mother were baking bread inside. No one knew exactly what was going on, and I was still trying to pretend all was casual.

I took photographs of her. We had a picnic on the coast by the lighthouse near Marineland, on the bluffs over the Pacific. It was foggy, mist upon us and the tall, droopy grasses in the field we walked through, but we made do. She wrapped herself in the blanket she'd brought for us to sit on. We were in the tall grasses of the headlands far from the coast road. She posed. I changed lenses, dropping film canisters, other things. She waved to me, unbuttoning the blouse she was wearing, her body full of a fragrance. The warm, yeasty scent of her skin smelled like bread under bronze silk.

We couldn't be seen together—not at the private, car-club-sponsored Japanese dances out in the Crenshaw District, not at the whites-dominated dances after school in the high school gym. Whites did not see Buddhas, and Buddhas did not see bloods. We were to stay with our own—*that* was the code—though we mixed some in the lunch line, in a few classes, on the football field, and in gym. We segregated ourselves.

Regina and I went to the Chicano dances in El Monte. Pacheco introduced us to them. Regina, tanned Portuguese, passed for Chicana, so long as she kept her mouth shut and her lashes long. Pacheco showed her what skirts to wear, his quick hands fluttering through the crinolines and taffetas in her closet at home. He advised me to grow a mustache and let my black hair go long in the back, to slick it down with pomade and to fluff it up in front, then seal it all in hair spray. I bought brown Pendletons and blue navy-surplus bell-bottoms. I bought hard, steel-toed shoes, We learned trots and tangos. We learned *cuecas* and polkas. We *passed, ese*, and had a good time for a couple of months.

One day, Regina got hurt. She was stopped by one of the football players at the beach. She was stepping onto a bus when he came up behind her and grabbed her arm. She tried to twist away, and the arm snapped. She crumpled. Everyone ran. She rode in a friend's car to the hospital that day and had the arm set. She didn't call me.

I heard about it after school the next day, crossing the street against the light. It was summer, and I was taking classes while Regina spent her days at the beach. I'd see her weekdays, stopping at her house on the way home. I was going to her when, just outside the gates of our school, a guy I knew taunted me with the news. He was Japanese, and it was strange to hear him say anything about Regina. I hadn't realized anyone from my crowd knew about us.

I wanted to run the rest of the way to her house. I crossed over a rise of bare earth, then down to a bedded railway—a strip line so that scrap steel and aluminum could be shipped from the switching stations and railyards downtown to steel and aeronautical factories near our school. Brown hummocks rose above eye level and masked the track of crossties, steel rails, and the long bed of gravel. I was set upon there by a troop of Japanese boys. A crowd of them encircled me, taunting, then a single gangly fellow I recognized from gym class executed most of the blows. They beat me, grinding my face in the gravel, shouting epithets like *inu* ("dog"), *cow-fucker*, and *paddy-lover*.

I've seen hand-sized reef fish, in a ritual of spawning, leave their singular lairs, gathering in smallish, excitable schools—a critical mass—and, electrified by their circling assembly, suddenly burst the cluster apart with sequences of soloing, males alternating, pouncing above the finning group, clouding the crystalline waters above the circle with a roll of milt.

All spring and summer, I'd been immune, unaware of the enmity of the crowd. I hadn't realized that, in society, humiliation is a force more powerful than love. Love does not exist in society, but only between two, or among a family. A kid from Hawaii, I'd undergone no real initiation in shame or social victimization yet and maintained an arrogant season out of bounds, imagining I was exempt. It was humiliating to have been sent to Camp. The Japanese American community understood their public disgrace and lived modestly, with deep prohibitions. I was acting outside of this history. I could cross boundaries, I thought. But I was not yet initiated into the knowledge that we Japanese were *not* like anyone else, that we lived in a community of violent shame. I paid for my naïveté with a bashing I still feel today, with cuts that healed with scars I can still run my fingers along. I can still taste the blood, remember the split skin under the mustache on my upper lip, and feel the depth of an anger that must have been *historical, tribal*, arising from fears of dissolution and diaspora.

Separated societies police their own separations. I was hated one day, and with an intensity I could not have foreseen. I was lifted by my clothes, the hands of my schoolmates at the nape of my shirt collar and the back of the waistband of my trousers, and I was hurled against the scrawny trunk of a little jacaranda tree and beaten there, fists cracking against my arms as I tried to cover my face, thumping along my sides and back, booted feet flailing at my legs. I squirmed, crawled, cried out. And I wept. Out of fear and humiliation and a psychic wounding I understand only now. I was *hated*. I was high and needed lowering. My acts were canceled. Regina was canceled. Both by our own peoples, enacting parallel vengeances of their own, taking our bodies from us.

Our trystings were over, and, later that summer, Regina simply moved away. Her father was retiring, she said, and had found a nice trailer park up by Morro Bay. She wouldn't see me before she left. I had to surprise her at a Laundromat one Saturday. She gave me a paperback book. She laughed, made light of everything, but there was a complete *fear* of me that I felt from her, deeply, one I had not felt before—at least, it had never registered. *Race*. It is an exclusion, a punishment, imposed by the group. I've felt it often since. It is a fear of *fraternity*. A fraternity that is forbidden. I wept, but let her go.

INTERPRETATIONS

1. In paragraph 1, Hongo describes his ethnic group. What portrait does he create?

2. "Gardena H.S. wasn't so much a mix or blend as a mosaic." What evidence supports his thesis?

3. "Dress and social behavior were a code one did not break for fear of ostracism and reprisal." What evidence resonates with your experiences in high school?

4. List the highlights of Hongo's relationship with Regina. Why does he devote so much space to this experience?

5. Hongo's brutal beating by his Japanese classmates was traumatic. Characterize your response to this incident.

CORRESPONDENCES

1. Review Fuentes's perspective on cultural interactions. To what extent do you agree with it? What conversation on this subject can you imagine Hongo and Fuentes sharing?
2. Review Santayana's perspective and show how Hongo's experience refutes it.

APPLICATIONS

1. Brainstorm about "fraternity." What images and associations does it evoke? What new meanings does Hongo's memoir create?
2. Discuss with your group Hongo's concept that "in society humiliation is a force more powerful than words." How does his concept of community compare to yours? Have you ever been punished for "crossing boundaries"?
3. Hongo describes race as "an exclusion," "a punishment," and a "fear of fraternity." Write an essay on your definition of race, supporting it as does Hongo with examples from your own experience.
4. In "Fraternity," Hongo tells a powerful story of his attempt to cross cultural boundaries. What story do you think Regina would tell? Create two journal entries written by Regina. Let the first one address her thoughts and feelings about culture before meeting Hongo. Direct the second entry to her thoughts and feelings after meeting him.

To Speak Patois

TANEISHA GRANT

Taneisha Grant received her B.S. degree from the City College of the City of New York in 1999. She received her medical degree in 2006 from Albert Einstein College of Medicine of Yeshiva University, Bronx, New York, and is currently a medical student at Yale Internal Medicine, New Haven, Connecticut.

Her essay "A Writing History: From Reluctant and Redundant to Raving and Rampant" was published in the December 1995 issue of "The Compositor," a newsletter from the CCNY English Composition Program. She also won the Lucia Santorsa/Beatrice Coviello Award for the same essay.

AT FOURTEEN YEARS OLD, I thought I knew everything there was to know about everything worth knowing—life, people, and relationships. My mind felt full, especially full of academic knowledge, and I felt that if given ample time for gathering a little experience in the field of teaching, I would be able to teach math and science. I had only completed the introductory levels of these classes but my ambition was not to be deterred by such trivialities. In my opinion, I was already armed with the foundation—more advanced math and science classes were mere applications of the basic concepts. I was also sure that if my "skills" as a relationship expert were to be tested, I would prove myself exceedingly gifted. I counselled all my peers because I knew how Kivette should cope with not having her boyfriend, Rory, call in all of a week, and why Tashika was "keeping malice" with Odetle over something Tashika supposedly hadn't done. I longed for the everyday rigors of life that my mother and her friends were always speaking about on my verandah. I was being anchored by high school—I needed a challenge.

I was born on the tropical West Indian Island of Jamaica, which is just south of Florida. I lived in a beautiful white house on a two-and-a-half acre plot of land. My neighbors and I were surrounded by the greenery that was mango, orange, cherry, avocado, guava, apple, and June plum trees. The neighborhood children would relish in sucking on the hard June plum covered with salt on their ways home until they got to the spiky seed. This sweetish-sourish fruit was particularly satisfying if eaten when "turned" (the point of just ripening). Those school evenings were filled with the lively chatter of noisy students, tired from the day's

355

work but with just enough energy left over to play a game of scruchie. This was a game in which two people stood about ten feet apart passing a ball between each other while all other participants ran back and forth to face the person with the ball. The object of the game was to skirt the ball as creatively as possible and not to get hit. Our "ball" was made from a juice box stuffed with paper and it really stung upon contact. Needless to say, none of us wanted to get hit and got quite a workout trying to avoid that juice box ball!

The rainy nights of May were a lot of fun because my sister and I were allowed to stay up past our bedtimes and await my cousins' return from crab hunting. The occasional sunshine warmed the water collected in the crab holes. These times were very unwelcomed by the crabs because they would have to leave their holes and would have nowhere to hide if attacked. It was on nights like these, under cover of the darkness, that my cousins went crab hunting by lamp light. Their catch was often plenty and the entire neighborhood would have a big feast of peppered crabs and boiled green bananas. On one of these nights, punctuated by the slightly hissing sounds of crickets, I happened to overhear my mother speaking on the verandah. She was telling Miss Vivene of our upcoming and permanent departure to the United States.

Growing up in Jamaica was everything one could wish for. From its white sandy beaches and crystal-clear waters to its unique reggae music, year-round sunshine, fruit trees, games of sidewalk scruchie, and delicious midnight crab feasts—this island was some sort of NICE! But quite unknown to me, sugar cane and spiced bun were not all that this island was made of. It also held a high cost of living and limited higher education. My parents thought it best for us to relocate (our home) and seize the more abundant educational opportunities offered by the United States.

I was very upset and afraid of leaving Jamaica's familiar sights, sounds, activities of daily living, my friends, my home, my country. My surroundings had always lent a partial definition to who I am. I was Taneisha who attended Titchfield High School, Taneisha who did scripture readings in church on Sundays, rode her bike to Mr. Browning's shop, and Taneisha who could find her way home blindfolded by counting the bumps in the road. I was now Taneisha leaving the familiar and all those other Taneishas behind, and that was heart-wrenching.

I had longed for a challenge and I certainly got one by moving to New York! Living here has been culturally shocking. Though the educational opportunities have been tremendously rewarding, the transition was difficult. Having to adjust to the drastic temperature change, the restrictions that go with being cautious in a more violent society, and the different educational system have quite fulfilled the challenge I sought. The sights and sounds are different, and the feeling of protection that is almost innate in a Jamaican society is lacking here.

There are many places in New York with high Jamaican populations, and there the culture and environment are closely simulated, but it's just not quite the same. I feel a deep-rooted guilt for leaving Jamaica. Though my family's situation was extenuating, I do feel as if I've abandoned my country. I speak Patois—the Jamaican dialect—as much as I can because one really can't help becoming a little culturally "dilute" when abroad. "Settled" is probably a better word, and it's an effort to keep yourself "shaken up" so as not to betray your country's memory by becoming too well-adapted/too well-mixed. I speak Patois because it serves as a verbal transport back to my homeland. I speak Patois to rekindle, "shake up" the memory of other identities and realize that I am still those Taneishas, the one who lives in New York State and also the Taneisha who will be going home.

I am now nineteen years old and I don't know a whole lot about life, relationships, or people. But I do know that I knew nothing of the rigors for which I longed or of change and the growth that it brings.

Turning points are moments
of conscious or unconscious
decisions to release stability
for a time.

Change is scary because
it means releasing the
comforts of the familiar
in order to embrace the
possibilities that newness
can bring.

Adjustments—coping mechanisms
to deal with changes—
can sometimes subdue the
memories of what was once
precious familiarity.

Dialects and other cultural
signatures help in maintaining
a firmer grasp on the old familiars.

I speak Patois.
Growth is the emotional and/or
physical manifestation of change
—of new.

INTERPRETATIONS

1. What characteristics does the author reveal about herself in the introductory paragraph?
2. How does she portray Jamaica visually, culturally, and psychologically?
3. Characterize her impression of life in New York City. Do you think she regrets having left her homeland? Cite evidence for your point of view.
4. What is the effect of ending the memoir with a poem? What does the poem mean?

CORRESPONDENCES

1. Compare and contrast the concept of assimilation presented in the essays by Rodriguez and Grant.
2. Review Kluckhohn's perspective on culture and discuss its application to Grant's essay.

APPLICATIONS

1. Review Geok-lin Lim's perspective and discuss its relevance to Grant's essay. What evidence is there of sorrow and guilt for leaving Jamaica?
2. Write a journal entry on the significance of Grant's title.
3. Analyze Grant's poem with your group. How do you respond? Are the issues raised in the poem different from those in the essay? How?

Passion and the Dream

LINDA STANLEY

Linda Stanley is a professor of English at Queensborough Community College in New York City, where she teaches many recent immigrants. She has a Ph.D. in comparative literature from New York University, and for many years has been interested in, and has published on, the changing responses of people in other countries to the American experience as F. Scott Fitzgerald portrays it in The Great Gatsby. *Brainstorm on your associations with Stanley's title. To what extent is it appropriate?*

RESIDENTS OF QUEENS, NEW YORK, we are on jury duty, and, as juries do, we find a lot in common. We learn early that most of us are Catholic, with a couple of Protestants and one Orthodox Jew for some variety. Almost all are college graduates (two teachers, two engineers, a copy editor, a nurse, a personnel officer, a sales manager), and each sex and age group are equally represented. Irish, English, Danish, French, German, Croatian, Cuban, Polish, Romanian, Italian, Austrian, African-American—we are representative of early, for the most part European, immigrations to Queens. With only one exception, we are at least second-generation Americans, and some of us go much further back.

Each day we spend most of our time together outside the court-room, either surrounding the table in the cramped closet of a jury room or, for at least an hour and a half each day, eating lunch together. We tell stories. Stories about childhood games, of what we were doing during the Vietnam War, of parenthood and grandparenthood, of travels, of sports and other leisure activities, of jobs, of events in the news. The stories form a fragile bond between us and keep us going for the two weeks, one day and one night of being almost constantly together.

Controversial topics, like the current trial of the four policemen accused of the Rodney King beating, are treated as newstories and not as topics for discussion. Those who are Republicans are matched by an equal number of Democrats, the young men drink alcohol while the middle aged feel the need to work out, and the single women are matched by the married and so we are careful. We know all Americans do not agree, and we do not want disharmony. By their sheer existence, our stories relieve us of our discomfort at being thrust in this situation. We also find pleasure in their content, and we laugh constantly.

We find varying degrees of pleasure in discussing the case. Some object to our doing so because the judge has admonished us not to. To ignore the courtroom is impossible because, next to the stories, we have the case in common. But our discussions are tangential to the issue of guilt as we admire the appearance of the young, female assistant district attorney, express wariness about the sternness of the judge, evaluate the cut of the defendant's suits, and relive the hilarity of the account of one of the witnesses. We do not feel we are prematurely closing our own minds or those of others through these discussions.

We discover early that the ethnic makeup of this defendant, plaintiff and witnesses represents much of the current immigration to Queens. The defendant and his brother, who witnesses for him, are Egyptian; his wife is from Ecuador; another witness is from India. Only one witness, from Greece, represents an earlier nationality on the scene, but he too is a first-generation American.

We on the jury are gradually gripped by the intensity of both the defendant and his wife. At first, we feel sorry for the wife, who sobs her way through her testimony. Too, we feel annoyed when the judge points out that the defendant does not have to testify because, as he tells us, in the American system the defendant is considered innocent and need not defend himself. Rather, he explains, it is up to the prosecution to prove he is guilty. Well, we think, that seems arrogant on the part of someone with so many charges of reckless endangerment against him. Our sympathies are with his wife, the tearful wife.

But when the defendant testifies, our sympathies slowly shift. An intense and nervous man, he blinks constantly. He also weeps. When the assistant district attorney finally gets up to cross-examine him, we wonder, with surprise, how she can ever hope to destroy such agonized testimony.

The passions are what move us. We cannot be told the reasons why the alleged crime has taken place, we can be told only the facts. The truth is denied us, but we can imagine their stories. They have come from so far with so many hopes to this city, the possessors of the same brave American Dream that all immigrants to America have dreamed. We know that he went first to Italy to learn to cook Italian food, perhaps knowing that Egyptian food is not in demand in America, and has prospered, now owning a medallion cab and a house. She has left behind a mother and a sister in Ecuador whom she returns to with her three children when all is not well between her and her Egyptian. Even when she comes back to New York, she leaves the children behind where they learn Spanish, a language their father cannot speak. The command of English of this pair is not conducive to easy communication and, we think, this has perhaps complicated their difficulties.

But their passion for their children is communicated in a universal language. His tears are for the children he had not been allowed to see for nine months, hers are for the terror of his taking them one pleasant Sunday morning in May on the street outside her new home in Queens.

We know that we will have to agree that what he has done is illegal. We have also discussed with disapproval how many Latin American women leave their children behind when coming to work in New York. We are suspicious of their actions, but we are not suspicious of their passions. Despite, or perhaps because of what we hear and know of many Americans' seeming callousness towards the fate of their own children, we are gripped by what these people so freely communicate to us about their love of their "babies."

Because of the many charges against the defendant, a unanimous decision does not come easily. We are taken to a hotel to be sequestered overnight. We eat dinner together and share rooms. For the first time, we share stories of significant events and people in our lives, of parents who have died and of the distress of their deaths. Breakfast finds us valued friends.

Back in the jury room, we unanimously decide we do not want to find him guilty of all charges. Yes, he hit his wife with a meat tenderizer when she protested his taking the children and, yes, he sped through the neighborhood with the three children held only by the arms of another person in the two-seater van, but we see his face even as we deliberate, and we cannot find him guilty of reckless endangerment in the first degree. He loves those children and is not callously indifferent to their fates. We settle on reckless endangerment in the second degree as well as to the assault charge and proceed to the courtroom.

There, the verdict is read by our foreman, a religious person who feels great sympathy for the defendant. The defendant, of course, is not aware of the foreman's agony as he begins to agonize himself. He shields his face with his hand and cries. His brother, who is present, cries also. When his lawyer asks for a poll of our votes, we have difficulty concentrating as each charge is read, and we must collect our thoughts occasionally before answering. Many of us feel tears welling up in our own eyes.

In the jury room once again, we feel the intensity of the experience keenly. We are very aware that we have supported each other through a difficult time. We make plans to meet again. We ask our court officer if all juries feel such intense camaraderie, and he can think of only one.

Fifteen minutes later, we prepare to leave the courthouse for the last time. As we pass through the lobby outside the courtroom, the defendant's brother stands weeping still.

Their passion has touched us profoundly. In losing their bright new world, they have shared with us the passions of an old world that they have been unable to leave behind. We have thought of inviting the defendant and his family to our reunion. We want them to understand what has transpired during the trial, that the dream is behind us all in its raw, most innocent form but that regeneration is possible. In a way that they can probably neither understand nor appreciate, they have made it possible for us.

INTERPRETATIONS

1. Why do you think Stanley implies that members of a jury always "find a lot in common"? From your own experience, do people thrown together always discover that they share common interests? To what extent does the essay suggest that, more than most groups, serving on jury duty might heighten common bonds?

2. What do we learn about the jurors from the essay? Why do they discuss stories rather than controversial issues? To what extent do you agree that the characteristics they have in common might have been overwhelmed by their political, marital, and sexual differences?

3. "The passions are what move us." How does the author build up to this statement? To what extent might the courtroom procedure of allowing only facts pertinent to the case encourage juries to interpret for themselves the "truth" of the case and to react to emotions expressed?

4. To what extent, based on the evidence Stanley presents, do you agree with the jury's decision to settle for "reckless endangerment in the second degree"? How convincing a rationale has she built for this lesser verdict?

5. Explain the meaning of the last paragraph of the essay. What "dream" does the author refer to? Why does this dream need regeneration and how does the author think the defendant and his wife have provided it?

CORRESPONDENCES

1. To what extent does Stanley's essay support Rodriguez's perspective that "Americans are wedded by proximity to a common culture"?

2. Is Stanley's purpose to inform or persuade? Is the tone of her essay similar to that of Hongo? Explain.

APPLICATIONS

1. Discuss the effect on our national life of the language barrier between many Americans. Is there, as the author suggests, a "universal language" that permits Americans to communicate with even the most recent immigrants?

2. To what extent do you think second- and third-generation Americans are generally as sympathetic to new immigrants as this jury is? How might you have responded as a member of the jury?

3. Alienation from the mainstream is a recurrent theme in several texts in this chapter. If you are a person of color who has felt like an outsider, write an analysis of that experience. If you are Caucasian and have felt excluded in a group, analyze the causes and effects in a brief essay.

4. Who is America? Check the following Web sites to learn the composition of inhabitants of the United States. Then, compare your findings to the jury described by Stanley in her essay.

   http://factfinder.census.gov

   http://www.socccd.cc.ca.us/ref/almanac/demographics/uspop.htm

   http://quickfacts.census.gov/qfd/index.html

Ragtime, My Time

ALTON FITZGERALD WHITE

Alton Fitzgerald White is a singer, actor, and dancer best known for his performances in "Smokey Joe's Cafe," "Miss Saigon," "Ragtime," and "The Lion King." A native of Cincinnati, Ohio, White attended the Cincinnati School for Creative and Performing Arts and majored in musical theater at the Cincinnati College Conservatory of Music. He made his Cincinnati Pops debut with Erich Kunzel at Riverbend Music Center on July 4, 2000, in a concert broadcast live nationwide on PBS. He has performed at Lincoln Center as part of the "American Songbook" series. White has released CDs and written a book of poetry, Uncovering the Heartlight. *The following essay about White's arrest was published in* The Nation *in 1999. Could it happen today?*

AS THE YOUNGEST OF FIVE GIRLS and two boys growing up in Cincinnati, Ohio, I was raised to believe that if I worked hard, was a good person and always told the truth, the world would be my oyster. I was taught to be courteous and polite. I was raised a gentleman and learned that these fine qualities would bring me one very important, hard-earned human quality: Respect!

While respect is indeed something one has to earn, consideration is something owed to every human being, even total strangers. On Friday, June 16, 1999, when I was wrongfully arrested while trying to leave my building in Harlem, my perception of everything I had learned as a young man was forever changed—not only because of the fact that I wasn't given even a second to use any of the wonderful manners and skills my parents had taught me as a child, but mostly because the police, who I'd always naïvely thought were supposed to serve and protect me, were actually hunting me.

I had planned the day to be a pleasant one. The night before was not only payday but also I received a rousing standing ovation after portraying the starring role of Coalhouse Walker Jr. in *Ragtime* on Broadway. It is a role I've worked very hard for professionally, and emotionally as well. A role that requires not only talent but also an honest emotional investment, including the morals and lessons I learned as a child.

Coalhouse Walker Jr. is a victim (an often misused word but in this case the true definition) of overt racism. His story is every black man's nightmare. He is hard-working, successful, talented, charismatic, friendly and polite. Perfect prey for someone with authority and not even a fraction of those qualities. The fictional character I portrayed on Thursday night became a part of my reality on Friday afternoon. Nothing in the world could have prepared me for it. Nothing I had seen on television. Not even stories told to me by other black men who had suffered similar injustices.

Most Fridays for me mean a trip to the bank, errands, the gym, dinner and then to the theater. On this particular day, I decided to break my usual pattern of getting up and running right out of the house. Instead, I took my time, slowed down my pace and splurged by making myself some homemade strawberry pancakes. It was a way of spoiling myself in preparation for my demanding, upcoming four-show weekend. Before I knew it, it was 2:45, and my bank closes at 3:30, leaving me less than forty-five minutes to get to midtown on the train. I was pressed for time but in a relaxed, blessed state of mind. When I walked through the lobby of my building, I noticed two light-skinned Hispanic men I'd never seen before. Not thinking much of it, I continued on to the vestibule, which is separated from the lobby by a locked door.

As I approached the exit, I saw people in uniforms rushing toward the door. I sped up to open it for them, especially after noticing that the first of them was a woman. My first thought was that they were paramedics, seeing as many of the building's occupants are retired and/or elderly. It wasn't until I had opened the door and greeted the woman that I recognized that they were the police. Within seconds I was told to "hold it" because they had received a call about young Hispanics with guns. I was told to get against the wall. I was searched, stripped of my backpack (which was searched repeatedly), put on my knees, handcuffed and told to be quiet when I tried to ask any questions.

With me were three other innocent black men. They had been on their way to their U-Haul, parked on the side of the building. They were moving into the apartment beneath me and were still glowing from the tour I'd given them of the beautiful historic landmark building. I had just bragged to them about how safe it was and how proud I was to have been living there for over five years. And now here the four of us were being told to get on our knees, handcuffed and not allowed to say a word in our defense. As a matter of fact, it was one of these gentlemen who got off his knees, still handcuffed, and unlocked the door for the policemen to get into the lobby where the two strangers were. Instead of being thanked or even acknowledged, we were led out the door past our neighbors, who were all but begging the police in our defense.

We were put into cars with the two strangers and taken to the 33rd Precinct at 165th and Amsterdam. The police automatically linked us to them with no questions and no regard for our character or our lives. No consideration was given to where we were going or what we were in need of doing before they came into our building. Suppose I had an ailing relative upstairs in my apartment waiting for me to return with her emergency remedy? Or young children who were told Daddy is running to the corner store for milk and will be right back? These three gentlemen weren't even allowed to lock their apartment or check on the U-Haul full of their personal belongings.

After we were lined up in the station, the younger of the two Hispanic men was immediately identified as an experienced criminal, and drug residue was found in a pocket of the other. I now realize how naïve I was to think the police would then uncuff me, apologize for their terrible mistake and let me go. Instead, they continued to search my back-pack repeatedly, questioned me and put me in jail with the criminals.

The rest of the nearly five-hour ordeal was like a horrible dream, putting me in a surreal state of shock. Everything from being handcuffed, strip-searched, taken in and out for questioning, to being told that they knew exactly who I was and my responsibility to the show and that in fact they knew they already had whom they wanted, left me in absolute disbelief.

When I asked how they could keep me there, or have brought me there in the first place with nothing found and a clean record, I was told it was standard procedure. As if the average law-abiding citizen knows what that is and can dispute it. From what I now know, "standard procedure" is something that every citizen, black and white, needs to learn, and fast. Even though they knew I was innocent, they made me feel completely powerless. All for one reason. Why do you think? Here I was, young, pleasant and successful, in good physical shape, dressed in clean athletic attire. I was carrying a backpack, containing a substantial paycheck and deposit slip, on my way to the bank and to enjoy a well-deserved great day. Yet after hours and hours I was sitting at a desk with two officers who not only couldn't tell me why I was there but seemed determined to find something on me, to the point of making me miss my performance.

It was because I am a black man!

I sat in that cell crying silent tears of disappointment and injustice with the realization of how many innocent black men are convicted for no reason. When I was handcuffed, my first instinct had been to pull away out of pure insult and violation as a human being. Thank God I was calm enough to do what they said. When I was thrown in jail with the criminals and strip-searched, I somehow knew to put my pride aside, be quiet and do exactly what I was told, hating it but coming to terms with the fact that in this situation I was powerless. I was a victim. They had guns!

Before I was finally let go, exhausted, humiliated, embarrassed and still in shock, I was led to a room and given a pseudo- apology. I was told that I was at the wrong place at the wrong time. My reply? "I was where I live."

As a result, what I learned growing up in Cincinnati has been shattered. Life will never be the same.

INTERPRETATIONS

1. White begins in paragraph 2 by relating his plans for the day. Cite specific examples that indicate his expectations for Friday, June 16, 1999.

2. Why is it effective to include paragraphs 3 and 4 in the context of what follows? Be specific.

3. Does what happens to White confirm or contradict your assumptions about the legal system in the United States? Explain your answer.

4. White reiterates several times that he was arrested because of his race. To what extent do you agree or disagree? Could it be argued that that his was a case of mistaken identity? Why or why not?

5. Why does White wait until paragraph 11 to describe his physical appearance? How does his description reinforce or weaken his charge that he was arrested because of his ethnicity.

CORRESPONDENCES

1. Read Baldwin's perspective and discuss its relevance to White's arrest and detention. How does paragraph 14 support or refute Baldwin's point of view?

2. Imagine a conversation between White and Hongo on racial profiling. In what ways were their emotional reactions to their experiences similar?

APPLICATIONS

1. Use the Internet to refresh your memory of the Bill of Rights of the U.S. Constitution. Write a journal entry on how your review affected your thinking on White's experiences.

2. Most people connect racial profiling with African Americans and Latinos. But after the events of September 11, 2001, Arab Americans as well as other people from the Middle East also became the focus of profiling and were arrested without cause. Write a letter to the editor of your college newspaper protesting this kind of discrimination.

3. Discuss with your group your various responses to White's experience. To what extent could you imagine yourself in a similar situation? Would you have reacted as White did? Would you have taken action after this occurrence?

4. Assume the persona of a police officer and write a justification of White's arrest because he "was at the wrong place at the wrong time."

Of My Friend Hector and My Achilles' Heel

MICHAEL T. KAUFMAN

Michael T. Kaufman (b. 1938) attended the City College of New York and Columbia University. He spent forty-two years at The New York Times *as a reporter, foreign correspondent, editor, and bureau chief. He also edited the George Soros publication* Transitions *that covered the post-Communist sphere in the Czech Republic. Kaufman's account of his experiences as* The New York Times *correspondent in Warsaw between 1984 and 1987 is* Mad Dreams, Saving Graces: Poland, A Nation in Conspiracy *(1989). Kaufman's most recent book,* Soros: The Life and Times of a Messianic Billionaire, *was published in 2003. Record in your journal your responses to Kaufman's introductory sentence.*

THIS STORY IS ABOUT PREJUDICE and stupidity. My own.

It begins in 1945 when I was a seven-year-old living on the fifth floor of a tenement walkup on 107th Street between Columbus and Manhattan Avenues in New York City. The block was almost entirely Irish and Italian, and I believe my family was the only Jewish one around.

One day a Spanish-speaking family moved into one of the four apartments on our landing. They were the first Puerto Ricans I had met. They had a son who was about my age named Hector, and the two of us became friends. We played with toy soldiers and I particularly remember how, using rubber bands and wood from orange crates, we made toy pistols that shot off little squares we cut from old linoleum.

We visited each other's home and I know that at the time I liked Hector and I think he liked me. I may even have eaten my first avocado at his house.

About a year after we met, my family moved to another part of Manhattan's West Side and I did not see Hector again until I entered Booker T. Washington Junior High School as an eleven-year-old.

The class I was in was called 7SP-1; the SP was for special. Earlier, I recall, I had been in the IGC class, for "intellectually gifted children." The SP class was to complete the seventh, eighth and ninth grades in two years and almost all of us would then go to schools like Bronx

Science, Stuyvesant or Music and Art, where admission was based on competitive exams. I knew I was in the SP class and the IGC class. I guess I also knew that other people were not.

Hector was not. He was in some other class, maybe even 7-2, the class that was held to be the next-brightest, or maybe 7-8. I remember I was happy to see him whenever we would meet, and sometimes we played punchball during lunch period. Mostly, of course, I stayed with my own classmates, with other Intellectually Gifted Children.

Sometimes children from other classes, those presumably not so intellectually gifted, would tease and taunt us. At such times I was particularly proud to have Hector as a friend. I assumed that he was tougher than I and my classmates and I guess I thought that if necessary he would come to my defense.

For high school, I went uptown to Bronx Science. Hector, I think, went downtown to Commerce. Sometimes I would see him in Riverside Park, where I played basketball and he worked out on the parallel bars. We would acknowledge each other, but by this time the conversations we held were perfunctory—sports, families, weather.

After I finished college, I would see him around the neighborhood pushing a baby carriage. He was the first of my contemporaries to marry and to have a child.

A few years later, in the 60s, married and with children of my own, I was once more living on the West Side, working until late at night as a reporter. Some nights as I took the train home I would see Hector in the car. A few times we exchanged nods, but more often I would pretend that I didn't see him, and maybe he also pretended he didn't see me. Usually he would be wearing a knitted watch cap, and from that I deduced that he was probably working on the docks as a longshoreman.

I remember quite distinctly how I would sit on the train and think about how strange and unfair fate had been with regard to the two of us who had once been playmates. Just because I had become an intellectually gifted adult or whatever and he had become a longshoreman or whatever, was that any reason for us to have been left with nothing to say to each other? I thought it was wrong and unfair, but I also thought that conversation would be a chore or a burden. That is pretty much what I thought about Hector, if I thought about him at all, until one Sunday in the mid-70s, when I read in the drama section of this newspaper that my childhood friend, Hector Elizondo, was replacing Peter Falk in the leading role in "The Prisoner of Second Avenue."

Since then, every time I have seen this versatile and acclaimed actor in movies or on television I have blushed for my assumptions. I have replayed the subway rides in my head and tried to fathom why my thoughts had led me where they did.

In retrospect it seems far more logical that the man I saw on the train, the man who had been my friend as a boy, was coming home from an Off Broadway theater or perhaps from a job as a waiter while taking acting classes. So why did I think he was a longshoreman? Was it just the cap? Could it be that his being Puerto Rican had something to do with it? Maybe that reinforced the stereotype I concocted, but it wasn't the root of it.

No, the foundation was laid when I was eleven, when I was in 7SP-1 and he was not, when I was in the IGC class and he was not.

I have not seen him since I recognized how I had idiotically kept tracking him for years and decades after the school system had tracked both of us. I wonder now if my experience was that unusual, whether social categories conveyed and absorbed before puberty do not generally tend to linger beyond middle age. And I wonder, too, that if they affected the behavior of someone like myself who had been placed on the upper track, how much more damaging it must have been for someone consigned to the lower.

I have at times thought of calling him, but kept from doing it because how exactly does one apologize for thoughts that were never expressed? And there was still the problem of what to say. "What have you been up to for the last forty years?" Or "Wow, was I wrong about you!" Or maybe just, "Want to come over and help me make a linoleum gun?"

INTERPRETATIONS

1. Comment on the significance of Kaufman's title. (If necessary, refer to a book on Greek mythology for the meaning of the names "Hector" and "Achilles.")

2. Evaluate the effectiveness of Kaufman's opening sentences. Does his essay support his self-judgment?

3. Analyze the causes and effects of the changes that occur in Kaufman and Hector's relationship over the years.

CORRESPONDENCES

1. Compare and contrast the significance of stereotyping in the essays by Kaufman and White. To what extent do you agree that people often make judgments based on stereotypes rather than their own experience? What is particularly disturbing about stereotyping in White's essay? How do you imagine yourself responding to such an experience?

2. Analyze the roles of ethnicity and social class in Kaufman's and White's texts. What insights did you gain from their experiences? How did they affect you emotionally?

APPLICATIONS

1. "This story is about prejudice and stupidity." Write a journal entry applying Kaufman's statement to your own experience.

2. Speculate about Kaufman's purpose in writing this essay. Is he trying to clarify this experience for himself? Is there evidence that he would like to influence his readers? Explain.

3. Brainstorm with your group on "racism" and "stereotyping." How do they differ in meaning and connotation?

   Were the policemen in White's essay racists because they responded to White as a stereotype? Summarize the highlights of your discussion.

The Man I Killed

TIM O'BRIEN

Tim O'Brien (b. 1946 in Austin, Minnesota) was drafted into the Vietnam War shortly after receiving a B.A. from Macalester College. After returning from two years in the service, O'Brien began postgraduate studies at Harvard. His war memoirs, If I Die in a Combat Zone, Box Me Up and Ship Me Home, *was named Outstanding Book of 1973 by* The New York Times. Going After Cacciato *(1978) was also based on O'Brien's war experiences. O'Brien's other novels include:* Northern Lights *(1975),* The Nuclear Age *(1985),* The Things They Carried *(1990, republished 2004) (from which the following selection is taken),* In the Lake of the Woods *(1994), and* Tomcat in Love *(1998). O'Brien's most recent novel,* July, July, *was published in 2002. O'Brien told an interviewer that in writing, one plays a semantic game, "lies" if necessary, "for a particular purpose and that purpose always is to arrive at some kind of spiritual truth that one can't discover simply by recording the world-as-it-is. We're inventing and using imagination for sublime reasons—to get at the essence of things, not merely the surface." Before reading O'Brien's text, record what responses to this killing—verbal or otherwise—you expect from the "I" character called "Tim."*

HIS JAW WAS IN HIS THROAT, his upper lip and teeth were gone, his one eye was shut, his other eye was a star-shaped hole, his eyebrows were thin and arched like a woman's, his nose was undamaged, there was a slight tear at the lobe of one ear, his clean black hair was swept upward into a cowlick at the rear of the skull, his forehead was lightly freckled, his fingernails were clean, the skin at his left cheek was peeled back in three ragged strips, his right cheek was smooth and hairless, there was a butterfly on his chin, his neck was open to the spinal cord and the blood there was thick and shiny and it was this wound that had killed him. He lay face-up in the center of the trail, a slim, dead, almost dainty young man. He had bony legs, a narrow waist, long shapely fingers. His chest was sunken and poorly muscled—a scholar, maybe. His wrists were the wrists of a child. He wore a black shirt, black pajama pants, a gray ammunition belt, a gold ring on the third finger of his right hand. His rubber sandals had been blown off. One lay beside him, the other a few meters up the trail. He had been born, maybe, in 1946 in the village of My Khe near the central coastline of Quang Ngai

373

Province, where his parents farmed, and where his family had lived for several centuries, and where, during the time of the French, his father and two uncles and many neighbors had joined in the struggle for independence. He was not a Communist. He was a citizen and a soldier. In the village of My Khe, as in all of Quang Ngai, patriotic resistance had the force of tradition, which was partly the force of legend, and from his earliest boyhood the man I killed would have listened to stories about the heroic Trung sisters and Tran Hung Dao's famous rout of the Mongols and Le Loi's final victory against the Chinese at Tot Dong.[1] He would have been taught that to defend the land was a man's highest duty and highest privilege. He had accepted this. It was never open to question. Secretly, though, it also frightened him. He was not a fighter. His health was poor, his body small and frail. He liked books. He wanted someday to be a teacher of mathematics. At night, lying on his mat, he could not picture himself doing the brave things his father had done, or his uncles, or the heroes of the stories. He hoped in his heart that he would never be tested. He hoped the Americans would go away. Soon, he hoped. He kept hoping and hoping, always, even when he was asleep.

"Oh, man, you fuckin' trashed the fucker," Azar said. "You scrambled his sorry self, look at that, you *did*, you laid him out like Shredded fuckin' Wheat."

"Go away," Kiowa said.

"I'm just saying the truth. Like oatmeal."

"Go," Kiowa said.

"Okay, then, I take it back," Azar said. He started to move away, then stopped and said, "Rice Krispies, you know? On the dead test, this particular individual gets A-Plus."

Smiling at this, he shrugged and walked up the trail toward the village behind the trees.

Kiowa kneeled down.

"Just forget that crud," he said. He opened up his canteen and held it out for a while and then sighed and pulled it away. "No sweat, man. What else could you do?"

Later, Kiowa said, "I'm serious. Nothing *anybody* could do. Come on, stop staring."

The trail junction was shaded by a row of trees and tall brush. The slim young man lay with his legs in the shade. His jaw was in his throat. His one eye was shut and the other was a star-shaped hole.

Kiowa glanced at the body.

---

[1]The Trung sisters led a Vietnamese rebellion against Chinese rule in A.D. 40; Tran Hung Dao repelled a Mongol attack in 1287; Le Loi defeated the Chinese in 1426.

"All right, let me ask a question," he said. "You want to trade places with him? Turn it all upside down—you *want* that? I mean, be honest."

The star-shaped hole was red and yellow. The yellow part seemed to be getting wider, spreading out at the center of the star. The upper lip and gum and teeth were gone. The man's head was cocked at a wrong angle, as if loose at the neck, and the neck was wet with blood.

"Think it over," Kiowa said.

Then later he said, "Tim, it's a *war*. The guy wasn't Heidi—he had a weapon, right? It's a tough thing, for sure, but you got to cut out that staring."

Then he said, "Maybe you better lie down a minute."

Then after a long empty time he said, "Take it slow. Just go wherever the spirit takes you."

The butterfly was making its way along the young man's forehead, which was spotted with small dark freckles. The nose was undamaged. The skin on the right cheek was smooth and fine-grained and hairless. Frail-looking, delicately boned, the young man would not have wanted to be a soldier and in his heart would have feared performing badly in battle. Even as a boy growing up in the village of My Khe, he had often worried about this. He imagined covering his head and lying in a deep hole and closing his eyes and not moving until the war was over. He had no stomach for violence. He loved mathematics. His eyebrows were thin and arched like a woman's, and at school the boys sometimes teased him about how pretty he was, the arched eyebrows and long shapely fingers, and on the playground they mimicked a woman's walk and made fun of his smooth skin and his love for mathematics. The young man could not make himself fight them. He often wanted to, but he was afraid, and this increased his shame. If he could not fight little boys, he thought, how could he ever become a soldier and fight the Americans with their airplanes and helicopters and bombs? It did not seem possible. In the presence of his father and uncles, he pretended to look forward to doing his patriotic duty, which was also a privilege, but at night he prayed with his mother that the war might end soon. Beyond anything else, he was afraid of disgracing himself, and therefore his family and village. But all he could do, he thought, was wait and pray and try not to grow up too fast.

"Listen to me," Kiowa said. "You feel terrible, I know that."

Then he said, "Okay, maybe I *don't* know."

Along the trail there were small blue flowers shaped like bells. The young man's head was wrenched sideways, not quite facing the flowers, and even in the shade a single blade of sunlight sparkled against the buckle of his ammunition belt. The left cheek was peeled back in three ragged strips. The wounds at his neck had not yet clotted, which made him seem animate even in death, the blood still spreading out across his shirt.

Kiowa shook his head.

There was some silence before he said, "Stop *staring*."

The young man's fingernails were clean. There was a slight tear at the lobe of one ear, a sprinkling of blood on the forearm. He wore a gold ring on the third finger of his right hand. His chest was sunken and poorly muscled—a scholar, maybe. His life was now a constellation of possibilities. So, yes, maybe a scholar. And for years, despite his family's poverty, the man I killed would have been determined to continue his education in mathematics. The means for this were arranged, perhaps, through the village liberation cadres, and in 1964 the young man began attending classes at the university in Saigon, where he avoided politics and paid attention to the problems of calculus. He devoted himself to his studies. He spent his nights alone, wrote romantic poems in his journal, took pleasure in the grace and beauty of differential equations. The war, he knew, would finally take him, but for the time being he would not let himself think about it. He had stopped praying; instead, now, he waited. And as he waited, in his final year at the university, he fell in love with a classmate, a girl of seventeen, who one day told him that his wrists were like the wrists of a child, so small and delicate, and who admired his narrow waist and the cowlick that rose up like a bird's tail at the back of his head. She liked his quiet manner; she laughed at his freckles and bony legs. One evening, perhaps, they exchanged gold rings.

Now one eye was a star.

"You okay?" Kiowa said.

The body lay almost entirely in shade. There were gnats at the mouth, little flecks of pollen drifting above the nose. The butterfly was gone. The bleeding had stopped except for the neck wounds.

Kiowa picked up the rubber sandals, clapping off the dirt, then bent down to search the body. He found a pouch of rice, a comb, a fingernail clipper, a few soiled piasters, a snapshot of a young woman standing in front of a parked motorcycle. Kiowa placed these items in his rucksack along with the gray ammunition belt and rubber sandals.

Then he squatted down.

"I'll tell you the straight truth," he said. "The guy was dead the second he stepped on the trail. Understand me? We all had him zeroed. A good kill—weapon, ammunition, everything." Tiny beads of sweat glistened at Kiowa's forehead. His eyes moved from the sky to the dead man's body to the knuckles of his own hands. "So listen, you best pull your shit together. Can't just sit here all day."

Later he said, "Understand?"

Then he said, "Five minutes, Tim. Five more minutes and we're moving out."

The one eye did a funny twinkling trick, red to yellow. His head was wrenched sideways, as if loose at the neck, and the dead young man seemed to be staring at some distant object beyond the bell-shaped flowers along the trail. The blood at the neck had gone to a deep purplish black. Clean fingernails, clean hair—he had been a soldier for only a single day. After his years at the university, the man I killed returned with his new wife to the village of My Khe, where he enlisted as a common rifleman with the 48th Vietcong Battalion. He knew he would die quickly. He knew he would see a flash of light. He knew he would fall dead and wake up in the stories of his village and people.

Kiowa covered the body with a poncho.

"Hey, you're looking better," he said. "No doubt about it. All you needed was time—some mental R&R."

Then he said, "Man, I'm sorry."

Then later he said, "Why not talk about it?"

Then he said, "Come on, man, talk."

He was a slim, dead, almost dainty young man of about twenty. He lay with one leg bent beneath him, his jaw in his throat, his face neither expressive nor inexpressive. One eye was shut. The other was a star-shaped hole.

"Talk," Kiowa said.

INTERPRETATIONS

1. How does the opening paragraph of O'Brien's story set up the pages that follow?

2. Who are Azar and Kiowa? What do they want O'Brien to do? Why?

3. Why does O'Brien, the writer, include the paragraphs of narration in his story? What do these paragraphs tell you about Tim, the soldier?

4. What facts does the narrator of the story absolutely *know* about the man he killed? What does he *surmise*?

CORRESPONDENCES

1. To what extent do you identify with the narrators in "Fraternity" and "The Man I Killed." Explain your answer.

2. Are Hongo and O'Brien seeking to persuade or inform their readers? How would you distinguish between the tone of each text?

APPLICATIONS

1. What do you learn about war from O'Brien's story? What preconceptions about war has this story changed? Within your small discussion group, talk with your classmates about the ideas you had about war before reading this story and those you formed after reading it. Write a journal entry about what you have learned as a result of this exploration.

2. "War is hell." Do you think that this maxim is true or false? Write an essay that explores fully your response to this statement.

3. O'Brien's story seems to end unresolved. What do you think he is feeling when the story concludes? Why doesn't he say anything to Kiowa? If you found the ending to be unsatisfying, rewrite the last several paragraphs after reflecting on the previous questions. Alternatively, pick up the action after a period of three months and continue the story in a way that presents your thoughts about the previous questions.

Literacy Narratives

Gloria Naylor and Kenneth Woo focus on the paradoxes of language. Naylor reveals the potential of language to wound, even destroy, while Woo discovers finally that words can create and liberate the self. As you reflect on their experiences, think about your encounters with language in the community and in other cultures. How do their cultural and educational experiences compare with yours? When did you first realize that words have the potential to imprison and liberate the self?

What's in a Name?

GLORIA NAYLOR

Gloria Naylor was born in 1950 in New York City to parents who were sharecroppers from Mississippi. She was, from her earliest years, a prodigious reader. After high school she worked as a missionary for the Jehovah's Witnesses from 1968 to 1975. After 1975 Naylor worked as a switchboard operator, pursued writing, and received a B.A. from Brooklyn College in English. She was greatly influenced by black women novelists such as Toni Morrison, Zora Neale Hurston, and Alice Walker. Naylor earned an M.A. in Afro-American studies at Yale in 1983. Her first novel, The Women of Brewster Place *(1982), won a National Book Award and was adapted as a miniseries, produced by Oprah Winfrey. Naylor's other novels include:* Linden Hills *(1985),* Mama Day *(1988),* Bailey's Cafe *(1990), and* The Men of Brewster Place *(1998). While reading Naylor's essay, which begins with theoretical remarks about language and soon turns to narrative examples, ask yourself how the two sections complement each other.*

LANGUAGE IS THE SUBJECT. It is the written form with which I've managed to keep the wolf away from the door and, in diaries, to keep my sanity. In spite of this, I consider the written word inferior to the spoken, and much of the frustration experienced by novelists is the awareness that whatever we manage to capture in even the most transcendent passages falls far short of the richness of life. Dialogue achieves its powers in the dynamics of a fleeting moment of sight, sound, smell and touch.

I'm not going to enter the debate here about whether it is language that shapes reality or vice versa. That battle is doomed to be waged whenever we seek intermittent reprieve from the chicken and egg dispute. I will simply take the position that the spoken word, like the written word, amounts to a nonsensical arrangement of sounds or letters without a consensus that assigns "meaning." And building from the meanings of what we hear, we order reality. Words themselves are innocuous; it is the consensus that gives them true power.

I remember the first time I heard the word nigger. In my third-grade class, our math tests were being passed down the rows, and as I handed the papers to a little boy in back of me, I remarked that once again he had received a much lower mark than I did. He snatched his test from me and spit out that word. Had he called me a nymphomaniac or a necrophiliac, I couldn't have been more puzzled. I didn't know what a nigger was, but I knew that whatever it meant, it was something he shouldn't have called me. This was verified when I raised my hand, and in a loud voice repeated what he had said and watched the teacher scold him for using a "bad" word. I was later to go home and ask the inevitable question that every black parent must face—"Mommy, what does 'nigger' mean?"

And what exactly did it mean? Thinking back, I realize that this could not have been the first time the word was used in my presence. I was part of a large extended family that had migrated from the rural South after World War II and formed a close-knit network that gravitated around my maternal grandparents. Their ground-floor apartment in one of the buildings they owned in Harlem was a weekend mecca for my immediate family, along with countless aunts, uncles and cousins who brought along assorted friends. It was a bustling and open house with assorted neighbors and tenants popping in and out to exchange bits of gossip, pick up an old quarrel or referee the ongoing checkers game in which my grandmother cheated shamelessly. They were all there to let down their hair and put up their feet after a week of labor in the factories, laundries and shipyards of New York.

Amid the clamor, which could reach deafening proportions—two or three conversations going on simultaneously, punctuated by the sound of a baby's crying somewhere in the back rooms or out on the street—there was still a rigid set of rules about what was said and how. Older children were sent out of the living room when it was time to get into the juicy details about "you-know-who" up on the third floor who had gone and gotten herself "p-r-e-g-n-a-n-t!" But my parents, knowing that I could spell well beyond my years, always demanded that I follow the others out to play. Beyond sexual misconduct and death, everything else was considered harmless for our young ears. And so among the anecdotes of the triumphs and disappointments in the various workings of their lives, the word nigger was used in my presence, but it was set within contexts and inflections that caused it to register in my mind as something else.

In the singular, the word was always applied to a man who had distinguished himself in some situation that brought their approval for his strength, intelligence or drive:

"Did *Johnny* really do that?"

"I'm telling you, that nigger pulled in $6,000 of overtime last year. Said he got enough for a down payment on a house."

When used with a possessive adjective by a woman—"my nigger"—it became a term of endearment for husband or boyfriend. But it could be more than just a term applied to a man. In their mouths it became the pure essence of manhood—a disembodied force that channeled their past history of struggle and present survival against the odds into a victorious statement of being: "Yeah, that old foreman found out quick enough—you don't mess with a nigger."

In the plural, it became a description of some group within the community that had overstepped the bounds of decency as my family defined it: Parents who neglected their children, a drunken couple who fought in public, people who simply refused to look for work, those with excessively dirty mouths or unkempt households were all "trifling niggers." This particular circle could forgive hard times, unemployment, the occasional bout of depression—they had gone through all of that themselves—but the unforgivable sin was a lack of self-respect.

A woman could never be a "nigger" in the singular, with its connotation of confirming worth. The noun girl was its closest equivalent in that sense, but only when used in direct address and regardless of the gender doing the addressing. "Girl" was a token of respect for a woman. The one-syllable word was drawn out to sound like three in recognition of the extra ounce of wit, nerve or daring that the woman had shown in the situation under discussion.

"G-i-r-l, stop. You mean you said that to his face?"

But if the word was used in a third-person reference or shortened so that it almost snapped out of the mouth, it always involved some element of communal disapproval. And age became an important factor in these exchanges. It was only between individuals of the same generation, or from an older person to a younger (but never the other way around), that "girl" would be considered a compliment.

I don't agree with the argument that use of the word nigger at this social stratum of the black community was an internalization of racism. The dynamics were the exact opposite: the people in my grandmother's living room took a word that whites used to signify worthlessness or degradation and rendered it impotent. Gathering there together, they transformed "nigger" to signify the varied and complex human beings they knew themselves to be. If the word was to disappear totally from the mouths of even the most liberal of white society, no one in that room was naïve enough to believe it would disappear from white minds. Meeting the word head-on, they proved it had absolutely nothing to do with the way they were determined to live their lives.

So there must have been dozens of times that the word "nigger" was spoken in front of me before I reached the third grade. But I didn't "hear" it until it was said by a small pair of lips that had already learned it could be a way to humiliate me. That was the word I went home and asked my mother about. And since she knew that I had to grow up in America, she took me in her lap and explained.

INTERPRETATIONS

1. Naylor writes that "words themselves are innocuous; it is the consensus that gives them true power." Do you agree with this position? Can you think of an example that supports it?

2. What are the effects of juxtaposing the rich multiple meanings of "nigger" in African-American culture with the derogatory label of the third grader? How does this juxtaposition support meanings being dependent upon context?

APPLICATIONS

1. Describe a time when you heard a familiar word in a new way.

2. In her opening paragraph, Naylor distinguishes between the *written* and the *spoken* word. To what extent do these different terms represent differences in *literacy*? Explain your answer.

3. What kind of literacy is the child in Naylor's narrative exposed to and forced to engage in? When was there a time in your life that you were thrown into the adult world and a new type of literacy? What kind of literacy were you confronted with? How did you begin to negotiate this new literacy?

4. What kind of literacy is being described and exemplified in paragraphs 4 through 13? As she becomes more aware of this type of literacy, what distinctions does Naylor come to understand?

Konglish

KENNETH WOO

I NEVER REALLY LIKED TO WRITE. Whenever I thought of English, or English class, there was only one word that popped into my head: essays. I always felt this feeling of nausea, "got to finish the essay by a certain date and what in the world am I supposed to write." I constantly saw myself as a science and math "buff" (majoring in computer science) and viewed English as an obstacle. I would think to myself, "why must I keep learning how to write, isn't the knowledge I already know enough to get by?" But there are a few instances in my life in which writing greatly affected my life, changing the way I perceived the art form of a brush (the pen) painting emotions on a blank white canvas (paper).

Moving from Flushing, New York to Douglaston was going to be a huge alteration in my life. Though I was only in second grade, I dreaded the thought of moving. What I feared the most was attending a new school: beady little eyes from strangers gazing at me because I was the new kid on the block. It was like those nightmares where I find myself standing naked in front of a laughing audience. The school I attended (P.S. 94) was one of the most academic achieving schools in the city, being number one or two in every imaginable category.

I remembered I had a poem to write about something that was close to your heart. I thought to myself, "I'm in the second grade, how am I supposed to write a poem?" I really thought a second grader writing a poem was outrageous. But I had no choice, and the poem was due the next day. So I sat in my miniature desk and tried to cook up something worthy since this was my first assignment at school. All of a sudden I thought about my grandfather. I had no idea what he looked like (since he died before I was born), what his favorite dish was; my grandfather was basically a stranger to me. So my pen started to dance and I called the poem, "I Wonder." I handed the poem to my teacher and waited for the poem to be marked. When the class received their poems back, I didn't receive back the piece I wrote. "Did I do something wrong? Great, what a great first impression." I never had the guts to ask her what happened to my poem, so I did what my father always said to do when in doubt: keep your lips shut. So I kept my lips shut. By the end of the class, I heard, "Ken, can you stay after school? I want to talk to you about your poem." What did I write in that poem? Was it wrong to write about my grandfather? I remembered my hands were sweating like bullets and my legs couldn't help but shake.

I approached the teacher cautiously, as if she were the enemy over the war line. I waited for my educator to shoot and assassinate my poem. "Yes, Mrs. Nazarro?" She leaned over my shivering body and said, "This is one of the best poems I read in my entire life. I read this piece in front of my Queens College lecture, and half the audience fell into tears. Ken, you have a gift—a gift of writing."

What my teacher said hit me like a ton of bricks. I couldn't understand what she was saying. I didn't want to write the poem, I didn't even feel like I put effort into it. But I kept all my emotions in and replied, "Thank you, Mrs. Nazarro." This was the first time I ever accomplished a writing experience, and I didn't like the feeling. I felt a sort of embarrassment, feeling "cheesed out." For some reason or another, I took this writing skill I had and shoved it deep into my soul, never seeing it again. I didn't see this ability to write until fifteen years later.

Time went by, from essays here and boring compositions there, and I finally graduated high school. When I attended SUNY Albany, I registered my classes so that I wouldn't have to take an English course for a while. After a semester, my mother decided it was time for me to go to the motherland, Korea. I didn't think much of the trip, "what's the big deal?" I thought going to summer school would have been a lot more productive in using my time but I had no say. So I jumped on a 747 and twelve hours later, ended up in this strange land they called the Land of the Morning Calm.

When my feet first touched Kimpo Airport, I was stunned and in awe. I never had seen a place where everyone was Korean. It took my eyes a while to get adjusted to, and I stared at the passengers that walked by. After my gazing, I took the next train to Korea University. At this university, I had registered for two courses, Business Management and Structure of Korea, and Introduction to Korean. I was really excited about the business course, but oh no, not Korean. Thinking about having to take a Korean course reminded me of the English courses I was forced to take.

For the first couple of weeks, we only attacked the basic stuff. From vowels to consonants, I felt like I was back in kindergarten. Han-gul (the Korean alphabet) is pretty much a simple concept to follow. It's basically our alphabet but circles and slashes are the A's, B's, and C's. The challenging part of the language, like English, is the numerous vocabulary words that had to be learned. Quickly, the Han-gul dictionary became a friend. When I was in Korea, it was hard. Everyone around me talked Korean while I struggled trying to say, "Hello, my name is Kenneth Woo, and how are you doing today?"

For lunch, I would walk to the local McDonald's. I preferred to eat there more than the local native cuisine because Ronald McDonald reminded me of home. I clearly remembered the first time I stepped in, as if it happened yesterday. I attempted to read the red and yellow alien language that gawked into my eyes. "What does that say?" I stood there for an eternity trying to figure out what it said when it finally whacked me. I was staring at Big Mac, only it was in the Korean alphabet. I suddenly noticed how much trouble I was in.

There was only one thing left to do—to conquer what I didn't know. I attacked the books and studied the Korean language as if my life depended on it (at the time, my survival in the country did rely on it). From the alphabet and days of the week, to learning their way of grammatical structure, it was a challenge I did not believe I could accomplish. However after some time, I was getting the hang of the language. I knew the consonants and vowels forwards and backwards, and was able to read the whole McDonald's menu.

Attending classes wasn't a problem. Most of the students never attended because they would get so drunk and wasted the night before, still drunk when they woke up. Wednesday was a problem for me. During the other days of the week I had classes and on the weekends I stayed at a relative's house, but Wednesday was a killer. I usually stayed in my room, smoking a cigarette as each minute passed by. Then one day in my dorm room, I approached a flier that read, "Free Brush-Painting classes on Wednesday . . . Rm 101 1:00 P.M." I decided to be brave and attend the mysterious class. When I walked in, there was one thing I noticed: I was the only male. This didn't bother me at all since a couple of my classmates looked attractive but I questioned myself what I was doing there. I ended up staying and I saw a dorky, black-dressed (like the WWF wrestler Undertaker), slothful man with a clean brush. He introduced himself as Mr. Lim, Master of the Brush. I chuckled at the title and waited for my lesson. Like the Korean language class, we went over the basic brush stroking techniques and went over some of the Chinese characters. What amazed me the most was how hard it was to hold an authentic Asian character brush. The tip was wide yet pointy, short yet heavy. The proper grip of the brush is the ambitious part. It's like when a person first approaches a billiard table and has no idea how to hold the cue stick.

Following a few practices, the Master of the Brush instructed that we had to paint our name in Chinese characters with a couple of words describing ourselves. I thought about the task and had a notion to make a poem out of the assignment. So I worked on the poem and brushed it out on the thin rice paper and handed it in to Mr. Lim. He read what I wrote and stared into my eyes. He replied, "Wow, this is a great poem, simple but deep. You have a talent. Your brushstrokes are another thing, but your poetry. God . . ." I snatched my piece and responded that I had to go eat lunch. I was enraged, I had no idea why. What he said made my blood pump. I knew it was the part about me having a talent. I didn't care about my techniques as a brushpainter, I could have cared less. But how can a typical Korean-American have a gift of writing poems, it made no sense to me. Once again I was determined to keep my talent buried within myself, forever.

I walked outside and it was so humid that the sun had a hard time peeking through the smog. Sweat was pouring out my pores like Niagara Falls and I wanted to go to a cool, air-conditioned place. I went to my spot (McD's) and ordered a No. 3 combo, super-sized. I sat by the window and ate gradually. As people walked by, I would stare at them thinking about where they were going, what part of Korea they were from, if they had a romance going. Then something caught my eye. Across the street there was an elderly woman with a mid-sized shopping cart packed with things, from clothing to a rice-cooker. This was the only homeless person I had seen in my native land since my feet touched here. I was in shock, not because she was homeless, but the way people on the street treated her. They passed by, as if she were a parking meter. She would shake a noiseless cup and hear no coins rattling. I stepped outside and lit my cigarette, trying to ignore the situation. I pondered to myself, "It was none of my business."

I flicked my cigarette and at the moment two guys approached the helpless grandmother and yelled in Korean, "What a disgrace to our country. Get the fuck off my land." They laughed and walked away. From across the street I saw two little droplets of water stream down her powerless face. My gut told me to do something, so I walked over and told her that it was all right. I reached into my pockets and gave her 50,000 won (equivalent to thirty American dollars) and told her it was a token from my heart. Then like my pores from the heat, her eyes started streaming with water like a broken faucet and she kept thanking me. She then uttered out of nowhere, "Don't close your soul, leave it open and share it among other people. It's a gift." I didn't think much of what she said assuming that she was drunk. I informed her that crying and gratitude were not needed and walked away. As my feet marched down the street, I heard the words of thank you all the way to my dorm.

This situation brought the Socrates out of me. Philosophical questions started to burn my cranium. How can a country like Korea ignore the unfortunate? I decided to talk to my aunt about what had happened and she told me the naked truth. She said that even though Korea excelled from the rubbles of the Korean War, the country still has a lot to do. The country has no social security, no welfare, and doesn't care for the people who need aid the most. I thought to myself, "how can a

Third World country that turned into a First World forget about the helpless?" Then I told her what the homeless woman said to me about my soul. My aunt paused, then slowly she said, "People like that know what they are talking about. Americans might think they are crazy, but here, they are the wisest. Consider what she said and open your soul." I felt like I was in an episode of the "Twilight Zone." What in the world is everyone talking about? Is the kimchee or the rice getting to their heads? I left the question unanswered and just looked forward to touching down on Uncle Sam's land.

The plane ride was exhausting and my parents were all over me. They showered their kisses on my weak pale face, and I returned the love. I arrived home and the whole family was exhausted. The lights turned out, but I had a problem called jet lag. So I unpacked and walked around my house. I stumbled upon an old Reebok box and opened the ancient treasure chest. The cloud of dust cleared and I found ratty old papers. It was a box filled with my old school work. It had my "A" paper on World War II, the 100's I received on those ridiculous spelling tests, and then "BAM." Under all the debris, I found my spirit, "I Wonder." I thought I was dreaming and pinched my arms a couple of times. It was reality, and I took the poem to a light source and read it out loud. Wow, this brought back memories. It then hit me like a freight train. This was my breath of life, my soul. What Mrs. Nazarro, Mr. Lim, the homeless grandmother, and my aunt were talking about was in this poem. My special gift is writing broken sentences into funny stanzas to express my emotions. This was my soul and my talent. I remembered what the poor grandmother said and smiled.

I woke up my mom and handed her the poem. She read the poem and her face shined. She hugged me and I left the room so she could continue her beauty sleep. I walked outside my abode and lit a cancer stick. I looked at the weak full moon and the beautiful dawn sky. I then closed my eyes, unlocked the door to my soul, and threw the key into the sun. I don't need the key. From now on, there were going to be visitors in and out reading my talent.

INTERPRETATIONS

1. Woo's narrative reflects on his journey to creativity from second grade to his second year in college. Why was he so reluctant to pursue his poetic self? What impresses you most about his journey?

2. Woo now thinks of words as being powerful enough to unlock the door to his soul. How does he explain this transformation? How do you respond to his metaphor?

APPLICATIONS

1. Imagine having the opportunity to talk with Woo. What would you ask him? What literacy experience would you share with him?

2. What kinds of literacy does the author encounter? Present specific examples from the essay to support your views.

3. Why is the homeless person presented in paragraphs 13–14 important to Woo? What kind of literacy does she represent to the author?

4. How does Woo use the concept of literacy as a theme in this essay? How do your experiences with literacy help you to understand your own life? Explain your answers fully.

The Knowing Eye

Tyler Hicks / *The New York Times*

READING IMAGES

1. At first glance, it might be difficult to discern the cultural encounter taking place in each photograph. What specific details show the encounter? What historical knowledge is useful to help you to see the cultural encounter as it applies to each photograph?

2. How do you feel when you see these photographs? How do they register a level of emotional energy?

Amanda Stellman

MAKING CONNECTIONS

1. How do these photographs relate to ones that you have seen previously? In particular, review the images presented in "Family and Community," "Work," and "Traditions" (Chapters 2, 5, and 6).

2. Which essays in this chapter seem to match these photographs best? What similarities do you notice between text and image?

Dora Sofia Caputo

WORDS AND IMAGES

1. Which of these images do you like more? Why? Present your findings in an essay using argumentation/persuasion or comparison/contrast. Be sure to include specific references to each photograph.

2. If you were creating a slide show, what kind of music might accompany each of these photographs? Produce a story board for the slides, explaining what influenced your musical selections. Provide specific examples from your soundtrack.

Additional Writing Topics

1. As college campuses become more ethnically diverse, how might administrators, faculty, staff, and students work together to create a climate of inclusiveness that enhances educational, social, personal, and cultural encounters? Interview a cross-section of the college community on this issue. What suggestions did they make? What responsibilities are they willing to assume? Write a summary of your findings for your campus or local newspaper.

2. In the context of the American Dream, analyze how Hongo, Grant, and Stanley explore the themes of immigration, exile, and displacement. Take into account generational as well as cultural differences.

3. Review the Norton perspective. Is it easier to support theoretically than practically? To what extent do the interactions presented in the selections in this textbook reflect the kinds of tolerance of individual differences Norton advocates?

4. Write about a group you participated in recently. Analyze how the group members interact with one another. By what means do they communicate with one another? How do they handle disagreement or friction? Write an essay on what you learned about group relations.

5. Lack of awareness of cultural differences or the assumption by one cultural group that another is inferior results in interactions that are painful power struggles. Apply this thesis to any three selections in this chapter.

6. Although "the melting pot" is the traditional metaphor associated with the immigrant experience in the United States, many sociologists now believe that "the fusion chamber" is a more accurate description of current cultural interacting. Contrast the implications of both terms and, using any three essays in this chapter, justify your choice of metaphor.

7. Who are you? Create a pie chart that accurately represents your cultural heritage. When you have finished, write an essay that describes and explains your thoughts about each section of your pie.

8. To what extent do you agree that in spite of our enormous ethnic diversity and the hyphenated identity of the children of most immigrant parents, we are on the whole shaped by a common culture.

9. Review Iyer's perspective on travel and analyze its relevance to any three cultural interactions in this chapter.

CHAPTER

8

Choices

CULTURE, ACCORDING TO ANTHROPOLOGIST BRONISLAW MALINOWSKI, is the "artificial, secondary environment that human beings superimpose on nature." We human beings, then, are "in" both nature and culture, and both influence our choices. A diversity of cultures, which the following texts illustrate, makes for great choices and sometimes great difficulty of choices.

Choices are part of daily life. Some are anticlimactic, even repetitive, such as training ourselves to set the alarm clock and getting up when it rings. It becomes "second nature" and we are on time for work or school without having to think about it. When life runs its traditional course, unconscious habit often replaces conscious choice, but when crises arise, social, personal, or political habit is useless, and all kinds of choices must be made, even painful ones. Such choices may involve a conflict of values or test our personal or social commitments. They also shape the kind of people we become.

Is culture a limitation on freedom of choice, or does it allow more free play of individual wisdom and imagination? Do we increase our own choices to the degree we free ourselves from culture? The first selection in the chapter poses such a possibility. The young man in the Swahili tale chooses a wife and finds that the choice involves such cultural requirements as a bride price. The wife's culture denies her the choice of husband, but her wisdom, which is even greater than her beauty, reveals to her subsequent choices that allow her to triumph.

Although our ability to choose may not be limitless, several texts in this chapter present choices open to us. Audre Lorde, for example, in "The Fourth of July," decides courageously in favor of confronting American racism, in contrast to her parents' passive acceptance and refusal to discuss their pain and humiliation. The narrator of "Honor

Bound" is forced into dramatic conversations with himself when confronted with unexpected choices; and in his memoir "Homeplace," Scott Russell Sanders defends his choice to stay in one community despite most peoples' lack of commitment to a particular place.

It would be hard to imagine more difficult choices than those which confront the family in Hana Wehle's memoir "Janushinka." Set in the Auschwitz concentration camp, a young mother is faced with the choice of saving herself or going to her death with her child.

A change of environment may also alter the significance of moral, economic, and social choices. In "To the Border," Richard Rodriguez sympathetically and poetically recreated the emotional and wrenching choices of a boy who is one of the lonely "Mexicans without Mexico," while in "The Fender-Bender," an illegal alien is the beneficiary of a moral choice by an Anglo driver.

Traditionally, college commencement speakers challenge students at what is viewed as a defining moment in their lives, and in her speech to the 1999 graduates of Mount Holyoke College, contemporary novelist and columnist Anna Quindlen urges the graduates to resist conformity and focus on making their own choices about their lives.

> This is the hard work of your life in the world: to make it all up as you go along, to acknowledge the introvert, the clown, the artist, the reserved, the distraught, the goofball, the thinker. You will have to bend all your will not to march to the music that all of those great "theys" out there pipe on their flutes. They want you to go to professional school, to wear khakis, to pierce your navel, to bare your soul. These are the fashionable ways. The music is tinny, if you listen close enough. Look inside. That way lies dancing to the melodies spun out by your own heart. This is a symphony. All the rest are jingles.

Perspectives

Growth demands a temporary surrender of security.

—*Gail Sheehy*

Life shrinks or expands in proportion to one's courage.

—*Anaïs Nin*

Which you want. A whipping and no turnips or turnips and no whipping?

—*Toni Morrison*

No trumpets sound when the important decisions for our lives are made. Destiny is made known silently.

—*Agnes de Mille*

. . . You don't get to choose how you're going to die or when. You can only decide how you're going to live now.

—*Joan Baez*

People are trapped in history and history is trapped in them.

—*James Baldwin*

If man's condition is unjust, he has only one alternative, which is to be just himself.

—*Albert Camus*

One doesn't throw the stick after the snake has gone.

—*Liberian proverb*

Once to every man and nation comes the moment to decide
In the strife of truth with falsehood, for the good or evil side.

—*James Russell Lowell*

A new place brings out a new thing in man.

—*D. H. Lawrence*

Two roads diverged in a wood, and I—I took the one less traveled by, and that has made all the difference.

—*Robert Frost*

Every time a man has contributed to the victory of the dignity of the spirit, every time a man has said no to an attempt to subjugate his fellows, I have felt solidarity with his act.

—Frantz Fanon

No day comes back again; an inch of time is worth a foot of jade.

—Zen proverb

There is, I think, an essential difference of character in mankind, between those who wish to do, and those who wish to have certain things.

—William Hazlitt

All life is an experiment. The more experiments you make the better.

—Ralph Waldo Emerson

If I had to choose between betraying my country and betraying my friend, I hope I should have the guts to betray my country.

—E. M. Forster

APPLICATIONS

1. What is implied in thinking about life as an experiment? Is it more appealing than a blueprint? How do they differ? To what extent are you free to conduct experiments in living?

2. Discuss with your group the perspective of the Zen proverb (above). What does it imply about time and choice? To what extent do you agree that time is more important than wealth?

3. Decisions are often the result of judgments. Consult a dictionary and thesaurus on the word and its connotations. Is there a choice that you made based on sound judgment? Write about it in your journal.

The Wise Daughter

SWAHILI FOLKTALE

Swahili is spoken widely in East Africa and is an official language of Kenya and Tanzania. What are your associations with the word "wise"?

THERE WAS ONCE A YOUNG MAN whose parents died and left him a hundred cattle. He was lonely after the death of his parents, so he decided to get married. He went to his neighbors and asked them to help him find a wife.

Soon one of the neighbors came to tell him that he had found the most beautiful girl in the country for him to marry. "The girl is very good and wise and beautiful, and her father is very wealthy," he said. "Her father owns six thousand cattle."

The young man became very excited when he heard about this girl. But then he asked, "How much is the bride price?"

"The father wants a hundred cattle," was the reply.

"A hundred cattle! That is all I have. How will we be able to live?" replied the young man.

"Well, make up your mind. I have to take an answer to the father soon," said the neighbor.

The young man thought, "I cannot live without this girl." So he said, "Go and tell the father that I want to marry his daughter."

So the two were married. But after they returned home, they quickly ran out of food, and the young man had to herd cattle for a neighbor to get anything to eat. What he got was not very much for a young lady who was used to eating well and living in style.

One day as the young wife was sitting outside the house, a strange man came by and was struck by her beauty. He decided to try to seduce her and sent a message to her. The young wife told him that she could not make up her mind and he would have to come back later.

Several months later, the girl's father came to visit. She was very upset because she did not have anything to feed him. But on that same day, the seducer came back. So the young wife told the seducer that she would give in to his requests if he would bring her some meat to cook for her father.

Soon the seducer returned with the meat and the girl went inside to cook it. Her husband returned, and he and her father sat down to eat and have a good time. The seducer was standing outside listening. Soon he became angry and went inside to see what was happening. The young husband, who was hospitable, invited him in.

The young wife then brought in the meat and said, "Eat, you three fools."

"Why do you call us fools?" the three men said all together.

"Well, Father," the girl replied. "You are a fool because you sold something precious for something worthless. You had only one daughter and traded her for a hundred cattle when you already had six thousand."

"You are right," said her father. "I was a fool."

"As for you, husband," she went on. "You inherited only a hundred cattle and you went and spent them all on me, leaving us nothing to eat. You could have married another woman for ten or twenty cows. That is why you were a fool."

"And why am I a fool?" asked the seducer.

"You are the biggest fool of all. You thought you could get for one piece of meat what had been bought for a hundred cattle."

At that, the seducer ran away as fast as he could. Then the father said, "You are a wise daughter. When I get home, I will send your husband three hundred cattle so that you shall live in comfort."

INTERPRETATIONS

1. Is this tale about how *not* to make choices? Explain your answer.

2. Evaluate the daughter's role in the story. Was she wise or just practical? What is the difference?

CORRESPONDENCES

1. Review the Liberian proverb. How does It apply to the Swahili tale? What does the latter suggest about making choices based on emotions? To what extent do you agree or disagree?

2. Review the Nin perspective and discuss its relevance to "The Wise Daughter." What courage does the young wife display? How does it affect her personal freedom?

APPLICATIONS

1. Write a journal entry about a choice you regret having made. What did you learn from this experience?

2. Consult a dictionary or thesaurus entry for wisdom. Which conno-
    tations best express your associations with wisdom? Can wisdom
    be taught? How might wisdom affect choices?

3. Create a portrait of someone you know or admire that you
    consider wise.

To the Border

RICHARD RODRIGUEZ

Richard Rodriguez (b. 1944) was born in San Francisco to Mexican immigrants. His memoir Hunger of Memory: The Education of Richard Rodriguez *(1982) deals with his sense of alienation from Mexican culture as a result of going through the U.S. school system, starting with a Sacramento, California, elementary school and leading to Stanford University and the University of California at Berkeley, where he earned a doctorate in English Renaissance literature. Rodriguez is also the author of* Days of Obligation: An Argument with My Mexican Father *(1992) and most recently,* Brown: The Last Discovery of America *(2002). He is also a contributing editor for* Harper's *and a commentator on public television's* The NewsHour with Jim Lehrer. *In preparation for reading Rodriguez's essay, write in your journal your memories of a conversation you had with your father about his childhood.*

YOU STAND AROUND. You smoke. You spit. You are wearing your two shirts, two pants, two underpants. Jesús says if they chase you, throw that bag down. Your plastic bag is your mama, all you have left: the yellow cheese she wrapped has formed a translucent rind; the laminated scapular of the Sacred Heart nestles flame in its cleft. Put it in your pocket. Inside. Put it in your underneath pants' pocket. The last hour of Mexico is twilight, the shuffling of feet. Jesús says they are able to see in the dark. They have X rays and helicopters and searchlights. Jesús says wait, just wait, till he says. Though most of the men have started to move. You feel the hand of Jesús clamp your shoulder, fingers cold as ice. *Venga, corre.*[1] You run. All the rest happens without words. Your feet are tearing dry grass, your heart is lashed like a mare. You trip, you fall. You are now in the United States of America. You are a boy from a Mexican village. You have come into the country on your knees with your head down. You are a man.

Papa, what was it like?

I am his second son, his favorite child, his confidant. After we have polished the De Soto, we sit in the car and talk. I am sixteen years old. I fiddle with the knobs of the radio. He is fifty.

[1]Go, run.

He will never say. He was an orphan there. He had no mother, he remembered none. He lived in a village by the ocean. He wanted books and he had none.

You are lucky, boy.

In the Fifties, Mexican men were contracted to work in America as *braceros*, farm workers. I saw them downtown in Sacramento. I saw men my age drunk in Plaza Park on Sundays, on their backs on the grass. I was a boy at sixteen, but I was an American. At sixteen, I wrote a gossip column, "The Watchful Eye," for my school paper.

Or they would come into town on Monday nights for the wrestling matches or on Tuesdays for boxing. They worked over in Yolo County. They were men without women. They were Mexicans without Mexico.

On Saturdays, they came into town to the Western Union office where they sent money—money turned into humming wire and then turned back into money—all the way down into Mexico. They were husbands, fathers, sons. They kept themselves poor for Mexico.

Much that I would come to think, the best I would think about male Mexico, came as much from those chaste, lonely men as from my own father who made false teeth and who—after thirty years in America— owned a yellow stucco house on the east side of town.

The male is responsible. The male is serious. A man remembers.

Fidel, the janitor at church, lived over the garage at the rectory. Fidel spoke Spanish and was Mexican. He had a wife down there, people said; some said he had grown children. But too many years had passed and he didn't go back. Fidel had to do for himself. Fidel had a clean piece of linoleum on the floor, he had an iron bed, he had a table and a chair. He had a coffeepot and a frying pan and a knife and a fork and a spoon, I guess. And everything else Fidel sent back to Mexico. Sometimes, on summer nights, I would see his head through the bars of the little window over the garage at the rectory.

The migration of Mexico is not only international, south to north. The epic migration of Mexico, and throughout Latin America, is from the village to the city. And throughout Latin America, the city has ripened, swollen with the century. Lima, Caracas, Mexico City. So the journey to Los Angeles is much more than a journey from Spanish to English. It is the journey from *tú*—the familiar, the erotic, the intimate pronoun—to the repellent *usted* of strangers' eyes.

It is 1986 and I am a journalist. I am asking questions of a Mexican woman in her East L.A. house. She is watchful and pretty, in her thirties, she wears an apron. Her two boys—Roy and Danny—are playing next door. Her husband is a tailor. He is sewing in a bright bedroom at the back of the house. His feet work the humming treadle of an old Singer machine as he croons Mexican love songs by an open window.

I will send for you or I will come home rich.

Mexico is poor. But my mama says there are no love songs like the love songs of Mexico. She hums a song she can't remember. The ice cream there is creamier than here. Someday we will see. The people are kinder—poor, but kinder to each other.

My mother's favorite record is *"Mariachis de Mexico y Pepe Villa con Orquesta."*

Men sing in Mexico. Men are strong and silent. But in song the Mexican male is granted license he is otherwise denied. The male can admit longing, pain, desire.

HAIII—EEEE—a cry like a comet rises over the song. A cry like mock weeping tickles the refrain of Mexican love songs. The cry is meant to encourage the balladeer—it is the raw edge of his sentiment. HAIII-EEEE. It is the man's sound. A ticklish arching of semen, a node wrung up a guitar string, until it bursts in a descending cascade of mockery. HAI. HAI. HAI. The cry of a jackal under the moon, the whistle of the phallus, the maniacal song of the skull.

Mexico is on the phone—long-distance.

A crow alights upon a humming wire, bobs up and down, needles the lice within his vest, surveys with clicking eyes the field, the cloud of mites, then dips into the air and flies away.

Juanito killed! My mother shrieks, drops the phone in the dark. She cries for my father. For light.

The earth quakes. The peso flies like chaff in the wind. The police chief purchases his mistress a mansion on the hill.

The door bell rings. I split the blinds to see three nuns standing on our front porch.

Mama. Mama.

Monsignor Lyons has sent three Mexican nuns over to meet my parents. The nuns have come to Sacramento to beg for Mexico at the eleven o'clock Mass. We are the one family in the parish that speaks Spanish. As they file into our living room, the nuns smell pure, not sweet, pure like candles or like laundry.

The nun with a black mustache sighs at the end of each story the other two tell. Orphan. Leper. Crutch. Dry land. One eye. Casket.

!Que lástima![2]
Tell me, Papa.
What?
About Mexico.

I lived with the family of my uncle. I was the orphan in the village. I used to ring the church bells in the morning, many steps up in the dark. When I'd get up to the tower I could see the ocean.

The village, Papa, the houses too . . .

The ocean. He studies the polished hood of our beautiful blue De Soto.

Relatives invited relatives. Entire Mexican villages got re-created in three stories of a single house. In the fall, after the harvest in the Valley, families of Mexican adults and their American children would load up their cars and head back to Mexico in caravans, for weeks, for months. The schoolteacher said to my mother what a shame it was the Mexicans did that—took their children out of school.

Like Wandering Jews. They carried their home with them, back and forth; they had no true home but the tabernacle of memory.

Each year the American kitchen takes on a new appliance.

The children are fed and grow tall. They go off to school with children from Vietnam, from Kansas, from Hong Kong. They get into fights. They come home and they say dirty words.

The city will win. The city will give the children all the village could not—VCRs, hairstyles, drumbeat. The city sings mean songs, dirty songs. But the city will sing the children a great Protestant hymn.

You can be anything you want to be.

Your coming of age. It is early. From your bed you watch your mama moving back and forth under the light. The bells of the church ring in the dark. Mama crosses herself. From your bed you watch her back as she wraps the things you will take.

You are sixteen. Your father has sent for you. That's what it means. He has sent an address in Nevada. He is there with your uncle. You remember your uncle remembering snow with his beer.

You dress in the shadows. You move toward the table, the circle of light. You sit down. You force yourself to eat. Mama stands over you to make the sign of the cross on your forehead with her thumb. You are a man. You smile. She puts the bag of food in your hands. She says she has told *La Virgen*.

---

[2]What a pity!

Then you are gone. It is gray. You hear a little breeze. It is the rustle of your old black Dueña, the dog, taking her shortcuts through the weeds, crazy Dueña, her pads on the dust. She is following you.

You pass the houses of the village, each window is a proper name. You pass the store. The bar. The lighted window of the clinic where the pale medical student from Monterrey lives alone and reads his book full of sores late into the night.

You want to be a man. You have the directions in your pocket: an address in Tijuana and a map with a yellow line that leads from the highway to an X on a street in Reno. You are afraid, but you have never seen snow.

You are just beyond the cemetery. The breeze has died. You turn and throw a rock back at La Dueña, where you know she is—where you will always know where she is. She will not go past the cemetery. She will turn in circles like a *loca*[3] and bite herself.

The dust takes on gravel, the path becomes a rutted road which leads to the highway. You walk north. The sky has turned white overhead. Insects click in the fields. In time, there will be a bus.

I will send for you or I will come home rich.

INTERPRETATIONS

1. Who is the "you" in the first (and subsequent) sentence? What choice has been made?

2. What attitude did the sixteen-year-old Rodriguez have toward the Mexican farmworkers he saw downtown in Sacramento? How far removed from their situation was his? How does this account for his attitude?

3. What attitude toward the United States is revealed by the last line of the essay?

4. The last vignette of this essay describes the beginning of a voyage from the known to the unknown: ". . . each window is a proper name." What are some of the "knowns" the Mexican boy is leaving? Why do you think Rodriguez chose to include each of them? What is their combined impact?

5. Rodriguez avoids a bald statement of his main point or thesis, apparently preferring to create a mood and force his reader to intuit meaning. What is the mood and the point?

[3]Crazy woman.

CORRESPONDENCES

1. "So the journey to Los Angeles is much more than a journey from Spanish to English. It is the journey from *tú*—the familiar, the erotic, the intimate pronoun—to the repellant *usted* of strangers' eyes." What is Rodriguez implying about the personal costs involved in "choosing" to cross the border? Apply the Nin perspective to Rodriguez's essay.

2. "The male is responsible. The male is serious. A man remembers." What point is Rodriguez making in these statements? What conversation can you imagine him having with Steffan (page 425)? On what issues might they agree?

APPLICATIONS

1. Rodriguez writes that the Mexican migrant workers are "[l]ike Wandering Jews. They carried their home with them, back and forth; they had no true home but the tabernacle of memory." What is the meaning here of "tabernacle"? In what sense does memory serve as a refuge? At what price does one "choose" to become a migrant worker? Discuss the questions with your group.

2. To what extent do the expectations of other people—parents, friends, peers, relatives—influence choices? Is there a decision that you made based on outside pressure? If so, describe your dilemma and the factors that motivated your choice. In retrospect, was it the "right" choice?

3. Has your family chosen to leave their native culture to emigrate to the United States? If so, how has this choice affected their cultural and linguistic identities? To what extent have they assimilated? What changes have occurred in your family's lifestyle?

4. What soundtrack might accompany the essay "To the Border"? Write an essay that describes the music that you hear. (Or, if possible, record a song or two that you have composed.)

The Fourth of July

AUDRE LORDE

Audre Lorde (1934–1992) was born in New York City of West Indian parents and grew up in Harlem. She was educated at Hunter College and Columbia University and taught at various colleges of the City University of New York. She was a professor of English at Hunter College from 1981 until her death. Her publications include Between Ourselves *(1976),* The Black Unicorn *(1978),* Zami: A New Spelling of My Name *(1982),* Sister Outsider: Essays and Speeches *(1984), and* Undersong: Chosen Poems Old and New *(1992).* The Cancer Journals *(1980) chronicles her fight with breast cancer.*

THE FIRST TIME I went to Washington, D.C., was on the edge of the summer when I was supposed to stop being a child. At least that's what they said to us all at graduation from the eighth grade. My sister Phyllis graduated at the same time from high school. I don't know what she was supposed to stop being. But as graduation presents for us both, the whole family took a Fourth of July trip to Washington, D.C., the fabled and famous capital of our country.

It was the first time I'd ever been on a railroad train during the day. When I was little, and we used to go to the Connecticut shore, we always went at night on the milk train, because it was cheaper.

Preparations were in the air around our house before school was even over. We packed for a week. There were two very large suitcases that my father carried, and a box filled with food. In fact, my first trip to Washington was a mobile feast: I started eating as soon as we were comfortably ensconced in our seats, and did not stop until somewhere after Philadelphia. I remember it was Philadelphia because I was disappointed not to have passed by the Liberty Bell.

My mother had roasted two chickens and cut them up into dainty bite-size pieces. She packed slices of brown bread and butter and green pepper and carrot sticks. There were little violently yellow iced cakes with scalloped edges called "marigolds," that came from Cushman's Bakery. There was a spice bun and rock-cakes from Newton's, the West Indian bakery across Lenox Avenue from St. Mark's School, and iced tea in a wrapped mayonnaise jar. There were sweet pickles for us and dill pickles for my father, and peaches with the fuzz still on them, individually wrapped to keep them from bruising. And, for neatness, there were piles of napkins and a little tin box with a washcloth dampened with rosewater and glycerine for wiping sticky mouths.

I wanted to eat in the dining car because I had read all about them, but my mother reminded me for the umpteenth time that dining car food always cost too much money and besides, you never could tell whose hands had been playing all over that food, nor where those same hands had been just before. My mother never mentioned that Black people were not allowed into railroad dining cars headed south in 1947. As usual, whatever my mother did not like and could not change, she ignored. Perhaps it would go away, deprived of her attention.

I learned later that Phyllis's high school senior class trip had been to Washington, but the nuns had given her back her deposit in private, explaining to her that the class, all of whom were white, except Phyllis, would be staying in a hotel where Phyllis "would not be happy," meaning, Daddy explained to her, also in private, that they did not rent rooms to Negroes. "We will take among-you to Washington, ourselves," my father had avowed, "and not just for an overnight in some measly fleabag hotel."

American racism was a new and crushing reality that my parents had to deal with every day of their lives once they came to this country. They handled it as a private woe. My mother and father believed that they could best protect their children from the realities of race in america and the fact of american racism by never giving them name, much less discussing their nature. We were told we must never trust white people, but *why* was never explained, nor the nature of their ill will. Like so many other vital pieces of information in my childhood, I was supposed to know without being told. It always seemed like a very strange injunction coming from my mother, who looked so much like one of those people we were never supposed to trust. But something always warned me not to ask my mother why she wasn't white, and why Auntie Lillah and Auntie Etta weren't, even though they were all that same problematic color so different from my father and me, even from my sisters, who were somewhere in-between.

In Washington, D.C., we had one large room with two double beds and an extra cot for me. It was a back-street hotel that belonged to a friend of my father's who was in real estate, and I spent the whole next day after Mass squinting up at the Lincoln Memorial where Marian Anderson had sung after the D.A.R. refused to allow her to sing in their auditorium because she was Black. Or because she was "Colored," my father said as he told us the story. Except that what he probably said was "Negro," because for his times, my father was quite progressive.

I was squinting because I was in that silent agony that character-ized all of my childhood summers, from the time school let out in June to the end of July, brought about by my dilated and vulnerable eyes exposed to the summer brightness.

I viewed Julys through an agonizing corolla of dazzling whiteness and I always hated the Fourth of July, even before I came to realize the travesty such a celebration was for Black people in this country.

My parents did not approve of sunglasses, nor of their expense.

I spent the afternoon squinting up at monuments to freedom and past presidencies and democracy, and wondering why the light and heat were both so much stronger in Washington, D.C., than back home in New York City. Even the pavement on the streets was a shade lighter in color than back home.

Late that Washington afternoon my family and I walked back down Pennsylvania Avenue. We were a proper caravan, mother bright and father brown, the three of us girls step-standards in-between. Moved by our historical surroundings and the heat of the early evening, my father decreed yet another treat. He had a great sense of history, a flair for the quietly dramatic and the sense of specialness of an occasion and a trip.

"Shall we stop and have a little something to cool off, Lin?"

Two blocks away from our hotel, the family stopped for a dish of vanilla ice cream at a Breyer's ice cream and soda fountain. Indoors, the soda fountain was dim and fan-cooled, deliciously relieving to my scorched eyes.

Corded and crisp and pinafored, the five of us seated ourselves one by one at the counter. There was I between my mother and father, and my two sisters on the other side of my mother. We settled ourselves along the white mottled marble counter, and when the waitress spoke at first no one understood what she was saying, and so the five of us just sat there.

The waitress moved along the line of us closer to my father and spoke again. "I said I kin give you to take out, but you can't eat here. Sorry." Then she dropped her eyes looking very embarrassed, and suddenly we heard what it was she was saying all at the same time, loud and clear.

Straight-backed and indignant, one by one, my family and I got down from the counter stools and turned around and marched out of the store, quiet and outraged, as if we had never been Black before. No one would answer my emphatic questions with anything other than a guilty silence. "But we hadn't done anything!" This wasn't right or fair! Hadn't I written poems about Bataan and freedom and democracy for all?

My parents wouldn't speak of this injustice, not because they had contributed to it, but because they felt they should have anticipated it and avoided it. This made me even angrier. My fury was not going to be acknowledged by a like fury. Even my two sisters copied my parents' pretense that nothing unusual and anti-american had occurred. I was left to write my angry letter to the president of the united states all by myself, although my father did promise I could type it out or the office typewriter next week, after I showed it to him in my copybook diary.

The waitress was white, and the counter was white, and the ice cream I never ate in Washington, D.C., that summer I left childhood was white, and the white heat and the white pavement and the white stone monuments of my first Washington summer made me sick to my stomach for the whole rest of that trip and it wasn't much of a graduation present after all.

INTERPRETATIONS

1. How do Lorde's description of the elaborate picnic food, the pretexts for avoiding the dining car, and the story of Phyllis's exclusion from her senior class trip foreshadow and increase the impact of the final event of her essay?

2. Where does Lorde reveal how she feels about her parents' general policy of trying to "anticipate and avoid" racial prejudice. To what extent do they succeed?

3. In similar circumstances would you feel the same way as Lorde? Why or why not?

4. The tone of the sentence (in the first paragraph) "I don't know what she was supposed to stop being" is somewhat ironic. Cite other passages using a similar tone. Is this also the tone of the last paragraph? What is the essay's prevailing tone?

CORRESPONDENCES

1. Review Nin's perspective and discuss its relevance to Lorde's essay.

2. Create a conversation between Lorde and Mabry (page 411) on how family member influence choices. What experiences can you add to the conversation?

APPLICATIONS

1. Write a journal entry on Lorde's use of color to enhance theme and reinforce the irony of her title.

2. View the 1989 movie *Born on the Fourth of July* and write an analysis of the importance of that date in Lorde's essay and Oliver Stone's film.

3. Compose the angry letter Lorde wrote to the president of the United States on her 4th of July trip to Washington DC. Be sure to include the relevant incidents climaxed by the visit to Breyer's soda fountain. Think carefully about an appropriate tone and what you want the letter to accomplish.

Living in Two Worlds

MARCUS MABRY

Marcus Mabry (b. 1967), raised by his mother and grandmother in an all-black section of Trenton, New Jersey, received a scholarship to the exclusive prep school Lawrenceville. He felt he had entered a different world, and the 1995 memoir White Bucks and Black-Eyed Peas: Coming of Age Black in White America *is his response. He received an M.A. from Stanford University and joined* Newsweek *in 1989 as an associate editor. In 1996, Mabry and a colleague won the Overseas Press Club's Morton Frank Award for Best Business Reporting for their cover story "End of the Good Life?" Mabry has also won the New York Association of Black Journalists award for Personal Commentary (1992), and a Lincoln University Unity Award in Media in 1991. He was named Chief of Correspondents for* Newsweek *in 2002. The following essay was originally published in the 1988 issue of* Newsweek on Campus. *Before reading Mabry's essay, record in your journal your responses to his title.*

A ROUND, GREEN CARDBOARD SIGN hangs from a string proclaiming, "We built a proud new feeling" the slogan of a local supermarket. It is a souvenir from one of my brother's last jobs. In addition to being a bagger, he's worked at a fast-food restaurant, a gas station, a garage and a textile factory. Now, in the icy clutches of the Northeastern winter, he is unemployed. He will soon be a father. He is nineteen years old.

In mid-December I was at Stanford, among the palm trees and weighty chores of academe. And all I wanted to do was get out. I joined the rest of the undergrads in a chorus of excitement, singing the praises of Christmas break. No classes, no midterms, no finals . . . and no freshmen! (I'm a resident assistant.) Awesome! I was looking forward to escaping. I never gave a thought to what I was escaping to.

Once I got home to New Jersey, reality returned. My dreaded freshmen had been replaced by unemployed relatives; badgering professors had been replaced by hard-working single mothers, and cold classrooms by dilapidated bedrooms and kitchens. The room in which the "proud new feeling" sign hung contained the belongings of myself, my mom and my brother. But for these two weeks it was mine. They slept downstairs on couches.

Most students who travel between the universes of poverty and affluence during breaks experience similar conditions, as well as the

411

guilt, the helplessness and, sometimes, the embarrassment associated with them. Our friends are willing to listen, but most of them are unable to imagine the pain of the impoverished lives that we see every six months. Each time I return home I feel further away from the realities of poverty in America and more ashamed that they are allowed to persist. What frightens me most is not that the American socioeconomic system permits poverty to continue, but that by participating in that system I share some of the blame.

Last year I lived in an on-campus apartment, with a (relatively) modern bathroom, kitchen and two bedrooms. Using summer earnings, I added some expensive prints, a potted palm and some other plants, making the place look like the more-than-humble abode of a New York City Yuppie. I gave dinner parties, even a *soirée française*.

For my roommate, a doctor's son, this kind of life was nothing extraordinary. But my mom was struggling to provide a life for herself and my brother. In addition to working 24-hour-a-day cases as a practical nurse, she was trying to ensure that my brother would graduate from high school and have a decent life. She knew that she had to compete for his attention with drugs and other potentially dangerous things that can look attractive to a young man when he sees no better future.

Living in my grandmother's house this Christmas break restored all the forgotten, and the never acknowledged, guilt. I had gone to boarding school on a full scholarship since the ninth grade, so being away from poverty was not new. But my own growing affluence has increased my distance. My friends say that I should not feel guilty: what could I do substantially for my family at this age, they ask. Even though I know that education is the right thing to do, I can't help but feel, sometimes, that I have it too good. There is no reason that I deserve security and warmth, while my brother has to cope with potential unemployment and prejudice. I, too, encounter prejudice, but it is softened by my status as a student in an affluent and intellectual community.

More than my sense of guilt, my sense of helplessness increases each time I return home. As my success leads me further away for longer periods of time poverty becomes harder to conceptualize and feels that much more oppressive when I visit with it. The first night of break, I lay in our bedroom, on a couch that let out into a bed that took up the whole room, except for a space heater. It was a little hard to sleep because the springs from the couch stuck through at inconvenient spots. But it would have been impossible to sleep anyway because of the groans coming from my grandmother's room next door. Only in her early 60s, she suffers from many chronic diseases and couldn't help but moan, then pray aloud, then moan, then pray aloud.

This wrenching of my heart was interrupted by the 3 A.M. entry of a relative who had been allowed to stay at the house despite rowdy behavior and threats toward the family in the past. As he came into the house, he slammed the door, and his heavy steps shook the second floor as he stomped into my grandmother's room to take his place, at the foot of her bed. There he slept, without blankets on a bare mattress. This was the first night. Later in the vacation, a Christmas turkey and a Christmas ham were stolen from my aunt's refrigerator on Christmas Eve. We think the thief was a relative. My mom and I decided not to exchange gifts that year because it just didn't seem festive.

A few days after New Year's I returned to California. The Northeast was soon hit by a blizzard. They were there, and I was here. That was the way it had to be, for now. I haven't forgotten; the ache of knowing their suffering is always there. It has to be kept deep down, or I can't find the logic in studying and partying while people, my people, are being killed by poverty. Ironically, success drives me away from those I most want to help by getting an education.

Somewhere in the midst of all that misery, my family has built, within me, "a proud feeling." As I travel between the two worlds it becomes harder to remember just how proud I should be—not just because of where I have come from and where I am going, but because of where they are. The fact that they live in the world in which they live is something to be very proud of, indeed. It inspires within me a sense of tenacity and accomplishment that I hope every college graduate will someday possess.

INTERPRETATIONS

1. Compare and contrast Mabry's two worlds. In which does he feel most himself?
2. Review the last paragraph of the essay. To what extent has his background contributed to his survival?
3. Identify the tone of his essay. Is it appropriate for the subject? Explain.

CORRESPONDENCES

1. Compare and contrast the ramifications of the personal choices made in "To the Border" and "Living in Two Worlds."
2. Review Baldwin's perspective on choices. How does it apply to "Living in Two Worlds"? To what extent is Mabry "trapped in history"? Cite evidence for your point of view.

APPLICATIONS

1. Discuss with your group the inequities of social class as described in Mabry's essay. What is ironic about his success?

2. Is Mabry a divided self? Characterize his "two worlds." How have his choices contributed to his emotional conflicts? To what extent is he an outsider in both worlds? Can you imagine making a similar choice?

3. Assume you and your family had to forcibly leave your home. What three items would you carry with you? Write a short essay on your emotional attachment to each.

4. What do you think one of Marcus Mabry's relatives would say to him after reading "Living in Two Worlds"? Using the voice of that individual, write a letter to Mabry that expresses your thoughts and feelings.

The Fender-Bender

RAMÓN "TIANGUIS" PÉREZ

Ramón "Tianguis" Pérez is an undocumented alien. Of necessity he does not disclose information about his life or his whereabouts. "The Fender-Bender" is an excerpt from his book Diary of an Undocumented Immigrant *(1991) and gives a glimpse of his life in this country.*

ONE NIGHT AFTER WORK, I drive Rolando's old car to visit some friends, and then head towards home. At a light, I come to a stop too late, leaving the front end of the car poking into the crosswalk. I shift into reverse, but as I am backing up, I strike the van behind me. Its driver immediately gets out to inspect the damage to his vehicle. He's a tall Anglo-Saxon, dressed in a deep blue work uniform. After looking at his car, he walks up to the window of the car I'm driving.

"Your driver's license," he says, a little enraged.

"I didn't bring it," I tell him.

He scratches his head. He is breathing heavily with fury.

"Okay," he says. "You park up ahead while I call a patrolman."

The idea of calling the police doesn't sound good to me, but the accident is my fault. So I drive around the corner and park at the curb. I turn off the motor and hit the steering wheel with one fist. I don't have a driver's license. I've never applied for one. Nor do I have with me the identification card that I bought in San Antonio. Without immigration papers, without a driving permit, and having hit another car, I feel as if I'm just one step away from Mexico.

I get out of the car. The white man comes over and stands right in front of me. He's almost two feet taller.

"If you're going to drive, why don't you carry your license?" he asks in an accusatory tone.

"I didn't bring it," I say, for lack of any other defense.

I look at the damage to his car. It's minor, only a scratch on the paint and a pimple-sized dent.

"I'm sorry," I say. "Tell me how much it will cost to fix, and I'll pay for it; that's no problem." I'm talking to him in English, and he seems to understand.

"This car isn't mine," he says. "It belongs to the company I work for. I'm sorry, but I've got to report this to the police, so that I don't have to pay for the damage."

"That's no problem," I tell him again. "I can pay for it."

After we've exchanged these words, he seems less irritated. But he says he'd prefer for the police to come, so that they can report that the dent wasn't his fault.

While we wait, he walks from one side to the other, looking down the avenue this way and that, hoping that the police will appear.

Then he goes over to the van to look at the dent.

"It's not much," he says. "If it was my car, there wouldn't be any problems, and you could go on."

After a few minutes, the long-awaited police car arrives. Only one officer is inside. He's a Chicano, short and of medium complexion, with short, curly hair. On getting out of the car, he walks straight towards the Anglo.

The two exchange a few words.

"Is that him?" he asks, pointing at me.

The Anglo nods his head.

Speaking in English, the policeman orders me to stand in front of the car and to put my hands on the hood. He searches me and finds only the car keys and my billfold with a few dollars in it. He asks for my driver's license.

"I don't have it," I answer in Spanish.

He wrinkles his face into a frown, and casting a glance at the Anglo, shakes his head in disapproval of me.

"That's the way these Mexicans are," he says.

He turns back towards me, asking for identification. I tell him I don't have that, either.

"You're an illegal, eh?" he says.

I won't answer.

"An illegal," he says to himself.

"Where do you live?" he continues. He's still speaking in English.

I tell him my address.

"Do you have anything with you to prove that you live at that address?" he asks.

I think for a minute, then realize that in the glove compartment is a letter that my parents sent to me several weeks earlier.

I show him the envelope and he immediately begins to write something in a little book that he carries in his back pocket. He walks to the back of my car and copies the license plate number. Then he goes over to his car and talks into his radio. After he talks, someone answers. Then he asks me for the name of the car's owner.

He goes over to where the Anglo is standing. I can't quite hear what they're saying. But when the two of them go over to look at the dent in the van, I hear the cop tell the Anglo that if he wants, he can file charges against me. The Anglo shakes his head and explains what he had earlier explained to me, about only needing for the police to certify that he wasn't responsible for the accident. The Anglo says that he doesn't want to accuse me of anything because the damage is light.

"If you want, I can take him to jail," the cop insists.

The Anglo turns him down again.

"If you'd rather, we can report him to Immigration," the cop continues.

Just as at the first, I am now almost sure that I'll be making a forced trip to Tijuana. I find myself searching my memory for my uncle's telephone number, and to my relief, I remember it. I am waiting for the Anglo to say yes, confirming my expectations of the trip. But instead, he says no, and though I remain silent, I feel appreciation for him. I ask myself why the Chicano is determined to harm me. I didn't really expect him to favor me, just because we're of the same ancestry, but on the other hand, once I had admitted my guilt, I expected him to treat me at least fairly. But even against the white man's wishes, he's trying to make matters worse for me. I've known several Chicanos with whom, joking around, I've reminded them that their roots are in Mexico. But very few of them see it that way. Several have told me how when they were children, their parents would take them to vacation in different states of Mexico, but their own feeling, they've said, is, "I am an American citizen!" Finally, the Anglo, with the justifying paper in his hands, says goodbye to the cop, thanks him for his services, gets into his van and drives away.

The cop stands in the street in a pensive mood. I imagine that he's trying to think of a way to punish me.

"Put the key in the ignition," he orders me.

I do as he says.

Then he orders me to roll up the windows and lock the doors.

"Now, go on, walking," he says.

I go off taking slow steps. The cop gets in his patrol car and stays there, waiting. I turn the corner after two blocks and look out for my car, but the cop is still parked beside it. I begin looking for a coat hanger, and after a good while, find one by a curb of the street. I keep walking, keeping about two blocks away from the car. While I walk, I bend the coat hanger into the form I'll need. As if I'd called for it, a speeding car goes past. When it comes to the avenue where my car is parked, it makes a turn. It is going so fast that its wheels screech as it rounds the corner. The cop turns on the blinking lights of his patrol car and leaving black marks on the pavement beneath it, shoots out to chase the speeder. I go up to my car and with my palms force a window open a crack. Then I insert the clothes hanger in the crack and raise the lock lever. It's a simple task, one that I'd already performed. This wasn't the first time that I'd been locked out of a car, though always before, it was because I'd forgotten to remove my keys.

INTERPRETATIONS

1. Compare and contrast the attitudes of the Anglo driver and the Chicano cop at the scene of the fender-bender.
2. Why do you think the Anglo chooses not to report the illegal alien to Immigration? Does it surprise you that the cop is intent on punishing the Mexican? Why or why not?
3. Characterize the tone of the narrative. Is it objective? Subjective? Ironic?

CORRESPONDENCES

1. Review Fanon's perspective on choices and discuss its relevance to "The Fender-Bender."
2. Rodriguez and Pérez portray aspects of the illegal immigrants' experience in the United States. Characterize your response to both selections.

APPLICATIONS

1. Discuss with your group stereotyping in "The Fender-Bender."
2. Review the last paragraph of the essay. What does it reveal about the attitude of the "illegal" toward his situation? Write an essay discussing the thematic implications of the author's use of irony in "The Fender-Bender."
3. The rights and status of illegal aliens became the subject of national debate in the last decade resulting in severe penalties and legal restrictions. What is your point of view? Do you think, for example, that "illegals" pose a threat to the job market given the fact that most of them are involved in menial tasks and paid below minimum wage? Summarize your discussion.

Janushinka

HANA WEHLE

Hana Wehle (1917–1997) was born in Czechoslovakia. She was a survivor of the Theresienstadt, Auschwitz, and Stutthof concentration camps. After the defeat of the Nazis in 1945, she returned to Czechoslovakia, where she remarried. In 1951, she and her husband, also a survivor of Auschwitz, emigrated to the United States. She published several essays about her concentration camp experiences.

This is how she described her purpose in writing "Janushinka."

For Franz Kafka, "writing is a form of prayer." For me, writing is a form of conveying a message. I remember the time in Auschwitz, when every prisoner in our part of the camp was destined to die in the gas chambers. How much did I then want to live, so that I could bring the message to the world about the absurdity of our existence during that period of madness. I survived and I want to help young people understand this event through a form which is easier to grasp than a strictly historical account. I like to share my experiences with a college-age audience on the threshold of adult life, since they are the makers of the future. I wish to give them certain awareness of things they would not encounter otherwise. Last, but not least, I want them to understand that what I write contains an important message for them.

As you read "Janushinka," determine what message it contains for you.

WITH JANUSHINKA'S BIRTH the passionate bond was sealed. She was swept into the happy orbit of her parents, Henry and Pepinka, and became the focal point of their life. Whenever they looked at her, they transformed their souls into that look. They tasted with pleasure bordering on reverence every move, touch and exploration of the child, as well as, later, the cascade of words scrambled in nonsense combinations. Today, forty years later, I am still able to draw from my memory the sweet melody of Janushinka's laughs and cries coming from the nursery.

Henry was my father's cousin, a successful, hard working businessman, in his thirties. Pepinka, a few years younger, was a beautiful woman with velvety brown eyes radiating with love and happiness.

419

I stayed with them for a short time, after arriving in Prague from the German-occupied Sudetenland in the northern region of Bohemia.

Before long, I too gravitated toward the sweet little child. I remember how one or the other of us would tip-toe in and out of the nursery to make sure that the sleeping Janushinka was not too cold or too hot. When the weather became chilly and rainy, we would brace ourselves with a surgical cotton mask so that germs would not invade her delicate system. Unquestionably, Henry and Pepinka's happiness was also heavily tinted by shadows of fear and anxiety for the safety of their precious jewel.

At a time when love and affection still warmed every corner of their home, the German army already occupied Prague. My recollection of being frightened as the clatter of marching soldiers could be heard through the windows is still clear. The dissonance between the dim winter morning when the Germans marched into our city and the sanctity of that loving home was an unbearable experience.

Very soon the tide of the events turned against the Jews. The curtains of their homes were drawn, the lights went out. They were deported to an unknown destination . . . Also the lights in the nursery were turned out, the curtains drawn. The chuckle of Janushinka was silenced.

After I was deported to Auschwitz, I never thought that I would see Henry and his family again. However, it did happen in the "Familienlager," one of the many sections of Auschwitz-Birkenau. I was on my way to the "latrine" (toilet), a large wooden barrack, used by prisoners under the watchful eyes of the SS guards. Inside the large area on one side were women, on the other side were men, exposed to one another in utter humiliation. The entrance was always crowded with prisoners waiting for their turn. For some of them it was too late: they collapsed into their own excrement, unable to lift themselves from the muddy ground. We had to bypass these human forms as we moved on in silence.

The air was damp and the rags of clouds hung over us. As we were slowly inching away, I heard somebody softly calling my name. Carefully, so as not to dispel the feeble voice behind me, I turned my head in the direction of a tiny cloud steaming from the frozen mouth of a man. I looked at the still face and suddenly felt as if a sword were splitting the web of my brain. There stood Henry! His sunken eyes were fixed upon me and the narrow line of his mouth twisted into a strange, almost embarrassed smile. The unshaven face hung between his shoulders, and the once translucent, blue eyes signaled an unspeakable anguish. His rasping voice cut through the silence around us: "Janushinka is very sick. Pneumonia. Pepinka is desperately trying to save her life."

In these words there was something that killed all hope. The memory of the gulf between Henry in the nursery and the man standing in front of me that day will never allow me to forget the perversity of fate. I remember the dreamer's dreams and how they were shattered under the wheels of the trains rushing through the German and Polish countrysides, carrying in their dark bellies thousands of little Janushinkas, Henrys, and Pepinkas . . .

I slipped back through time and recaptured the fragrance of the little child in the nursery and the sight of Pepinka pulling the soft pink blanket over the sleeping Janushinka. Henry is lovingly watching the young woman in the bright opening of the door, as she steps out of the nursery. She then sets a bowl of steaming soup on the table covered with a starched, hand-embroidered table cloth; the silver spoons touching the fine porcelain send pleasant tinkles through the cozy dining room.

The urgency in Henry's eyes jolted me back into the present. I looked past Henry and glanced at the watch towers above the barbed wire surrounding the camp. What consolation could I offer to this man? I felt so cold and hungry. A picture of Pepinka and Janushinka struggling in some dark corner of a barracks pushed its way upon me. Janushinka's body is so thin that it appears translucent. Pepinka bends over the little girl and with an almost childlike expression hopes for a miracle. Her hand caresses the sweet forehead, covered with beads of sweat and her gentle lips brush the feverish face as she intently follows the quickening breath of her child, fighting for life . . . I leaned toward Henry and whispered: "Meet me here tomorrow at this time, I will bring you some soup." The crowd behind pushed us into the latrine barrack. As we parted, it seemed to me that Henry's face somewhat brightened.

Once in a while the workers at the camp post office got an additional portion of soup. I was one of them and, therefore, was able to share that precious "premium" with my mother, who had been deported with me to Auschwitz. Suddenly I panicked. What if I did not get the special soup tomorrow? Henry would be waiting . . . and what about my mother? How could I deprive her? Would she be able to understand?

The night seemed long because I could not sleep. Will I get the additional soup, and if I do, how shall I divide it? We all are so hungry! The barrels of soup paraded endlessly in front of my tired mind. Will any of them stop in front of me? Will there be some soup for Henry? The last barrel is finally set in front of me. What a relief! Eagerly I bend over the slippery edge of the barrel and realize with horror—the vessel is empty!

Finally daylight crept into our barrack. The dead were carried behind the barrack, the half dead and the healthy filed out for the roll-call. That day the counting and recounting of prisoners was endless. It was almost midday before we could return. I could not rest. My eyes were glued to the road stretching between the rows of the wooden barracks. At last two women surfaced in the fog. Between them, they carried the long awaited barrel of soup. I followed eagerly the wooden clogs marching in unison with the swinging barrel suspended from two heavy poles. They headed toward us, the poles in the grip of their bony hands. Around their necks, attached to the poles, was a strong strap, which pulled their heads forward. As they came closer I could see their distorted faces reflecting the enormous strain of their bodies as they struggled to distribute the weight of the barrel between their arms and necks.

Finally they arrived at our barrack. Amid the pushing of the hungry prisoners a line was formed. There stood the vessel with a grayish, slimy liquid dripping down its sides. We all followed eagerly every drop. One full ladle was dropped into each bowl. My turn came . . . in an almost hypnotic trance I traced the movement of the ladle. It emptied once and dipped in—and emptied into my bowl again!

Victoriously I carried the full bowl to my place, where my mother was waiting for her share of the soup. I reluctantly explained to her why we would from now on divide the soup into three parts. She understood the urgency and shared in the sacrifice. I hurried with the rest of the soup to the latrine barrack. As I pushed my way through the waiting crowd to meet Henry, icy rain dropped into the soup. The hand on my shoulder was Henry's. His face seemed thinner than the day before. As I was transferring the soup into his dish, Henry's eyes were transfixed on that thick, gray stream barely filling the bottom of his bowl. He just nodded and disappeared into the crowd.

I met Henry several times, sometimes with the soup, sometimes without it. Meanwhile, Janushinka, he told me, was still in the grip of death. The question as to whether I could actually prevent her imminent death never left me. What if the recovery never took place?

The subhuman conditions in the camp were sapping the strength of Henry's frail body. His walking had become visibly slower, his back stooped increasingly and he was more listless. One day, however, I noticed some change. He tried to straighten his haggard body and across his face the cruel play of fear and hope was gone. The words rolled from his mouth like pieces of gold: "Janushinka's fever has subsided—she ate the soup!" Henry's and my eyes connected in a new alliance with life. In his face lingered a flicker of hope. For myself, I freed my conscience from the burden of guilt about having deprived my mother of the additional soup.

As Janushinka's health slowly improved so Henry's strength quickly evaporated. One day Henry did not show up. As usual, I waited in front of the latrine barrack, the gelatinous soup cold in my bowl . . . That day I returned to my mother's place, overtaken by fatigue. We shared Janushinka's soup in silence.

The only place where men and women were able occasionally to share a fleeting moment was the latrine barrack. For a long time I looked into the faces around me in vain. I never saw Henry again. At the far end of our camp was the so called children's block where some of the mothers and their young children were housed; they helped take care of the youngsters' needs. There Pepinka and Janushinka lived also. Any contact between the occupants of the children's block and the rest of the camp prisoners was forbidden. Apparently, Henry had found some clandestine way to get the soup to Janushinka during her sickness. After his disappearance I lost track of their whereabouts.

Not until the beginning of July 1944, when the prisoners of the "Familien-lager" were about to be gassed, did I learn about Pepinka's and Janushinka's fate. Daily selections, grouping and regrouping of the old and young, the sick and healthy, took place. The younger and more healthy men and women were transported to other camps for work; the old and sick were exterminated in the gas chambers and to the mothers of young children a choice was given: "Leave your child behind and save yourself by joining the group of working women, or—go to your death together with your children." Three hundred young mothers made their choice: Pepinka was one of them. She held the tiny hand of Janushinka as if she would lead the child to school, like other mothers, in another world. In her lonely hour of anguish once again Pepinka hoped for a miracle. This time, however, there was none . . . Janushinka had to die, before she even learned to live. By a twist of fate Janushinka's recovery had led to Pepinka's death. Such was the notorious "law" in the world of Auschwitz!

INTERPRETATIONS

1. What is Wehle's relationship to Janushinka and her family? What do the details of their lifestyle before the war suggest about their social class?

2. Reread paragraphs 3 through 5. Which details foreshadow the fate of many Jewish people during the Nazi regime?

3. What is the connotation of "rags" in the phrase "the mass of clouds" (paragraph 7)? Of "crept" in "Daylight crept into our barrack" (paragraph 12)?

4. How does Wehle's mother's presence make her decision to help Janushinka more difficult? Would you have chosen differently? Explain.

5. Do you think more people would have survived the war if they had not had parents, spouses, or children in the camp? Explain.

6. How does Janushinka's recovery lead to Pepinka's death? Do you agree that "fate" was involved here? If so, how would you define "fate"? Is character also involved? Love? How would you characterize Pepinka?

Honor Bound

JOSEPH STEFFAN

Joseph Steffan (b. 1964) was a senior in 1987 when he was discharged from the United States Naval Academy after admitting that he was gay. After his discharge, Steffan filed a lawsuit against the academy, became an advocate for gay and lesbian military members, and wrote about his military career in Honor Bound (1992). Steffan received a law degree from the University of Connecticut in 1994. Before reading Steffan's essay, speculate as to the meaning of his title.

I WALKED INTO THE COMMANDANT'S outer office and reported to his executive assistant, a junior officer assigned to serve as his aide. He said the commandant would be right with me, and asked me to take a seat. The strange quietness of the hallway seemed to permeate everything, and although the EA's greeting had been cordial, there was an obvious tension in the air. He undoubtedly knew the purpose of this meeting as well, and I began to wonder how long it would take before it leaked to the rest of the brigade.

I tried to keep calm, but it was difficult to ignore the obvious importance of this meeting. What would happen in the next few moments would likely determine, to a very large extent, the rest of my life. My feelings were a strange mixture of fear, anger, and pride, and I was determined that, no matter what, I was going to maintain my sense of dignity.

Finally, the EA signaled that the commandant was ready and led me into his office. The commandant of midshipmen, Captain Howard Habermeyer, was waiting just inside the door as we entered. He greeted me, shaking my hand, and motioned for me to sit as he returned to his desk. The office was relatively opulent by military standards, with dark wood paneling and blue carpeting. Behind the commandant's large wooden desk stood the United States flag and the blue-and-gold flag of the Brigade of Midshipmen. The walls were covered with pictures and plaques, memorabilia from his service as an officer in the submarine service.

Captain Habermeyer was tall, bespectacled, and quite thin, almost to the point of frailty. He and the superintendent had taken over during the previous summer, replacing Captain Chadwick and Admiral Larson,

425

both of whom I had come to know quite well during my previous years. I regretted that they were not here now, and that my fate rested in the hands of two officers who barely knew me. I sometimes wonder if they had been there instead whether it would have changed the outcome at all. Perhaps it would at least have been more difficult for them.

I had first met Captain Habermeyer at a small leadership retreat held for the top incoming stripers of my class. The retreat was relatively informal and was held at an Annapolis hotel. At the time, he impressed me as an intelligent and articulate officer, and we had shared a conversation about his admiration of Japanese culture. It was an interest that had grown through several tours of duty he had in Japan.

I had heard since then that Captain Habermeyer was a stickler for regulations. He played everything exactly by the book. My suspicion was confirmed when the EA remained standing in the doorway as the commandant began to question me about my request. He had apparently been ordered to remain as a witness to the conversation. Despite an outward sense of cordiality, I was beginning to feel like a criminal under interrogation.

As with the previous officers, I refused to discuss the purpose of my request with the commandant, but he continued to question me. He finally stated that no one in the military has an inherent right to meet with anyone above his own commanding officer, which for midshipmen is technically the commandant. If I refused to disclose the purpose of the meeting, he would deny my request. When he again questioned me, I finally answered, "The meeting concerns a situation of which you are already aware."

"You're referring to the NIS investigation presently under way?" he asked.

"Yes, sir."

He responded, "Are you willing to state at this time that you are a homosexual?"

The moment of truth had arrived. In a way, I was surprised that he was even asking the question. Captain Holderby had already basically told him the answer. Was he offering me an out, a chance to deny it, to say that it was all a big misunderstanding? Was he offering me a chance to lie?

I looked him straight in the eye and answered, "Yes sir, I am."

It was a moment I will never forget, one of agony and intense pride. In that one statement, I had given up my dreams, the goals I had spent the last four years of my life laboring to attain. But in exchange, I retained something far more valuable—my honor and my self-esteem.

In many ways, the commandant's words were more than a simple question—they were a challenge to everything I believed in, and to the identity I had struggled to accept. In giving me the opportunity to deny my sexuality, the commandant was challenging that identity. He could just as well have asked, "Are you ashamed enough to deny your true identity in order to graduate?" More than anything I have ever wanted in my entire life, I wanted to be an outstanding midshipman and to graduate from the Naval Academy. And I firmly believe that if I had been willing to lie about my sexuality, to deny my true identity, I would have been allowed to graduate.

I had come to the academy to achieve my potential as an individual. These four years had been filled with trials and lessons from which I learned a great deal about life and about myself. But none of these lessons was more difficult, important, or meaningful than coming to understand and accept my sexuality—in essence, to accept my true identity. By coming out to myself, I gained the strength that can come only from self-acceptance, and it was with that added strength that I had been able to persevere through the many trials and difficulties of life at Annapolis.

The commandant's question was also a challenge to my honor as a midshipman. The Honor Concept at Annapolis is based on the tenet that personal honor is an absolute—you either have honor or you do not. No one can take it from you; it can only be surrendered willingly. And once it is surrendered, once it is compromised, it can never again be fully regained.

I knew that my graduation would mean absolutely nothing if I had to lie to achieve it, especially if that lie was designed to hide the very fact of my own identity. I would have given up my honor, destroying everything it means to be a midshipman. And I would have given up my identity and pride—everything it means to be a person.

The only way to retain my honor and identity, both as a midshipman and a person, was to tell the truth. I was honor bound not simply by the Honor Concept, but by its foundation: the respect for fundamental human dignity. The academy had the power to take away everything tangible that I had attained, but only I had the power to destroy my honor. Even if the academy discharged me for being gay, I could live with the knowledge that I had passed the ultimate test. I was willing to give up everything tangible to retain something intangible but far more meaningful: my honor and my identity. Even the military could not take them away from me now.

Captain Habermeyer said that he could not grant my request to speak with the superintendent because he would eventually sit in judgment over me. A performance board would be scheduled the next day, the first step toward discharge from Annapolis. Although I explained that I still desired to graduate, the commandant assured me that he did not believe the superintendent would allow it.

Before leaving, I looked at the commandant and said, "I'm sorry it had to end this way." He answered, "So am I." I truly believed him, which didn't make the imminent destruction of my life much easier to deal with. It would have been so much easier to have someone to hate, a person to blame for everything that was happening. But there was no one to blame. I couldn't blame myself because I had done what I believed right. There was only a military policy, a rule like countless others that define life in the military, rules that we learn to instinctively enforce and obey.

My perception of what was happening seemed almost detached at times, and I wondered how long it would be before I woke up to realize this was all a horrible dream. In retrospect, I don't doubt that I was suffering from shock, so completely overcome by emotion that I couldn't feel anything at all. I wanted to scream or cry or something, but there was too much to deal with, and I wondered if I would be able to stop once I started.

Not only was the nature of my life changing rapidly, but I was also anticipating how each of my relationships with other people would change. Would my parents and friends reject me as I had feared for so long, or was I not giving them enough credit? In any case, I knew it would be only a short time until the news of my disclosure would leak to the brigade, and I had to be prepared before then. I had heard a story about two male mids who were caught in bed together a year or two before I was inducted. That evening, they were both dragged from their rooms, wrapped in blankets and beaten by other mids in what was called a "blanket party." In a way, I doubted whether anyone would dare do that to me, but I wasn't too excited about the possibility.

There was no doubt in my mind that the story would leak, probably within twenty-four hours. After that, it would spread like wildfire. Annapolis is such a rumor mill that I could expect to hear about five hundred colorful variations of the story within a few hours. I decided that the best way to combat this inevitability was through a controlled release of information, and that release had to start with my closest friends at the academy.

I spent the rest of the afternoon telling six of my friends what was going on. Each of them was shocked and surprised, but they were universally supportive, even more so than I had hoped. I told them I wanted them to hear it from me first, but that they should keep it under wraps for now. I also took the time to go to each of the teachers I had in classes that semester to inform them personally. I felt a need to do this first out of respect for them, and second, to make sure that they knew I was not ashamed to face them. If I was going to leave the academy, I wanted it to be with the same level of pride I had felt as a battalion commander. I didn't want anyone to think I was running away, departing under a cloak of deserved shame. I wanted to show them I was the same person as before—exactly the same.

INTERPRETATIONS

1. Explain the significance of the title of Steffan's essay. Do you respect his courage to tell the truth about his sexuality in spite of the consequences he would confront? Why or why not?
2. What prompted Steffan to later tell his closest friends about his decision? To what extent were you surprised by their reactions? How might you have responded in their situation?
3. Why does Steffan describe the setting and the captain in such detail? How do these descriptions affect meaning?

CORRESPONDENCES

1. Review Camus's perspective on choices and discuss its relevance to Steffan's decision. Do you agree that his situation was unjust? Why or why not?
2. Wehle and Steffan take risks because of their commitments to individual integrity. Under what circumstances can you imagine taking a similar risk to protect your honor?

APPLICATIONS

1. Rent the 1982 movie *Sophie's Choice* and write an extended journal entry on your responses to the choices made by young mothers in the film. To what extent did the film confirm or change your response to Pepinka's choice in Wehle's essay?
2. The realities written about by Hana Wehle are unthinkable. In the final sentence of her essay she writes: "Such was the notorious 'law' in the world of Auschwitz!" What was the "world of Auschwitz"?

   http://remember.org/then-and-now/index.html

   http://www.holocaust-trc.org/wmp17.htm
3. In the last paragraph of this essay, Joseph Steffan informs his friends and teachers of his situation. What do you think he might have said to them? Create a conversation about twenty lines in length that you think might have taken place between Steffan and a friend or a teacher.

Homeplace

SCOTT RUSSELL SANDERS

Scott Russell Sanders (b. 1945 in Memphis, Tennessa) writes essays, stories, and novels that show an equal interest in nature and in literature, in science, and in the arts. He is a distinguished professor of English at Indiana University, where he currently directs the Wells Scholars Program. At Brown University, he earned a B.A. (summa cum laude) in 1967 and at Cambridge University a Ph.D. in 1971. Sanders is a frequent contributor to journals such as Audubon, Harper's, Orion, North American Review, *and* Utne Reader, *among others. His novels include* Terrarium *(1985),* Bad Man Ballad *(1986),* The Engineer of Beasts *(1988), and* The Invisible Company *(1989). Sanders's nonfiction books include:* Wilderness Plots *(1983),* Fetching the Dead *(1984),* The Paradise of Bombs *(1987),* Secrets of the Universe *(1993),* Staying Put *(1993),* Writing From the Center *(1995), and* Indiana *(2005). His latest book is the memoir* A Private History of Awe *(2006). Sanders's work has also been selected for* Best American Essays, *the PEN Syndicated Fiction Award, and the Gamma Award. Write a journal entry on your associations with the word* homeplace, *and how it might differ from the word* home.

As a boy in Ohio, I knew a farm family, the Millers, who suffered from three tornadoes. The father, mother, and two sons were pulling into their driveway after church when the first tornado hoisted up their mobile home, spun it around, and carried it off. With the insurance money, they built a small frame house on the same spot.

Several years later, a second tornado peeled off the roof, splintered the garage, and rustled two cows. The Millers rebuilt again, raising a new garage on the old foundation and adding another story to the house. That upper floor was reduced to kindling by a third tornado, which also pulled out half the apple trees and slurped water from the stock pond. Soon after that I left Ohio, snatched away by college as forcefully as by any cyclone. Last thing I heard, the family was preparing to rebuild yet again.

Why did the Millers refuse to move? I knew them well enough to say they were neither stupid nor crazy. Plain stubbornness was a factor. These were people who, once settled, might have remained at the foot of a volcano or on the bank of a flood-prone river or beside an earthquake fault. They had relatives nearby, helpful neighbors, jobs and stores and schools within a short drive, and those were all good reasons to stay. But the main reason, I believe, was that the Millers had invested so much of their lives in the land, planting orchards and gardens, spreading manure on the fields, digging ponds, building sheds, seeding pastures. Out back of the house were groves of walnuts, hickories, and oaks, all started by hand from acorns and nuts. April through October, perennial flowers in the yard pumped out a fountain of blossoms. This farm was not just so many acres of dirt, easily exchanged for an equal amount elsewhere; it was a particular place, intimately known, worked on, dreamed over, cherished.

Psychologists tell us that we answer trouble with one of two impulses, either fight or flight. I believe that the Millers exhibited a third instinct, that of staying put. They knew better than to fight a tornado, and they chose not to flee. Their commitment to the place may have been foolhardy, but it was also grand. I suspect that most human achievements worth admiring are the result of such devotion.

The Millers dramatize a choice we are faced with constantly; whether to go or stay, whether to move to a situation that is safer, richer, easier, more attractive, or to stick where we are and make what we can of it. If the shine goes off our marriage, our house, our car, do we trade it for a new one? If the fertility leaches out of our soil, the creativity out of our job, the money out of our pocket, do we start over somewhere else? There are voices enough, both inner and outer, urging us to deal with difficulties by pulling up stakes and heading for new territory. I know them well, for they have been calling to me all my days. I wish to raise here a contrary voice, to say a few words on behalf of staying put, learning the ground, going deeper.

Claims for the virtues of moving on are familiar and seductive to Americans, this nation founded by immigrants and shaped by restless seekers. From the beginning, our heroes have been sailors, explorers, cowboys, prospectors, speculators, backwoods ramblers, rainbow chasers, vagabonds of every stripe. Our Promised Land has always been over the next ridge or at the end of the trail, never under our feet. In our national mythology, the worst fate is to be trapped on a farm, in a village, in the sticks, in some dead-end job or unglamorous marriage or played-out game.

Stand still, we are warned, and you die. Americans have dug the most canals, laid the most rails, built the most roads and airports of any nation. In a newspaper I read that, even though our sprawling system of interstate highways is crumbling, politicians think we should triple its size. Only a populace drunk on driving, a populace infatuated with the myth of the open road, could hear such a proposal without hooting.

Novelist Salman Rushdie chose to leave his native India for England, where he has written a series of brilliant books from the perspective of a cultural immigrant. In his book of essays *Imaginary Homelands* he celebrates the migrant sensibility: "The effect of mass migrations has been the creation of radically new types of human being: people who root themselves in ideas rather than places, in memories as much as in material things." He goes on to say that "to be a migrant is, perhaps, to be the only species of human being free of the shackles of nationalism (to say nothing of its ugly sister, patriotism)." Lord knows we could do with less nationalism (to say nothing of its ugly siblings, racism, religious sectarianism, and class snobbery). But who would pretend that a history of migration has immunized the United States against bigotry? And even if, by uprooting ourselves, we shed our chauvinism, is that all we lose?

In this hemisphere, many of the worst abuses—of land, forests, animals, and communities—have been carried out by "people who root themselves in ideas rather than places." Migrants often pack up their visions and values with the rest of their baggage and carry them along. The Spaniards devastated Central and South America by imposing on this New World the religion, economics, and politics of the Old. Colonists brought slavery with them to North America, along with smallpox and Norway rats. The Dust Bowl of the 1930s was caused not by drought but by the transfer onto the Great Plains of farming methods that were suitable to wetter regions. The habit of our industry and commerce has been to force identical schemes onto differing locales, as though the mind were a cookie cutter and the land were dough.

I quarrel with Rushdie because he articulates as eloquently as anyone the orthodoxy that I wish to counter: the belief that movement is inherently good, staying put is bad; that uprooting brings tolerance, while rootedness breeds intolerance; that to be modern, enlightened, fully of our time is to be displaced. Wholesale displacement may be inevitable in today's world; but we should not suppose that it occurs without disastrous consequences for the earth and for ourselves. People who root themselves in places are likelier to know and care for those places than are people who root themselves in ideas. When we cease to be migrants and become inhabitants, we might begin to pay enough heed and respect to where we are. By settling in, we have a chance of making a durable home for ourselves, our fellow creatures, and our descendants.

The poet Gary Snyder writes frequently about our need to "inhabit" a place. One of the key problems in American society now, he points out, is people's lack of commitment to any given place;

> Neighborhoods are allowed to deteriorate, landscapes are allowed to be strip-mined, because there is nobody who will live there and take responsibility; they'll just move on. The

reconstruction of a people and of a life in the United States depends in part on people, neighborhood by neighborhood, county by county, deciding to stick it out and make it work where they are, rather than flee.

But if you stick in one place, won't you become a stick-in-the-mud? If you stay put, won't you be narrow, backward, dull? You might. I have met ignorant people who never moved; and I have also met ignorant people who never stood still. Committing yourself to a place does not guarantee that you will become wise, but neither does it guarantee that you will become parochial.

To become intimate with your home region, to know the territory as well as you can, to understand your life as woven into the local life does not prevent you from recognizing and honoring the diversity of other places, cultures, ways. On the contrary, how can you value other places if you do not have one of your own? If you are not yourself *placed*, then you wander the world like a sightseer, a collector of sensations, with no gauge for measuring what you see. Local knowledge is the grounding for global knowledge. Those who care about nothing beyond the confines of their parish are in truth parochial, and are at least mildly dangerous to their parish; on the other hand, those who *have* no parish, those who navigate ceaselessly among postal zones and area codes, those for whom the world is only a smear of highways and bank accounts and stores, are a danger not just to their parish but to the planet.

Since birth, my children have regularly seen images of the earth as viewed from space, images that I first encountered when I was in my twenties. Those photographs show vividly what in our sanest moments we have always known—that the earth is a closed circle, lovely and rare. On the wall beside me as I write there is a poster of the big blue marble encased in its white swirl of clouds. That is one pole of my awareness; but the other pole is what I see through my window. I try to keep both in sight at once.

For all my convictions, I still have to wrestle with the fear—in myself, in my children, and even in some of my neighbors—that our place is too remote from the action. This fear drives many people to pack their bags and move to some resort or burg they have seen on television, leaving behind what they learn to think of as the boondocks. I deal with my own unease by asking just what action I am remote *from*— a stock market? a debating chamber? a drive-in mortuary? The action that matters, the work of nature and community, goes on everywhere.

Since Copernicus, we have known better than to see the earth as the center of the universe. Since Einstein, we have learned that there is no center; or alternatively, that any point is as good as any other for observing the world. I find a kindred lesson in the words of the Zen master Thich Nhat Hanh: "This spot where you sit is your own spot. It is on this very spot and in this very moment that you can become enlightened. You don't have to sit beneath a special tree in a distant land." If you stay put, your place may become a holy center, not because it gives you special access to the divine, but because in your stillness you hear what might be heard anywhere.

I think of my home ground as a series of nested rings, with house and family and marriage at the center, surrounded by the wider and wider hoops of neighborhood and community, the bioregion within walking distance of my door, the wooded and rocky hills of southern Indiana, the watershed of the Ohio Valley, and so on outward—and inward—to the ultimate source.

The longing to become an inhabitant rather than a drifter sets me against the current of my culture, which nudges everyone into motion. Newton taught us that a body at rest tends to stay at rest, unless it is acted on by an outside force. We are acted on ceaselessly by outside forces—advertising, movies, magazines, speeches—and also by the inner force of biology. I am not immune to their pressure. Before settling in my present home, I lived in seven states and two countries, tugged from place to place in childhood by my father's work and in early adulthood by my own. This itinerant life is so common among the people I know that I have been slow to conceive of an alternative. Only by knocking against the golden calf of mobility, which looms so large and shines so brightly, have I come to realize that it is hollow. Like all idols, it distracts us from what is truly divine.

I am encouraged by the words of a Crow elder, quoted by Gary Snyder in *The Practice of the Wild*: "You know, I think if people stay somewhere long enough—even white people—the spirits will begin to speak to them. It's the power of the spirits coming up from the land. The spirits and the old powers aren't lost, they just need people to be around long enough and the spirits will begin to influence them."

As I write this, I hear the snarl of earth movers and chain saws a mile away destroying a farm to make way for another shopping strip. I would rather hear a tornado, whose damage can be undone. The elderly woman who owned the farm had it listed in the National Register, then willed it to her daughters on condition they preserve it. After her death, the daughters, who live out of state, had the will broken, so the land could be turned over to the chain saws and earth movers. The machines work around the clock. Their noise wakes me at midnight, at three in the morning, at dawn. The roaring abrades my dreams. The sound is a reminder that we are living in the midst of a holocaust. I do not use the word lightly. The earth is being pillaged, and every one of us, willingly or grudgingly, is taking part. We ask how sensible, educated, supposedly moral people could have tolerated slavery or the slaughter of Jews. Similar questions will be asked about us by our descendants, to whom we bequeath an impoverished planet. They will demand to know how we could have been party to such waste and ruin.

What does it mean to be alive in an era when the earth is being devoured, and in a country that has set the pattern for that devouring? What are we called to do? I think we are called to the work of healing, both inner and outer: healing of the mind through a change in consciousness, healing of the earth through a change in our lives. We can begin that work by learning how to inhabit a place.

"The man who is often thinking that it is better to be somewhere else than where he is excommunicates himself," we are cautioned by Thoreau, that notorious stay-at-home. The metaphor is religious: To withhold yourself from where you are is to be cut off from communion with the source. It has taken me half a lifetime of searching to realize that the likeliest path to the ultimate ground leads through my local ground. I mean the land itself, with its creeks and rivers, its weather, seasons, stone outcroppings, and all the plants and animals that share it. I cannot have a spiritual center without having a geographical one; I cannot live a grounded life without being grounded in a *place*.

In belonging to a landscape, one feels a rightness, an at-homeness, a knitting of self and world. This condition of clarity and focus, this being fully present, is akin to what the Buddhists call mindfulness, what Christian contemplatives refer to as recollection, what Quakers call centering down. I am suspicious of any philosophy that would separate this-worldly from other-worldly commitment. There is only one world, and we participate in it here and now, in our flesh and our place.

INTERPRETATIONS

1. How effective is it that Sanders begins his essay with the story of the Millers? Do you share his admiration for their choosing to rebuild their house after each tornado? Why or why not?

2. Review paragraph 6. How do you interpret "national mythology"? To what extent do you agree that Americans are seduced by the virtues of moving on?

3. Sanders believes that people who remain in one place are more likely to be involved in community service. To what extent do you agree? Do you share his commitment to civil responsibility? Cite reasons for your answer.

CORRESPONDENCES

1. Imagine a conversation between Rodriguez and Sanders on the subject of home. What points are they likely to disagree on? What experiences would you bring to the discussion?

2. Review Lawrence's perspective on place. What is your response? How does it apply to Sanders's essay?

APPLICATIONS

1. Are you someone who likes to be on the move or who prefers to stay in one place? As you contemplate the future, are you likely to change your opinion? Depending on your stand on this issue, what factors would you consider in deciding to stay or move? Write a brief essay on the subject.

2. Freewrite on your concept of home. Focus on the images and associations that the word evokes. Then write an essay defining what home means to you.

3. Discuss with your group Sanders's thesis that "Committing yourself to a place does not guarantee that you will become wise, but neither does it guarantee that you will become parochial." Frame your discussion by defining "wise" and "parochial" and make a summary of your findings.

4. Being in motion or staying still—these are the choices explored by Sanders in his essay. Walk around a room briskly for five minutes. Then sit still for five minutes. Write down your thoughts pertaining to what you perceive about each of these five-minute sessions. How do your responses relate to what Sanders has written about in his piece?

One of These Days

GABRIEL GARCÍA MÁRQUEZ

Gabriel García Márquez (b. 1928) was born in Aracataca, Colombia and raised by grandparents who told him many fables and fairy tales. García Márquez dropped out of law school to pursue a career in journalism, and was a regular contributor to El Espectador *and other newspapers before dedicating himself to writing fiction full time. His first book* Leaf Storm and Other Stories, *was published in 1955.* One Hundred Years of Solitude, *García Márquez's most successful and popular novel, was written in 1967. García Márquez's other major literary works include:* Chronicle of a Death Foretold *(1981),* Love in the Time of Cholera *(1988),* The General in His Labyrinth *(1990),* Of Love and Other Demons *(1994), and* News of a Kidnapping *(1996). García Márquez's memoir,* Living to Tell the Tale, *was published in the United States in fall 2003. Before reading Márquez's story, record in your journal your thoughts on the concept of revenge.*

Márquez's Colombia, which is about the size of California and Texas, is located in northwestern South America and bordered by Panama, Venezuela, Brazil, Peru, and Ecuador. Like many South American countries, Colombia has a long history of violence and political upheaval. A brutal civil war began in 1899 and lasted until 1902. The period 1946–1958 is known as La Violencia, because hundreds of thousands of lives were lost due to insurrection and banditry. The emergence of the infamous guerilla Marxist groups like the National Liberation Army (ELN) and the Revolutionary Armed Forces of Colombia (FARC) in the 1960s and 1970s drove the country further into violence and instability. During the 1970s and 1980s Colombia was known around the world for its international drug cartels. Colombia's long history of political and social instability accounts for the millions of natives who have fled in recent years. Alvaro Uribe, who won the presidential election of 2002, has been working with the United States to implement an aggressive campaign against Colombia's drug trade.

MONDAY DAWNED WARM and rainless. Aurelio Escovar, a dentist without a degree, and a very early riser, opened his office at six. He took some false teeth, still mounted in their plaster mold, out of the glass case and put on the table a fistful of instruments which he arranged in size order, as if they were on display. He wore a collarless striped shirt, closed at the neck with a golden stud, and pants held up by suspenders. He was erect and skinny, with a look that rarely corresponded to the situation, the way deaf people have of looking.

When he had things arranged on the table, he pulled the drill toward the dental chair and sat down to polish the false teeth. He seemed not to be thinking about what he was doing, but worked steadily, pumping the drill with his feet, even when he didn't need it.

After eight he stopped for a while to look at the sky through the window, and he saw two pensive buzzards who were drying themselves in the sun on the ridgepole of the house next door. He went on working with the idea that before lunch it would rain again. The shrill voice of his eleven-year-old son interrupted his concentration.

"Papá."

"What?"

"The Mayor wants to know if you'll pull his tooth."

"Tell him I'm not here."

He was polishing a gold tooth. He held it at arm's length and examined it with his eyes half closed. His son shouted again from the little waiting room.

"He says you are, too, because he can hear you."

The dentist kept examining the tooth. Only when he had put it on the table with the finished work did he say:

"So much the better."

He operated the drill again. He took several pieces of a bridge out of a cardboard box where he kept the things he still had to do and began to polish the gold.

"Papá."

"What?"

He still hadn't changed his expression.

"He says if you don't take out his tooth, he'll shoot you."

Without hurrying, with an extremely tranquil movement, he stopped pedaling the drill, pushed it away from the chair, and pulled the lower drawer of the table all the way out. There was a revolver. "O.K.," he said. "Tell him to come and shoot me."

He rolled the chair over opposite the door, his hand resting on the edge of the drawer. The Mayor appeared at the door. He had shaved the left side of his face, but the other side, swollen and in pain, had a five-day-old beard. The dentist saw many nights of desperation in his dull eyes. He closed the drawer with his fingertips and said softly:

"Sit down."

"Good morning," said the Mayor.

"Morning," said the dentist.

While the instruments were boiling, the Mayor leaned his skull on the headrest of the chair and felt better. His breath was icy. It was a poor office: an old wooden chair, the pedal drill, a glass case with ceramic bottles. Opposite the chair was a window with a shoulder-high cloth curtain. When he felt the dentist approach, the Mayor braced his heels and opened his mouth.

Aurelio Escovar turned his head toward the light. After inspecting the infected tooth, he closed the Mayor's jaw with a cautious pressure of his fingers.

"It has to be without anesthesia," he said.

"Why?"

"Because you have an abscess."

The Mayor looked him in the eye. "All right," he said, and tried to smile. The dentist did not return the smile. He brought the basin of sterilized instruments to the worktable and took them out of the water with a pair of cold tweezers, still without hurrying. Then he pushed the spittoon with the tip of his shoe, and went to wash his hands in the washbasin. He did all this without looking at the Mayor. But the Mayor didn't take his eyes off him.

It was a lower wisdom tooth. The dentist spread his feet and grasped the tooth with the hot forceps. The Mayor seized the arms of the chair, braced his feet with all his strength, and felt an icy void in his kidneys, but didn't make a sound. The dentist moved only his wrist. Without rancor, rather with a bitter tenderness, he said:

"Now you'll pay for our twenty dead men."

The Mayor felt the crunch of bones in his jaw, and his eyes filled with tears. But he didn't breathe until he felt the tooth come out. Then he saw it through his tears. It seemed so foreign to his pain that he failed to understand his torture of the five previous nights.

Bent over the spittoon, sweating, panting, he unbuttoned his tunic and reached for the handkerchief in his pants pocket. The dentist gave him a clean cloth.

"Dry your tears," he said.

The Mayor did. He was trembling. While the dentist washed his hands, he saw the crumbling ceiling and a dusty spider web with spider's eggs and dead insects. The dentist returned, drying his hands. "Go to bed," he said, "and gargle with salt water." The Mayor stood up, said goodbye with a casual military salute, and walked toward the door, stretching his legs, without buttoning up his tunic.

"Send the bill," he said.

"To you or the town?"

The Mayor didn't look at him. He closed the door and said through the screen:

"It's the same damn thing."

Translated by J. S. Bernstein

INTERPRETATIONS

1. What kind of man do you think Aurelio Escovar is? What specific details can you find to support your view?

2. Aurelio Escovar chooses to remove the Mayor's tooth without using anesthetic. Why does he do this? Do you believe him? Why or why not?

3. Note the dialogue between Aurelio Escovar and his son (see paragraphs 4 through 16). What do you learn about the dentist from these paragraphs? How does this information prepare you for what comes next in the story?

4. Why does the dentist open the drawer in paragraph 17? What do you think he intends to do with the object he finds inside? Explain your reasoning fully.

5. In paragraph 29, the dentist says, "Now you'll pay for our twenty dead men." Why did he choose to utter this statement exactly at this time? What does this statement add to your understanding of the relationship between the dentist and the mayor? How might it help explain the dentist's behavior earlier in the story?

CORRESPONDENCES

1. Both Joseph Steffan and Aurelio Escovar are men concerned with honor. How is honor defined and lived up to in "Honor Bound"? What is the point of honor in "One of These Days"? To what extent are Steffan and Escobar similar to and/or different from each other in the choices they make and the actions they perform in the name of honor?

2. How do Rodriguez and García Márquez use setting (time, place, atmosphere) in their respective works? How does setting help the authors get their points across? How does their use of setting affect a reader's responses to the works?

APPLICATIONS

1. What do you think is the primary theme of the story "One of These Days"? Write an essay that explains this idea and that supports it with carefully presented examples from the text.

2. How do you feel when you go to the dentist? How do your experiences compare with those depicted in paragraphs 22–33? What writing techniques does Márquez use to capture this moment?

Write a narrative essay that tells the story of a meaningful dental visit. Try to emulate Márquez in making your experience come alive to a reader!

3. Oftentimes, writers *tell* about an experience or situation by explaining and analyzing carefully. It is also possible to achieve the same purpose by *showing* what has occurred or is occurring. Generally, *showing*, rather than *telling*, will help you to gain and retain a reader's interest, thereby making this descriptive technique quite effective. For example, what specific details do you notice in "One of These Days"? Why do you think that Márquez has chosen to include them?

   Review an essay that you have written. Where might you include specific details to *show* a reader what you mean? What exact details will accomplish the goal of showing rather than telling?

4. How does Márquez use *setting* to bring readers into the world he has created in the story "One of These Days"? Which specific details stick out to give you a sense of *time, place*, and *atmosphere*?

   Now, write a story that has as its first sentence: "_____ rode into the _____ on horseback." Supply the name of a person in the first blank and a type of place (e.g., mansion, apartment building, shack, log cabin, hunting lodge) in the second. Continue to write! As you work, pay particular attention to setting. Notice how elements of your first sentence help you to establish setting. Try to apply some of the techniques you observe Márquez using to bring *your* readers into *your* world!

Flight by Night

YAMIT NASSIRI

Yamit Nassiri (b. 1976) was born in Israel and moved to New York City with her American husband in 2000. She graduated from Queensborough College in January 2004 and is currently enrolled in the Linguistic Degree program at Queens College (CUNY). Record in your journal your memory of your "first flight" and your responses to this experience.

THE WEDDING RING on my left ring finger carries an essential part of my life behind it. Not only does it symbolize a change in my personal status, but the significant choices I have made. Every time the sheen of the white-gold metal reflects towards my eye, or when my thumb naturally plays with it, I recall my wedding night underneath the huppah (canopy). I remember the decisive moment when I said "I do" to my husband who was standing to my left, looking into my eyes with such excitement and adoration. He understood perfectly that my part of the vow "I do," meant that I agreed to leave my family and my country in order to become his wife.

It was a hot June night and everyone's face was covered with sweat. I noticed the tears on my mother's cheeks, but never dared to ask her why, so that she would not get the chance to say the unnecessary words: "I miss you already," or "I need you." How could I possibly deal with that then? It would have hurt too much. But . . . maybe it was only my imagination. Mothers always cry on their children's wedding day. Certainly my mother cried out of happiness and gratitude to God for sending her daughter a sweet, loving and caring man. She prayed all her life for that to happen, and indeed, her wish was granted.

As a little girl, I remember my mom saying that "no matter what happens to you, it is determined in advance by your fate," she explained, "but in a way, you can control your destiny by making your own decisions and making the choice to act upon them." Her philosophy regarding fate and destiny was not so clear to me, until I met Maurice and decided to marry him. To do so, I had to desert my family, my homeland, and move to the United States. Although I liked the idea of acquiring more freedom, it did not make my decision easier.

After my parents' divorce, I became an important figure at home, fulfilling the roles of mother and father. While my mother was working hard, I was taking care of the household, working outside to help pay the bills, and basically raising my sister (who is nine years younger than me). It hurt me that I could not afford college or even a driver's license, while my friends easily could. I was not able to discover myself or explore my abilities or talents. As a result, I grew resentful and felt deprived of opportunities for personal growth.

By accepting Maurice's proposal, I was letting go of my duties and responsibilities to my family. Part of me felt guilty. Yet the guilt did not make me give up my love. Had I done so, I would have hated myself. The uncertainty was my main concern, since I did not know what to expect. I was leaving the familiar behind and heading towards a new beginning.

My first year in New York City was difficult to deal with. I was terrified by the new environment, the unfamiliar faces, language, and customs. Unlike Israel, everything around me looked extremely big: buildings, roads, shopping malls, and streets. New York was a gigantic mountain compared to Israel, which was like a grain of sand. I was completely lost. Immigration laws made me wait to get my social security card, work permit, driver's license, and eventually my green card. I hated the jobs that paid the minimum salary and felt exploited, which filled me with bitterness. More than anything, I felt lonely. There was no one to confide in since all my friends lived in Israel.

My unhappiness affected my relationship with Maurice, and we argued more often. I cried a lot. Even small arguments made me cry. I accused him of tearing me away from my family and friends. He kept saying that it was only a matter of time and that I needed to be more patient. The idea of going back to Israel had crossed my mind a few times. Yet I wasn't ready to give in and let myself down. It would have been too easy.

Significant changes occurred in the following year and thereafter that shaped my identity and future goals. College contributed a lot. At first, I was worried about having difficulties with the language, and I was confused about choosing a major. But with strong will and determination I managed to set goals for myself and receive excellent results. The fact that English wasn't my first language required me to work harder than the other students (in class) in order to keep up. In my first semester I took ESL classes to improve my reading and writing skills. It was fulfilling to see myself advancing, and it was then that I got the idea of becoming an ESL teacher, with encouragement from my professor. I started taking advanced English classes and combined them with dance classes, since I have always loved to dance ballet, jazz, latin, and hip-hop. It was (and still is) a sort of relaxation and escape.

It was interesting also to meet so many people from different cultures and countries, since I felt less like a stranger. My social life improved significantly as well when I made good friends in school, which also contributed to my education. Now that I had my own circle of friends, I craved the independence, the space that I had in Israel. So I told Maurice that once a week I needed to spend some time with my girlfriends, because that would give me time to breathe. At first, he wasn't thrilled about the idea of "girls' night out," but gradually he understood its importance. He realized that it was my way of surviving in this new country, and furthermore, it improved our relationship.

Consciously or unconsciously, I became part of my new environment. Today, after four years, the process of Americanization continues. I speak the language, watch American movies, eat American food, wear American clothes, and "hang out" with American friends. Everyday I absorb more information about the country and the people, about the history, customs, and values. Yet accepting American values has not made me forget my own customs and traditions. I feel that my heart is closer to my country today, and as a result, I care more about observing Jewish holidays. I constantly think about my mom in Israel, and wherever I go I carry with me the small Bible she gave me ten years ago, which gives me strength.

Being with Maurice, I have a lot more opportunities. I am able to grow and find new dimensions in myself, which I wasn't able to do when living with my mom. Besides his love and affection, Maurice makes me feel confident and secure, which I cherish. My achievements in college make me believe in myself more, and I am less afraid of challenges. Sometimes I try to imagine what is possible and then hope to surpass the boundaries. Doing the things I want to do gives me peace of mind, so that I am better to myself and to the people around me. Despite all the initial obstacles, I am now able to look at my ring with such delight.

INTERPRETATIONS

1. What symbol does Nassiri use to unify her essay? How does it also enhance theme?

2. Characterize Nassiri's mother. How has her philosophy of fate and destiny affected the writer?

3. Nassiri has to negotiate between her responsibilities to her mother and her husband. What strategies does she use to accomplish this while creating space for herself?

4. To what extent has the process of assimilation affected her attitude toward the customs and traditions of her homeland? Explain.

5. Characterize Maurice. How does he contribute to her "new self"?

CORRESPONDENCES

1. Review Emerson's perspective and discuss its relevance to Nassiri's essay. What evidence is there of experimentation?
2. Review Lawrence's perspective and discuss its application to Nassiri's essay. What new things did she discover about herself in her new country?

APPLICATIONS

1. To what extent is pain an element of choice? What role does emotion play in making choices? Write an essay on a choice that you made involving pain—your own or others.
2. Imagine yourself in Nassiri's situation. Would you have made a different choice? Explain. Compare your responses to those of your group and summarize your responses.
3. Write an essay analyzing the reasons for a choice you would make between the security of the familiar (job, vocation, person) and taking a risk involving the unknown. What factors would influence your choice?

The Knowing Eye

Thomas Lee

READING IMAGES

1. The first photo is an archetypical image representing *choice*. Why do you agree or disagree with this statement?
2. What are some of the choices that may be interpreted from each of these photographs?
3. Which photograph are you able to relate to most? Be sure to explain how the *tone* of each photograph influences your response.

Tamar Michal Friedner

MAKING CONNECTIONS

1. Compare the photograph of the person in the doorway with the image of the partial faces in Chapter 3 (page 137). How do these representations seem similar or different?

2. How would you characterize the choices written about in this chapter's essays? Which of these photographs best characterizes the nature of choice that you have read about?

WORDS AND IMAGES

1. What is the person standing in the doorway thinking? Make a drawing of what you perceive to be this individual's thoughts. Write a journal entry that describes how you came to your conclusion and the process you went through to create your drawing.

Bianca Henriquez

2. In our lives we are always making decisions. Write an essay about
    a decision that you had to make. As you think about your topic, let
    your responses to the photographs guide you. For example, will
    you write about a decision that you made privately or one that
    was made in the company of others?

Additional Writing Topics

1. Review the Frost perspective. What does it imply about the nature of choice? Under what circumstances might you make a similar choice? In an essay, analyze your reasons for a choice you would make to take "the road less traveled."

2. View the 1983 movie *El Norte* and/or review the selections by Rodriguez and Pérez, and write an analysis of the cost of being a migrant worker or illegal alien in the United States.

3. Although in many ways the Holocaust was "unthinkable," Wehle is asking her readers to think about it. What are some of the conclusions thinking might force on one who reads about the Holocaust?

4. Each chapter in this textbook begins with a myth, a folktale, or a story that teaches a lesson. Collaborate with members of your group on composing a moralistic tale that, like "The Wise Daughter," teaches a moral lesson on choices.

5. To what extent are the selections by Rodriguez, Mabry, and Pérez concerned with the "American Dream"? How do their dreams compare with yours?

6. Is culture, like nature, a limitation on freedom of choice, or does it allow more free play of individual wisdom and imagination? Do we increase our own choices to the degree that we free ourselves from culture? Limit your discussion to any three selections in this chapter.

7. What place do you most associate with "coming home"? Write an essay in which you describe the physical space as well as the emotions it evokes. You will be combining narration and description, so choose sensory and sensual details that will enable your reader to both visualize the space and experience it emotionally.

8. Wehle and Steffan discuss the importance of individual integrity. Write an essay discussing your views on integrity and its impact on choices you have made.

9. Imagine yourself confronting a choice that involves taking a risk. Write an essay analyzing the reasons for the choices you would make between the security of the familiar (job, vocation, person), and taking a risk involving the unknown. What factors would influence your choice?

CHAPTER

9

Popular Culture

IN PREVIOUS CHAPTERS WE EXPLORED the degree to which our identities, relationships, education, and careers are influenced by the many people in our private and public worlds. In this chapter we will focus on another instrument for shaping our thoughts and behavior: popular culture. Traditionally, as we have seen, cultures are social. They inculcate human achievements, particularly those that serve the good of the people. The world of culture is a world in which values are realized and conserved. What then is popular culture? "Popular" may be defined as "in relation to the general public, the majority," and the culture it encompasses includes media images of contemporary life and culture. Popular culture is dynamic, transitory, and an initiator of change. Through sophisticated technology it introduces us to worlds far from our local communities, enlarging our perspectives of cultural realities at home and abroad. Popular culture also creates a commonality that cuts across traditional barriers of geography, language, education, economics, ethnicity, and class.

The essays in this chapter reflect aspects of popular culture you encounter daily in magazines, television, films, and music, and when you use a cell phone or computer. As you analyze each medium individually and in your groups, you will be asked to think critically about issues in contemporary culture and to develop an awareness of the extent to which the medium not only influences our ideas but often directs our daily actions, including how to "talk," what music to listen to, films to see, television programs to watch, and games to play.

Popular culture is manifested in the people responsible for creating it and the spaces where it is created. Two places that embody popular culture are the mall and the school. Robyn Meredith examines the implications of the decision by the owners of Minnesota's Mall of

America to place a curfew on teenagers on weekend nights. "Arnie's Test Day," by Barry Peters, is a story for anyone who has either gone through high school or knows anyone who has ;-). (Extra points for anyone who correctly identifies Peters's secret organizational strategy!)

The influences of film and television are all-pervasive. No consideration of the forces that have helped shape the history of the century could ignore the impact of the media. From the birth of film, movies have—among other things—documented events, and informed our ideas of romantic love, physical beauty, heroism, and personal and national identity. Culturally, they have exposed us not only to subcultures and countercultures within the United States but throughout the world.

Film is the focus of two essays in this chapter. In "I wouldn't have nothing if I didn't have you," Martin Kutnowski writes about the themes present in the film, *Monsters, Inc.* and their significance to him as a parent. Stephen King is himself no stranger to the creation of monsters and the manufacture of scream. In "Why We Crave Horror Movies" he discusses just that. As King explains, the audiences captivated by horror films represent all of us to a degree, as we must "keep the gators fed."

Today, new technologies compete for our attention, in our homes, at school, and in the workplace. Cell phones and computers have made significant changes to the way we work and play. In "The Pleasures of the Text," Charles McGrath explores the world of text messaging, whose homophones, emoticons, and acronyms have enabled us to live and love through a cell phone keypad. In direct competition with television and movies for our leisure time, the personal computer has made possible a new venue for entertainment: the video game. John Misak, in his essay "Is That Video Game Programming You?" explores videogaming and videogamers. Questions of game content and control are central to this new medium.

Perhaps the aspect of popular culture that has most influenced the values of the present generation is music. Tom Lee, in "A Timeless Culture," initially addresses the concept of popular culture and then extends his analysis to consider what transforms a popular work into a "classic." James Geasor ("Whatever Happened to Rock 'n' Roll?") and Todd Craig (". . . well, if you can't hold the torch . . . then why pass it . . .?") both work with this second idea: Geasor's focus is on rock and roll music and Craig centers his attention on hip-hop. These three essays work together, and we have treated them as a mini-unit. You will find the Correspondence questions for all three readings at the end of Craig's essay.

In sum, the icons and images of popular culture pervade all aspects of contemporary culture, nationally and globally. Critical analyses of the texts in this chapter should provide catalysts for your evaluation of the issues they address, as well as their impact on your life.

Perspectives

It is a misunderstanding of the American retail store to think we go there necessarily to buy. Some of us shop. There's a difference. Shopping has many purposes, the least interesting of which is to acquire new articles. We shop to practice decisionmaking. We shop to be useful and productive members of our class and society. We shop to remind ourselves how much is available to us. We shop to remind ourselves how much is to be striven for. We shop to assert our superiority to the material objects that spread themselves before us.

—Phyllis Rose

Two out of every three adults in the United States say they fidget, fuss, take furtive glances in windows and mirrors, and study other people's reaction to the way they look. It is not overstating it to report that a solid majority of the American people are close to being obsessed with their physical appearance.

—Louis Harris

Hip-hop has reached well beyond its urban roots to diverse national dimensions and has been an integral part of American culture for almost 30 years.

—Brent D. Glass

Resigning one's self to living off the table scraps of the American Century is what twentystuff culture is all about. It's about recycling anger into irony, pain into poses.

—Walter Kirn

The mall is a common experience for the majority of all youth: they have probably been going there all their lives.

—William Severini Kowinski

The image is freedom, words are prison.

—Jean Luc Godard

The success of modern advertising, its penetration into every corner of American life, reflects a culture that has itself chosen illusion over reality.

—Jack Solomon

453

Movies are still the most seductive and powerful of artistic mediums, manipulating us with ease by a powerful combination of sound and image.

—Jessica Hagendorn

Piercing is a return to flesh as fashion—and a revitalized rite of passage.

—D. James Romero

All objects, all phases of culture are alive. They have voices. They speak of their history and interrelatedness. And they are talking at once.

—Camille Paglia

I am my body.

—Marge Piercy

In America, the photographer is not simply the person who records the past but the one who invents it.

—Susan Sontag

It is easier to understand a nation by listening to its music than by learning its language.

—Anonymous

What's swinging in words? If a guy makes you tap your foot and if you feel it down your back, you don't have to ask anybody if that's good music or not. You can always feel it.

—Miles Davis

Along with the idea of romantic love, she was introduced to another— physical beauty. Probably the most destructive ideas in the history of human thought. Both originated in envy, thrived in insecurity, and ended in disillusion. In equating physical beauty with virtue, she stripped her mind, bound it, and collected self-contempt by the heap. She forgot lust and simple caring for. She regarded love as possessive mating, and romance as the goal of the spirit. It would be for her a well-spring from which she would draw the most destructive emotions, deceiving the lover and seeking to imprison the beloved, curtailing freedom in every way.

—Toni Morrison

The truest expression of a people is in its dances and its music. Bodies never lie.

—Agnes de Mille

Movies are not a good source of role models or heroes. It appears that the majority of today's films focus on violence and crime. Since we live in a nation where crime is the cause of many social problems that exist, I do not think that portraying criminals and violent characters as heroes is good for children. By doing this, the film industry tells the audience that violent people are admirable and that their values should be embraced. I feel there should be more positive role models in movies and on television so that young people can actually have someone to look up to who represents positive values.

—*Celeste Armenti*

If Poe were alive, he would not have to invent horror; horror would invent him.

—*Richard Wright*

APPLICATIONS

1. Review the perspectives on movies and discuss each with your group. On what issues did you agree and disagree?

2. The perspectives of Harris and Morrison focus on the preoccupation with physical beauty in contemporary American culture. To what extent do you and your group members disagree with their points of view? Compose three perspectives of your own on the topic.

3. Is piercing as important as clothing in constructing identity? Does it also make a statement about individuality or is it a reflection of conformity to current fashion trends? Discuss these issues in a short essay.

The Pleasures of the Text

CHARLES MCGRATH

Charles McGrath (b. 1947 in Boston, Massachusetts) was deputy editor of The New Yorker *from 1974 to 1997, when he became book review editor for* The New York Times. *In the following essay you will see how he feels about one type of concision or abbreviation. When he took the book review job, McGrath wrote that wanted less concise reviews. "My main notion is that the reviews themselves need to be informative and entertaining. I'm impatient with the kind of review in which one expert picks at another writer's work without giving the reader the big picture of what the book is about. And I want reviews that stand on their own." He is currently a writer at large for* The Times, *appearing frequently in the* New York Times Magazine, *in which the following essay was published in January, 2006. McGrath received a B.A. (summa cum laude) from Yale in 1968. He is the editor of* Books of the Century: A Hundred Years of Authors, Ideas and Literature *(1998), and (with David McCormick) of* The Ultimate Golf Book: A History and a Celebration of the World's Greatest Game *(2002). Does McGrath practice what he preaches in this selection?*

THERE USED TO BE AN AD ON SUBWAY CARS, next to the ones for bail bonds-men and hemorrhoid creams, that said: "if u cn rd ths u cn gt a gd job & mo pa." The ad was promoting a kind of stenography training that is now extinct, presumably. Who uses stenographers anymore? But the notion that there might be value in easily understood shorthand has proved to be prescient. If u cn rd these days, and, just as important, if your thumbs are nimble enough so that u cn als snd, you can conduct your entire emotional life just by transmitting and receiving messages on the screen of your cellphone. You can flirt there, arrange a date, break up and—in Malaysia at least—even get a divorce.

Shorthand contractions, along with letter-number homophones ("gr8" and "2moro," for example), emoticons (like the tiresome colon-and-parenthesis smiley face) and acronyms (like the ubiquitous "lol," for "laughing out loud"), constitute the language of text-messaging—or txt msg, to use the term that txt msgrs prefer. Text-messaging is a refine-ment of computer instant-messaging, which came into vogue five or six years ago. But because the typical cellphone screen can accommodate no more than 160 characters, and because the phone touchpad is far less versatile than the computer keyboard, text-messaging puts an even greater premium on concision. Here, for example, is a text-message version of "Paradise Lost" disseminated by some scholars in England: "Devl kikd outa hevn coz jelus of jesus&strts war. pd'off wiv god so corupts man (md by god) wiv apel. devi stays serpnt 4hole life&man ruind. Woe un2mnkind."

As such messages go, that one is fairly straightforward and unadorned. There is also an entire code book of acronyms and abbreviations, ranging from CWOT (complete waste of time) to DLTBBB (don't let the bedbugs bite). And emoticonography has progressed way beyond the smiley-face stage, and now includes hieroglyphics to indicate drooling, for example (:-) . . .), as well as secrecy (:X), Hitler (/.#( ) and the rose (@$);-). Keep these in mind; we'll need them later.

As with any language, efficiency isn't everything. There's also the issue of style. Among inventive users, and younger ones especially, text-messaging has taken on many of the characteristics of hip-hop, with so much of which it conveniently overlaps—in the substitution of "z" for "s," for example, "a," for "er" and "d" for "th." Like hip-hop, text-messaging is what the scholars call "performative"; it's writing that aspires to the condition of speech. And sometimes when it makes abundant use of emoticons, it strives not for clarity so much as a kind of rebus-like cleverness, in which showing off is part of the point. A text-message version of "Paradise Lost"—or of the prologue, anyway—that tries for a little more shnizzle might go like this: "Sing hvnly mewz dat on d :X mtntp inspyrd dat shephrd hu 1st tot d chozn seed in d begnin hw d hvn n erth @$);- outa chaos."

Not that there is much call for Miltonic messaging these days. To use the scholarly jargon again, text-messaging is "lateral" rather than "penetrative," and the medium encourages blandness and even mindlessness. On the Internet there are several Web sites that function as virtual Hallmark stores and offer ready-made text messages of breathtaking banality. There are even ready-made Dear John letters, enabling you to dump someone without actually speaking to him or her. Far from being considered rude, in Britain this has proved to be a particularly popular way of ending a relationship—a little more thoughtful than leaving an e-mail message but not nearly as messy as breaking up in person—and it's also catching on over here.

Compared with the rest of the world, Americans are actually laggards when it comes to text-messaging. This is partly for technical reasons. Because we don't have a single, national phone company, there are several competing and incompatible wireless technologies in use, and at the same time actual voice calls are far cheaper here than in most places, so there is less incentive for texting. But in many developing countries, mobile-phone technology has so far outstripped land-line availability that cellphones are the preferred, and sometimes the only, means of communication, and text messages are cheaper than voice ones. The most avid text-messagers are clustered in Southeast Asia, particularly in Singapore and the Philippines.

There are also cultural reasons for the spread of text-messaging elsewhere. The Chinese language is particularly well-suited to the telephone keypad, because in Mandarin the names of the numbers are also close to the sounds of certain words; to say "I love you," for example, all you have to do is press 520. (For "drop dead," it's 748.) In China, moreover, many people believe that to leave voice mail is rude, and it's a loss of face to make a call to someone important and have it answered by an underling. Text messages preserve everyone's dignity by eliminating the human voice.

This may be the universal attraction of text-messaging, in fact: it's a kind of avoidance mechanism that preserves the feeling of communication—the immediacy—without, for the most part, the burden of actual intimacy or substance. The great majority of text messages are of the "Hey, how are you, whassup?" variety, and they're sent sometimes when messenger and recipient are within speaking distance of each other—across classrooms, say, or from one row of a stadium to another. They're little electronic waves and nods that, just like real waves and nods, aren't meant to do much more than establish a connection—or disconnection, as the case may be—without getting into specifics.

"We're all wired together" is the collective message, and we'll signal again in a couple of minutes, not to say anything, probably, but just to make sure the lines are still working. The most depressing thing about the communications revolution is that when at last we have succeeded in making it possible for anyone to reach anyone else anywhere and at any time, it turns out that we really don't have much we want to say.

INTERPRETATIONS

1. According to McGrath, why do people use text messaging? Where does he state these reasons?

2. What conclusion does McGrath come to regarding text messaging? Explain why you agree or disagree with these ideas.

3. How does this essay's title, "The Pleasures of the Text," represent McGrath's viewpoint? How does the title itself represent the writer's tone?

CORRESPONDENCES

1. Review some of the literacy narratives presented previously (Alexie, page 71; Madera, page 76; Marshall, page 196; Cremona, page 206; Naylor, page 379; Woo, page 383). Which of these narratives, in your opinion, is most clearly allied with, or anticipates, text messaging? What type of literacy is recalled by text messaging (see page 000)? Explain your answers.

2. What do you think McGrath would say about interactive ("live") videogame play, where gamers communicate electronically with others as they play? How might McGrath address the form and content of the ongoing conversations?

3. How is text messaging, as described by McGrath, an expression of popular culture? What specific arguments does Tom Lee ("A Timeless Culture") make that best apply to text messaging?

APPLICATIONS

1. Write a text message that you would send to a friend. Now write this message in formal English, perhaps embellishing the original message. Which version do you think best conveys your meaning to your audience? Explain your answer fully in an essay that makes reference to McGrath's.

2. "If u cn rd this," check out the following Web sites:

   http://www.snopes.com/language/apocryph/cambridge.asp

   http://www.bisso.com/ujg_archives/000224.html

   http://www.computeruser.com/resources/dictionary/
      emoticons.html

   http://www.environmental-studies.de/SIM-Card/SMS/
      SMS-glossary/sms-glossary.html

2a. What have you learned about literacy from these Web sites? Write down your own definition of literacy. How does your definition compare with one that you find in the dictionary?

2b. What have you learned about a human being's ability to read? How do these ideas inform your understanding of literacy? Provide specific examples from the Web sites above in your analysis essay.

3. Write (or translate) a poem or song into the language of text-messaging. Add emoticons to represent your reactions to the work in appropriate places.

Now, share your poem, including the in-text responses, with your group. How well were your groupmates able to understand your poem? Did they have reactions similar to yours in the same places as you?

Discuss the poems submitted by all members of your group. What conclusions have you come to regarding translating in general?

Big Mall's Curfew Raises Questions of Rights and Bias

ROBYN MEREDITH

Robyn Meredith writes about Asian business for Forbes *and* Forbes Global *magazine. She was the Detroit correspondent for* The New York Times *and a business reporter for* USA Today. *This article was originally published in the September 4, 1996* New York Times. *Brainstorm on your associations with malls. Is there a particular age group to which they appeal?*

BLOOMINGTON, MINN., AUG. 29—Marcus D. Wilson, eighteen, has been coming to the Mall of America here once or twice a week since it opened four years ago. He buys tapes, plays video games and sees his friends, especially his girlfriend.

But starting September 20, his habits will be disrupted by the mall's new chaperon policy. People under 16—including his 15-year-old girlfriend, Stephanie E. Jones—will be barred from the mall on Friday and Saturday nights unless they bring a parent or other grownup over 21. Teenage shoppers who were interviewed recently said they would not be caught dead with their parents at the Mall of America, the biggest mall in the country and the coolest spot in town.

The Mall of America is one of the nation's first shopping centers to impose curfews on unchaperoned teenagers. Malls from New Jersey to California are watching the effort as they, too, struggle to control rowdy teenagers.

The new policy here touches on many serious social issues: safety, race relations, parental responsibility and civil liberties. Malls have always been magnets for teenagers, but rising levels of juvenile violence have put pressure on shopping centers to limit who walks in the door.

Although the rule means that his girlfriend will be excluded on Fridays and Saturdays after 6 P.M., Mr. Wilson favors the rules because he thinks they will make the mall safer. But Miss Jones, who works at a shoe store, said "If I can work in the mall, I know how to handle myself." But she added, "I understand what they're trying to get at."

Every weekend night, at least 2,000 teenagers gather at the Mall of America. On wintry Minnesota Saturday nights, 3,000 teenagers swarm

461

the shopping mall, disturbing other shoppers with chases, practical jokes and fistfights, said Teresa A. McFarland, a mall spokeswoman.

Still, Mr. Wilson called the policy "a little racist" because weekend nights are the only time large groups of black teenagers, like him, show up at the suburban mall, which is near the Minneapolis airport. Mall workers already tend to hand him a copy of the mall's rules for behavior as he walks in the door, not bothering to give copies to the white teenagers nearby, he said. Ms. McFarland bristled at the suggestion, saying the mall's policy was to hand all young people a copy of the rules.

That sentiment is one reason some local community groups are concerned about the mall's policy and how it will be enforced. Yusef Mgeni, president of the Minneapolis chapter of the Urban Coalition, a public policy research and advocacy group, said, "This policy has been drawn up in reaction to and in large part because of the large number of young people of color who congregate in the mall in the evening."

"The policy itself is neutral," said Mr. Mgeni (pronounced em-JANE-ey). "How they implement it will determine whether it is unfair."

Virgil H. Heatwole, a mall manager, denied that the policy was directed at children of color. "It is fair; it is across the board," he said. "We are not targeting any individual, any group, any ethnic group."

Under the policy, security officers posted at each of the mall's twenty-three entrances will ask unchaperoned youths to prove that they are at least 16 before letting them inside. Other workers will sweep the halls, ejecting those who are under 16.

Mr. Heatwole said he hoped the policy would result in children bringing their parents to the mall. "I think society itself, we need to look at where parents are today," he said.

The mall's policy is opposed by the American Civil Liberties Union. "It infringes on the rights of young people," said Chris Hansen, a senior staff counsel at the A.C.L.U. in Manhattan. "It ought to be the parents, not the mall or the government who decide whether unchaperoned children can come to the mall," he said.

"We don't object at all to the mall setting up rules of behavior," Mr. Hansen said. "But we do object to punishing the good kids for the behavior of kids that aren't behaving."

Federal courts have ruled in past cases that shopping malls are not considered public spaces and that First Amendment rights may be restricted inside them, Mr. Hansen said. But state courts are nearly evenly divided on the issue. New York holds that malls are private property, while California courts have ruled that shopping centers "now occupy the civic role that downtown used to," Mr. Hansen said.

Minnesota does not apply First Amendment principles to shopping malls, said Kathleen M. Milner, legal counsel for the Minnesota Civil

Liberties Union, part of the A.C.L.U. For that reason, her group does not plan to sue over the chaperon rules.

While many shopping centers draw customers from only their immediate communities, the Mall of America draws people of differing generations and cultures. Families from across the country, here on two-day shopping binges, mix with local teenagers, who include rebellious suburbanites with spiked hairdos as well as poorer children from nearby Minneapolis and St. Paul. It is an uneasy combination.

Of course, security concerns at the mall pale compared with those in cities like New York. "This is not like walking into the Port Authority at 3 o'clock in the morning," said Billy Ellis, a Manhattan native who manages the mall's Rainforest Cafe, where there has never been a drunk at the bar. Many people here leave their cars unlocked in the mall's parking lot, he said.

While the mall has more than 400 stores and is so big that its indoor amusement park sports a roller coaster and log ride, teenagers congregate on the weekends along the railings to the mall's four floors, where they can peer at one another. Parents are nowhere to be seen, and mall workers have found children as young as 12 caring for 2-year-old siblings as they wander the mall.

Young people and adults agree that the teenagers can be obnoxious. They race down the halls in groups, scattering shoppers in their paths. They use foul language when shouting to their friends two floors above. Some even drop food or spit over the railings, aiming at shoppers below.

Recently, the fun and games have taken an alarming turn. Security officers broke up a fight between two 15-year-old boys who were quarreling about a pair of red tennis shoes. One boy had lifted the other's feet off the ground as if he intended to throw him over the railing, which "could have killed him," Mr. Heatwole said.

Perhaps the worst incident came one Saturday in June. Nancy A. Bordeaux and her family came to the Mall of America from Portland, Oregon. They were eating hot dogs when a gang of Asian-American teenagers chased a group of black teenagers through a food court. One boy pointed a gun at her 16-year-old son, Felix, who is black, apparently mistaking him briefly for one of those being chased, Mrs. Bordeaux said.

Although no one was seriously hurt, "it was really pretty frightening," said Mrs. Bordeaux, who praised the mall's chaperon policy.

While the problems seem magnified here because of the mall's sheer size, they are common on a smaller scale at shopping centers around the country, mall managers and others in the industry said.

"It is a subject that was probably hardly ever discussed fifteen years ago, and now it is at the top of the agenda for a lot of management companies, and that reflects societal changes," said Mark J. Schoifet, a spokesman for the industry trade group, the International Council of Shopping Centers, based in New York.

"Malls are put in the position of being baby sitters," Mr. Schoifet said. "These are mall managers, not social workers."

The Mall of America said it had partly patterned its policy after a shopping center in Asheville, North Carolina, that three years ago began requiring teenagers to have chaperons on Saturday nights. Sunrise Mall in Corpus Christi, Texas, requires children under 14 to be accompanied by an adult at all times. But the mall's general manager, Brian K. Giffin, said the rule was enforced only when unaccompanied children caused trouble.

Few malls restricted teenagers' access, Mr. Schoifet said, because their spending power tops $90 billion a year. "Nobody in our business wants to alienate this group in any way," he said. "It is a quandary."

Malls around the country will watch to see if the Mall of America's approach works, and some might follow its example, he added.

Some stores at the Mall of America have had their business hurt by the teenage crowd. One is the Security Store, which sells personal security items on the first floor, near a stage where families, most of them white, gather by day to hear storytellers or children's songs.

But on Friday and Saturday nights, that part of the mall seems transformed, said the store's manager, Paul T. Barnes. One evening, as he stood outside his store, someone poured a chocolate shake on his head from the floor above.

On weekend nights, Mr. Barnes said, the crowds are younger. Thousands of teenagers swarm near his store, "seventy percent of them under the age of 20 and minority and wearing gang-related apparel," Mr. Barnes said. Many of his older customers are scared away. "A lot of people are not used to seeing large numbers of kids and large numbers of minority kids," he said.

Some young black shoppers said the new chaperon policy would only add to their sense that they were under added scrutiny at the Mall of America. Martino M. Landrum, 15, said. "Every time we go to a store, we've got the owner following us, and they let the white people alone." Mr. Landrum said he knew that black gang members came to the mall, but he said white skinheads did as well. He opposes the mall's policy and said it was aimed at blacks.

Most teenagers interviewed in the mall last week said they thought the policy was unfair because it would punish all young people, not just the ones who cause trouble.

Jackie M. Soucek, 14, one of three girls outside the mall waiting for a bus to her suburban home one night, said, "They just took away the best shopping days." She and her friends had already visited the mall twice that week, and they vowed never to be seen there with their parents.

INTERPRETATIONS

1. Meredith begins by interviewing people who frequent the mall. What is their attitude toward the decision of the mall owners to ban unescorted teenagers on weekend nights? What is your reaction?

2. Are you convinced that the curfew decision was not ethnically based? Why or why not?

3. Where do you stand on the issue of malls as private or public properties? What arguments on this issue do you find convincing?

4. What points regarding mall security does Meredith raise? Are the concerns legitimate in your view?

CORRESPONDENCES

1. Which side of the mall curfew debate would those people who are antigaming be more likely to support? Defend your opinion with examples from Meredith's and Misak's (page 467) essays.

2. Is Meredith's purpose to inform or is she also seeking to persuade her audience? How does the tone of her essay compare with that of McGrath?

APPLICATIONS

1. Speculate with your group as to why the mall is the hangout of choice for many teenagers. You might conduct interviews with several adolescents of both genders and use their responses as a basis for your discussion.

2. Visit your local mall and interview personnel including shop owners, shoppers, and security guards on their impressions of how teenagers affect life at the mall. Using their responses, write an essay analyzing the effects of their presence on the mall's social and economic environment.

3. Visit your local mall and jot down your visual and sensory impressions. What are its dominant colors? Is the space designed to stimulate social interactions? How do people use the space? What does their body language indicate about their responses to being there? Write an analysis of your findings.

4. In her essay, Meredith reports varied perspectives presented by several individuals. From the essay, select *one* person in favor of the curfew and *one* who is not. In the voice of *each* person you have chosen, write a letter to the president of the city council that either supports or does not support the mall restrictions.

Is That Video Game Programming You?

JOHN MISAK

John Misak (b. 1970) teaches English at Queensborough Community College and The New York Institute of Technology. He has written for several gaming magazines and is an editor at Gamesworld Network. Many of his articles have focused on the impact of games on gamers and society as a whole. He is the author of four mystery novels: Soft Case, Time Stand Still, All in a Row, *and also* Death Knell, *which will be released in 2007.*

THE GRAVEL UNDERFOOT crunches just a bit louder than you hoped, as you try to quietly position yourself to take out the enemy perched high on his watchpost. Crouched down alongside the barracks, you check your ammunition. With a sigh, you count four rounds for your silenced machine gun. Sure, you have over a hundred AK-47 rounds, but you might as well go and sound the security alarm instead of firing that thunderous weapon. You have to make those four rounds count. The guard seems content to stare off into space, unaware of your presence and your intention to stop his breathing permanently. A quick view in the binoculars confirms his exact position. A light breeze kicks up some dust and you use all of your willpower to hold in a cough. You feel the sweat on your hands as you raise the machine gun, recheck your aim, and squeeze off the remaining rounds in a quick burst. The gun throbs into your shoulder. Your target goes down, and you experience a satisfying thrill. Your elation is cut short, however, by the realization that you forgot about the guard in the check station. He reminds you of this by putting a few piercing rounds in your side. You're dead.

The above, on first read, may appear violent. In a time of war and fear of war, reading about machine guns and stealth kills seems out of place. Glorifying violence, even that of heroes fighting in a war, just isn't done anymore. John Wayne's dead, along with George C. Scott and Lee Marvin, and Arnold just doesn't do that sort of thing any more. Violence, and the glorification of it, seems to have crept into the background of society.

Unless you are a gamer.

That's right, the exchange above did not take place in Iraq or Afghanistan. There's a good chance something like it took place next door or in your own living room. Usually it happens on a computer screen or television. There's a lot of button mashing and gamepad fiddling, and sometimes some yelling and screaming. But, at first glance, the participants do not seem violent. Now it's gone mobile. You can kill someone with a device smaller than a paperback or even with your phone. Killing's a global business, and as it appears, business is good. Billions of dollars good. With more to come.

Maybe you've done it yourself, put a bullet in someone's digital brain. People you know have killed, and they have reveled in it. Is this technology gone too far? Not only are we killing on the screen but with today's processing power we can learn the intricacies of a high-tech weapon. We know the kickback of a .45 caliber handgun. We know the best place to aim for is not the head but the heart because it is an easier target. Information normally given out only in Basic Training or the police academy is not only readily available but known by civilians. What's more, it's not just nameless computer generated enemies on the TV screen we're killing. It's little Bobby down the block, or perhaps even a college professor from the Midwest. Either way, they have identities. They have hopes and dreams and families. And a gamer's goal is to kill them.

Gamers are being sought after with constant legislative attempts to calm down their hobby. Fists are being pounded on podiums and places like Columbine are mentioned with anger and purpose. Video game violence is spilling into real life. The line between fantasy and reality is blurred and people are dying because of it. Little Bobby is using weapons. Little Bobby knows the blast radius of a grenade. Little Bobby goes on killing rampages and loves it. His mother has drawn the line, an anti-gaming activist says with a sneer, so he can only experience killing a police officer at his friend's house. His mother won't allow *that* sort of activity to grace her widescreen TV. She has morals and strict behavioral guidelines for little Bobby.

A few months later, a group of outcast teenagers lock and load and sweep through their high school, killing everyone in their path. On their computers are violent videogames. It turns out the kids re-enacted a level from one of the games. They followed it to the letter, using all they learned in the game to kill more efficiently. No headshots here. If only they had never played these games, all of their innocent classmates would still be alive. If they never used a pipe bomb in the video game *Duke Nukem* how would they have ever known what one was? They would never have turned violent if not for the bloody images on their computer screens.

Or would they have?

Saying the games caused the killing takes a logical leap many are not willing to make. In a sense, it is a form of profiling. To say that the killers' video game habit fed their murderous rampage means that all gamers have that rampage inside waiting to come out. It means Little Bobby is a killer in waiting. It is only a matter of time.

I've been around videogames pretty much since their inception. I've played them, reviewed them for magazines, even learned a little bit about making them. My first gaming experience was playing PONG in the arcade. I then upgraded to a home system with bad graphics. It wasn't until my family bought an Apple computer that I was introduced to real gaming. The first PC game I played involved going into a dungeon and killing monsters to get to an evil wizard. The game was called *Wizardry*. I kept stats of my characters' proficiency at killing. My mother thought nothing of it, though she preferred I spend more time outside. I told her putting out the garbage covered that. So, instead of playing ball and getting tanned outside, I was pasty white and sweated over the well being of my characters.

That game specifically developed my love of videogames. The graphics were paltry and sparse, so the entire story and action took place in my head. I imagined the dank, acrid smell of the dungeon as I led my party of characters down its entrance. I never saw a picture of my characters but I knew what they looked like. They had their own personalities. That was, wow, over twenty years ago, and I can still see them. Other games offered me the same level of imagination. Could they have helped me become a fiction writer? Writing, above all else, takes imagination. A car pinstriper once told me he couldn't find employees to do his job. When I guessed it was because he couldn't find someone with steady hands, he shook his head. "I can *teach* anyone that. It's the eye for the lines of the car that is rare." The same goes for fiction, in a way. Anyone can learn grammar and structure; imagination is the real requirement of a creative writer. These games exercised that part of my brain and strengthened it. Now, with dazzling graphics, they don't develop imagination so much. Now they help in an even tougher area, the sense of place. This is always one of the toughest things to teach a new writer. So, for me, video games didn't make a mass murderer, but instead a writer. My writing might not win any prizes, but to say it is murderous is a bit much, I think. Torturous for some, perhaps, but they have little taste in fiction I've decided.

The question that begs to be asked is, does digital violence desensitize us to real world violence? Those that argue for this say that watching explosions and gunfire make it more acceptable to our brain in real life. I disagree, and strongly. I defy someone who has experienced a real bomb blast to say that my Xbox recreates it perfectly. (I am sure Microsoft wants us to think so.) Also, not only have I played violent video games, I watched Tom and Jerry annihilate each other on television. Rambo single-handedly took on entire armies on the silver screen when I was a kid. My cousin introduced me to the odd thrill of blowing up plastic army men with firecrackers. Mom never let me do that but I did watch in awe. I've never gotten violent with anyone. In fact, I probably got myself out of such instances more than anyone I know. I could never hunt. I could never shoot someone, even in anger. I might want to strangle the random bad driver, but that's about it. Digital violence has not affected my life. Maybe I am a rare case.

What about boys playing with army men or G.I. Joe? Last time I checked, Joe doesn't make floral arrangements or study math. No, he blows things up, and with efficiency. With millions of Joes sold over the years, I would venture to say he hasn't made someone kill. Well, I am sure there is some wacko out there who followed the murderous commands coming from his refrigerator, but let's just say I think the line here melds with sanity. Going across the mall with a machete and a rifle takes a certain lack of sanity. Thinking you are the main character from *Grand Theft Auto* and trying to shoot at police goes in the same box, the one labeled "Nuts." I hesitate to say it but it needs to be said; normal people don't do these things whether they play video games or not. And by normal, I mean functional. If you go to church in a clown suit carrying a chicken, you need not apply.

We do have to take into account that *some* people are affected. The movie *Money Train* led to the mimicking of killing a subway token clerk. A few football players from Long Island died by lying on the yellow line of a highway because they saw it done in *The Program*. Touchstone pictures and their parent company, Disney, took the scene out of the movie. Someone surely sees a correlation. Or, perhaps more correctly, someone was worried about the bottom line. Dead teenagers don't go to the movies. Neither do their parents.

Of course, along with the sanity idea comes intelligence, or the lack thereof. I don't think I need to tell anyone that plopping yourself down in the middle of a highway is stupid. If I do, then the movie or video game or television show isn't to blame. A person like that might be apt to put a plastic bag over his or her head. Call me Darwinian but this smacks of survival of the fittest. The fittest, or the smartest, don't lie down on a highway. Someone please let me know if I missed a memo on that.

A more compelling argument might be the relationship I mentioned earlier between the Columbine killers and the video game *Doom*. This is the constant mention by those people pounding their fist on the podium. They digitally killed and they killed in reality. Surely one leads to the other. Because we can't tell who is impressionable enough to make this leap, should we ban these games to save people? Would the Columbine killers have done nothing if they hadn't played the game? The answer, at best, is elusive. It becomes personal. If you play these games you want them to stick around. If you don't, there exists a dark mysterious aura around them. Video game killers *could* be a dangerous breed and the only way to protect society is to not have them get the gratification from them. Preeminently wipe out bad behavior at the earliest indication of it, a la *Minority Report*. Wait, that didn't work out too well, did it?

If we stop these violent games, in my opinion, then we need to wipe out violent movies. And, if people get ideas from movies and games, then what of the murder mysteries we read? As a mystery writer myself, one of my jobs is to think of new and creative ways for a character to get away with murder. Therefore, my novels might be informational to a murderer in training. My books, and the four or so people who read them, must go. Can't have people watching *CSI* either. Someone might learn something there. Violent cartoons? They're no good. You might have Little Bobby dropping an anvil on his brother. Anvils, though not readily available, are dangerous to kids. Somewhere, some kid has his eyes on a 100 pound anvil for his little brother. Save the whales but eliminate the anvils, *CSI*, violent movies, and whatever else might give someone an idea how to off someone.

Stated that way this all seems drastic. Most people don't want the government telling them what to do too often. People also don't want young children exposed to excessive violence. Firing a rifle in a WWII video game re-enactment is one thing. Killing police officers wantonly in *Grand Theft Auto* might be something else. Think about it the next time you are at the video game store. Did the company create a game that has violence in the storyline or are they cashing in on unnecessary violence? Right now, the government isn't making the decision for us. Tomorrow might be another story. The podium-pounders are hard at work to convince the government to get involved.

For now, the choice is ours. Keep the games out of Little Bobby's hands, sure. No kid should be able to play a game like *Grand Theft Auto* and its ilk. I question whether anyone should be able to play a game centered around killing police officers and prostitutes. If you want to make a difference, use the best power you have in our society, your wallet. Gaming is a billion dollar industry and growing. The game companies are pumping out more and more violent games. They think that's what gamers want. If you agree, buy them. If you don't, don't. This is democracy at its finest. Using your buying power is like casting a vote in the booth. The only difference is, this vote really counts. The corporate bigwigs don't rely on confusing ballots, just dollars and cents.

INTERPRETATIONS

1. After reading only the first paragraph of Misak's essay, what do you think will come next? Why do you think Misak has chosen to begin his essay in this way?

2. What is Misak's primary argument? What evidence does he supply to convince you?

3. How does Misak's choice of language help to convey his meaning and retain a reader's interest? Find five images, allusions, or descriptive details that catch your attention. Explain how you respond to each of these items.

4. What good does Misak see in video games?

CORRESPONDENCES

1. How do you think video games represent popular culture, as written about by Lee (page 474)? Explain your answer, referring to both Lee and Misak.

2. According to Misak, why do people play violent video games? How are these reasons related to why people watch horror movies, as analyzed by King (page 496)?

APPLICATIONS

1. Misak states that some people are asking the government to prevent the sale of violent video games. Do you think that censorship is the best solution to the perceived problem? Create a formal argumentation and persuasion essay that defends your position. At some point in your composing process, probably when you are satisfied that you have set down your primary arguments, review the examples and exact language you use in your essay. Review how Misak uses language and imagery in his essay.

2. Do you like to play video games? Freewrite for five minutes about your answer to this question. Next, create a list of those reasons that appear in your freewriting. What examples can you generate to support each reason in your list? Finally, select a few primary reasons and their examples as the basis for a formal essay. When

you write your introduction, how might you begin with a situation that will grab a reader's interest?

3. With the members of your peer group, decide on a movie that you will all see independently over the weekend. After you view the film, write a journal entry that responds to Misak's question about video games: "Did the company create a game that has violence in the storyline or are they cashing in on unnecessary violence?"

    In your next class session, each group member should read his or her journal entry. What ideas does the group have in common? What answer might the group provide to Misak's question in relation to the film they have seen, written about, and discussed?

A Timeless Culture

TOM LEE

Tom Lee (b. 1988) is a graduate of Sewanhaka High School in Floral Park, New York. Tom enjoys playing the sax, guitar, and piano. He is majoring in music at Queens College.

POP CULTURE IS TODAY, always has been, and always will be an immense part of our lives. We are aware of its existence; we are aware of its unavoidable effect on us; we are even aware of our society's sometimes-dangerous obsession with it. All the same, pop culture remains at the acme of importance in our culture. While writing this essay, I found myself focusing on mainstream pop culture vs. the lesser-known factions of it, and debated which one is better. However, I realize now that pop culture of any type is merely a reaction to another type or a combination of two or more others. So, what purpose in society does popular culture fill?

Pop culture brings to attention or combats certain political or social issues so that, possibly, somebody with more power can do something about it. In the early nineties art world, a lot of emphasis was placed on the theme of surveillance, the idea that people were not able to do anything unobserved. In the seventies, particularly 1977, the counter culture movement reached its peak with the punk rock explosion. Punk rock had very anti-establishment morals. This was so partly because of the disgust with the awesome power of government at the time, the other part being that the people involved were the children of the baby boomers who were abandoned and lost in the mediocrity of families with a large number of children. During the sixties, rampant in the world of literature, authors would write short stories about environmental issues such as mankind's harmful effect on the Earth. For example Rachel Carson wrote *Silent Spring* to point out the pollution problem that people were causing.

Even in music earlier than the seventies, genres have been created to oppose accepted values of the time. For example, post WWII music, inversely with the animosity of the war, had a very light, happy feel to it. American songwriters like Glenn Miller and the Andrews Sisters produced happy upbeat love songs such as "Don't Sit Under the Apple Tree," and "I'll Be With You In Apple Blossom Time." This change didn't only appear in America in the later years of the big band era and swing's evolution into solo singers, but it was also evident in other countries, such as Jamaica and its birth of ska. Jamaican songwriters like Byron Lee and the Dragonnaires conceived this idea as a way to evoke unity in the world. Social issues, too, have always been addressed in popular culture. Langston Hughes, a black poet during the Harlem Renaissance, empowered black people and gave them pride despite the strong prejudices that existed at the time.

Popular culture, no matter what it is, is usually a direct commentary on an idea and has a definite beginning and a definite end. Once the idea that is being commented on is addressed, the idea is supposed to fizzle out. However, in each generation of pop culture there are always a few timeless survivors. So, what is it that makes something timeless? What is the perfectly disjunct vision that separates Toni Morrison from Stephen King; the picture-perfect image that separates Ansel Adams from the paparazzi; what is that perfect fifth that separates The Beatles and Public Enemy? Is there even one definitive reason that something will remain with us throughout history? Is it written in the stars, the decided fate of the gods, or is it simply just good publicity?

It's on the tip of your tongue, but you can't give it a name. You don't know how to explain it, but you have a sixth sense that always knows when something is going to simply fade away. Of course, pop culture, quite obviously, affects kids first and foremost. Unfortunately, this inherent sixth sense is absent in the adolescent (for those of you who thought that Hanson or 'N Sync were going to last) breathing life into the commercial industry. Not to worry, as the old saying goes "with age comes reason," and, as the reasonable can vouch for, with reason comes clarity of judgment. The reasonable can easily distinguish a classic from a flavor of the week . . . usually. The things that become classics, I find, are the ones that create clichés. By this I mean the ones that create something so innovative and different that everybody tries to mimic it. For example Charlotte Bronte, Pablo Picasso, and even Louis Armstrong all shaped their fields of expertise and created fresh new ideas. I take depth into account as well. Have you ever heard a song, saw a painting or read a novel months or years after you had first encountered it? Have you ever seen an entire universe of underlying subtleties that you hadn't noticed; taken a new interpretation of it; or simply just relived a moment in your life that you had forgotten about? That is depth. If you have experienced depth, you've probably stumbled upon a classic.

Traditional ideas are continuously revamped. Most people, and this has always been true, attempt to recapture the past. They want it to be "like the good old days," "the way mom and pop used to do it," "classic," "retro," or "old school." Nowadays especially, it is a growing trend in clothing (the "vintage look"), music (the reintroduction of classical instruments and the use of old songs in beats), art (the modern day replications of classic works), and movies (the remakes of old movies with new directors) to recreate ideas of the past. Of course, how can we not forget VH1 reality shows which bring old pop culture idols back into the limelight and shows like "I Love the 80s" and "Best Week Ever" which talk about both past and current pop culture alike? One doesn't find it ironic that the electronic downloading of music is at its peak, and at the same time more and more people have been going to live music concerts, and, yes, vinyl records have been reintroduced into the market. Technology designed merely to mimic the object it replaces never fully manages to deliver the same impact.

Human beings seem to have this fascination with the things of the past that have become dated. It gives us a nostalgic feeling and allows us to connect with our historical roots. It is human nature to strive for the past and attempt to reinvent what we once had: it is the great themes of the past such as the permanence of nature, the eternal plight between knowledge and ignorance, or the power of human emotion, that are always seen in the timeless artists. Despite the fact that these themes are often seen as cliché, it takes a true artist to just, in the words of TV fashion personality, Tim Gunn, "make it work." The universality of these themes allows human beings from any time, any place, any nationality, or social class to connect with the pool of humanity's collective unconscious.

INTERPRETATIONS

1. Lee ends his opening paragraph with the question: "So, what purpose in society does popular culture fill?" What answers does he provide in his essay? Where are they stated?

2. What do you think Lee means by his use of the term "popular culture"? What is your definition of this term? What is the dictionary definition of it?

3. In the final paragraphs of his essay, Lee theorizes about why people are interested in popular culture. What reasons does he provide? Explain why you agree or disagree with his analysis.

APPLICATIONS

1. Lee asks in paragraph 4, "So, what is it that makes something timeless?" What movies or music groups were popular when you

were younger, say between the ages of ten and thirteen? Select one of those that you revered and write a journal entry about your memories of this film or group and how you felt about it/them at the time. (Try to get yourself back into that same mind-set you had as a young teenager!)

Sometime in the next few days, view that film or listen to the music of that group again. Write another journal entry about your feelings and reactions.

Now, in a formal essay, attempt to define "popular culture" and establish those qualities found in films or movies that last, that are timeless. Use your two journal entries to formulate your definition and your analysis.

2. Write a letter in which you try to convince a friend that a new and popular musician or actor has the stuff of stardom. Explain your reasons carefully, and provide specific details and examples.

Whatever Happened to Rock 'n' Roll?

JAMES GEASOR

James Geasor was born in Brooklyn, New York in 1958. After more than twenty-two years in the printing business, he decided to pursue a degree in secondary education, and is currently a liberal arts student at Queensborough Community College (CUNY). For as long as he can remember, James has had an active interest in music that embraces many genres and cultures. He has attended innumerable concerts, hearing artists that included the Beatles, Issac Stern, Maestro and the Brooklyn Bridge, The Beach Boys, the Grateful Dead, Marc-Andre Hamelin, Bob Marley, David Bowie, Murray Perahia, Billy Taylor, John Williams, Buddy Rich, Black Sabbath, Chick Corea, Itzhak Perlman, U2, and Talking Heads. He lives in Westbury, New York with his son Bryan.

THE SUMMER OF 1964 was my first personal experience with rock 'n' roll. I was six years old when my father packed me and five of my siblings into the family station wagon and took us to see the Beatles at Forest Hills Tennis Stadium one late August evening. Although only a child at the time, I was raised in a home that had a steady background of music and constant chatter, with what seemed an endless parade of visiting friends and relatives. As for the concert itself, I don't recall much other than there was an awful lot of hysterical screaming and that you couldn't hear much of the music. Countless girls would rush the stage only to be bear-hugged, lifted, and carried off by an obviously beleaguered security force. Although witness to a phenomenon that would only grow larger in the ensuing years, I didn't come to appreciate until much later that by the end of the decade the Beatles, and a few other up and coming rock bands, would change the face of popular culture in the Western Hemisphere. And change popular culture not only in music, but in fashion, art, political awareness, and attitude. By the late 1960s, the Civil Rights Movement and Vietnam War had become signposts for the maelstrom of youthful discontent, and the music of that generation would become the voice that helped them articulate their fears and concerns about their future and the future of the American psyche.

Between 1963 and 1970, the year they disbanded, the Beatles had released more than fifteen studio albums, many of which sold in the millions. But I'm not writing this in praise of the prolific songwriting talents of John Lennon and Paul McCartney. Rather, I wish to point out that the Beatles were one of the first musical groups who wrote songs about social issues and the human condition, and in doing so would create an intimate relationship with their audience. This artist and listener relationship was something that other rock groups would begin to emulate. In a sense they charted the course that many other groups would follow. Bands like the Grateful Dead, the Rolling Stones, and the Who would have long careers that their fans could follow along with, and it would create an intimacy which would allow their fans to grow with them. This feeling of belonging to something progressive and meaningful helped create a culture that hitherto was missing from the popular music scene. The admiration went as far as copying their hair styles, clothing, social discourse, and attitude.

But the prior mentioned break-up of the Beatles brought an end to a certain aura of the popular culture they had spawned. Part of the culture of the 1960s was the experimentation with drugs. At that time, rock music in particular was inextricably linked to the drug culture. Marijuana, LSD, barbiturates, and other even harder drugs had become part of a cultural phenomenon that ostensibly allowed those participating in this shared experience to expand their minds and free themselves of their perceived socially indoctrinated inhibitions. In the end it cost many people either their lives or a life of addiction and misery, and many famous musicians lost their lives to the overdose of drugs or to alcohol addiction, all in the attempt to "break on through to the other side."

As popular culture in America began to adjust to the changing political climate and burgeoning technological advancements of the 1970s, rock music began to change along with it. By the second half of the 1970s, disco and punk rock had burst onto the scene, and both had a rather weakening effect on the culture of rock music and popular culture in general. Where 60s bands like the Beatles and the Grateful Dead emphasized, to a certain degree, social and political awareness, punk rock preached anarchy and disillusionment. As for disco, the mindless strains of vacuous, pointless music, along with a vial of high quality cocaine, was all that was needed to feel part of a culture that was void of anything significant, other than dancing the night away. Although bands like the Rolling Stones and the Grateful Dead carried on, their output became uneven, and obligations to recording contracts forced their creative energies to wax and wane to the point that even some of their die-hard fans began to question their commitment. Some artists who began their careers in the 1970s, such as Bruce Springsteen and Billy Joel, did carry on the tradition of growing as artists within their music, and both released albums that contained songs about social and political awareness along with artistic merit. But as the 1980s began, the influence of technology would begin to change rock music and popular culture unlike anything before.

Although Bob Moog created his music synthesizer in the early 1960s, and certain late 60s and early 70s rock bands utilized its other-worldly sounds to great effect, its high cost kept it out of the hands of the average musician. By the early 1980s, other manufacturers began pro-ducing synthesizers that were more affordable. The electronic sounds and synthetic drum beats that began percolating on the airwaves ushered in a new type of rock music and a changing trend in popular culture. Up until the 1980s, the electric guitar was the undisputed, instantly recognizable sound of rock 'n' roll. The advent of cheaper key-boards and the start of what was to become known as sequencing allowed musicians to "program" their songs using drum machines and keyboard synthesizers. Although some bands used both guitars and synthesizers, by the end of the 80s the synthesizer was the predominant instrument in popular music. The electronic based popular music that carried over into the 90s was becoming dance oriented, rock music in general was starting to lose its focus, and many subcategories of popular music began to emerge.

A simple search on the Internet revealed more than one hundred of these subcategories of popular music. Death metal, speed metal, hard core, grunge, hip-hop, trip-hop, rap, trance, dance, electronica, dub, club, alternative, Christian . . . the list seemed endless. With the advent of sampling (where "artists" sample, or copy, small phrases of other people's music then twist it, i.e., string it together via sequencing, into something they can legally put their name on), technology had now begun to empower people whose musical talent was, at best, suspect. The growing cult of celebrity in the 90s had now completely blurred the lines as to what music had come to represent in its relationship with popular culture. Nowadays, it is not uncommon to find "musicians" using nothing more than laptop computers and maybe a keyboard sequencer to enthrall the crowds. Actual musical instruments are almost nowhere to be found, and the majority of music being piped out to the audience is pre-sampled and pre-sequenced prior to the concert. While there are artists who use sampling for effect rather than pure con-tent, and they can still retain that elusive spark of originality, technol-ogy (particularly the computer) has now created a vast overkill and bewildering amount of music that basically has no value other than as distractive entertainment. The energy and thrill of seeing a talented group of musicians perform live, warts and all, seems a thing of the past. Most popular music concerts today resemble aerobics videos with a soundtrack of sterile music, lip-synched vocals, and performers who care more about image and choreography than musical content.

And that is the underlying current of popular music and culture in the twenty-first century. Back in the 60s and through the early part of the 70s, artists and musicians helped define the segment of popular culture they wished to reach. In today's music, the opposite is true. Musicians and artists try to keep up with the fickle, changing trends of popular culture to stay afloat and in the public eye. To their dismay most up and coming artists, within a matter of months, wind up as flotsam and jetsam washed up on the shores of the vast coastline of popular culture. It seems that today's popular music and culture simply lacks curiosity. And that's not a dangerous thing, it's just kind of sad.

It takes time to nurture a talent and create a unique form of expression that others can identify with. And hopefully as your talent grows, your audience stays with you and eagerly awaits what you have to say both musically and lyrically with great anticipation. Unfortunately, in today's cultural climate of instant gratification and shortened attention spans, even artists that do have the ability to commit to long term artistic views have to deal with the uncertain and unsteady opinions of popular demand. And to the artists who turn a blind eye to public opinion and forge their own careers out of sheer will and artistic integrity, I applaud you one and all. But it seems there's not much of that going on anymore.

I'm not one who longs for the good old days of rock 'n' roll. I like to see trends and people change and grow, they just have to have meaning and direction, and that's what appears to be lacking in modern culture and music. As for the Beatles, I did like their music, but they were far from my favorite band and they weren't much of a musical influence on me personally. But what they represented as songwriters and their influence in changing popular culture in their time is something I understand and respect. If that six-year-old boy could have seen what was to come of popular music and culture in the 21st century, even he would have asked, "Whatever happened to rock 'n' roll?"

INTERPRETATIONS

1. In his title, Geasor asks, "Whatever Happened to Rock 'n' Roll?" What explanations does he provide to answer this question?

2. What writing techniques does Geasor use to organize his ideas and retain reader interest? Which do you find to be most effective?

3. According to Geasor, what contributions did the Beatles make to popular culture? To what extent do you agree with his opinions?

APPLICATIONS

1. Geasor begins his essay with his recollection of attending a Beatles concert when he was six years old. What is the first musical event that you remember going to? What was most memorable about this event to you?

    Write a first-person narrative about this experience that captures the moment. Remember to pay particular attention to your five senses in recalling specific details. Bring your reader into the scene itself!

2. How do you think history will judge the era of popular culture written about by Geasor? Create a chart that lists both the positives and negatives of "rock 'n' roll" as presented by him. Now create a formal essay that argues for either a positive or negative historical assessment.

... well, if you can't hold the torch ... then why pass it ...?[1]

TODD CRAIG

Todd Craig hails from Queens, New York. A product of the Queensbridge and Ravenswood Housing projects in his youth, he left Queens for New England in hopes of a better education and life. A graduate of Harvard School of Education, Todd is a writer and a deejay; it is in fact, his love of music that opened the door to his writing. Todd has returned to his native borough of Queens and presently teaches English Composition while working on his first novel and third screenplay.

ONE DAY I WAS AT WORK talking to one of my students by the name of Jose. Jose is a deejay, and since we share this common interest, at any given time, you could catch the two of us talking about music and the climate of hip-hop as it stands right now in 2006. In one of our various conversations, we got on the topic of the new Ghostface album "Fishscale."

"Yo son, how you like that new Ghost?" was the natural question I had.

"Eh, its aight . . ."

"What?!? It's aight?"

"Yeah, its aight, but I don't think its one of Ghost's illest albums."

From this point in the conversation, I began to fill the role of hip-hop historian. But it was in the midst of this conversation I began to really think about the climate of hip-hop music, especially in 2006. What was most disconcerting to me was that this had been a similar response to the one I received when talking about Busta Rhymes's latest effort entitled "The Big Bang." What bothered me most was in a musical world where all people want to do as listeners is lean back, lean with it and rock with it, or even shoulder lean while consuming some chicken noodle soup with a soda as a beverage on the side, the next generation coming of age in hip-hop are only concerned with listening to what they've been programmed to like. Meanwhile, veteran artists like Ghostface, Busta Rhymes, and many more who have been integral to the foundation of hip-hop are not getting the credit they deserve for their albums

[1]Busta Rhymes featuring Q-Tip and Chauncey Black, "You Can't Hold the Torch," *The Big Bang,* Aftermath/Interscope Records, copyright 2006.

musically, specifically because they have made a conscious decision to NOT do what's "hot." Instead, while everyone else went left, they went right, and decided to make something we rarely see these days: a "classic" album.

This really hurts my feelings because of where I stand when it comes to hip-hop. Because when it comes to the music, I grew up in it, and was fortunate enough to experience what many people categorize as the "golden era" of hip hop, the mid-90s, where the focus was on the music as opposed to money and sales. See, I stand as a hip-hop understudy, a historian of sorts through listening to and analyzing the music. In my youth, every Sunday when I got my allowance, I ran to QP's flea-market after Sunday school to purchase the next and newest hip-hop album on cassette tape. And as Biggie so eloquently put it "I let my tape rock 'til my tape pop."[2] I've been a deejay since 1990, and was buying records before then. So growing up, I didn't just listen to hip-hop—I studied it. I'm a vinyl enthusiast and hip-hop purist, dedicated to the sound and qualities of great music. Unfortunately that is turning into vintage music given the state of the game at this point.

Now, there are a number of ways that one could go about this conversation. For example, one could very easily make the argument that I, in my age of thirty-two a.k.a. Gen X'er gone grown-up, have gotten to the same point that my elders got to when I was younger: that being "Boy, you think that's good music . . . that ain't music . . . they got that song from this older record . . . When I was coming up, we listened to *music* . . . boy, you don't know the type of music we used to listen to . . . *that* was *music* . . . that crap you listening to, is garbage!" I hated that argument back then, so to avoid hypocrisy, I try hard not to make that argument now.

I'd rather go a different angle; see, hip-hop music is one of the first cultures that comes both with and out of the music that has gone from the "underground" subculture to actually overtake what we know as mainstream popular culture. It's really one of the first times we see grandkids learning to dance to the same genre of music their parents listen to at the same time those parents are listening to and sharing with *their* parents . . . all simultaneously. Thus the question for me is rooted in intellectual thought; mainly, how has this game we call hip-hop changed musically? And I've always said to myself, "At the point where I listen to the radio and the popular 'Old School at Noon' shows are all my favorite songs, I'll know I'm old." So in thinking about this, I've merely decided to just look at the difference in the music between

---

[2]The Notorious B.I.G., "Juicy," *Ready to Die*. Bad Boy Entertainment/Arista Records, copyright 1994.

now and what might be considered the crux of the golden era: January of 1994 to December, 1996. Given the fact that I can look back on hip-hop for a decade and have formative memories is interesting in and of itself given when I was growing up, hip-hop was a "faze that'll soon die out" or "a fad" like the thousands if not millions of one-year one-hit wonder songs it's generated. Now, McDonalds and Dunkin Donuts, Starbucks, Jeep and Sprite have all used elements of hip-hop in their advertising schemes. Even Volkswagen is throwing up Ws, and shouting "Vee Dub": all elements of hip-hop slang, language and culture.

For me, as a hip-hop fan and deejay, the best time for this music was encapsulated by the following albums: Nas's first album "Illmatic"; Mobb Deep's second album "The Infamous" (even though most people think it's the first album because they missed "Juvenile Hell"); Notorious B.I.G.'s first album "Ready to Die"; and finally Wu-Tang Clan's own Raekwon the Chef's first solo album "Only Built 4 Cuban Linx." What became apparent to me was when I asked the question "Give me your top ten albums between the years of January 1994 to December 1995," no one I asked could give me just ten. However, when asking about the albums of today, the usual response was "Todd, I don't even really listen to hip-hop like that anymore" or "the game's changed so much, I can't even give you ten quality albums." No one could give me only ten albums from a decade prior because of the oversaturation of good quality hip-hop music during that time. This was a time in hip-hop music when the focus was on making quality music. And because the music and culture at that time were evolving, all forms were heard and accepted based on the criteria of creativity, originality and sound quality. This artistry held true for both the lyrics and music. Whether it was in the lyrics, which showed creativity through subject matter—specifically gauged by use of mental brainwork to decipher the words—or with production that stemmed from Jazz, Soul, Blues, Latin, Funk loops or even R&B remakes with live instruments (check Stevie J. and The Roots), the ultimate goal and endeavor of the artist(s) involved was primarily focused on making good music. It wasn't necessarily about the trend or what was popular, it was in fact about going against the grain.

Part of that very clearly comes from the hunger of some of these artists, some leaving troublesome situations in order to find a better way of life in the music. As well, while some may argue that this was the time in which rap changed from the conscious pro-black lyrics and visuals to the "gangsterization" of rap, I look at it differently. Rap music has always been that subculture people have wanted to belong to and understand. You can easily make the argument that part of the shift in popular culture in regards to music entails being included in that new style, that mystery music, language and dress—and being able to fully understand what it means and from where it emanates. This was the sentiment of hip-hop music during these years. The walk, talk and dress of rappers, b-boys and hip-hoppers were similar to the DaVinci Code—complex to unravel but necessary to understand. But even then, there was so much more to understand; and not only was the music exclusive, but it was highly balanced. For every O.D.B., you had A Tribe Called Quest. For Smif-N-Wessun you had Common. For Boot Camp and D.I.T.C.,[3] you had Native Tongues and Digable Planets. For Gangstarr and Brand Nubian, you had 2Pac and CNN. There was such balance musically, it was all too easy to switch and shift gears in order to consume a balanced "hip-hop diet"; I could wake up grimy for breakfast to "The Infamous," have a pensive lyrical lunch with The Roots, then straddle both sides with dinner and dessert over Jeru.

And even for that era of the genre where the lyrics became more violent, it was far from glorification; it was, in fact, a lyrical war report. Essentially, what C-SPAN, CNN, MSNBC, and BBC are for news, hip-hop music was the news report for our people: the urban inner-city disenfranchised youth who see hundreds of black men murdered on a daily basis but never get to see their friends on the news. What ABC, CBS and NBC wouldn't give us on the news, artists like Nas, Mobb Deep, Capone and Noriega, Black Moon, Gangstarr and Wu-Tang Clan would give us in three minutes and thirty seconds or sometimes more. And really, if you listen to the songs and are immersed in the music of that time, you could realize like I do: there was always a message that came with this violent depiction of life. The message, was indeed, don't go *that* way. Unfortunately, the stereotype says that the music has influenced the youth to lead lives of crime. Interestingly enough, the main character in the new Volkswagen commercial is "throwing up" a W in a way that could be construed as a gang sign—somehow though, we as a society don't necessarily label that as negative reinforcement of the stereotype, right? And never once, as a society, have we thought about the simple question: What does it mean that we know through music that a certain part of society lives like this? Do we begin to change the way people live, or do we turn a blind eye to it in order to let the negativity perpetuate itself across generations of particular races and cultures? (Because isn't the saying that "life imitates art" and not vice-versa?)

Now in 2006, we have reached the era where hip-hop is no longer the subculture, but is indeed popular culture. We see it on a daily basis in the fashion choices of youth, the words they choose to speak in everyday language, and the shift in lifestyle. And now, the music, which was

---

[3]Diggin' In The Crates Crew—Hip-Hop rapper/producer team featuring: Lord Finesse, Fat Joe, Show and A.G., O.C., BuckWild, Big L.

at the forefront of the culture then, can be looked at as secondary, as it is engrossed in the corporate world of big business. Hip-hop is no longer new, and with the loss of this mysterious newness, gone are the days of the balance that was prevalent in the music over a decade ago. Coupled with the monetary success and super-star status of many rappers turned actors, fashion designers, company CEOs, and entrepreneurs, there has been a shift in the music, because everyone wants to be a rapper and make money. But not everyone wants to make good music first and foremost. This can obviously be linked to the incorporation of hip-hop as big business in terms of sales for record executives throughout the industry. And as unfortunate as it is, it has taken place how it has for just about every form of African-American music and culture: it has been appropriated by a larger system that is not concerned with the roots and fundamental teachings and lessons of hip-hop, but instead merely with reaching kids to make more sales to make more money, cash bigger checks for the companies who can write even smaller checks to the artists who make and have made the system work for them in a way no one thought it would. Thus, for these artists to make all the money, someone else has to get a cut. And with this appropriation through big business, hip-hop has translated to the youth of today in a way it never spoke to us. For now, the focus is not on the love of the game, the culture or even the music, it's on making money, selling millions of records, counting BBS radio spins and tracking SoundScan sales. The absence of the love for the music has corrupted what was once a pure culture. It has shifted the focus from the purely idealistic love of the music to the fiscally business-driven materialistic desire of more money, more money . . . and—more money!

It's clear to me that a decade ago, we—specifically, members of hip-hop culture—educated children on the diversity of life, because if hip-hop is culture, we educated through a unique form of cultural diversity. We were not only shown how to be conscious and pensive, but we were also taught to be strong or "hard" and given examples of how *both* lifestyles played themselves out. The diversity was intrinsically infused within the music, simply because the range of content within the music was so overwhelming, accessible, and apparent. With hip-hop now, however, we educate kids on being only thugs and gangsters, and reaping the spoils without any major work. We are not primarily infusing morals or even reporting, but instead now, we are brainwashing . . . in the worst way. Because all we are telling kids is that this is what you need to be to be "that dude" or "that nigguh."[4]

---

[4]And how this word has changed from such a negative connotation to an acceptable greeting and categorization of people, I will never truly understand!

Through a majority of the music now, youth are subliminally told "you wanna shine shorty, you gotta go at it like this . . ." But how is a 14 or 15-year-old teenager who lives in an urban inner-city environment supposed to afford foreign cars and SUVs, chrome 24+ inch tire rims, platinum and diamond chains and rings, bracelets and watches, and the latest and greatest in technology?

Nowadays, there's very little in the music to balance the scales as much as there was a decade ago. Unfortunately now, there's only one path and vantagepoint musically based on the financial gain of the corporate culture that has appropriated and commodified hip-hop, and made big business of what once was our own unique movement and underground culture. And yes, I know, it goes down with every generational change—in fact, this is probably where my age comes in and plays a role in my analysis. But with hip-hop now spanning multiple generations, at bare minimum, we can begin to see the effects of how such significant changes to both the music and culture are really taking place and essentially affecting our youth and generations beyond them. So with this in mind, this historical viewpoint is indeed critical, as it has the potential to allow us to possibly anticipate or even predict the future trends using knowledge of the past, based on the history's ironic cyclical nature.

For me, the conversation culminated in a discussion I had with hip-hop producer Alchemist. As we were talking about this subject, he brought up an interesting point: "we are now in an era, with Jay droppin' an album, where a parent and son can listen to the same thing. But youth culture by nature is designed for rebellion, for kids to NOT want to like and listen to what their parents like. So now what's gonna happen to hip-hop?" Even though every hip-hop fan felt a loss when Jay-Z, rapper turned President of Def Jam Records, claimed retirement. However, Jay has made a comeback, creating a long time buzz within the hip-hop industry for the release of his new album, "Kingdom Come." While we have seen in hip-hop music a time where two to three generations are listening to the same genre of music, this can indeed be a time where they are all listening to the *same* artist, the *same* album—the *same* exact music. But youth culture indeed functions off the premise of rebellion. It is an ironic twist of fate that can and will truly be a test and testament to hip-hop music and culture as we know it. Because essentially, you are left in one of two places. The first shows two to three generations coming together what could be a monumental moment for not only hip-hop as a music, but also as an art form and culture that has truly weathered the storm in outlasting the infamous test of time. The second, there is discord amongst the youth and the different generations, and a rebellion to what could be considered "good music" in order to preserve this specific premise of youth culture. It could potentially swing us back into an era where the only hip-hop music that'll be tolerated is good quality music, or swing us further into the dark side of what I do like to refer to as "something else." I guess only time and an album release date can tell . . .[5]

I've always promoted the simple fact that history does repeat itself, and in order to truly know where you are going, at some point you have to look back to see exactly where you've been. So I'd be all the more happy for the pendulum to swing back to the right as opposed to the extreme left it sits on for our culture now. But to me, it's really always been just as simple as this: can we get back to the days where the love was truly for the music and the preservation of the culture and artistry?

Idealistic?

Of course.

Optimistic?

Without question.

Hopelessly romantic?

Let's allow time to call judgment on that one.

My request: focus strictly on the music . . . and the love of it. Because the money will always follow behind that lost, yet retrievable and obtainable goal—

The classic album.

INTERPRETATIONS

1. How would you characterize Craig's writing style? Use specific examples from the essay to support your interpretation.

2. How does Craig portray the "golden era" of hip-hop? Where in the essay are these qualities presented?

3. In paragraph 12, Craig discusses the connection between hip-hop music and politics. What specific arguments does he make? Explain why you agree or disagree with him.

4. According to Craig, what messages about life and the world are now being conveyed by hip-hop artists?

CORRESPONDENCES

1. In his essay, Craig addresses the state of hip-hop then and now. How are his perceptions similar to and/or different from James Geasor's views of rock and roll?

[5]Jay-Z sold over 600,000 albums in his first week. This amidst the climate of the majority of artists trying to sell 1,000,000 albums in a quarter.

2a.   In their essays, Craig, Lee, and Geasor all consider the relationship between popular culture and the political climate of the time. What historical period is discussed by each writer? How does each popular music reflect its historical/political moment?

2b.   How does today's popular music represent what is happening in your world today?

3.   Tom Lee defines a "classic" as "something so innovative and different that everybody tries to mimic it." How do Geasor and Craig apply this definition to the kinds of popular music they write about? What characterizes classic rock and roll and hip-hop?

APPLICATIONS

1.   Choose a current song, album, or music video that you think will transcend popular culture and become a "classic." Write an essay explaining why you think your selection will accomplish this feat. In framing your argument, think about the historical, sociological, and personal arguments used by Lee, Geasor, and Craig in their essays. Try to apply such a long view to the subject of your essay.

2.   When does an artifact of popular culture (a song, painting, movie, or book) become a classic? Create a conversation that Lee, Geasor, and Craig might have in response to this question. Use quotations from their essays as much as possible, so that it seems that they are actually talking to each other. Have each writer "speak" at least four times.

"I wouldn't have nothing if I didn't have you"

MARTÍN KUTNOWSKI

Martin Kutnowski (b. 1968) is a composer, music theorist, and teacher. Born and raised in Buenos Aires, Argentina, in 1995 he emigrated to the United States, and lived in New York for ten years. In 2005 he emigrated again, this time to Fredericton, Canada, where he currently lives with his wife and children. As a composer, he has so far published two collections of piano pieces for children: Echoes, Pictures, Riddles, and Tales *(2005) and* Watercolors for Ten Fingers *(2007), and contributed individual pieces to compilations published both in America and in Europe. His art music, which often references the folk idioms of Argentina, can also be heard in commercial recordings by Bertrand Giraud, Marcela Fiorillo, and* Incontri di Musica Contemporanea; *his commercial music has been used in shows such as MTV's* Room Raiders *and* Soapography. *As a teacher and writer, Kutnowski often explores the issue of music and meaning, both in the tonal repertoire of the past—where music can still be treated as a self-sufficient art—and in TV and film. In these media, Kutnowski analyzes music as but one more component within a multistream, multimedia message. He has also published articles, both solo and in collaboration, about the scholarship of teaching and learning. Currently affiliated with Saint Thomas University at Fredericton, where he directs the Fine Arts Program, Kutnowski previously taught at Queensborough Community College of The City University of New York, The Aspen Music Festival and School, and Conservatorio Municipal Manuel de Falla of Buenos Aires. More information can be obtained at* www.contrapunctus.com.

"THERE IS NOTHING MORE TOXIC or deadly than a human child!"

Once again, I am watching *Monsters, Inc.* I have watched it a million times, but my two little ones, aged two and three, seem to never become tired of it, and constantly ask me to play the DVD. So, today I indulge them once more. It's also *my* pleasure; *Monsters* is an enjoyable, incredibly imaginative story about a world in which monsters of different shapes and sizes work long hours visiting what they call the "human world." They do so by passing through the closet doors in rooms where children are sleeping, as if each one of these magical doors were some kind of "dimensional" threshold—not unlike the hole through which

Alice falls to enter Wonderland. Waking children up in the middle of the night, monsters scare them off, then go back from whence they came, collecting their screams and storing them in oxygen-like tanks so that these screams can be later recycled as an energy source for the monster world. For the most part, the story unfolds within this alternate reality—a half-fantastic, half-science-fiction universe of sorts.

As I keep watching, I wonder: What is it that is so good about this film? Why do my children like this movie so much? And why do *I* like it?

The easy answer is that these monsters, far from being scary, are puffy, funny and lovable. As we see them working in the scream factory, we realize that in fact they are not evil per se; rather, their scaring is a professional role, just a job they're doing—like many of us, who must wear a hat at work and another one at home. Once they're off, these monsters behave like any other Joe: they go out with friends for a drink, they worry about unemployment and energy crises, they feel proud about simple everyday accomplishments such as being named the "Employee of the Month," and so on.

The story focuses on two characters, James Sullivan ("Sulley") and Michael Wazowski ("Mike"), who are very close friends. When we first see Mike, he is waking Sulley up, who is also his roommate, getting him ready for his training session. These two seem to be united not only by personal affinity but also by professional ties. The trust between them becomes clear by the familiar way Mike addresses Sulley, unceremonious and matter-of-factly, the way only a close friend can do it.

But the moment when we find out just how close they really are is immediately after the training session—still within their introductory scene—where both characters sit down to watch a TV commercial, which is promoting the company where they both work, Monsters, Inc. Sulley is featured as the star scarer; in the final shot, where Sulley and Mike are shown in the foreground with the complete staff standing in the background, the round trademark logo of the company completely blocks Mike, so that only Sulley is seen on the screen. Right after the commercial, the camera turns to Mike; he seems devastated. In turn, Sulley's facial expression, deeply worried at the possibility of his friend getting hurt—it would have been Mike's first time in TV, now just a shattered dream—speaks volumes about Sulley's feelings for his friend. Soon after, both Sulley—and the audience—find out that Mike is elated anyway, oblivious to reality, as he screams: "I was on TV! . . . I am a natural!" He's funny, alright.

On the other hand, the two sinister characters of the story, Mr. Waternoose (CEO of Monsters, Inc.) and Randall Boggs (another scarer employed by the company, jealous of Sulley's success) just want to find the way to produce more and more scream, regardless of the additional suffering that it may inflict on children. Mr. Waternoose says, with a hint of nostalgia: "children nowadays are not so easy to scare," probably referring to a late nineteenth-century, violence-and-fear-based educational philosophy. Presumably, raising children then was much easier than now, thanks to terror. The reference is enhanced by Mr. Waternoose's countenance, Victorian dress code, grave and stern voice—marvelously brought to life by James Coburn—and overly formal language.

The moral of the story is profound: it's always better to communicate with children through humor and kindness, rather than using abusive means. As I nod to myself, thinking about what Mr. Waternoose represents and how even my parents—in their childhood—were terrorized with monsters et al., I take a glance at my own children, now quietly sitting at the TV—sure enough, without electronic candy they would be, right now, making a mess all over the house. Indeed, under certain conditions nothing seems "more deadly or toxic than a human child"; there are days when I return home from work and it would seem that my house was just vandalized: books strewn all over the kitchen, liquids and body fluids spilled on the wooden floor, remains of yesterday's food in the bed, abstract crayon-based artwork on the newly painted walls . . . I shudder, and take a second look at my children, my dearly beloved little monsters. It's not hard to imagine why hard-working parents—like me—would be tempted to resort to any conceivable measure to restore order and feel some peace. To be sure, in a Victorian-style home, children like mine would be nothing but intolerable. A parent at wits end—like me!—would see the appeal of scaring his or her children, because no physical "harm" would seem to be involved. But the movie makes its point, and teaches me, and hopefully every other parent: "laughter is ten times more powerful than scream." In other words, more "energy"—a more positive type of energy, a better emotional bond, one might read—can result from communicating through laughter than through fear.

There is another fundamental theme in the story, which is the evolving relationship between the hero, Sulley—the big monster who is the top scarer at Monsters, Inc.—and Boo, the little girl who, also like Alice, is accidentally drawn to an alternate reality. Children are delighted when they see that Boo is not only unafraid of Sulley, but, rather, it's Sulley who's terrified of Boo. Beyond this refreshing reversal, an affectionate, Beauty-and-the-Beast kind of bond develops, giving serious depth to Sulley's character, who in the process gets in touch with his own, gut-wrenching parental instincts. He comes to understand the vulnerability of children's soul—children just like the ones he had been scaring before—and the intense emotional bond that he himself is capable of establishing with Boo. He also discovers the crucial fact that scaring children does cause them much harm, and consequently also distances them from their parents or caregivers. When forced to let Boo go, Sulley also gets to experience the bittersweet pinch—shared by any loving parent—at the sight of one's children growing up, an indication that they will slowly but surely leave their childhood behind, venture beyond the parental nest, and eventually take off to live their own lives. At the end of the movie, in a kind of snail-and-the-whale scheme, it's Mike's chance to return the favor to his friend: he's the one who brings much missed Boo back to Sulley's life.

The ultimate, hidden theme of the story, then, is also a borrowed one. It's the ageless theme of friendship between the straight guy and the funny guy, the big guy and the small guy, the strong one and the weak one. In essence, *Monsters, Inc.* revisits the unbreakable bond between the two unlikely, impossible friends. It's the same asymmetrical pairing which American popular culture has exploited so much in the last one hundred years: from computer-animated films (Shrek and the Donkey in *Shrek,* Manfred and Sid in *Ice Age*), to sitcoms (Jerry Seinfeld and George Costanza in *Seinfeld,* Felix Unger and Oscar Madison in *Odd Couple*), to stand-up shows (Abbot & Costello, Martin and Lewis), all the way to the earliest silent films (Laurel and Hardy, among others). Of course, the idea of association by contrast goes back even further, and can be found in the archetypes of Italian *commedia dell'arte* (agile Arlecchino vs. old and dumb Pantalone), in Cervantes's eternal characters, Don Quixote and Sancho, and even in the oldest piece of literature, *Gilgamesh's Epic* (Gilgamesh and Enkidu).

While I am lost in these thoughts, the movie ends and the final credits start. I have never stuck around for this portion of the DVD. Today, my wife takes the children for their bath without my help, and I have a unique chance to sit down and relax a bit longer. The lyrics of the final credits complete the picture. There, Mike finally confesses how he had been secretly jealous of Sulley's success, whom everyone seemed to love. But the story has taught Mike much about his friend and also about himself, and he sums it up: "I wouldn't have nothin if I didn't have you." Sulley concurs: "one without the other/don't mean nothing to me."

In this movie, then, it's not only the ghosts of Victorian education that are exorcized. In another crucial reversal, the fixed roles of the "odd couple" formula are also revisited. Despite his size, the little guy finally has the opportunity to excel, be a hero, and ultimately feel an equal to his dear, admired friend.

INTERPRETATIONS

1. In his third paragraph, Kutnowski asks, "What is it that is so good about this film? Why do my children like this movie so much? And why do *I* like it?" Why *does* Kutnowski like the movie? What reasons does he provide in his essay?

2. What primary theme does Kutnowski find in *Monsters, Inc.?* What do you believe to be the primary message of the movie?

3. What do you think is the purpose of paragraph 11?

CORRESPONDENCES

1. In "Why We Watch Horror Movies," (page 496) Stephen King writes, "If we share a brotherhood of man, then we also share an insanity of man." How do you think this statement applies to *Monsters, Inc.* and what Kutnowski says about the film?

2. In "A Timeless Culture," Tom Lee explores the idea of what constitutes a classic artistic work. What elements of *Monsters, Inc.* would qualify it as a classic, according to Kutnowski?

APPLICATIONS

1. "Hey, that's a great idea for a movie!"

    Write a plot summary for a children's movie that you would like to create. As you briefly outline events, be sure to convey your characters clearly. Also, think about the message you want children to receive. How may plot and characterization be used to express this message?

2. It seems that almost every film for children has its share of heroes and villains. Create two drawings, one of a hero in a children's movie and one of a villain. (You might try to invent these characters entirely from your imagination and not rely on anything that you have actually seen.) What visible characteristics does each one have? How do you think people from other cultures might interpret these visual cues?

3. These days in theaters, there always seems to be a movie made for children. Go see one, and then write a review of it. (Check the form of a movie review in your local newspaper.) In your review, stress how you think parents will respond to this movie and what they may learn from it.

Why We Crave Horror Movies

STEPHEN KING

Stephen King (b. 1947) is one of the best-selling novelists of our time and is famous worldwide for his horror fiction. He graduated from the University of Maine and began writing short stories in order to supplement his teaching salary. Carrie *(1974), King's first novel, was a phenomenal success in both print and on the screen. Among King's many novels are:* The Shining *(1977),* Pet Sematary *(1983), and* Misery *(1989). King's most recent books are* Dream Catcher *(2001),* From a Buick 8 *(2002), and* Cell *(2006). As you read King's essay, underline the statements with which you are in agreement or disagreement.*

King's works have often been made into successful movies and include "Stand By Me" (1986), "The Shawshank Redemption" (1994), and "The Green Mile" (1999). "Storm of the Century" (1999) was written as a television mini-series.

I THINK THAT WE'RE ALL MENTALLY ILL; those of us outside the asylums only hide it a little better—and maybe not all that much better, after all. We've all known people who talk to themselves, people who some-times squinch their faces into horrible grimaces when they believe no one is watching, people who have some hysterical fear—of snakes, the dark, the tight place, the long drop . . . and, of course, those final worms and grubs that are waiting so patiently underground.

When we pay our four or five bucks and seat ourselves at tenth-row center in a theater showing a horror movie, we are daring the nightmare.

Why? Some of the reasons are simple and obvious. To show that we can, that we are not afraid, that we can ride this roller coaster. Which is not to say that a really good horror movie may not surprise a scream out of us at some point, the way we may scream when the roller coaster twists through a complete 360 or plows through a lake at the bottom of the drop. And horror movies, like roller coasters, have always been the special province of the young; by the time one turns 40 or 50, one's appetite for double twists or 360-degree loops may be considerably depleted.

We also go to re-establish our feelings of essential normality; the horror movie is innately conservative, even reactionary. Freda Jackson as the horrible melting woman in *Die, Monster, Die!* confirms for us that no matter how far we may be removed from the beauty of a Robert Redford or a Diana Ross, we are still light-years from true ugliness.

And we go to have fun.

Ah, but this is where the ground starts to slope away, isn't it? Because this is a very peculiar sort of fun indeed. The fun comes from seeing others menaced—sometimes killed. One critic has suggested that if pro football has become the voyeur's version of combat, then the horror film has become the modern version of the public lynching.

It is true that the mythic, "fairytale" horror film intends to take away the shades of gray . . . It urges us to put away our more civilized and adult penchant for analysis and to become children again, seeing things in pure blacks and whites. It may be that horror movies provide psychic relief on this level because this invitation to lapse into simplicity, irrationality and even outright madness is extended so rarely. We are told we may allow our emotions a free rein . . . or no rein at all.

If we are all insane, then sanity becomes a matter of degree. If your insanity leads you to carve up women like Jack the Ripper or the Cleveland Torso Murderer, we clap you away in the funny farm (but neither of those two amateur-night surgeons was ever caught, heh-heh-heh); if, on the other hand your insanity leads you only to talk to yourself when you're under stress or to pick your nose on the morning bus, then you are left alone to go about your business . . . though it is doubtful that you will ever be invited to the best parties.

The potential lyncher is in almost all of us (excluding saints, past and present; but then, most saints have been crazy in their own ways), and every now and then, he has to be let loose to scream and roll around in the grass. Our emotions and our fears form their own body, and we recognize that it demands its own exercise to maintain proper muscle tone. Certain of these emotional muscles are accepted—even exalted—in civilized society; they are, of course, the emotions that tend to maintain the status quo of civilization itself. Love, friendship, loyalty, kindness—these are all the emotions that we applaud, emotions that have been immortalized in the couplets of Hallmark cards and in the verses (I don't dare call it poetry) of Leonard Nimoy.

When we exhibit these emotions, society showers us with positive reinforcement; we learn this even before we get out of diapers. When, as children, we hug our rotten little puke of a sister and give her a kiss, all the aunts and uncles smile and twit and cry, "Isn't he the sweetest little thing?" Such coveted treats as chocolate-covered graham crackers often follow. But if we deliberately slam the rotten little puke of a sister's fingers in the door, sanctions follow—angry remonstrance from parents, aunts and uncles; instead of a chocolate-covered graham cracker, a spanking.

But anticivilization emotions don't go away, and they demand periodic exercise. We have such "sick" jokes as, "What's the difference between a truckload of bowling balls and a truckload of dead babies?" (You can't unload a truckload of bowling balls with a pitchfork . . . a joke, by the way, that I heard originally from a ten-year-old.) Such a joke may surprise a laugh or a grin out of us even as we recoil, a possibility that confirms the thesis: If we share a brotherhood of man, then we also share an insanity of man. None of which is intended as a defense of either the sick joke or insanity but merely as an explanation of why the best horror films, like the best fairy tales, manage to be reactionary, anarchistic, and revolutionary all at the same time.

The mythic horror movie, like the sick joke, has a dirty job to do. It deliberately appeals to all that is worst in us. It is morbidity unchained, our most base instincts let free, our nastiest fantasies realized . . . and it all happens, fittingly enough, in the dark. For those reasons, good liberals often shy away from horror films. For myself, I like to see the most aggressive of them—*Dawn of the Dead*, for instance—as lifting a trap door in the civilized forebrain and throwing a basket of raw meat to the hungry alligators swimming around in that subterranean river beneath.

Why bother? Because it keeps them from getting out, man. It keeps them down there and me up here. It was Lennon and McCartney who said that all you need is love, and I would agree with that.

As long as you keep the gators fed.

INTERPRETATIONS

1. An effective introduction should capture the reader's interest. Review King's first paragraph. What is his thesis? What evidence does he offer to support? Do you agree or disagree with his point of view? Did he gain your attention? Why or why not?

2. What are King's three main reasons for the popularity of horror movies? Which did you find most convincing?

3. What is King's purpose in writing this essay? Is he mainly seeking to inform or does he want also to persuade his reader? Explain.

CORRESPONDENCES

1. Review Wright's perspective on horror and discuss its application to King's essay.

2. Review Armenti's perspective on movies. What conversation can you imagine his having with Stephen King? To what extent does Armenti's point of view on movies reflect yours?

APPLICATIONS

1. Many of King's novels, including *The Shining* (1980), *Pet Sematary* (1989), or *Sleepwalkers* (1992), have been adapted for the screen. View one of them and write two paragraphs responding to King's comment that "Horror isn't a hack market now, and never was. The genre is one of the most delicate known to man, and it must be handled with great care and more than a little love."

2. Review paragraphs 12–14 and write a journal entry agreeing or disagreeing with King's thesis.

3. King writes in paragraph 12: "The mythic horror movie, like the sick joke, has a dirty job to do. It deliberately appeals to all that is worst in us." To what extent do you agree or disagree? Does King's claim describe why you like horror movies? What other reasons are there? Write a brief essay explaining your point of view.

Arnie's Test Day

BARRY PETERS

Barry Peters lives in Ohio. He received his M.A. from Wright State University in 1995 and teaches English at Centerville High School.

ARNIE WATSON, facing five tests on a spring Friday of his junior year at Riverdale High School, sat in his bedroom at five a.m. and wrote all over his clothes. Beneath the bill of his Chicago Bulls cap, Arnie wrote in Spanish twenty of the vocabulary words from a list that he was provided with by Señora Martin on Monday and told to memorize by Friday. Certainly Arnie would have memorized those words, just as he had done with vocabulary lists all year, had he not been on the phone for two hours Thursday night trying to convince Marilou Spencer not to break up with him. Dismayed when Marilou slammed the phone in his ears, Arnie couldn't concentrate on his Español the rest of the night. Exasperated, he rose early on Friday and meticulously wrote those twenty words and shorthand definitions in fine black ink on the underside of the cap's red bill.

Frankly, Arnie didn't have the chance to study history, either, that week. Gus Finley and Arnie were going to meet at the Riverdale Library on Tuesday and study the amendments to the Constitution, but Arnie got stuck in the house after a fight with his parents. How are you going to get into a real college, they yelled, a Michigan or a Duke or a Stanford, if you fall out of the top five percent of your class, if you bring home any more eighty percents in your honors classes? It won't be possible, they said. Just you wait and see, Arnie retorted, storming upstairs to his bedroom.

Knowing that he couldn't leave the house after such a scene, Arnie didn't meet Gus at the library, which is why on that Friday morning before school, Arnie wrote abbreviated versions of the amendments on the inside collar of his Reebok polo shirt, actually needing to write on the inside of the shirt itself, repealing Prohibition just above his heart.

Luck ran against Arnie that week in English, too. Mr. Phelan, the Riverdale basketball coach, told his players they had better be at spring conditioning OR ELSE. Naturally, Arnie wanted to stay on Phelan's good side for his senior season, so Arnie ran and lifted weights with the rest of the team after school that week, precluding him from reading all but the first chapter of *The Great Gatsby*. On Friday morning, then, Arnie wrote "Jay Gatsby" and "Nick Caraway" and "Tom Buchanan" and "Daisy Buchanan" on the tanned inside of his belt along with a very brief synopsis of their literal and metaphorical roles in the novel; on the pale blue inside waistband of his jeans, Arnie elaborated on Fitzgerald's symbolism, even drawing a pair of spectacles overlooking a map of East Egg and West Egg, Gatsby's mansion, a heap of ashes and a skyscraper representing New York City, praying that the information he had gleaned from *Cliff's Notes* would be useful on Mrs. Schenck's in-class essay.

Possibly the most difficult test for Arnie would be physics. Quantum theory was hard enough for Arnie to understand during lectures and labs: finding time to memorize formulas for Friday's test was another problem.

Right when he opened his notebook on Wednesday night, Arnie's grandmother called to say that Grampa had been admitted to Riverdale Hospital with chest pains. So Arnie and his parents spent three hours at the hospital, where Arnie read *People* magazine instead of *Introduction to Physics* while waiting for the doctors to report Grampa's condition. They said Grampa would have surgery on Friday—Arnie's test day— only a few hours after Arnie wrote quantum physics formulas on the outside of his polyester white socks.

Unusual as it was, Arnie faced a fifth test that Friday in trigonometry. Vindicating himself for being required to attend Riverdale Lutheran Church choir practice last night—after basketball conditioners and before his devastating phone call to Marilou Spencer, after lying to his parents that no, he did not have any tests on Friday, after answering countless questions from other choir members about his grandfather's impending heart operation—Arnie wrote trigonometry notes on the bottom white soles of his Air Jordan basketball shoes. Why me, Arnie thought, and next to the silhouette logo of Michael Jordan flying above the world, Arnie charted trigonometic patterns. X-axis: the function of pressure is on the rise. Y-axis: the probability exists that Arnie will be forced to use his crib notes. Z-axis: the arc of trouble in Arnie's life increases at an extremely sharp angle, the black line speeding unheeded toward infinity.

INTERPRETATIONS

1. What specific *facts* does Barry Peters provide about Arnie Watson? What might you guess at about Arnie from information that has been stated indirectly?

2. Why has Arnie decided to cheat on his tests? What priorities has he established for himself?

3. What do you observe about the writing style that Peters has used for this story? How do you think the style is related to the content of "Arnie's Test Day"?

CORRESPONDENCES

1. To an extent, the essays by James Geasor and Todd Craig concern self-perception. Rockers, rebels, and rappers might see themselves one way, and society might see them another. How is illusion and reality a theme of each of these essays? To what extent is the character Arnie Watson's perception of himself truth or fiction? From your own experiences, how effective—in terms of illusion and reality—is Peters's depiction of the world that Arnie inhabits?

2. In "Arnie's Test Day," Peters takes a snapshot of the story's protagonist. What realities confront Arnie Watson? What does the story's last line predict for his future? Given Arnie's current situation— and his fate—how does he fit into the partial portrait of today's youth provided by Meredith in "Big Mall's Curfew Raises Questions of Rights and Bias"?

APPLICATIONS

1. "Español," "the amendments to the Constitution," *The Great Gatsby*," "Quantum theory," "trigonometry." These are the subjects Arnie is to be tested on. Remembering back to your high school days, did you find these topics to be valuable? Should they have been replaced by other—more relevant—subjects? Write an essay explaining your position.

2. "To cheat or not to cheat . . .?" Why do you agree or disagree with Arnie's solution to his dilemma? What arguments are you able to develop in support of your decision?

3. Create a list of specific details that you find in "Arnie's Test Day." Look over your list carefully. Which details do you like the most? Which are most striking?

    When writers use exact details, they hope to generate interest in their work and to draw a reader into the world inhabited by their characters. How does Peters's use of details affect *your* response to the story?

Choose something that you have written for this class that you would like to revise. When making your changes, focus upon how you might include specific details to engage your readers as you make your point. Remember to pay attention to your five senses—they will often reveal details that are clear and effective. As you work on your text, do you think there is a point at which a piece cannot support additional details? If so, why is this the case?

The Knowing Eye

Elissa R. Schlau

READING IMAGES

1. What is your response to the photograph with the bicycles? Would you classify the objects in the photograph as popular culture or as art? If there is a difference between these terms, what is it and how might it influence your interpretation of the objects in the photograph and the photograph itself?

2. What kind of music is being played by the person in the second photograph? What details in the image help you to form your opinion? What kind of music do you think would be played by the people in the group portrait?

MAKING CONNECTIONS

1. What specific aspects of popular culture do you find in these photographs? What additional kinds are identified in the essays presented in this chapter?

Arnold Asrelsky

2. Review the photographs that have appeared in earlier chapters. Which ones show evidence of popular culture? What specific details can you locate to support your claims?

WORDS AND IMAGES

1. What music do you think would be listened to by the musician in the second photograph? Create a tune in this style and write a brief explanation of the music you have composed and how you came to create it.

2. Popular culture or classic? Consider the analyses contained in the essays by Tom Lee, James Geasor, and Todd Craig. For each of the photographs, consider whether the artifact depicted or implied (the installation of objects, the music produced by the guitar

Elissa R. Schlau

player, the music played by the band) is more likely to be classified as "popular culture" or "classic." As you set up your analysis essay, first establish clear and complete definitions of these terms before applying them to your exploration of the photographs.

Additional Writing Topics

1. Both Tom Lee and James Geasor hold the Beatles up as a paragon of popular culture. Is such attention and tribute deserved? Do some research about John, Paul, George, and Ringo. Listen to their records, watch their films, read some articles, and ask your parents (or someone of their generation) about them.

   Next, write an article for your college newspaper about rock and roll's first supergroup from the vantage point of history. Consider creating a headline such as "The Beatles: Yay or Nay," "She Loves You, Yeah, Yeah . . . So?," "The Beatles: Hype or Hip?" or anything that reflects your undertaking to separate truth from fiction. Here are two Web sites to get you started:

   http://en.wikipedia.org/wiki/The_Beatles

   http://www.beatles.com

2. Now that you have read Martín Kutnowski's essay, view *Monsters, Inc.* In addition to interpreting the film's story, pay careful attention to the score. How do you think the music relates to what is happening on screen? What specific examples can you provide to support your observations? Cite two other films in which the music plays a role in theme, characterization, or setting.

3. Custom ("vanity") license plates for automobiles also make use of shorthand text. Using the concepts presented by Charles McGrath (see paragraphs 2–5 on p. 457), design a license plate that describes you. Then use your license plate as the title for a descriptive essay about yourself.

4. Write a comparison and contrast essay about the films *8 Mile* and *Hustle & Flow*. What is the main idea that you will present to your reader? What specific similarities or differences will you choose as the basis for your arguments? Reading Todd Craig's analysis of hip-hop should help to provide you with points to focus upon.

5. Choose an influential rock, hip-hop, or movie star popular with your generation. Review tapes and interviews with him or her, and write an essay analyzing the causes and effects of his or her influence on your age group. Support your analysis with creative, specific examples.

6. Write a persuasive essay comparing and contrasting your responses to seeing a movie in a theater as opposed to viewing it at home on a DVD. Provide as many specific examples as you can to convince

your target audience. Remember to take into consideration the genre of your film: comedy, thriller, romance, action, or horror.

7.   Todd Craig writes "Now in 2006, we have reached the era where hip-hop is no longer the subculture, but is indeed popular culture. We see it on a daily basis in the fashion choices of youth, the words they choose to speak in everyday language, and the shift in lifestyle." In their respective essays, James Geasor and Tom Lee also note the power of popular culture to minister to prevailing ideas and trends.

Explore the music, dress, and lifestyles of a bygone era or another culture. Examine photographs, movies, paintings, recordings, and newspaper and magazine articles. Write a consolidated report of what you have discovered, defining "popular culture" for that time or place.

You will find the Internet to be an invaluable tool for locating source material. Plugging search terms such as "the 1880s" or "the 1920s" or "Mexico 'popular culture'" or "modern Japan" into a Web search engine will present you with many options for finding information. Be creative with the search terms you use. You can even limit your search to images or sound clips, and access to full-text original documents might be available in the licensed resources subscribed to by your college library.

8.   Some teachers and administrators argue that cell phone usage by students is getting in the way of their educational mission and have called for legislation that would ban the phones from schools. As the leader of a student governance group, prepare a speech that you will deliver to either support or refute such an iniative. Included in the group you will address are students, teachers, and parents.

9.   Check out the following Web sites:

Movies:

http://www.ericenders.com/100films.htm

http://www.bfi.org.uk/sightandsound/topten/poll/critics.html

Music:

http://www.xpn.org/885ATGA.php

http://www.listsofbests.com/list/38

Television:

http://43best.weblogswork.com/
    pmwiki.php?n=Main.43BestTVShows

http://www.the-top-tens.com/lists/top-ten-tv-shows.asp

Each list reflects the opinion of the webmaster who maintains it. Select only one "best of" list to work with. Do you agree or disagree with the choices? When you explain your answer to this question, identify those qualities that the webmaster seems to value in choosing his or her favorites. Also in your essay, present the criteria *you* would use for including an item in *your* "best of" list. Fully explain why you favor your criteria as opposed to those of the webmaster. Conclude your essay with your list!

Rhetorical and Cultural Glossary

Abstract   Without physical, tangible existence in itself; a concept as opposed to an object. A "child" is a concrete object that our senses can perceive, but "child-ishness" is an abstract quality. *See* Concrete.

Addition   A revising technique that enables you to add information to your draft. Words, phrases, or paragraphs may be inserted to clarify or enhance what you have written.

Analogy   A comparison that points out a resemblance between two essentially different things. Sleep and death are analogous, although certainly not identical. Often an analogy is drawn to explain simply and briefly something that is complex or abstract by pointing out one way in which it resembles something that is simpler or more concrete. To explain how the mind processes and stores information in its memory, an analogy might be drawn to the way in which a bank processes and stores deposits.

Antonym   A word of opposite meaning from another word, "Good" is an antonym of "bad." *See* Synonym.

Argumentation   In persuasive essays, a unit of discourse meant to prove a point or to convince; the process of proving or persuading.

Audience   A work's intended readership, the author's perception of which directly affects style and tone. As a rule, the more limited or detailed the subject matter, the more specific the audience. An author may write more technically if the intended audience is composed of specialists in the field and may write less technically if the writing is for the general public.

Brainstorming   A prewriting technique in which you rapidly write down ideas in list form. Each idea is usually represented by only one or two words.

Cause and Effect   A type of exposition used primarily to answer the questions "Why did this occur?" and "What will happen next?" The structure of a cause-and-effect essay is a series of events or conditions, the last of which (the effect) cannot occur without the preceding ones (causes). When you write a cause-and-effect essay, it is helpful to keep chronology clearly in mind: remember, causes always create effects and effects are derived from causes.

Class   A group of related objects or people. Those who share the same economic status in a society are said to be of the same social class, such as working class, middle class, upper class.

Cliché   An expression so overused that it has lost its ability to convey a sharp image or fresh idea. Clichés, such as "busy as a bee," diminish clarity and precision. Familiarity reduces them to little more than vague generalizations.

Coherence   The sense of connection and interrelationship present among the parts of a work. In a coherent piece of writing each sentence leads reasonably to the next sentence, and each paragraph follows reasonably from the preceding paragraph. A lack of coherence is evident when gaps are left between parts. The reader of a poorly written essay might begin to ask, "Why does the writer say this here?" or "How did the writer get to this idea from the preceding idea?" *See* Transition and Unity.

Colloquialism   A conversational or folksy word or phrase deemed inappropriate in formal writing. Using colloquialisms ("booze" for "whiskey" or "loosen up" for "relax") imparts a less dignified, less studied quality to one's writing. *See* Slang.

Combining   A rearrangement strategy that helps you to concentrate information in a draft by taking ideas expressed in two or more locations and placing them together. Such a change can improve essay organization and the logical presentation of main ideas.

Comparison and Contrast   A type of exposition that states or suggests similarities and differences between two or more things. Two types of organization for comparison and contrast essays are point by point and subject by subject.

Conclusion   A summing up or restatement of the writer's thesis. A strong conclusion imparts a sense of completion and finality to a piece of writing. The conclusion may be no more than a sentence in a short essay; it may be many paragraphs in a long report. A short conclusion may restate the writer's thesis in a memorable way, place the specific topic being discussed within or against a broader framework, or suggest answers to questions raised in the essay. A summary of the writer's main points may be effective as the conclusion to a long paper, but in a short essay it will seem unnecessarily repetitious.

Concrete   Specific and tangible as opposed to general and abstract. "Wealth" is an abstract concept of which "gold" is a concrete form. The use of concrete details, examples, and illustrations is a key to clear and effective writing. *See* Abstract.

Connotation   The implication(s) and overtones, qualities, feelings, and ideas a word suggests. Connotation goes beyond literal meaning or dictionary definition. "Sunshine" denotes the light rays of the sun, but connotes warmth, cheer, happiness, and even prosperity. *See* Denotation.

Culture   The total pattern of human (learned) behavior embodied in thought, speech, action, and artifacts. It is dependent on the human capacity for learning and transmitting knowledge to succeeding generations through the use of tools, language, and systems of abstract thought.

Deduction   A logical or argumentative appeal in persuasive essays; deductive reasoning elicits a specific conclusion from a generalization. Deduction as a logical approach proceeds from the general to the particular. For example, if we assume that cigarette smoking causes cancer, we may deduce that a person who smokes is liable to contract the disease. *See* Induction.

Definition   A type of exposition that explains the meaning of a word or concept by bringing its characteristics into sharp focus. An **extended definition** explores the feelings and ideas you attach to a word. Extended definitions are suited to words with complex meanings, words that are subject to interpretation, or words that evoke strong reactions. Such definitions are an appropriate basis for organizing exposition. A **dictionary definition** places a word in a class with similar items but also differentiates it from members of the same class.

Deletion   The revising strategy that enables you to remove unnecessary information from your draft. Words, phrases, or paragraphs may have to be dropped if you find they clutter or digress.

Denotation   The literal meaning of a word as defined in a dictionary. *See* Connotation.

Description   A method of paragraph development that conveys sensory experience through one or more of the five senses: sight, hearing, touch, taste, and smell. Description is generally either objective or subjective and can be organized in three broad categories: spatial, chronological, or dramatic. *See* Mode.

Diction   The writer's choice of words. Writers are said to employ proper diction when the words they choose to express their ideas are accurate and appropriate; that is, when what they write says exactly what they mean. Poor diction stems from choosing words whose denotation does not accurately convey the author's intended meaning or from choosing words regarded as inappropriate because they are nonstandard ("ain't"), colloquial, or obsolete.

Editing   The final stage of revising, not to be substituted for careful revision. Changes in punctuation, spelling and word choice are all editing changes.

Epiphany   A moment of insight for a character, often resulting in a turning point.

Exposition   A mode or form of discourse that conveys information, gives directions, or explains an idea that is difficult to understand.

Fetishism   The worship of inanimate objects believed to have magical or transcendent powers. Some people obtain sexual arousal and satisfaction from an object, for example, gloves or shoes.

Figure of Speech   An imaginative phrase and comparison that is not meant to be taken literally. "He ran as fast as the wind" is a figure of speech known as a simile. *See* Analogy, Hyperbole, Metaphor, Personification, Simile, and Understatement.

Freewriting   A prewriting activity that requires you to write down thoughts about a subject as they occur to you. Essentially, you are taking dictation from your brain.

Function   The utility of an object, as opposed to its cultural meaning.

Generalization   A broad statement, idea, or principle that holds a common truth. Despite many possible exceptions, it is generally true that a soldier's job is to go to war. Writing that relies too much on generalization is likely to be vague and overly abstract. *See* Specificity.

High Culture   Classical music, serious novels, poetry, dance, high art, and other cultural products that are usually appreciated by a small number of educated people.

Hyperbole   Obvious exaggeration, an extravagant statement, intentionally designed to give the reader a memorable image. A fisherman who brags that the one that got away was "big as a whale" almost certainly is speaking hyperbolically. *See* Understatement.

Image   In writing, an image is a picture drawn with words, a reproduction of persons, objects, or sensations that are perceived through sight, sound, touch, taste, or smell. Often an image is evoked to visually represent an idea. *See* Symbol.

Impressionistic   Depicting a scene, emotion, or character so that it evokes subjective or sensory impressions. An impression is an effect produced upon the mind or emotions. The more writing emphasizes the effects on the writer of scenes, persons, and ideas, the more impressionistic, and hence the less objective, it will be. *See* Objectivity and Subjectivity.

Induction   The process by which one draws a generalized conclusion from specifics. If it is a fact that a high percentage of people who die from lung cancer each year also smoke cigarettes, one might safely induce that cigarette smoking is a contributing factor in the disease. *See* Deduction.

Introduction   An introduction sets forth the writer's thesis or major themes and establishes tone (attitude toward one's subject), and—particularly in a long paper—suggests an organizational plan. The introduction, or opening, of an essay should capture the reader's attention and interest. Like the conclusion, it may be no more than a sentence or it may be many paragraphs.

Irony   The undermining or contradicting of someone's expectations. Irony may be either verbal or dramatic. **Verbal irony** arises from a discrepancy, sometimes intentional and sometimes not, between what is said and what is meant, as when a dog jumps forward to bite you, and you say, "What a friendly dog!" **Dramatic irony** arises from a discrepancy between what someone expects to happen and what does happen: for example, if the dog that seemed so unfriendly to you saves your life. *See* Sarcasm and Satire.

Jargon   The specialized language of a trade, profession, or other socioeconomic group. Truck drivers employ a jargon on their citizen's band radios that sounds like gibberish to most people. Writing that employs contextless jargon is inappropriate.

Journal   A daily written record of ideas, memories, experiences, or dreams. A journal can be used for prewriting and as a source for formal writing.

Journalism   The profession of writing for newspapers, magazines, wire services, and radio and television. Journalistic writing emphasizes objectivity and factual reportage; the work of editorial writers, columnists, and feature writers often is a more subjective form of reportage.

Literal   The ordinary or primary meaning of a word or expression. Dwelling on literal meaning can promote erroneous thinking. The sentence "Childhood is a time of sunshine" should be read figuratively, not literally. (The sun does not always shine during childhood: rather, childhood is a happy time.)

Metaphor   A figure of speech in which, through an implied comparison, one object is identified with another and some qualities of the first object are ascribed to the second. *See* Simile.

Mode   A conventional form or usage. Writing includes four customary modes of discourse: description, narration, exposition, and persuasion (argumentation).

Multiculturalism   Assimilation of several cultures while allowing each culture to retain its separate identity.

Myth   A traditional or legendary story with roots in folk beliefs.

Narration   A narrative essay is a story with a point; narration is the technique used to tell the story. When writing a narrative essay, pay close attention to point of view, pacing, chronology, and transitions.

Objectivity   Freedom from personal bias. A report about a scientific experiment is objective insofar as facts in it are explained without reference to the writer's feelings about the experiment. But not even the most factual piece of writing is completely uncolored by the writer's attitudes and impressions. Objectivity is best thought of as a matter of degree, increasing in direct proportion with the writer's distance from the work. *See* Subjectivity.

Paradox   A statement that sounds self-contradictory, even absurd, and yet expresses a truth. It is paradoxical, though nonetheless true, to say that one person can simultaneously feel both love and hatred for another person.

Parallel Structure   The association of ideas phrased in parallel ways, thus giving a piece of writing balance and proportion. "He loves wine, women, and singing" lacks parallelism. "He loves wine, women, and song" is parallel; the verbal noun "singing" interrupts the series of nouns.

Personification   A figure of speech in which abstract concepts or inanimate objects are represented as having human qualities or characteristics. To write that "death rides a pale horse," for example, is to personify death.

Persuasion   The art of moving someone else to act in a desired way or to believe in a chosen idea. Logic and reason are important tools of persuasion. Equally effective may be an appeal either to the emotions or to the ethical sensibilities.

Point of View   The vantage point from which an author writes. In expository prose, an author may adopt a first-person or a third-person point of view. *See* Style and Tone.

Politics   The practice of promoting one's interests in a competitive social environment. It does not only have to do with running for government office; there are office politics, academic politics, classroom politics, and sexual politics.

Popular Culture   Sometimes called mass culture. It is accessible to everyone and is dominated by sports, television, films, and popular music.

Purpose   A writer's reason for writing. A writer's purpose is clarified by his or her answer to the question "*Why* am I writing?"

Rearrangement   The revising process that enables you to reorganize your draft by changing the placement of information. Three subsidiary rearrangement techniques are moving, combining, and redistributing.

Redistributing   A rearrangement strategy that helps you to reorganize your essay by taking a block of information and breaking it up into smaller units. Such a revision might help you to explain ideas more carefully or divide main ideas into more understandable units.

Revising   The writing process that enables you to change what you have written. Revising implies rethinking, rereading, and rewriting and does not necessarily come after a whole essay is created. Revising helps you bring what you have written into line with what you want to write.

Sarcasm   An expression of ridicule, contempt, or derision. Sarcastic remarks are nasty or bitter in tone and often characterized by irony that is meant to hurt. You might express your displeasure with those who have given you a hard time by sarcastically thanking them for their help. *See* Irony.

Satire   A genre of writing that makes various use of irony, sarcasm, ridicule, and broad humor in order to expose, denounce, or reform. Satires dwell on the follies and evils of human beings and institutions. The satirist's tone may range from amusement and gentle mockery to harsh contempt and moral indignation.

Simile   A figure of speech including *like* or *as* and stating a direct, explicit comparison between two things: he ate *like* a pig; her heart felt light *as* a feather. *See* Metaphor.

Slang   Colloquialisms and jargon are deemed inappropriate in formal writing. Whether a word or phrase is considered colloquial or slang is often a matter of personal taste. Also, slang often gains acceptance in time. A word such as *uptight*, once considered slang by cultivated people, is now an acceptable colloquialism. *See* Colloquialism and Jargon.

Specificity   Precision, particularity, concreteness. Specificity, like generalization, is a matter of degree; the word *horse* is more specific than *animal* but more general than *stallion*. *See* Generalization.

Style   The "fingerprint," the identifying mark, of a writer—both as an individual and as a representative of his or her age and culture. An author's style is the product of the diction employed, sentence structure and organization, and the overall form and tone in which thoughts are expressed. Style is variously described, depending on the analyzer's purpose. It may be simple or complex, forthright or subtle, colloquial or formal, modern or classical, romantic or realistic, "logical" or poetic. It may be anything, in short, that reflects the writer's personality, background, and talent. *See* Point of View and Tone.

Subjectivity   The personal element in writing. The more subjective a piece of writing, the more it is likely to be focused on the writer's opinions and feelings. *See* Objectivity.

Substitution   A revising strategy that allows you to replace unsatisfactory words, phrases, or paragraphs with ones that are more desirable. Substitution uses both addition and deletion in the same place in the draft.

Syllogism   A high formal three-part form of deductive logic. The syllogist argues that if a generalization (major premise) is true and a specific case of the generalization (minor premise) is also true, then any conclusion reached is necessarily true. If the major premise is "smoking causes cancer" and the minor premise is "John Doe smokes," then the conclusion is "John Doe will contract lung cancer." Syllogisms often sound logical, but are not true because one or both premises are faulty. *See* Deduction.

Symbol   Something that stands for something else. An eagle is a conventional symbol of the United States. Any word, image, or description, any name, character, or action that has a range of meanings and associations beyond its literal denotation may be symbolic, depending on who is interpreting it and the context in which it appears. The word eagle, therefore, may bring to mind different images or ideas; it may connote freedom or power or solitude.

Synonym   One of two or more words having approximately the same meaning. "Happiness" and "joy" are synonyms. *See* Antonym.

Tautology   Inherent or pointless repetition. To write that a person was treated with "cruel inhumanity" is tautological: inhumanity is always cruel.

Thesis   The main idea or theme of an essay. In expository prose, the writer usually states the thesis clearly in the introduction. The thesis statement should establish point of view, the primary point(s) intended for discussion, and the writer's attitude toward it.

Tone   Tone of voice; an author's attitude toward his or her subject, and, at times, audience. Tone is caught in the "sound" of a piece of writing. The tone of an essay may be angry, resigned, humorous, serious, sentimental, mocking, ironic, sarcastic, satirical, reasoning, emotional, philosophic—anything, in short, that echoes the voice of the author. One tone may predominate or many tones ("overtones") may be heard in any work. *See* Style.

Topic Sentence   The sentence in a paragraph that states clearly the main theme or point of the paragraph.

Transition   A bridge between one point or topic or idea and another. The logical movement from sentence to sentence and paragraph should be easy to follow if a piece of writing is coherent. This logic is often emphasized by means of transitional expressions such as *therefore, hence, similarly, however, but, furthermore, also,* and *for example. See* Coherence.

Understatement   An obvious downplaying or underrating of something. It is the opposite of hyperbole, although use of either may create a memorable image or an ironic effect. To say that "after they ate the apple, Adam and Eve found life a bit tougher," is to understate their condition. *See* Hyperbole.

Unity   The basic focus or theme that permeates a piece of writing, thus lending the piece a sense of wholeness and completeness. The words and sentences and paragraphs, the images and ideas, the explanations and examples, the characters and actions, the descriptions and arguments—all should be relevant to the overriding purpose or point of a work. *See* Coherence.

Geographic Index

Africa

Asia

Central America and the Caribbean

South America

Europe

Middle East

North America

United States: Ethnic Groups

United States

Credits